Educational Need
in the Public Economy

National Educational Finance Project
and Institute for Educational Finance

University of Florida

Educational Need
in the Public Economy

Editors and Primary Authors
Kern Alexander
K. Forbis Jordan

Contributing Authors
Richard Perlman
George Psacharopoulos
John Due
C. M. Bernd
William K. Dickey
James A. Hale
Carol E. Hanes
Thomas Melcher
William E. Sparkman
James R. Stultz
Stephen Thomas
Lillian D. Webb

A University of Florida Book

The University Presses of Florida
Gainesville / 1976

Library of Congress Cataloging in Publication Data

Main entry under title:
Educational need in the public economy.

   Final publication of the National Educational
Project.
   "A University of Florida book."
   1. Education—Economic aspects—United States.
2. Education—United States—Finance. I. Alex-
ander, Kern. II. Jordan, Kenneth Forbis, 1930-
III. Perlman, Richard. IV. National Educational
Finance Project.
LC66.E255   379'.121'0973   75-33898
ISBN 0-8130-0530-2

COPYRIGHT© 1976 BY THE BOARD OF REGENTS
OF THE STATE OF FLORIDA

PRINTED IN FLORIDA, U.S.A.

Authors

Kern Alexander
> *Director, National Educational Finance Project, and Professor, Educational Administration, University of Florida*

C. M. Bernd
> *Research Associate, National Educational Finance Project*

William K. Dickey
> *Research Associate, National Educational Finance Project*

John Due
> *Professor of Economics, University of Illinois*

James A. Hale
> *Associate Professor of Educational Administration, University of New Mexico*

Carol E. Hanes
> *Research Associate, National Educational Finance Project*

K. Forbis Jordan
> *Research Director, National Educational Finance Project, and Professor, Educational Administration, University of Florida*

Thomas Melcher
> *Research Associate, National Educational Finance Project*

Richard Perlman
> *Professor of Economics, University of Wisconsin, Milwaukee*

George Psacharopoulos
> *Professor, London School of Economics, University of London*

William E. Sparkman
> *Assistant Professor, Educational Administration, Kansas State University*

James R. Stultz
  Research Associate, National Educational Finance Project

Stephen Thomas
  Assistant Professor, Madison State College, Virginia

Lillian D. Webb
  Research Associate, National Educational Finance Project

Preface

Designed as a basic resource document for public policy makers and school finance program planners, this final publication of the National Educational Finance Project (NEFP) presents a variety of data and discussion to support the concept of increased public funding for education, identifies the target populations to be served and the level of funding required to support adequate programs and services, and includes a discussion of potential revenue sources and distribution formulas. As legislatures continue to enact statutes which mandate programs and services for all pupils and as the scope of the educational program is broadened to provide for unique needs associated with the physiological and psychological differences among pupils as well as the variations in occupational goals, the intent of the staff has been that this book would provide basic data and information which could be used as a supporting document for increased educational funding.

This publication is intended for use by state education agency fiscal planners, members of state legislatures and their staffs, local school district administrators, professors and students of educational finance and economics, members of Congress and their staffs, staff members in federal agencies responsible for various aspects of fiscal planning, and others at the state and national level who have a continuing interest in providing adequate educational opportunity for American youth.

The National Educational Finance Project was initiated in June 1968 and operated for a period of six years. The major portion of the funds came from Title V, Section 505, of the Elementary and Secondary Education Act with additional funds being provided from the Bureau for Education of the Handicapped and the Education Professions Development Act through the U.S. Office of Education and from the Department of Agriculture for the school food service component. As the first comprehensive national study of school finance since 1933, the National Educational Finance Project has gained national recognition as a landmark study in the field of school finance. The availability of the basic research findings of the study in the summer and fall of 1971 was very timely in view of the state and federal court decisions which were announced in that period.

Since its inception, the National Educational Finance Project has been a cooperative endeavor involving the state departments of education of all fifty states as well as several major universities scattered throughout the nation. The project was administered through the Florida Department of Education and the University of Florida, Gainesville. The central staff of the project was located at the University of Florida. For Phase II of the project, 1972–74, the project committee consisted of the chief state school officers from Delaware, Florida, Kentucky, Mississippi, South Dakota, and Texas. Special recognition is due the following chief state school officers for their guidance and support during Phase II of the project: Kenneth Madden (Delaware); Floyd Christian and Ralph Turlington (Florida); Lyman Ginger (Kentucky); Garvin Johnston (Mississippi); Donald Barnhart (South Dakota); J. W. Edgar and M. L. Brockette (Texas). Program administrators for the U.S. Office of Education were James Gibbs, Thomas Johns, David Phillips, and Harry Phillips. The staff wishes to recognize the guidance and support which has been provided by these persons during the course of the project. Appreciation is also expressed to Ralph Sharp of the Florida Department of Education for his assistance as state agency fiscal officer during the course of the project.

Special recognition is extended to R. L. Johns who served as project director and senior staff member for the first four years of the project. Professor Johns and other members of the project committee, as well as many individual researchers from throughout the nation, made significant contributions to the research and dissemination efforts conducted during Phase I of the National Educational Finance Project.

In addition to expressing appreciation to those individuals who contributed to various portions of this final publication, we would like to give recognition to Elaine Buckley, Nelda Cambron, Carol Hanes, and other staff members of the Institute for Educational Finance for their technical assistance with the preparation of the manuscript and the logistics associated with the publication.

The reader of this volume is cautioned that the content in no way reflects the official position of the U.S. Office of Education or the position of the project committee or any of its members. Additionally, contributing authors of individual chapters have only assumed responsibility for the content and concepts in that chapter. Only the two editors are responsible for the totality of the content, concepts, and ideas expressed in this publication.

KERN ALEXANDER
K. FORBIS JORDAN

Contents

Overview and Observations

Each year in every state in the nation, citizens are faced with the major public policy decision of how much to invest in various public services. Even though all services may be justified in terms of public benefits, some may warrant greater financial consideration than others. Of primary concern in this publication is the level of funding for public elementary and secondary education; each state has seen fit to establish and support this public enterprise as essential to the general welfare. Even though the appropriateness is beyond question and the investment may be fully justified on sound social, economic, and moral grounds, the level of the public financial commitment continues to be a major and undefined political decision.

In recent years the soundness of continued and increased investments in public education has been questioned by various critics. The primary objections have been that the economic and social effectiveness of public education cannot be shown to be statistically significant and that the benefits derived therefrom do not generally justify an increase in the public's financial commitment to the public schools. These criticisms, although performed in a climate of objective academic inquiry, in many cases have been misinterpreted or overemphasized by those seeking to restrict, for various reasons, the public financial interest in the public schools. In the face of this onslaught of criticism, there has been a noticeable paucity of response on behalf of public education. The purpose of this publication is to address this situation and to present material which may be used to support requests for increased investment in public elementary and secondary education.

The authors assume an advocacy position for greater investment in public elementary and secondary schools. Within the various chapters, an economic rationale is presented which justifies this investment, and educational finance data provide the educational need justification for a major

1

commitment of public funds. Further, tax capacity and effort of the fifty states are examined, and sources of revenue to support the proposed educational expenditures are identified. Finally, some guidelines are presented regarding the design of state school finance formulas which may better serve to equalize educational opportunity.

From this study certain conclusions and recommendations may be drawn which bear directly on future educational policy decisions.

BENEFITS OF EDUCATION

Increased investment in public education will produce continued, positive individual and societal benefits. A variety of external benefits accrue to society as a result of the effective operation of the public schools. Cost-benefit studies have shown that, to both the individual and society, the economic gains derived from elementary and secondary schooling far exceed the cost.

EQUALITY OF EDUCATION

Education is a socially and economically profitable investment which results in increased earnings and promotes social mobility. Greater returns can be secured through more selective investments which result in increasing the quality of education at various levels rather than merely expanding the breadth and scope of educational programs and opportunities. To enhance the social and economic returns from education, emphasis should be placed on increasing the quality of programs for educationally deprived and preschool children.

ECONOMIC REDISTRIBUTION FROM EDUCATION

Low-income families receive benefits from the public schools far in excess of the taxes they pay. The ratio between taxes paid and benefits received varies among states; however, the redistribution effect clearly shifts benefits to low-income persons, promoting vertical equalization among income classes.

A continuing basic problem is that unequal educational programs are still present among school districts. This inequality results in a poor child receiving much lower financial benefits in a poor school district than a similar poor child would receive if he happened to live in a wealthier school district. To gain more positive and equal redistributional benefits, both within and among income classes, states should enact school support programs which assure fiscal equalization among school districts while increasing the level of funding to improve the quality of educational programs.

TEACHER SUPPLY AND DEMAND

Presently a nationwide teacher surplus exists in both elementary and secondary education. However, under the economic system in which public schools operate, the demand for additional teachers is determined to a great extent by the number of teachers school districts can afford to hire. The surplus may in reality be largely attributable to the underfunding of public education programs. If funds were increased to provide for programs to meet children's particular educational needs not now being met, in all probability a greater balance would be achieved in teacher supply and demand.

EDUCATIONAL PRODUCTIVITY

The measurement of educational output is in a primitive state, and educational decision makers should be extremely cautious in formulating substantive educational policies on the basis of present productivity studies. From the limited data available, though, certain variables contributing to higher educational productivity may be identified. For example, teacher quality has been shown to be associated with educational productivity, thereby suggesting that funds to improve the quality of the teaching force would be a worthwhile public investment.

EDUCATIONAL NEEDS AND COSTS

The absence of adequate educational programs for all pupils dictates that increased funds be allocated for public elementary and secondary education to assure equality of educational opportunity for all children within each state. Projections of the funds required for public education can be made from recent studies of the educational needs of children and the program costs required to accommodate these needs. By quantifying the number of children by state in need of early childhood education, exceptional education, vocational education, and compensatory education programs, and adding this number to the normal increase for regular children, it is possible to determine the elementary and secondary educational needs for the entire country. By aggregating these needs and applying them to appropriate cost differentials for the particular programs, a total educational dollar projection is obtained.

Educational need and cost projections made in this book, state by state for the entire nation, produce an accurate view of the financing necessary to support education if enrollment, inflation, educational needs, program costs, and certain equalization standards are taken into account. The precision of this projection has been enhanced by use of full-time equivalent students in projecting costs, thus preventing duplication of pupil counting which unnecessarily inflates the total expenditure estimate. This projection reveals that the total elementary and secondary financial needs, exclusive of transportation and capital outlay, will amount to $75 billion in 1980, an increase of $29.4 billion over 1972–73.

Regular or basic educational programs will require $49.7 billion in 1980, an increase of $11.6 billion over 1972–73. This estimate is probably conservative since the inflation factor was based on years prior to 1972–73, years admittedly representing much lower rates of inflation than the country is likely to witness between now and 1980. The remainder of the additional funds needed in 1980 can be attributed to special programs, with kindergarten having the greatest increase from $1.7 billion in 1972–73 to $6.4 billion in 1980. Estimates of the other major special program categories show exceptional education increasing from about $2.1 billion to $6.5 billion, vocational education from $2.9 billion to $6.4 billion, and compensatory education from approximately $2.2 billion to $6.2 billion.

PUPIL TRANSPORTATION NEEDS AND COSTS

Even though an overall decline in pupil enrollments and number of pupils transported can be projected, increased funds will be required for transportation programs. In 1972–73 approximately 19.6 million pupils were transported to and from school at public expense; in the absence of an unforeseen intensification of busing, this figure should decline to about 18.4 million in the 1979–80 school year. Using very conservative estimates of increase in costs, the projected transportation expenditure should be near $1.6 billion in 1980. Of course, current inflationary trends, particularly in view of the recent oil crisis, probably render this estimate unreasonably low. Additionally, social requirements, technological developments, and legislative requirements could contribute to increases in this projection. However, some additional efficiencies of operation will and should be gained as school fiscal management techniques become more sophisticated.

SCHOOL FACILITY NEEDS AND COSTS

The decline in projected pupil population in the near future mitigates to some extent the overall need for school building construction, but it by no means eradicates the problem. The NEFP survey of building needs of the states showed a great need to replace temporary and obsolete structures and to relieve overcrowded classrooms. In 1972–73, the nation needed 301,401 additional classrooms, the total cost of which would exceed $20 billion. Since it is extremely doubtful that capital outlay costs of this magnitude would or should be met in a single year, a long-range plan for the new facilities was projected from 1972–73 through 1979–80. Assuming that the building backlog was not met on an equal yearly basis for these years, that a 2 per cent additional obsolescence of existing buildings occurred each year, and that the annual inflation factor would be about 6.5 per cent, the total costs of construction to meet all of these building needs by 1979–80 would probably more than double. This projection is based on pay-as-you-go financing and does not include debt service costs which would be incurred if the capital outlay program were financed by long-term borrowing.

STATE SCHOOL FINANCE FORMULAS

State school finance formulas should possess the qualities to guarantee full fiscal equality while providing an adequate level of funding to assure that all pupils have access to programs oriented to their psychological and physiological conditions, economic and cultural backgrounds, or occupational aspirations. However, if the nation's elementary and secondary schools are to retain the qualities of diversity which this nation holds in such high esteem, opportunities should be provided for each district to supplement the state program. This dynamic quality has been a major factor in the continued growth and development of American public education and should be enhanced rather than stifled. However, care should be taken by the states to equalize these funds in such a manner that a child's education will not be contingent on unreasonable variations in educational aspirations. State efforts to fund education should focus on assuring greater fiscal and educational equalization among districts. Funding mechanisms should also provide for equalized fiscal encouragement for districts desiring to exert levels of effort beyond that required for an adequate program. The opportunity to supplement educational programs and seek higher levels of quality should not be a privilege available only to the wealthy, but an opportunity extended to all.

STATE TAX SOURCES TO SUPPORT EDUCATION

Additional funds for financing education cannot be found on any significant scale in the local property tax or in the expansion of local nonproperty taxes. Instead, new revenues must be derived from increasing the state sales and income taxes, in addition to placing greater reliance on federal grants.

Most states can make more effective use of the sales tax. Using certain assumptions, the NEFP found that all states together in 1972–73 could have reasonably increased the sales tax yield by over $16 billion. Reasonable adjustments in excise taxes on liquor and tobacco products could have produced a total of $5.4 billion in new tax funds in 1972–73. Of the other major tax sources, income taxes could have been utilized to a much greater degree in most states, without excessive tax burden, with the side benefits of increasing the redistributional effect of the entire tax system. If all states in 1972–73 had levied a similar personal income tax with rates from 4 to 10 per cent, their combined efforts could have produced revenues of $31.5 billion, or about $14.5 billion more than state income taxes actually yielded. Approximately 1.7 billion additional dollars could have been obtained from levying a 9 per cent corporate income tax in all states in 1972–73.

By generally increasing the major taxes at reasonable rates, and assuming uniform application among states, with certain adjustments for equity to low-income persons, the 1973 total potential revenue capacity exceeded $38 billion.

FEDERAL FINANCING INVOLVEMENT

To date, the federal role in financing public schools has been minimal; however, conditions appear to mandate greater federal commitment. In 1971, the NEFP recommended that legitimate national interests required that approximately 30 per cent of the public school revenues be provided by the federal government. These original recommendations also sought federal consolidation of the many categorical aids into a few major block grants for vocational education, compensatory education for low-income children, aid for tax-exempt federal property, education of handicapped children, school food service, and educational research and development. To this list now should be added a block grant for early childhood education. The economic and educational welfare of the country strongly supports an increased federal involvement to make kindergarten programs accessible to all five-year-old children in America.

The reluctance of the federal government to enter into the financing of elementary and secondary education as a full-fledged partner must be overcome if elementary and secondary education is to be funded at an adequate level. For even though state government appears to have considerable additional tax capacity, a closer view comparing educational needs to tax potential reveals that state funds are not sufficient to cover all needs even if the assumption is made that states would suddenly make the revenues accessible through a massive tax revision policy. The sheer volume of educational financial needs is of sufficient magnitude to give good reason for federal intervention. To recapitulate these needs: first, school facility needs are projected to range from $20 to $50 billion depending on when the funds are provided and the facilities constructed; second, some additional transportation costs are inevitable, especially with the recent explosion in oil prices; third, and most important, the immediate and continuing educational needs of children will directly require an ongoing annual outlay for current operation expenses of $75 billion by 1980.

To acquire state revenues sufficient to cover the financial gap between current revenue patterns and the needed educational expenditures may not be possible or politically feasible for the states to achieve alone. With this in mind some rather broad but realistic assumptions are in order. First, assume that the states do have the $38 billion additional tax potential as ascertained for the base year of 1972–73 by the NEFP and are willing to make the funds accessible through major tax revisions. Second, assume that the present policy of property tax relief will continue and significant revenues cannot and will not be obtained from this source. Third, assume that this revenue capacity would increase at the same rate as the increase in school expenditures as projected from 1973 to 1980, producing a state revenue potential of about $58 billion in 1979–80. From this amount past history would indicate that elementary and secondary education could expect to obtain about $22.6 billion, representing 39 per cent of state general fund dollars, the average that state governments have historically allocated to elementary and secondary education.

With such admittedly favorable assumptions, the states would still have a deficit of about $6.8 billion between the required additional educational operating needs ($29.4 billion) and education's traditional share of the tax potential ($22.6 billion). If the states committed resources to these documented educational needs for operating school programs, no additional revenue capacity would be available for the massive school facility needs, the smaller financial needs of school transportation, the expansion of other programs in school food services, or development activities.

Since the states are unlikely to respond as fully and cooperatively to changes in taxation as projected above, and since the projected educational needs and costs are conservative, the realistic role of the federal government would be to move affirmatively toward the 30 per cent share as previously recommended by the NEFP, an amount which would constitute approximately $22.5 billion of the projected $75 billion operating needs for elementary and secondary education in 1980.

Further, the federal government has educational, economic, and moral interests in equalizing education in all states. This interest should be met by allocating funds to states in the manner best suited to achieve fiscal equality. The problem of fiscal inequality among the states should be met with a large general purpose equalization grant.

Even though a large increase in federal funding may mitigate the problems of financing school facilities at state and local levels, it nevertheless will not erase them. Therefore, the federal government should intervene to provide new school facilities through major construction grants or subsidized loan programs.

Participation and cooperation by both state and federal governments will be required, with much greater effort by both, if the vast educational needs documented in this book are to be met.

KERN ALEXANDER

Indirect Returns to Early Education

Richard Perlman

While the direct financial returns to elementary and secondary education, called for brevity here "early education," are difficult enough to measure, the indirect returns—those apart from later earning gains attributable to schooling—defy quantification. Nevertheless, since they play an important part in private and social decisions on additional schooling, they must be considered and weighed.[1]

These indirect returns fit, although a little uncomfortably, into two broad classifications, monetary and nonmonetary benefits.[2] Obviously, assigning dollar values to the nonmonetary benefits cannot be easily translated into additions to a calculated direct return. Thus, except for determining the value of the option to acquire higher education, which is fostered by completion of early education, no attempt is made to adjust the rate of return of investment in early schooling for indirect benefits. Instead, these benefits serve as added factors, albeit of uncertain weight, on the favorable side of the decision to invest in schooling over other private investment alternatives.

In discussing both types of indirect returns, reference will be made to their effect on both private and public decisions on additional investment in schooling. In fact, though, laws and custom severely limit the scope for private choice in early education. With compulsory education extending to age sixteen or seventeen in most states, individual choice between leaving or continuing school is more or less confined to the last year or two of high school. These years, though, are important in the investment decision because they are the first during which the student has a meaningful alternative, gainful employment, to further schooling.

Any benefit to a single individual is also a gain to society as a whole, as long as the individual's gain is not offset by a related loss to another individual. While certainly the private benefit is much more important to the individual recipient than to the whole society to which he belongs, advantages from education broaden into significant social benefits as more and more individuals take the opportunity to capture the indirect returns from additional schooling.

There are also important indirect benefits that redound to society as a consequence of the schooling of its members that add little to each individual's welfare. Thus, these "externalities" weigh heavily in social educational investment decisions, but count for little in the individual's judgment of the value of further investment in schooling.

Since this study focuses on public sector decisions, the need for examination of indirect returns from the individual viewpoint seems open to question, especially since most private benefits become socially important as many individuals pursue them. But apart from tracking down the sources of social benefits, which in many cases originate with the individual, careful analysis of the indirect benefits that enter the social decision mix must screen out those individual benefits gained at the expense of others, which thereby net nothing to society as a whole.

Keeping in mind these insuperable problems of measurement and the caution needed in even detecting the presence of social benefits, analysis of the indirect monetary and nonmonetary benefits from early schooling can be conducted with more realism and validity.

INDIRECT MONETARY BENEFITS

Option Value of Education

Early schooling is the stepping-stone to higher education. Whatever gains, economic or otherwise, that are attributable to the highest levels cannot be realized unless the student moves up from the bottom of the schooling ladder; it is the rare individual who can skip rungs. Hence, successful early schooling provides the student with the option to higher schooling levels, college and graduate school. This option has a value to the extent that investment in higher education yields returns above those on alternative investments.

In introducing this concept of the option to higher education that early schooling offers, Weisbrod suggests a way of measuring its value.[3] The difference between the direct rate of return to college investment over the rate on alternative investments is weighted by the ratio of college to high school investment costs and multiplied by the probability of college attendance to derive the value of the option, measured in additional points to the high school rate of return.

A numerical example will perhaps clarify this process. Assume a calculated direct rate of return of 15 per cent for high school and 12 per cent for college, and an average yield of 8 per cent on other investments. If college investment costs are twice those of high school, then completion of the lower schooling level creates an option for making this investment heavier and more profitable by a net of 4 per cent (12 per cent − 8 per cent). Thus, for the student who finishes high school, this option has a net value of 8 per cent—4 per cent multiplied by 2 (the weight of the heavier college investment). But if the probability that a student who finishes high school will also finish college is 0.25, a realistic value for today's educational attainment pattern, then the total value of the option to the average student beginning high school is 2 per cent (8 per cent × 0.25), and the rate for high school should be adjusted upward from 15 per cent to 17 per cent.

A casual viewer might claim that this procedure commits the egregious bookkeeping error of double counting. Returns to college education are included in the rate of return to both high school and college investment. But closer examination shows that this is not the case. The logic in the method arises from the difference in the time horizon from which the respective rates are calculated. Using the values of the above example, a fourteen-year-old beginning high school student has an expected rate of return of 17 per cent, including the option value of a college education. At eighteen, after high school completion, the investment decision for further schooling must be made again. At this starting point, the youth has an expected return from college of 12 per cent. There is no question of double counting since the investment decisions are made at different times; that is, the option value is independent of, not additive to, the college investment decision.

Note that the option-value adjustment makes the direct returns to higher education an indirect benefit to earlier schooling. But college, too, has its considerable indirect benefits. These, no less than the direct benefits of higher incomes derived from college training, are available only to those who have completed high school. The indirect benefits from college, therefore, also contribute to the option value of the high school diploma, no less so because they are difficult to measure and far removed from the source that generates them.

The option value has interesting policy applications for the direction of educational investment resources. Public investment decisions differ from private ones in that while the state can choose additional investments in high school over college, economics is not so irrational a science as to have its analysis yield a recommendation that an individual's welfare would be served by repeating high school instead of moving on to college.

In a critical appraisal of the option-value concept, Ribich points out that when the direct rate of return is higher for the lower level of schooling, as in the above numerical example, the option value has no influence in decision-making.[4] With many alternatives for public investment, optimum resource allocations would indicate increases in investment in both high school and college, if the rate of return on each exceeded that on the alternatives. But, assuming a limited choice between investment in the two levels of schooling, the choice would be for high school over college investment even without the option-value adjustment.

What if the college rate were higher than the high school rate? While rate-of-return studies invariably find a higher rate for the earlier schooling level, greater indirect benefits might make the true rate for college higher even if the measured rate cannot include these benefits. Furthermore, the fact that past experience reveals a higher high school return rate does not absolve policy makers from preparing for contrary contingencies.

Ribich presents an interesting numerical example which yields "peculiar" policy signals. Assume a high school rate of 8 per cent, a college rate of 15 per cent, an alternative public investment rate of 5 per cent, the ratio of college to high school investment costs two to one, and a 50 per cent probability of college completion by high school graduates. According to the Weisbrod formulation, the high school rate of return adjusted for the option value becomes 18 per cent $(0.08 + [0.15 - 0.05] 2/1 \times 0.50)$. The peculiarity of the policy prescription is that it calls for investment in high school where half the students average an 8 per cent return and the other half average an additional 15 per cent from college, instead of investment in college where all average a 15 per cent return.

This is another instance, though, in which close examination finds sense in an apparently illogical policy. Educational investments can take many forms, and the values in Ribich's example call for investments that increase the flow of college students rather than investments that expand services and facilities for existing college enrollment. Theoretically, this flow can be widened by further investment in high school facilities to allow for more graduates, but as a practical matter there is little evidence that a shortage of schools restricts the number of graduates.

Instead, public educational investment should be focused on projects and programs that would increase the number of high school graduates —specialized teaching, expanded remedial efforts, career education, expanded guidance resources, for examples. These investments would increase the potential flow to college, to say nothing of raising the rate of return on public investment in high school.

Measures that merely keep the student from dropping out of high school do not help expand the flow of college students, which requires that the option to attend college be exercised. In short, passive measures would lower the average probability (P) that high school graduates will go to college. The measures noted above, though, are designed to make high school education a better preparation for both work and college. At worst they would probably leave P unchanged; at best they would raise P, allowing for a double stimulus to the college flow of a larger number of high school graduates and a stronger probability for the average member of this more numerous group to continue his schooling.

Thus, in cases in which the direct net returns on college are above those on high school investments, the option-value concept aids in directing both the location and type of educational investment toward increasing the flow of college graduates by efforts to raise the number of high school graduates and to increase the probability of college attendance. Not to claim exclusive concentration on high school investments for this purpose, it should be conceded that selective investments in college that attract more students can also serve the purpose of expanding college enrollments. Finally, not to overstate the policy significance of the option-value concept, it is worth repeating that when the rate of return, with indirect benefits considered, is higher for the lower education level, the option value plays no part in public decision-making. Insofar as economic efficiency is the standard for public resource allocation, investment would be concentrated on the lower level in any case.

Education and Unemployment Reduction

A close inverse relationship between educational attainment and unemployment level has been a dominant characteristic of our labor markets. The unemployment rate for college graduates lies well below that for high school graduates, with the dwindling number without their high school diplomas suffering the most from both the incidence and duration of unemployment.

To calculate the direct private rate of return, all analysts agree that adjustment should be made for unemployment. For example, earnings forgone by students who attend school instead of working for pay are modified by the probability of not finding market work, measured, albeit imprecisely, by the average unemployment rate for high school graduates. Similarly, correct procedures for estimating the net earnings gain from college after graduation adjust average earnings for college graduates and the high school graduate group with which they are compared downward by their respective unemployment rates.

There is some dispute over whether adjustment for unemployment should be made in calculating the direct social rate of return. While the individual must accept the risk of unemployment as a fact of economic life, society acting through government programs has the power to affect the rate. Even if public policy has followed a goal of achieving full employment, it has been eminently unsuccessful in reaching this goal. The argument holds that government has the means of reducing unemployment, and the measured social gains from education should not be dependent on society's failure to realize full employment potential.[5]

Although the inclusion of an unemployment adjustment factor in calculating the direct social rate of return can be debated, there is no doubt that a rise in education levels which leads to a reduction in unemployment rates should count as a contribution to indirect returns. A monetary benefit is clearly produced if unemployment is reduced because the supply of labor becomes more fully utilized, yielding higher earnings to the work force. A nonmonetary benefit, in this case an externality, also arises because of the improved social environment that always accompanies mitigation of the economic blight of unemployment.[6]

However, it is not inherently necessary that just because unemployment rates are lower for those with higher education, a rise in the education level will reduce total unemployment. Perhaps unemployment will fall even more heavily on those with less education, and, as long as there are differences in educational attainment, there will always be some with less education than others. Unless there are reasons for education, in itself, to contain elements that widen and deepen a worker's employment opportunities, a policy of raising education levels to reduce unemployment has all the logic of removing the last car from trains to improve railroad safety because most accidents involve this car.

There are reasons for believing that the education process itself does improve employability. Low unemployment rates for the highly educated partially reflect a strong trend in labor demand toward professional and technical manpower, that is, toward jobs requiring a high level of education to acquire the skills needed. That the emphasis is on skills provided by post–high school education only reinforces the need for widening the flow of college students through high school investment, in the manner described in the discussion of the option-value concept. Not only are unemployment rates lower for professional and technical groups, the occupational classification requiring the most education, but, as seen in Table 1, their relative employment has risen the most in recent years. The employment rise, accompanied by the low unemployment rate, suggests strong demand for this type of labor. Thus, to the extent that an upward movement in the average schooling level meets rising demand for the skills developed through education, expansion of educational investment to widen the flow of students into higher levels eases potential labor bottlenecks.

This shift in demand toward the skills of the educated is further substantiated by the downward movement in demand for the unskilled, uneducated individual. Not only is the unemployment rate for the less well-educated high, but, in addition, Table 1 shows the weakening demand for the unskilled expressed in the relative employment decline and high unemployment rates among lower echelon occupations.

TABLE 1
RELATIVE RISE IN DEMAND FOR PROFESSIONALS AND DECLINE
IN DEMAND FOR OPERATIVES AND NONFARM LABORERS

Occupation	Employment Percentage of Labor Force		Unemployment Rate	
	1959	1972	1959	1972
Professional and technical	11.0	14.0	1.7	2.1
Operatives	18.0	16.6	7.6	6.9
Nonfarm laborers	5.6	5.2	12.6	10.3

SOURCE: *Manpower Report of the President*, 1973. The overall unemployment rate was almost the same for both years, at 5.5 per cent in 1959 and 5.6 per cent in 1972.

Besides a growing demand for highly trained manpower, education further insulates workers from unemployment by making them more adaptable to technological change. Weisbrod speaks of the "hedge" that education provides against displacement by new production methods that require new skills. It might seem that education limits flexibility by narrowing the recipient's career development toward particular occupations. But the trend is for firms themselves to train and retrain workers for specific company needs. Education provided by the schools, called general training for labor market purposes, is financed by students and taxpayers, while the firm underwrites specific, task-oriented, on-the-job training.[7]

Thus, the firm tends to favor those with the most general training for its on-the-job training programs. These workers, long practiced in the basic tools of learning, can most easily adapt to further education, albeit of the vocational type. In fine, the firm seeks those workers who have best developed the capacity to graft on new skills, taught at company expense, who more than likely are those workers with the broadest educational base, acquired at their own or the taxpayer's expense—at least not the company's. The data support this argument. In his study of company practices, Mincer found a close positive relationship between educational attainment of workers and the amount of on-the-job company training they received.[8]

Besides having lower unemployment rates in normal times, the educated are less likely to lose their jobs during periods of economic weakness. Firms that have invested in their further specific training are reluctant to lay these workers off during recessions for fear of losing them without realizing the full returns from training costs sunk into their productive development. In a sense, then, workers training at company expense, mainly the more educated workers, become fixed production factors for firms, which as a result cut out their services only under greatest financial stress.[9]

In summary, three factors which tend to lower the relative incidence of unemployment among the educated are the increased demand for workers of greatest skill developed through schooling, the greater employment flexibility of the educated in adjusting to technological change, and the large volume of on-the-job training received that both strengthens worker adaptability to changing manpower requirements and reduces the worker's chances of being laid off during recessions.

Despite these factors, a balanced view of the employment advantages of education must include the view that perhaps all the employment advantages of the educated do not result from qualities developed by the process of education itself. These advantages also result from the preferential treatment those with more schooling enjoy in the labor market, and a concomitant bias against those with fewer years of schooling.

The issue is an important one for government investment policy. To examine an extreme position, suppose lower unemployment for the educated was not in the least dependent on skills developed by schooling, but rather reflected only employer preferences and prejudices. Under these conditions, there would be no indirect social gain from extra schooling, although the private benefits would be substantial. The gain to the educated in lower unemployment would be exactly offset by the higher rates for the less educated, with overall unemployment unaffected by these employer attitudes. Expressed differently, if we consider the extent to which the educated enjoy lower unemployment rates because of employer preference and assume a change in attitude so that all workers are judged on their merits and not on their diplomas, the overall unemployment rate would remain unaffected. This is not to deny that removal of employment discrimination against the less educated has its own special social value.

Certainly social consciousness has been less aroused by the evils of educational discrimination than by racist or sexist employment practices, probably because those who suffer unfair treatment because of limited education can accommodate the prejudice—they can continue their schooling. From society's viewpoint, though, investment in schooling that caters to employer preferences for the educated yields no net returns, and it further exacerbates the labor market weakness of the remaining less educated.

The preceding discussion of the social evils of educational preference and prejudice in the labor market, and of its misleading yield of indirect benefits of reduced unemployment through schooling, does not suggest that all measured employment gains from schooling are socially spurious, any more than the prior review of the unemployment-reducing features of schooling argued that the significantly lower unemployment rates for the educated were entirely derived from qualities provided by the educational process itself. In fact, it is impossible to measure the shares of the benefits attributable to the qualities of schooling and to labor market bias, even though they are conceptually distinct.

Miscellaneous Indirect Monetary Benefits

Weisbrod noted several other indirect monetary benefits from education.[10] They are discussed here under the tepid title of miscellany not so much because their contribution is minimal—on the contrary, some yield substantial dollar returns—but because they are far removed from the education process of imparting knowledge and developing skills and aptitudes.

Furthermore, many accrue to elementary education. There is no denying that there are important public educational investment decisions to be made at the elementary level, such as optimal expenditures for special education, remedial work, smaller classes, and extracurricular facilities. But elements that contribute to the basic rate, such as the ones to be discussed, only add excess support to the incontestable wisdom of sufficient investment to educate all children through grade school. The direct rate of return on elementary education is extremely high—some estimates go over 30 per cent. Law and custom preclude earning alternatives for children's school time, and, if these factors were not enough, social needs for the provision of minimal elementary education dominate economic factors, which are highly favorable in any case.[11]

The few indirect monetary benefits to be discussed only touch upon the favorable financial ramifications that reach out from the learning tree. Those benefits which arise from higher levels of schooling, for which the basic investment decision is less clear cut, are of particular relevance. Again, social or external benefits usually accompany the more obvious financial returns.

Child-care services.—While grade schools certainly do not pose as substitute day-care centers, child-care services are nevertheless offered in joint supply with their fundamental work of providing basic education. Despite their incidental source, these services have a great monetary value.

Weisbrod attempted to measure their total dollar contribution based on the average earnings of mothers who would not have been able to work if the public grade schools had not provided these free services. This estimate does not even count the benefits of added leisure time to those mothers who do not work. This method of calculation overstates the actual monetary benefits, which would be more accurately measured by the amount parents would have to pay for alternative day care.

While we may cavil at Weisbrod's estimation method, the fact remains that substantial implicit monetary benefits of child care are provided as a by-product of elementary education. Unfortunately, these large returns provide no policy guidance. For the early years of schooling the direct rate lies far above that on alternative public investments; for the later years, when the rates are more competitive, the value of the child-care services offered by the school disappears.

Intergenerational effect of education.—There is a strong tendency for the children of highly educated parents to attain a high level of schooling themselves. In fact, there is a high correlation between parent and child educational attainment for all levels of schooling.

Intergenerational transfer of education undoubtedly stems partially from income differences. Those with much education have higher incomes and can afford to spend more money on their children's schooling. Other contributing factors to more schooling for the children of the educated are effective parallel home instruction, which enhances the child's chances for academic success, inherited aptitude for schooling, a favorable home attitude toward education, and more information on education's benefits.

Whatever the factors that attract the children of the educated to more schooling, they will gain the benefits which higher education will provide. A facetious recommendation, then, would advise children to have educated parents. There is, however, a valid social policy implicit in the intergenerational transmission of education. From a social as well as private or family viewpoint, educating children to a higher level today strengthens the odds that their children will demand higher education tomorrow. Using the option-value terminology discussed above, P, the probability that a group of students will advance through a higher level of education, rises in the long run, allowing for the social benefits of higher education.

Do-it-yourself educational by-products.—Weisbrod speaks of "non-market options" developed by education. Through acquisition of the basic tools of learning, an individual can perform many necessary services himself without the need for hiring others to do this work.

While it takes no schooling to wash a car, it requires more than functional literacy in these days of complicated directional signs and mysterious parking information to drive it safely and legally. Without at least several years of elementary schooling, the individual would be confined to public transportation or would have to hire others to drive him about to satisfy his travel needs. Perhaps the picture of chauffeured semiliterates does seem unrealistic, but, nevertheless, the value of the self-driving educational requirements provided by early schooling is a real one.

Some current tax schedules challenge the expertise of an accountant. Filling out even the standard form requires more than basic literacy and the rudiments of reading comprehension; schooling into high school is required for filling out the average tax return. The social gain of self-service tax filing is the sum of all private implicit earnings from this effort. The value of this effort is measured by the costs that would have provided the services of tax accountants or consultants to do the job. Of course the income of tax experts is lower than it would be if most people were unable to file their own reports. But the issue of whether a social gain results from self-service tax-filing centers on the effects of an expansion of tax accounting knowledge for the general public.

Suppose high schools offered courses in "taxpayer education."[12] Income of tax experts would fall and eventually unemployment among tax consultants and accountants would rise. From a national point of view it seems as if there is no net social benefit; what the taxpayers gain in savings, the tax experts lose in earnings. But the question is one of efficient resource allocation and increases in overall productivity. If more people learn to fill out their own tax forms, then those currently doing this work professionally will find other uses of their time and effort that will add to the national product.

To argue that there will be chronic unemployment among those doing tax work is to deny the employment flexibility of the labor force and, in the long run, the rationality of occupational choice, because of the implicit assumption that large numbers will continue to enter the field. Those who would have specialized in tax work will seek other careers. The economy will grow because of the effective increase in human resources derived from the released time and effort formerly devoted to professional tax services. There is the threat of unemployment from all technological changes and rise in work force productivity, but the only way to avoid the danger is to sacrifice economic development for the security of low-output full employment.

NONMONETARY BENEFITS

The nonmonetary benefits which accrue mainly to the recipients of schooling are called consumption benefits. Perhaps the designation is somewhat misleading. These benefits to the individual extend beyond his role as purchaser of goods and services, and even apart from it. Rather they are labeled consumption benefits to differentiate them from measured investment returns. A speculative economist could try to put dollar values on these benefits, but given their unquantifiable nature no one has made the attempt. Instead, they are kept in the background ready to prop up a low rate of return in cases of indecision regarding the wisdom of educational investment.

While these returns accrue to those receiving education, they also benefit the society to which these individuals belong. The issue of public gain from private consumption benefits receives fuller treatment below. Three externalities, or nonmonetary benefits mainly to society apart from the individual receiving education, are also discussed. First, there are, for want of a more descriptive designation, the "general benefits" of a more informed citizenry. Then there are the increases in overall productivity and the related contributions to economic growth that an educated work force yields.

Consumption Benefits from Education

Besides the obvious financial gain of higher lifetime earnings and returns on money invested in schooling, education expands the capacity to enjoy life. This psychic, ineffable development of a feeling of well-being is difficult to describe and impossible to measure. The general rule, though, is to separate consumption gains into the two classes of "leisure-related" and "work-related" benefits. While the individual may compartmentalize his time, he cannot isolate his attitude so that there is no interrelationship between the two; he enjoys his leisure-related psychological gains while at work, and vice versa.

Leisure-related consumption benefits.—Whether any net consumption benefits arise during the period of education itself is certainly debatable. School is work, and more than a few people who believe studying requires more effort than market labor subscribe to the old aphorism "Man invented work to avoid thinking." Schools offer a variety of extracurricular activities, but the industrial worker is not without his social life.

Some would even question whether education raises the satisfaction of leisure hours after schooling. Education undoubtedly changes tastes, and, just as interpersonal comparison of utility cannot be measured, so too do intertemporal changes in tastes for the same individual defy qualitative comparison. To speak figuratively, who is to say that the individual who would have enjoyed beer if he had not gone to college has greater psychic benefits from the wine he drinks after college? Thus, if education only alters tastes, claiming consumption benefits from schooling reflects weak logic and more than a modicum of academic arrogance. It is no coincidence that analysts who measure the economic gains from schooling and add an imponderable plus for leisure-related consumption benefits are college professors.

Education does more than alter tastes. While schooling may take the edge off the simpler pleasures, it does not destroy them. New tastes and interests are grafted on to the old, and learning widens the option for enjoyment of free time. Viewed in this light, education can only benefit the individual with widened opportunities for satisfying leisure hours. He can enjoy both beer and wine, movies and plays, rock and the classics, best sellers and belles-lettres, and enjoy life as the modern counterpart of the Renaissance man.

That these psychic benefits from additional schooling might issue more from college than from high school training does not make them irrelevant to the early schooling investment decision. By adding to the rewards of college they contribute to the option value of a high school diploma. Furthermore, that these benefits go to the individual with little spillover to the rest of society still adds to the nation's welfare, the whole in this case being equal to, or greater than, the sum of its parts.

Work-related consumption benefits.—Adam Smith recognized that the nature of a man's work determined the satisfaction or dissatisfaction he derived from it, and more to the mercenary point, the wages he received. Work that was secure, pleasant, and prestigious paid less than other occupations which required the same level of preparatory investment in training time and money; similarly, unsafe, unpleasant, or insecure jobs paid more. Smith called these positive and negative work-related consumption effects "compensatory." That is, they compensated for wage differences that otherwise would not have arisen under competitive conditions for jobs requiring equal investments except for those consumption effects that were attached to them.

Education undoubtedly brings positive work-related consumption effects. The jobs the highly educated hold tend to be prestigious and responsible. The tasks involved are varied and often require independent action and judgment. Smith's standards for explaining earnings differences among the educated cannot be applied because for the most part the highly educated hold only jobs with these characteristics. While there may be little difference in fringe consumption benefits among the various occupations of the educated, there is still the question of whether the monetary benefits of higher education understate the total returns to college; that is, Smith's explanation of earnings differences can be applied across educational investment levels. A comparatively low rate of return on college investment may be compensated for by the fringe benefits of job-related psychic income from positions the educated hold. This conclusion, though lacking quantitative elegance, is more defensible than one that, with little regard for numerical accuracy, attempted to estimate (guess) dollar values for these benefits to include them in the calculated rate of return.

Consumption benefits attract people to particular fields. As a consequence, under competitive conditions the increased number lowers the value of the marginal product of these workers and depresses wages. To the extent wages measure productivity, consumption benefits, by crowding particular fields, lower potential national output and misallocate human resources which could produce more in other, less personally satisfying work. As Bowen notes in his analysis of the effect on the social returns of work-related consumption benefits, the drag on wages these benefits impose is already considered in the calculation of the rate of return.[13]

The issue in question, though, is whether we should make a mental addition of these benefits to the calculated rates in our evaluation of total social returns to education. We assumed away the question with our earlier statement that society benefits from the improved well-being of its educated members, but the issue deserves more careful review since public educational policy may be affected by the result.

Whether these benefits represent a net addition to a society depends on that society's goals and social philosophy. Under extreme nationalism with goals of unencumbered economic growth and military power, no addition should be made, and the work-related consumption benefits should be looked upon as sinister, if not treasonable, forces designed to thwart the national purpose.

We have come to expect more from our society. Our basically humanitarian political philosophy considers the individual's well-being the criterion for public policy decisions and counts an improvement in his welfare a national gain. Thus, if lower rates of return are realized because many seek and acquire education which leads to self-satisfying employment, our true national gain rises above the calculated rate of return as our citizenry derives greater satisfaction from its work effort.

Unfortunately, forces are operating against this idealistic viewpoint. International competition presses an emphasis on technology over the arts. Private loan financing of education is made with more confidence if the student prepares for a career whose monetary returns are more promising. While private lending institutions may not be expected to take a broad view of psychic benefits—banks cannot collect from the job satisfaction of their borrowers—it is incumbent on public policy makers and budgetary administrators to recognize the social value of the emotional welfare of citizens.

General Benefits

There is no disputing the need for some level of schooling to assure the maintenance of a free society. Authoritarianism feeds on ignorance, and an uninformed population cannot resist oppression from the few armed with the weapons of learning. This is not to say that education tends to be abused as a means to power, but to claim that without learning a people lacks capacity to resist those who might wish to control its attitudes and behavior. By the same token, a subjugated people cannot rise without educated leaders. The less considerate imperial powers recognized this fact by limiting the educational opportunities of their colonials; in our own country, consistent with the inhumanity of slavery, teaching slaves to read and write was in many places illegal. History, unfortunately, is filled with examples of totalitarianism in highly literate societies; nevertheless, generalized learning is a necessary if not sufficient condition for freedom.

While there is no disputing the need for some education for all to assure preservation of our political institutions, the issue is over the quantity of education to be provided. Only an educational extremist would argue that maintenance of our individual and collective liberty requires that everyone receive a college education. Pursuing this policy for the sake of the general benefits to society would waste resources that could be more beneficially directed to other uses.

But on the other hand, the complexity of modern life and the plethora of mass communications media demand more than rudimentary literacy to differentiate between information and propaganda, and to make rational political choices that do not surrender individual liberty by default because of lack of knowledge and developed reasoning power. A conservative estimate of the level of education needed to provide the general social benefits that create an intellectual climate favorable for the preservation of our democratic institutions would set a goal of universal secondary school completion.

An advance in national educational attainment to this level would not require much additional investment in basic facilities compared with the needs of other large-scale public expenditure projects. About 70 per cent of the work force has at least a high school diploma, but, more to the point, the percentage of sixteen- and seventeen-year-olds not enrolled in school in 1971 was only 10 per cent (800,000 out of 8 million).[14] In other words, only 10 per cent of those not covered by compulsory education of high school junior and senior age are not attending school. This dropout rate has fallen dramatically over the past generation. In 1953, 26 per cent in this age group were not enrolled in some form of secondary schooling (1.1 million out of 4.2 million).

Thus, compliance with a recommendation of universal secondary school completion would not require much additional investment in physical plant. Nevertheless, considerable care would have to be taken to channel funds in the right direction to make school continuation a worthwhile undertaking for those who would drop out under current programming. Forcing youths to remain in school without developing incentives other than a need to cooperate with regulations would be about as effective in securing the general social benefits from more schooling as smoking expensive cigars would be in making an individual wealthy.

Under current programs for most of the crucial 800,000 or so who now quit school immediately upon reaching the minimum school leaving age, dropping out is a rational step. Further schooling for them would not yield adequate financial returns on the extra time spent that delayed their earnings from work, nor would they likely find success in college if they struggled through the last high school years.

In short, if the state required school attendance up to age eighteen, it should make the extra school years advantageous to those who would be affected by the new regulation, those who, given the choice, would quit under current curricula. A holding operation does not develop maturity nor does it generate social values. More than an expansion of vocational training within the school program would be needed. Career education in the broadest sense, including preparation for the work environment and exposure through site visits and in-school discussions with those in different fields is required to increase understanding and appreciation of career preparation offered by formal schooling. This type of schooling would both provide an incentive to continue school and produce general social benefits of a more informed society. Many school systems are developing such programs. They are innovative, personalized, and expensive investments, but they might yield the greatest benefits in direct returns, in reduced unemployment, satisfied workers, increased probability of continuing schooling through college, and improved social and political climates—in short, in producing all the socioeconomic values that comprise education's potential.

The discussion on general benefits should not close without noting other social gains that schooling produces besides the strengthening of our democratic institutions. Education raises society's cultural level. This statement does not deny the uncertainty of positive leisure-related consumption benefits for some individuals whose tastes have simply been changed because of schooling which attributes positive cumulative benefits for all of high educational attainment. There is even more implied than the obvious conclusion that if some enjoy greater consumption benefits because of expanded tastes, the society to which they belong also profits. Such social benefits are not externalities but simple extrapolations of private gains to society as a whole.

Apart from education leading to consumption of more mentally demanding leisure activities, schooling also produces culture. Genius or even talent requires discipline and training to become productive. The literal meaning of the word education, "drawing out," explains its purpose. Even a discussion limited to the economic benefits of schooling should acknowledge that it does more than bring out the recipient's maximum earning capacity. Education helps develop whatever latent cultural expression the individual possesses, whether to perform or even to evaluate, which can bring satisfaction to all those exposed to the trained faculties of the artist or critic.

The role of education as producer of social values can also be applied to the general benefits previously described. Not only does schooling help preserve democracy by educating the electorate; it also produces leaders who are more likely to rule guided by reason rather than emotion. Outside of the political and cultural spheres, education helps increase the productivity of civic and organizational leadership.

Perhaps we attribute too much to schooling and uncritically accept years of schooling as a measure of leadership capacity, not only in business and national politics, but even in our social groups and other organizations. There is a danger of an elitism of the educated, with those not fortunate enough to have a large number of school years to their credit precluded from positions of responsibility, decision-making, and trust, despite their abilities. Currently, though, the risk is not very great. For one thing, as more people have received more schooling, awe of education has noticeably diminished to the point where many are questioning the intrinsic value of college. Also, the growing number of those attaining college has greatly reduced the less educated group suffering from the preference given the educated, and a majority is not usually considered an elitist group regardless of the unfair benefits it enjoys.

Although it takes a certain amount of schooling to become a successful embezzler, crime rates drop off sharply as the educational level rises. How much crime reduction, especially for offenses involving violence, is attributable to education, and not to other factors related to schooling, is hard to say. Wealthier students receive the most years of schooling, and crime goes down with wealth. Millionaires do not hold up grocery stores. Education also raises incomes and in doing so indirectly benefits society with reduced crime. We hope that school instills a more positive sense of civic responsibility that discourages antisocial behavior over and above the obvious deterrent to a life of crime that higher incomes consequent to schooling usually cause. Education not only disciplines the mind; it also puts the student in a social setting which requires adaptability to group activity and a degree of conformity to established norms and procedures—a combination of elements, which, if properly blended, allows for intellectual curiosity and questioning on one hand and cooperation with social requirements on the other. Of course, if schools do their job badly, there might result stultified minds and blind conformity or, on the other extreme, unchanneled, random, emotionally opinionated viewpoints and lawlessness.

There does not seem to be any tendency toward a reduction in teen-age crime despite the expansion of education for youths. This pattern does not deny the potential social gains from schooling—lowered crime rates—but rather suggests the failure of education to reach the needs and aptitudes of all its recipients. Again, a challenge arises to a recommended program of universal educational attainment through the high school years. Besides the failure of other general benefits to be realized if the schooling experience is not made fruitful for the new captive enrollment, crime rates could even rise if extended compulsion led to frustration instead of positive values.

We revert to economic factors in a last example of general benefits. The educated are big spenders. Translated into more elegant economic terminology, this means that the ratio of consumption expenditures to income rises with the level of schooling. Broadened tastes of the educated increase their demand for a variety of goods and services. This stronger demand related to schooling thus helps keep production and employment high and meets the increase in output that results from the increase in national productivity which is associated with a highly educated work force.

Education and Productivity

The gains in productivity of the educated that result in their high earnings in postschool work life are counted as direct returns to education and are included in the calculation of the rate of return on investment in schooling. To some extent, though, projection of financial gains from education by earnings differences between those who have attained a given level of schooling and those who only attained the next highest educational level overestimates the net social returns from schooling. Before discussing the indirect returns related to productivity increases from education, it is worth noting the source of overestimation of direct returns in the conventional measurement method.

Earlier we noted that employers might retain the educated and lay off the less educated during periods of economic weakness, partially explaining the higher unemployment rates of the less educated. The same preference for the educated appears in hiring. When workers are selected because of their schooling level to fill well-paying jobs in which others of less schooling could just as adequately serve, there is no national social gain in the consequent higher earnings of the educated; there has been no increase in productivity, the basis for higher earnings, because of extra years of schooling. This use of education as a screening device for employment has been called "credentialism," the acceptance by employers of a degree or diploma as a symbol of productive efficiency, without regard to the abilities of the lesser educated to satisfy job requirements. While there are no definitive data on the extent of the practice, Berg, a strong critic of credentialism, found no evidence of superior job performance for those with more schooling among a number of occupations.[15]

TABLE 2
MEDIAN YEARS OF SCHOOL COMPLETED BY THE EMPLOYED CIVILIAN LABOR FORCE, 18
YEARS AND OVER, IN SELECTED OCCUPATION GROUPS AND YEARS (1948–72)

Occupation Group	1972	1967	1962	1957	1952	1948
Professional and technical workers	16.3	16.3	16.2	16.0+	16.0+	16.0+
Managers and administrators	12.9	12.7	12.5	12.4	12.2	12.2
Craftsmen and foremen	12.2	12.0	11.2	10.5	10.1	9.7
Operatives	11.5	10.8	10.1	9.5	9.1	9.1
Nonfarm laborers	11.0	9.5	8.9	8.5	8.3	8.0
Service workers	12.0	11.0	10.2	9.0	88.8	8.7
All occupation groups	12.4	12.3	12.1	11.7	10.9	10.6

SOURCE: *Manpower Report of the President*, 1973. Data for 1972 relate to persons 16 years of age and over.

Whether or not credentialism is an important factor in employment selection, there is evidence that the recent expansion in educational attainment has surpassed industrial needs. Rather than raising productivity of the workers involved, schooling has gone beyond the limits of job requirements.

Table 2 shows the change in educational attainment for selected occupational groups over the past generation. Note that the years of schooling for the most highly trained segment of the work force, professional and technical workers, have not changed much over the years. Educational requirements for these jobs have always been exacting. Similarly, the educational attainment of managers and administrators has not changed much over time; however, sharp changes have occurred in schooling experience further down the occupational skill ladder. The growing complexity of industrial tasks, with reasoning power gradually replacing mechanical aptitude even in the trades, probably demands the extra schooling the craftsmen group has received over the past generation. But can the same be said of operatives and unskilled nonfarm laborers and service workers?

The argument here is not that these last three groups are now over-educated in the broadest sense of filling modern society's need for a more educated citizenry, but that they are overeducated for their employment schooling needs. Custodial work, for example, does not demand four years of high school to fulfill job requirements, even though general social benefits may be derived from universal high school completion.

If firms make high school graduation a requirement for employment at any level, and custodial work can be performed just as well by those with only eight years of schooling, then there are no economic returns from the extra schooling that custodians receive. There is no increase in productivity from the extra schooling, and consequently no secondary rise in output per unit of labor effort from co-workers.

The issue here is not whether there is employer preference or credentialism present, but simply whether, as seems evident from the data, workers at low-level jobs have more schooling than required for satisfactory job performance. In the latter case, as in the former, "extra" education does not contribute to output.

There is much discussion and concern over "worker alienation"—low morale of employees who do not feel challenged by their jobs. This attitude is partly attributable to advances in mass production techniques and separation of tasks from the final product, but it also undoubtedly arises from work that does not make demands on learning skills acquired through education and not held by past generations of industrial workers.

The psychological difficulties that arise from jobs that lie far below the worker's intellectual potential are customarily discussed with reference to the college work force. The data in Table 2 suggest that this modern industrial problem also reaches high school educated workers. In fact, the professional jobs, the only ones held by those who average college graduation level of schooling, required this heavy commitment to schooling in the past. Thus, it appears on the surface that the strong upward trend in the number of college graduates has no more than met the fresh demand for these highly educated workers. Table 2, however, only shows average educational attainment for each occupational group, and the number with college training in those lower groups who average close to twelve years of schooling is undoubtedly substantial. It is safe to assume their negative attitude to the nonmonetary aspects of work in these jobs is even stronger than that of the high school trained worker.

The policy implication of these facts is not that ambitions for schooling should be tempered and the amount of education reduced. Education's primary purpose is not the satisfaction of industrial demand, nor should its general benefits be sacrificed to avoid the harmful psychological effects of occupational overqualification. Instead, education for nonworking activities should be stressed and a movement made toward a cultural instead of vocational orientation in higher education. At the same time, the data do show strong demand for the educated in professional and other occupations requiring a high level of formal education and training.

Further discussion of worker alienation or adjustment to excessive employment preparation would take us too far afield. While the point has been made that the direct social rate of return is somewhat overestimated, since the lesser educated could fill many of the jobs now held by the educated, and that earnings differences do not entirely reflect productivity gains from education, the importance of this element in reducing social returns should not be overemphasized. There are certainly considerable increases in productivity resulting from expanded education. The work force has to a great degree upgraded its skills through schooling to meet the changing demand for labor toward professional and skilled workers. In short, while direct productivity gains from education may be exaggerated by unqualified rate-of-return estimations, these gains are nevertheless substantial.

Although the major growth in productivity appears in the workers who have received extra education themselves, improvements spill over in the productive efficiency of others. Workers do not produce in isolation, and the interdependence of the work force tends to diffuse productivity gains originating in one sector throughout the cooperating work force. It is not just that the educated may introduce more efficient work techniques or that their example stimulates others to greater output, though these factors do contribute to total productivity; in addition, the output of others who work closely with the educated rises as a result of the greater efficiency of their cooperating productive factors, in this case educated workers.

This derived improvement in productive efficiency can be explained by reference to the capital created by education. This is the human capital resulting from educational investment. Just as machines aid the productivity of the work force, so capital embodied in particular workers adds to the productive efficiency of other workers. The only difference between the two forms of capital, which does not affect the indirect productivity gains that result from increased output of those working with additional capital, lies in the ownership of the capital. Physical capital is owned by the firm which receives most of the returns of added output that the capital produces; human capital is embodied in the educated workers, who receive most of the returns in higher wages. In both cases, residual gains in productivity and earnings accrue to the supporting work force.

Since education raises to some extent the productivity and earnings of the less educated, direct rate-of-return calculations underestimate the social benefits of education. Earnings differences between the educated and those with less schooling shrink with a derivative rise in earnings of the latter, which lowers calculated rates of return on investment in education. The private rate of return is undoubtedly reduced, but is society worse off because of the positive spillover effects on production and earnings of the less educated? Correct social accounting should add an implicit amount to the calculated amount to arrive at an adjusted value of social gains from schooling.

These secondary gains look very much like indirect monetary returns. In fact they are, and another example of the weakness of our simple expository taxonomy must be admitted because they are also nonmonetary returns under certain social attitudes. A rise in productivity leads to increased national product and is the key to economic growth. The question, then, of whether society, as contrasted with individuals whose benefits are measured in higher earnings, is better off because its members produce and consume more goods and services determines whether nonmonetary benefits accrue from the secondary rise in productivity associated with education. This question is best discussed with reference to the relationship between education and growth.

Education and Growth

After World War II the United States, and for that matter all other advanced economies, eagerly followed economic growth as the path to national fulfillment. In an overemphasis of economic values, national greatness became equated with productive power and national output. This national outlook received further strength from Russian technological advances, and, in the early post-Sputnik years, patriotism seemed to demand that all our intellectual energies be devoted to further mechanical progress, with educational emphasis on science and technology. What little attention to the humanities which was not given to Russian language study was devoted to soul-searching for the source of our technological backwardness.

This description contains some hyperbole, but, in any case, by the mid-sixties unremitting pursuit of economic growth as a national goal began to come under criticism. The cry was raised that "Man cannot live by gross national product alone." Then the antimaterialists were joined by the ecologists in the attack against growth. More production meant more garbage, more squandering of our natural resources, and more damage to our environment. In any case the same improvement in productive capacity resulting from education that could lead to more consumption goods and a higher consumption level could be directed to the production of goods and services that increased our standard of living by improving our environment.

National output can rise through an expansion in productive factors and improvement in their quality. To increase production we must have more of this and/or more efficient labor and capital.[16] Concentrating on the labor input, we can ignore the effect of an expanded labor force on growth. More workers will increase production, but per capita product may not rise. Growth through these means promises no gain in individual economic welfare and may possibly reduce the average standard of living. Thus, narrowing our interest to labor quality changes, we see that education plays an important role in raising total output.

Education improves the productive capacity of the nation in two ways. The first and most obvious path to growth appears from upgrading the skills of the work force. Over the years the increased supply of skilled and highly trained workers has paralleled the growth in educational attainment of the nation's work force. Closely related to the gains in productivity of the educated has been the increased efficiency of the cooperating less educated work force.

Then, too, education helps improve the quality, or productive efficiency, of capital as the increased numbers of the highly educated add to the development of new machinery and processes. Further advances arise in production methods and business and office management. In short, education raises productivity within skill levels.

It is difficult to measure the contribution of education to overall productivity; even the direct gains of increased productivity of the educated, using earnings as a proxy for productivity, cannot be accurately calculated. It is even more difficult to measure its contribution to growth. Denison has made the greatest effort to measure education's share among the factors that have induced growth in the American economy, but his estimate still leaves a wide range for possible error.[17]

The measured importance of education to growth is of more than academic interest. Public investment policy designed to maximize growth wishes to be guided on information regarding the relative contribution of human and physical capital. The issue is sharper for developing countries, but it also enters decision-making in this country, though with less urgency.

Denison notes that, at least for private investment decisions, the growth element in investment in education is independent of the rate of return. Since much of private investment in schooling is made with funds that would have otherwise been used for consumption and not as an alternative to physical capital investments which were financed by conscious savings effort, the money spent on education added more to growth than if it had been invested in physical capital, even though the rates of return on the two forms of investment have moved closely together.

For the future, then, if private educational investments continue to be made as substitutes for consumption, the growth potential, or total possible investment, will continue to rise faster from educational investment than from the same amount of physical capital investment. As for public investment decisions, the question of source of funds, whether from would-be consumption expenditures or allocated savings, has less significance. The state uses taxes as its principal source of funding and whether tax money would have been saved or consumed is immaterial in its investment decision. There is some parallel to private financing, though in that, at least until recently, the public showed preference for levies that financed schooling over most other public investment projects.

The issue of separation of investment decisions from rate-of-return considerations in its effect on growth has much broader application to this entire study. The question is why individuals, and to a lesser extent the state, tend to favor educational investments over other types, a favoritism expressed in a willingness to reduce consumption to squeeze out investment funds for schooling, when rates of return are similar on educational and physical capital expenditures. Assuming rational behavior by investment decision makers, whether private individuals or public officials, this preference for educational investment indicates that direct rate-of-return estimates do not capture all the returns educational investment yields. What is missing from the calculations are the indirect benefits described in this chapter.

SUMMARY

Every empirical cost-benefit study shows that the financial gains from elementary and secondary education, measured by later earnings attributable to this schooling, far exceed costs. Furthermore, rates of return on investment in this early education greatly surpass those on alternative private and public investment projects.

Since the direct rate of return is so high and clearly above the critical level of forgone returns on alternative programs, a question might arise concerning the need for detailed discussions of benefits from early schooling not included in calculations of the rate of return. The high rate itself explains this need. Taxpayer reluctance to support more early educational investment and public decisions to finance projects competing for state funding despite high calculated rates on early schooling suggest that these rates need all the support they can get to sway investment decisions toward education. This support takes the form of indirect benefits not included in the calculation of the basic rate discussed in this chapter.

All these indirect benefits add to the positive side of public early schooling investment decisions. But the day has passed when the easily planned investments in expanded basic facilities to meet a burgeoning school-age population could gain these high returns. Now, if sizeable benefits are to be captured, investment in education must be carefully directed to programming and curriculum development that can make education a more worthwhile economic and social undertaking.

REFERENCES

1. Many of the topics discussed here are also treated in the author's *Economics of Education: Conceptual Problems and Policy Issues* (New York: McGraw-Hill, 1973).

2. The words "returns" and "benefits" are used interchangeably throughout, even though in the language the former carries a strong connotation of monetary gains.

3. Burton Weisbrod, "Education and Investment in Human Capital," *Journal of Political Economy* 70, supp. (October 1962).

4. Thomas Ribich, *Education and Poverty* (Washington: Brookings Institution, 1968), Appendix C.

5. Mary Jean Bowman, "The Costing of Human Resource Development," in *Conference on the Economics of Education* (New York: Macmillan, 1966), p. 479, advises against adjusting for unemployment in measuring the social rate, since "we are measuring resources, not failure to use them."

6. While in this section I try to focus only on monetary benefits, the purity of my methodology gladly yields to an element that yields monetary and nonmonetary benefits jointly.

7. This pattern for financing training is described by Gary Becker, *Human Capital* (National Bureau of Economic Research, 1964).

8. Jacob Mincer, "On-the-Job Training: Costs, Returns, and Some Implications," *Journal of Political Economy* 70, supp. (October 1962).

9. This explanation of retention of the skilled during recession is advanced by Walter Oi, "Labor as a Quasi-Fixed Factor," *Journal of Political Economy* 70 (December 1962).

10. For a further discussion of these indirect benefits, see Martin O'Donoghue, *Economic Dimensions in Education* (Aldine, 1971).

11. This view has been accepted since the earliest modern studies of human capital. For example, J. R. Walsh, "Capital Concept Applied to Man," *Quarterly Journal of Economics* 44 (February 1935), p. 256, writes: "The training children receive . . . is not primarily intended to develop vocational skills. Rather, it is the intent of their parents and the state to promote the education of citizens. The purpose is to provide political and cultural education in the widest sense. And although abilities which have their economic significance are developed as

a part of the process of training an intelligent electorate, these abilities are by no means the preconceived object of the training. Their appearance is incidental to the major purpose.''

12. The same analysis that follows could apply to the effect of the introduction of driver-education courses on the income of driving schools and, ultimately, on society's welfare.

13. William Bowen, *Economic Aspects of Education* (Princeton: Princeton University Press, 1964).

14. *Manpower Report of the President* (Washington, 1973).

15. Ivar Berg, *Education and Jobs: The Great Training Robbery* (New York: Praeger, 1970).

16. Confining the discussion to these two factors for the sake of simplicity loses more than a little realism, especially these days when we have become increasingly aware of the latent limitation to production imposed by a scarcity of natural resources.

17. Edward Denison, *The Sources of Economic Growth in the United States* (Committee for Economic Development, 1962).

Investment in Education and Equality of Opportunity

George Psacharopoulos

"Investment in education" and "equality of opportunity" are becoming increasingly popular concepts.* Lip service is paid to them daily by politicians, administrators, journalists, and academics alike. Yet surprisingly, we know little about the relationship between education and equality in general.

It has been taken for granted for a long time that schooling is a universally good investment and more education leads to a more equal distribution of income. But both views have been challenged. Recent evidence seems to indicate that returns to higher education (at the graduate level, in particular) are below returns to alternative forms of investment (Bailey and Schotta, 1972) and that education accounts for a small part of income inequality in our society (Jencks, 1972). Therefore, the initial enthusiasm surrounding education as a form of profitable investment and equalizer of opportunities has given place to scepticism. Possibly, other types of capital may yield higher returns, and income may be more equally distributed via direct tax subsidy schemes than via the indirect provision of educational opportunities.

This scepticism is quite valid. The field is relatively young (less than two decades), and the theoretical links have not yet been fully delineated. In addition, the data on which many analyses are based leave much to be desired.

The purpose of this paper is to attempt a clarification and integration of a number of issues centering around the efficiency and equity dimensions of education. Moreover, several pieces of empirical evidence are brought together in an effort to assess the quantitative relationship between education and equality.

The first part deals with the efficiency aspect of investment in schooling. After explaining the rate of return concept as applied to education and

*Useful discussions on this paper were provided by Nicholas Barr and Richard Layard.

discussing the usual objections to it, evidence is presented on the returns to education covering nearly forty countries. The yield of investment in education is classified into several dimensions, such as the level of schooling, and whether it refers to the individual investor or to society as a whole. Moreover, the returns to education are compared with the returns to physical capital.

The second part deals with the equality aspect of education. The concept of equality of opportunity is clarified by means of a simple model of earnings determination where ability, socioeconomic background, and years of schooling are the only independent variables. The results of existing earnings functions are utilized to assess the importance of various links in the model.

The final part brings together the efficiency and equity aspects of education within a policy context. Several educational planning methodologies are examined with emphasis on how their policy prescriptions relate to the efficiency of resource allocation in education and the distribution of income in our society.

INVESTMENT IN EDUCATION

In the post–World War II period economists faced this puzzle: Why did war-devastated countries such as Germany and Japan recover fast, while other countries such as India failed to grow in spite of masses of international aid? The clue was to be found in differences in human rather than physical capital (Schultz, 1961). Germany grew quickly because German know-how survived the war ruins. India did badly because the physical capital aid was not enough; it should have been supplemented by human know-how.

Know-how can be obtained either by experience or by formal schooling. Since learning by doing is a lengthy process, the emphasis in development planning has been on investment in education. The underlying hypothesis is that this kind of investment creates human capital and therefore helps a country to grow.

The human-capital hypothesis was further strengthened by the solution to another puzzle. When accounting for all measured conventional inputs (like raw labor, physical capital, and land), outputs in the United States seemed to grow faster than inputs (Abramovitz, 1956). What accounted for this unexplained surplus, more commonly known as the "residual"? The clue was again to be found in that raw labor (i.e., a simple head count) failed to take into account labor quality improvements via education (Denison, 1962, 1967, Jorgenson and Griliches, 1967).

There exist many analogies between human and physical capital. Physical capital is created by accumulating past investments, namely by forgoing today's potential consumption. For example, an entrepreneur invests a sum of money that he could otherwise have consumed to construct a machine. He would certainly expect a yield on his capital, say x per cent per year, the size of which would depend on the market conditions for the machine's product.

Human capital is created in a similar manner. The student (and/or his family and/or the state) incurs for a number of years some direct costs of schooling like tuition and books. Furthermore, he forgoes the salary he would be earning if he were not in school. As this salary represents potential consumption that is forgone, it must be counted as part of the indirect cost of schooling. On graduation from the highest educational level completed, the individual possesses human capital equal to the discounted sum of past investments in schooling. Of course, he would expect a return on his investment, r per cent per year, the size of which would again depend on the market conditions for graduates of the same educational level.

Let us carry this analogy further by considering a numerical example. When an entrepreneur wants to decide whether or not to invest in a machine, he has to take into account at least these data: cost of the machine, $C = \$100$; expected net annual revenue from selling the machine's products, $R_t = \$45$; expected life of the machine, $n = 3$ years (i.e., $t = 1, 2, 3$); the market rate of interest (or the discount rate), $i = 10$ per cent.

Given these data, he can estimate the net present value (NPV) of the machine, namely, NPV = sum of discounted benefits − cost. If the net present value is positive he will buy the machine. In our particular example,

$$\text{NPV} = \sum_{t=1}^{n} \frac{R_t}{(1+i)} - C = 45 \sum_{t=1}^{3} \frac{1}{(1+0.1)^t} - C \doteq 110 - 100 = \$10.$$

Since the machine gives a net surplus of $10, the rational entrepreneur would decide to invest in it. An alternative calculation which amounts to virtually the same decision is to set the net present value equal to zero and solve for the discount rate. There are cases where the rate of return and present value criteria would yield different answers (Hirshleifer, 1958). Such cases, however, are rarely encountered when evaluating educational projects. Namely,

$$\text{NPV} = 0 = 45 \sum_{t=1}^{3} \frac{1}{(1+r)^t} - 100.$$

The only unknown in the first equation is r, which is the yield, or rate of return, or profitability, of investing in this particular machine. The approximate value of r in this case is 11 per cent, and since this is higher than the alternative rate of discount (i = 10 per cent) the rational entrepreneur would decide to buy the machine.

In applying this approach to the human capital equivalent, assume that a high school graduate behaves like an entrepreneur in deciding whether to invest in a four-year college education. The investment cost in this case would comprise four years of direct outlays plus forgone earnings. The benefits would consist of the differential between what college graduates and high school graduates earn. The relationship between costs and benefits of this particular investment is depicted in Figure 1.

Cross-sectional data of people with different amounts of schooling at different ages give the earnings profiles Y_c for college and Y_h for high school graduates. Note that the earnings of college graduates start four years later, grow faster, and reach their peak at a later age, relative to the earnings of high school graduates. The benefits the student would expect from this type of investment over his lifetime are equal to area B, namely the difference between the two profiles. The costs of the investment consist of two parts, the direct costs, area C_1, and the forgone earnings, area C_2. Therefore, the total schooling cost, C, is equal to $C_1 + C_2$.

Let us now bring in the time dimension. Since costs and benefits occur at different ages, they should be discounted to a common point in time in order to be compared, i.e.,

$$\text{NPV} = B - C = \left[\sum_{t=1}^{43} \frac{B_t}{(1+i)^t} \right] \frac{1}{(1+i)^4} - \sum_{t=1}^{4} \frac{C_t}{(1+i)^t}.$$

In this expression B_t stands for the benefits at any given age, namely, $B_t = (Y_c - Y_h)_t$; C_t stands for the sum of direct plus indirect costs, namely $C_t = (C_1 + C_2)_t$; and i stands for the discount rate.

In other words, the annual benefits are discounted to age twenty-two and then their sum is discounted back to the common point in time (age eighteen) to be compared to the sum of discounted costs. If the net present value is positive, the investment-oriented student would enroll in higher education. The student's decision could also be taken by setting NPV = 0 in the second equation and solving for i, now called the rate of return to investment in education. In view of the fact that comparison of absolute net present values is awkward, further discussion will proceed exclusively in terms of rates of return.

Rates of return to education can be classified by many dimensions depending on the adjustments made in the data, the point of view of the investor, or the educational level to which they refer. Of the many existing rate-of-return species, consideration will be given to two that are relevant to the analysis in this paper—social versus private rates and rates by completed educational cycles.

The yield to investment to any form of capital (physical or human) can be seen from two points of view, that of the individual investor and that of society as a whole. Consider the case of investment in a new factory. If the

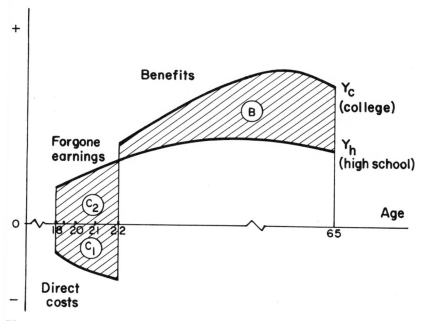

Fig. 1. Costs and benefits of investment in college education

government judges that the factory would alleviate unemployment in the region, it might subsidize it. Since the government covers part of the cost, the entrepreneur would enjoy a higher private rate of return than would society as a whole. Alternatively, if the government taxes away a part of the profits of a brewery, investment in this kind of capital would yield a lower private rate of return to the entrepreneur. To put it in other words, taxes and subsidies create discrepancies between private and social rates of return.

Since earnings are taxed and educational costs are subsidized, the private-social distinction is a must when considering the returns to investment in schooling. A social rate of return to investment in education results when costs are accounted in full and benefits are accounted gross of taxes. Full costing means to compute as part of the costs what a university place really costs, not just what the student pays in the form of tuition (if he pays any tuition at all). Free education means that it costs nothing to the individual in terms of direct costs, but it certainly costs something to the government that provides for university places and also to society as a whole, as well as to the student himself in terms of forgone production.

The rationale for dealing with the earnings gross of taxes in a social rate-of-return calculation lies in the nature of taxes as transfer payments. What an individual pays in the form of income tax, another individual (or even himself) receives back in the form of government services. Conversely, a private rate of return is calculated on the basis of after-tax earnings, as this is what the individual realizes. Costs include only what the individual pays, which is, of course, less than the full social cost of education.

The example depicted in Figure 1 dealt with the estimation of the rate of return to higher education. Similarly, one can use pairs of age-earnings profiles for adjacent educational levels and compute the rate of return to secondary or to primary schooling. All rates of return carry a notion of marginality, as the investment refers to a schooling *increment* (e.g., to higher education) over a base level (secondary education). But this marginality is not strict in any economic sense as it refers to the full educational cycle encompassing many years. The term "marginal" therefore is simply used to avoid confusion with an "average" rate of return to all levels of schooling, which would be much harder to define.

Qualifications

This analysis, although simple, raises a series of objections. Let us list the most common ones along with the human-capital theory counter-arguments.

1. *You cannot treat human beings as machines.* Let us dismiss this objection as old-fashioned; it could have been valid if slavery were still common practice. All human-capital theory does is treat human beings *as if* they were machines in order to permit the estimation of costs and benefits associated with the investment in education and their comparison. It does not treat human beings *as* machines.

2. *No student would behave like an investment analyst on the question of whether or not to go to college.* Yes, of course, although the "as if" argument applies here as well. Moreover, we could ask the profitability question in an ex post rather than an ex ante way—what has been the

profitability of investment in higher education for someone who has decided, *for whatever reason*, to enroll in college? It is in this historical sense that most of the returns to education have been estimated.

This is similar to asking what is the profitability of a machine that has already been bought. For that we would not have to wait until the machine ends its working life. All we have to do is look around at similar machines of different ages, record their annual cash flow, and arrive at an estimate of the profitability of a machine of this kind.

3. *Part of the earnings differential is due to ability, not to education.* If graduates are on the average abler than nongraduates (assuming they have a higher IQ level), part of the earnings differential should be attributed to ability rather than education. Denison (1964) suggested that the earnings differential should be adjusted downward by 40 per cent in order to take into account ability and other factors correlated positively with more education. Since then, however, a flood of empirical evidence has suggested an ever decreasing adjustment factor for ability (e.g., see Griliches and Mason, 1972, Griliches, 1970, and Hause, 1972).

4. *The salaries on which the returns to education are based do not correspond to the social marginal product of labor.* This is the most repeated criticism of human-capital theory. If wages are determined by nepotism, custom, need, or the like, how could one talk of the social returns to education? This objection and the following one refer only to the social rate of return. Private rates of return would remain valid even if objections 4 and 5 were correct. There are ways one can bypass this objection. First, there exist econometric techniques that can yield the so-called shadow wage rates on which the rate of return calculation can be based (Psacharopoulos, 1970, Layard et al., 1971). Second, one can concentrate on the earnings in a competitive sector of the labor market not likely to be subject to institutional or other distortions (Harberger, 1971).

5. *Education is simply a screening device and carries no social product.* This is the most recent attack on the economics of education. All schooling does is stamp people with a certificate, the possession of which enables access to highly paid jobs. (For a mild version of this theory see Wiles, 1974.) Thus the social returns to education should be drastically reduced (up to 50 per cent, according to Taubman and Wales, 1973), as part of the earnings differential between graduates and nongraduates represents a private transfer payment, not a social gain.

But the screening hypothesis does not stand against empirical tests. As we have demonstrated elsewhere (Layard and Psacharopoulos, 1974), the screening hypothesis yields three unverified predictions. First, employers would have devised cheaper methods for screening candidates for ability. But those tests are not common practice. Second, the returns to completed educational levels would have been higher than the returns to dropouts of the same level. But this is not universally true. Last, age-earnings profiles for different educational levels would converge over time. This is because employers would later correct hiring mistakes if the employee's productivity were less than his wage. But, in practice, such age-earnings profiles diverge rather than converge.

The Evidence

Once the concept of human capital was established, researchers started to estimate the profitability of the new form of investment. The major part of the estimation activity centered in the United States for the simple reason of data availability, but it soon spread to all five continents.

In this section we will present evidence on the returns to education in the U.S. and in other countries classified by two dimensions—the level of schooling they refer to and whether they refer to the individual investor or to society as a whole. The returns to education will then be compared to the returns to physical capital in an effort to assess the allocative efficiency of investment in education both within the educational sector and between education and the rest of the economy.

The returns to education in the United States have been studied by Becker (1960), Hansen (1963), Hunt (1963), Hanoch (1967), Rogers (1969), Ashenfelter and Mooney (1968), Hines et al. (1970), Weiss (1971), Taubman and Wales (1973), Eckaus (1973), Johnson and Stafford (1973), and many others. The comprehensiveness of the different studies varies enormously. Some used census data while others used special surveys. Some report the returns to education at all levels while others deal exclusively with graduate education. Further, the comparability of the different studies is limited by the fact that their authors used different adjustments in order to arrive at the rates of return.

In this paper we will concentrate on those studies that have used 1960 U.S. Census data. There exist three such studies that have produced rates of return for more than one level: Hines et al. (1970), Hanoch (1967), and Eckaus (1973). All three produced private rates of return, but Hines et al. reported social rates as well. The rates of return from these studies are reported in Table 1. The reader should be warned that these rates are not strictly comparable. Although the rates in all studies refer to white males and are free from ability or growth adjustments, Eckaus' rates are adjusted for hours worked. Moreover, the base line for the returns to primary education differs among the studies. (See footnote to Table 1.)

In spite of these differences, however, one can discern a common

TABLE 1
PERCENTAGE RATES OF RETURN TO INVESTMENT IN EDUCATION BY LEVEL, U.S., 1959

Educational Level	Social	Private		
	Hines et al. (1970)	Hines et al. (1970)	Hanoch (1967)	Eckaus (1973)
Elementary (8 versus 0)	17.8	155.1	> 100.0	31.5
High school (12 versus 8)	14.0	19.5	16.1	4.0
College (16 versus 12)	9.7	13.6	9.6	12.0

NOTES: All rates are based on census data and refer to white males. Hanoch's rates refer to white males in the North. Hanoch's control group for the returns to elementary education is 0–4 years of schooling; Eckaus' corresponding control group is 0–7 years. Eckaus' rates are adjusted for hours worked.

pattern in the returns to education. With one exception (Eckaus' 4 per cent rate for secondary schooling), private rates are higher than social rates. This is because the tax-subsidy interplay results in a net subsidization of education at all levels. Moreover, the rates of return decline as the level of education rises. This is an indication of diminishing returns to investment in education.

Regarding absolute magnitudes, all studies support the proposition that the returns to primary education are extremely high. Moreover, the returns to a bachelor's degree vary little around the 10 per cent mark. This last finding has been confirmed by other studies that have used special sample surveys instead of census data to produce returns to a bachelor's degree. The results of three such studies are reported in Table 2.

There also exists evidence on the returns to education beyond the B.A. The results of seven such studies are reported in Table 3. They show that

TABLE 2
PERCENTAGE RATES OF RETURN TO A B.A. USING SPECIAL SAMPLE SURVEYS

Source	Social	Private
Rogers (1969)	NA	8
Taubman and Wales (1973)	10	11
Johnson and Stafford (1973)	9	NA

NOTE: Johnson and Stafford's estimates are for colleges of average quality.

the returns to graduate education are in all cases below the returns to a first degree. Moreover, some studies report zero or even negative social rates of return to graduate study.

It might be argued that this rate-of-return pattern—i.e., the declining rates by educational level and the very low returns to graduate education—is specific to the United States. Examination of the returns to education in other countries, however, shows that this is the prevailing pattern. As I have demonstrated elsewhere (Psacharopoulos, 1973a), the returns to education in thirty-one countries are on the average consistent with the above U.S. pattern. These countries are Canada, Puerto Rico,

TABLE 3
PERCENTAGE RETURNS TO GRADUATE EDUCATION IN THE U.S.

Source	Social		Private		
	M.A.	Ph.D.	Unspecified (1 year +)	M.A.	Ph.D.
Hunt (1963)	NA	NA	NA	−1.0	0.0
Hanoch (1967)	NA	NA	7.0	NA	NA
Ashenfelter and Mooney (1968)	NA	NA	NA	7.5	9.1
Weiss (1971)	NA	NA	NA	6.6	4.8
Bailey and Schotta (1972)	NA	1.4	NA	NA	2.5
Taubman and Wales (1973)	8.0	4.0	NA	8.0	4.0
Eckaus (1973)	NA	NA	4.5	NA	NA

NOTES: Weiss' rates refer to normal completion time and assume zero student part-time earnings. Bailey and Schotta's rates refer to all teaching ranks. Eckaus' rate is adjusted for hours worked but not for growth.

Mexico, Venezuela, Colombia, Chile, Brazil, Great Britain, Norway, Sweden, Denmark, The Netherlands, Belgium, Germany, Greece, Turkey, Israel, India, Malaysia, Singapore, the Philippines, Japan, South Korea, Thailand, Nigeria, Ghana, Kenya, Uganda, Rhodesia, New Zealand, and Hawaii (before becoming a state). In spite of the many difficulties in arriving at comparable rate-of-return figures between countries, the large number of case studies (fifty-three in all) lends support to this finding. Moreover, an additional set of studies for the same countries has largely confirmed the earlier results. (See Hoerr [1973] on Malaysia, Blaug [1973] on the Philippines, Stoikov [1973] on Japan, Klevmarken [1972] on Sweden, and Dodge and Stager [1972] on Canada.)

There have also been profitability studies in countries not included in the original survey, and their results are shown in Table 4. This table also confirms the high profitability of the primary school level. Moreover, Table 5 shows that the social returns to graduate education in countries other than the U.S. are on the low side and never exceed the 10 per cent mark.

TABLE 4
PERCENTAGE RETURNS TO EDUCATION IN FIVE ADDITIONAL COUNTRIES

Country	Social			Private		
	Primary	Secondary	Higher	Primary	Secondary	Higher
Australia (a)	NA	NA	NA	NA	14.0	13.9
Australia (b)	NA	NA	8.4	NA	NA	15.0
France	NA	NA	NA	NA	13.8	12.2
Iran	27.0	5.0	9.0	> 100.0	5.0	12.0
Taiwan	27.0	12.3	17.7	> 50.0	12.7	15.8
Morocco	40.4	28.5	5.5	74.3	35.7	13.0

SOURCES: Australia (a), from Blandy and Goldsworthy (1972); Australia (b), from O'Byrne (1971); France, from Mingat and Lévy-Garboua (1973), preliminary estimates; Iran, from Psacharopoulos and Williams (1973); Taiwan, from Gannicott (1972); Morocco, from Psacharopoulos (1972).

Based on the evidence of all existing profitability studies in nearly forty countries, I have attempted to present in Table 6 worldwide averages of the returns to education by level. In view of the variability of the returns and methodologies used, this is an extremely difficult task. Nevertheless, what appears in Table 6 is what I consider to be a set of typical returns to education.

The returns to primary education are stated as minimum values. This is because in some cases the profitability of education at this level reaches infinity, due to the zero earnings forgone at young ages. The returns to secondary education and to higher education (first degree) are taken from Psacharopoulos (1973a, Table 4.2). This is because the new evidence is largely consistent with the averages of the older survey. Lastly, the returns

TABLE 5
PERCENTAGE RETURNS TO GRADUATE EDUCATION IN COUNTRIES OTHER THAN THE U.S.

Country	Social		Private	
	M.A.	Ph.D.	M.A.	Ph.D.
United Kingdom (a)	2.6	2.6	NA	NA
United Kingdom (b)	2.5	4.5	18.0	17.5
United Kingdom (c)	NA	4.2	NA	8.2
France	NA	NA	NA	NA
Canada	8.2	3.5	13.7	7.8
Iran	9.0	6.0	13.0	9.0

SOURCES: U.K. (a) from Morris and Ziderman (1971); U.K. (b) from Ziderman (1973); U.K. (c) from Metcalf (1973); Iran, from Psacharopoulos and Williams (1973); Canada, from Dodge and Stager (1972); figures are maximum rates regardless of field of study.

at the graduate level are stated as the observed range of values in the United States. This is in order to avoid averaging of what may be the most heterogeneous and least comparable educational level across countries.

Subject to the qualifications presented earlier, these propositions can be derived from Table 6: (1) It is almost meaningless to talk about "the returns to education" without reference to a particular educational level. The reason is that the returns vary among levels as much as from about zero to infinity. (2) When the variance of the returns by level is taken into account, it is the lower educational levels that exhibit the highest profitability. (3) There exists a severe misallocation of resources devoted to education, both within the education sector and between education and the rest of the economy.

TABLE 6
PERCENTAGE OF WORLD AVERAGE RATES OF RETURN BY EDUCATIONAL LEVEL

Educational Level	Social	Private
Primary	> 25	> 50
Secondary	14	16
Higher, first degree	11	18
Graduate level	1 to 8	− 1 to 9

SOURCE: See text.

NOTE: Figures are rough orders of magnitude.

Efficient allocation of resources devoted to education would mean equalization of the social rates of return at all educational levels and, moreover, equalization of this common social rate of return of investment in education to the yield of investment in physical capital.

There have been many studies whose authors attempted to find the returns to investment in physical capital (e.g., Minhas [1963], who developed estimates of the returns to physical capital in a number of countries). Although the results of these studies vary enormously according to the methodology used, the values of the estimated returns are less dispersed than the returns to human capital. Whether one adopts as the alternative discount rate the yield of long-term bonds, the before-tax rate of profit of corporations or any other before-tax measure of the rate of interest, the value par excellence of the returns to physical capital has centered around the magic 10 per cent mark. This also happens to coincide with the value estimated by Jorgenson and Griliches (1967) in the United States. Since this rate refers to 1959, i.e., the same year as that to which the U.S. returns to education refer, it may be adopted for comparison with the returns to education. To repeat, the exact choice of the rate of return to physical capital is not crucial, as this rate is not as sensitive as the returns to education.

If we use the 10 per cent bench mark, the figures in Table 6 suggest that investment in education in general is more profitable than investment in physical capital. In other words, there exists a worldwide underinvestment in education. It is in this sense that a country might consider giving priority to investment in schools rather than to the construction of another steel mill.

If we consider the social returns to education by level, the figures in Table 6 suggest that higher education (at the bachelor's level) is just socially profitable. Resources devoted to secondary and particularly primary education exhibit a larger payoff than investment in physical capital. The social (monetary) payoff of graduate education is low in comparison to the returns to the other levels or to the alternative discount rate. This structure of the rates of return by level suggests a budgetary reshuffling of expenditures toward primary and secondary levels in order to achieve an efficient allocation of resources within the education sector.

These propositions resulting from the profitability estimates examined in this section are consistent with the results of alternative analytical techniques, like production function analysis. For this purpose one can define an aggregate cross-country production function of the type

$$Y = f(K_h, K_m, L),$$

where Y is the country's level of output, say, Gross National Product (GNP), K_h is a measure of the country's human capital stock (measured as the sum of past accumulated investments in education), K_m is a measure of the country's stock of physical capital (measured as the sum of past investments in conventional capital), and L is a measure of the country's labor force. When this function is fitted across countries, it is possible to assess the relative strength of the three independent variables in determining the level of income. In an earlier study I found that human capital was a more important variable in determining output than either physical capital or brute labor (Psacharopoulos, 1973a). In another work along the same lines based on a never-fitted aggregate production function, Krueger (1968) derived inequality statements regarding the part of income differences attributable to three human factors—differences in the number of years of schooling, age distribution, and urban-rural distribution of the population. She concluded that "differences in human resources between the United States and the less developed countries account for more of the difference in per capita income than all other factors combined." These results are consistent with and moreover confirm the above proposition that priority might be given to human versus physical capital in the development process.

An alternative way one can specify the above function is

$$Y = f(L_o, L_p, L_s, L_h, K_m),$$

where subscripts refer to different categories of human inputs, namely, labor with primary (p), secondary (s), higher (h), or no (o) qualifications. When this function is fitted across countries one can assess the relative importance of each category of educated labor in determining the level of output. In my earlier work I found that labor with secondary qualifications contributes more to output than labor with higher qualifications (Psacharopoulos, 1973a). Moreover, the Organization for Economic Cooperation and Development (OECD) (1971) found that when labor was split into two categories, those with higher qualifications and the rest, it was the rest that contributed most to output. These results are consistent with and confirm the rate-of-return structure by educational level presented earlier.

Differentiation of a production function of the last type with respect to one category of labor yields the social marginal product of this category of labor. This can in turn be compared to the actual market wage rate. The result of an exercise of this kind was that labor with secondary qualifications was paid less than it contributed to output (Psacharopoulos, 1973a).

A further use of an aggregate production function is in assessing the sources of economic growth. When labor was classified by three educational levels, it was the primary and secondary levels that accounted for most of the rate of growth of output attributed to education in general in a large number of countries (Psacharopoulos, 1973a).

By way of summary, the superiority of the lower levels of education is not only supported by evidence from a large number of countries, but by using alternative analytical techniques as well.

This discussion has concentrated on the efficiency aspect of investment in education—more education of the right kind means higher social output. But how is this output distributed among different people? This question refers to the equity aspect of education and will be discussed in the rest of this chapter.

EQUALITY OF OPPORTUNITY

Equality of opportunity is a very popular slogan. It may well be that this popularity is responsible for the loose way in which this term is often used and for the fact that it means different things to different people. Therefore, our first task here is to ask what we really mean when we use this phrase, and we find three main areas of confusion. (For additional discussion see Blaug [1970] and Klappholz [1972].)

To begin with, equality of opportunity is a vague concept since it is not always specified to what the opportunity refers. Does equality refer to educational opportunity, employment opportunity, occupational opportunity, income-earning opportunity, or to what sociologists call opportunity for "success" in life?

Even if the reference of opportunity is given, the way in which opportunities should be equalized is not always made explicit. For example, the most popular concept of equality of educational opportunity does not specify whether equality should be judged via an input measure, e.g., by an equal expenditure on all children, or by an output measure, e.g., by equal achievement, which would require unequal expenditure on children to compensate for differences in ability and cultural background.

Let us consider equality of employment opportunity, namely, that equally productive workers receive equal pay irrespective of age, sex, education, and the like (Corazzini, 1972). How can the productivity of an individual be assessed? As Arrow (1973) has shown, employers faced with uncertainty of the productivity of *individual* workers adopt a policy of offering higher wages to *groups* of individuals classified by ascending educational level. Therefore, equality of employment opportunity reduces to equality of educational opportunity. Evidently, most of the items the opportunity refers to are likely to be highly correlated, e.g., success in life, income, education, and employment.

The second point of vagueness is a confusion between equality of opportunity and equality itself. In a strict sense, equality of opportunity ends with equalizing the chances of achieving something. The eventual outcome is left to the individual, e.g., to his effort or chance.

Alternatively, concern with equality itself, e.g., income distribution, refers to a step beyond the concept of equality of opportunity. This is because equality of opportunity means (or should mean) equal distribution of *access* toward, say, a higher level of income. It does not (or should not) refer to the distribution of income itself. In other words, equality of opportunity can be thought of as a necessary but not a sufficient condition for equality of income distribution, when other factors like chance are held constant.

The third, and maybe the major, source of confusion regarding the concept of equality of opportunity is the determination of which characteristics governing the individual's chances of success should be controlled and which should be allowed free play.

According to one definition, equality of opportunity exists when a representative individual of one social group has the same probability of succeeding as does a representative individual of any other social group (Ribich, 1972). But what if the "representative" individuals of the two groups differ in IQ levels? Should one allow success differences because of talent or not?

At this point it is useful to distinguish between the weak (older) and the strong (more recent) versions of equality of opportunity (O'Donoghue, 1971). The former reflects the classic meritocratic view, namely, Talent (e.g., IQ) + Effort = Merit (i.e., income). (For an elaboration see Young [1958].) According to this version, one's chances of success should be allowed to vary with ability, but differences in socioeconomic background should be compensated for, e.g., by providing scholarships to poor students.

The strong version, in contrast, requires that differences in abilities are compensated for as well. This is associated with the view that most IQ differentials are environmentally rather than genetically determined. This view, therefore, advocates positive discrimination in schools in favor of less able students and abolition of culturally determined examinations.

Equality of Opportunity in the Earnings-Determining Process

In view of these ambiguities, we will try to outline in this section a simple model of equality of opportunity. The purpose of this model is to provide an integrating framework of the various concepts discussed in the preceding paragraphs. Results of existing research will be utilized to assess the importance of the various links in the model.

It will be assumed that the ultimate aim of equalizing opportunities is to achieve a certain level and structure of earnings (Y). This is, of course, a very narrow view of what success in life means, but it has the advantage of being a concrete and measurable variable, not to mention the fact that many in our society, rightly or wrongly, would identify success with income.

It will be further assumed that the individual's earnings (dependent variable) are determined by three independent variables: his level of educational attainment (S), his ability (A), and his socioeconomic background (B). Consideration of these variables would enable us to specify in a concrete way the criterion of equality of opportunity, to distinguish between equality of opportunity and equality itself, and also to accommodate both the weak and strong versions of equality of opportunity. The inclusion of only four variables (Y, S, A, and B) is an abstraction to simplify exposition. Each variable can be easily expanded into a set of more specific variables.

Y is narrowly defined as the level of money labor earnings. This is in order to exclude effects of property income determined by inheritance and institutional conditions. A broader definition of Y might include nonmoney income (like leisure time), but we exclude this on pragmatic grounds; Y might be defined on a lifetime rather than annual basis so as to take into account differently shaped age-earnings profiles.

S is measured as number of years of schooling, or it could represent the highest level of educational attainment. This variable abstracts from quality differences among schools but it can be easily expanded into a broader view of attainment by including a quality dimension.

A refers either to genetic IQ ability (e.g., IQ measured at an early age) or to acquired ability because of a better socioeconomic background. The "either" is crucial if we want to distinguish between the strong and weak versions of equality of opportunity.

B can be measured by any proxy of socioeconomic background, such as father's occupation, family income, etc.

The structure of earnings (or income distribution) will be measured by the variance of the logarithm of earnings (Var log Y). The higher the variance of the log of earnings, the more unequal the income distribution. The reason why this particular measure of inequality is chosen (and not, say, the Gini coefficient) will be made clear in what follows.

The relationships among the four variables are presented in Figure 2. It is assumed that the level and structure of earnings are determined in a sequential process. Socioeconomic background and ability determine one's highest educational attainment which in turn determines one's earnings (link 3) and also the structure of earnings in society (link 4). Links 1, 2, and 3 refer to *one* individual, whereas link 4 refers to income distribution when *all* individuals are taken into account. Note also that socioeconomic background can independently determine the level of ability (broken link 5). Given this model, the concept of equality of opportunity becomes more clear and concrete and, moreover, is easily linked to our beginning discussion.

Equality of opportunity means the removal of obstacles in paths 1 and/or 2 in this model. The removal of obstacles only in route 1 refers to the weak version of equality of opportunity. The removal of obstacles in both routes 1 and 2 refers to the strong version. Our earlier discussion concentrated on link 3.

This argument can also be presented another way. The weak version of equality of opportunity requires that the expected earnings of all individuals, regardless of social background, is equal to a constant k, i.e.,

E (Y | A, S) = k, for all B.

The strong version, however, requires correction for A as well, namely,

E (Y | S) = k, for all B and A.

Note that the *actual* value will not necessarily be equalized, as there

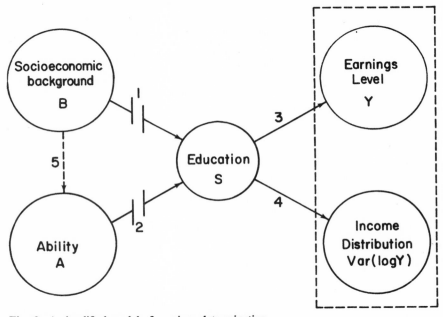

Fig. 2. A simplified model of earnings determination

exists a host of other factors (Z), such as luck, operating in the income-determination process, which are beyond policy control. It is only the *expected* or *average* value that is equalized.

Regardless of the controversy between the two versions, equality of opportunity means that success (measured by earnings in our case) should be independent of some factors we regard as unacceptable in the determination of income (like family background).

It should also be noted that this model defines a one-way relationship: equality of opportunity ⟶ (investment in) education. In this sense it is an intragenerational model. However, more education today would mean more equality of opportunity for tomorrow's children. Therefore, a relation of the type (investment in) education ⟶ equality of opportunity can be defined only in an intergenerational sense.

Although the intergenerational effects of equality of opportunity cannot be denied (see Bowles, 1972, 1973), our main concern here is with more short-term, intragenerational effects of equality of opportunity on earnings.

Some Evidence on the Model's Links

The relationship that we know most about in the model presented is link 3. The explained variance of earnings by all independent variables in earnings function analysis seldom exceeds 40 per cent. "Other" main variables

TABLE 7
PERCENTAGE INCREASE IN EARNINGS ASSOCIATED WITH ONE EXTRA YEAR
OF SCHOOLING IN THE UNITED STATES

$\dfrac{\Delta Y}{\Delta S}$ %	Main Variables other than Years of Schooling	Source
2.0	Age, sex, race, occupation	Hirsch and Segelhorst (1965)
6.4	Age, race, region, residence	Hanoch (1965)
8.0		Lassiter (1966)
7.8		Griliches (1970)
6.7	Age, weeks worked, marital status	Weiss (1970)
3.5	Age	Hansen et al. (1970)
0.8	Age, race, occupation, experience	Rees and Shultz (1970)
4.6	Age, ability, schooling before service	Griliches and Mason (1972)
3.8	Ability, interaction schooling ability	Hause (1972)
4.3	Family background	Bowles (1972)
4.0	Experience, ability	Solmon (1973)
7.3		Becker and Chiswick (1966)
8.0		Chiswick (1970)
11.0	Experience, (Exp)^2, weeks worked	Chiswick and Mincer (1972)
7.0		Mincer (1972)

include occupation, age, family background, ability, sex, and weeks worked. Although the percentage of the variance of earnings explained by education alone is usually small (e.g., on the order of 3 per cent in Jencks, 1972), the regression coefficient of Y on S (controlling for other factors) is in most cases statistically significant. Tables 7 and 8 show the effect of one extra year of schooling on earnings, both in the United States and in other countries. The percentage increase in earnings associated with one extra year of education centers around the 5 to 7 per cent mark. But as demonstrated earlier, this increase, when compared to the costs of schooling, is sufficient to generate rather high rates of return to investment in education.

The strength of the other links in the model has not been investigated as much. Although there exist nearly a hundred applications of earnings

TABLE 8
PERCENTAGE INCREASE IN EARNINGS ASSOCIATED WITH ONE EXTRA YEAR
OF SCHOOLING IN COUNTRIES OTHER THAN THE UNITED STATES

Country	$\frac{\Delta Y}{\Delta S}$ %	Main Variable in the Function other than Years of Schooling	Source
Sweden	5.3	Ability	Griliches (1970)
Mexico	17.0		Carnoy (1967)
	15.0	Age	
	12.0	Age, father's occupation, city, attendance	
S. Vietnam	16.8	Age, multiple jobs	Stroup and Hargrove (1969)
Colombia	6.6	Age, family background, migration	Schultz (1968)
Thailand	5.0		Blaug (1971)
	4.6	Age	
	4.7	Age, sex	
Taiwan	7.5		Gannicott (1972)
	6.0	Age, family background, sector	
Malaysia	5.3		Hoerr (1973)
Kenya	6.4		Thias and Carnoy (1972)
	4.8	Age, father's literacy, tribe	
Iran	5.7	Age, sex, civil service status	Psacharopoulos and Williams (1973)

functions, the relationship among ability, socioeconomic background, and education has been analyzed in the context of a single regression equation and not in a sequential way. However, Bowles (1972) found that link 1 is stronger than link 3. In his work, socioeconomic background explains over 50 per cent of the variance of years of schooling attained, whereas education usually explains much less of the earnings variance. Morgenstern (1973) has also found strong indirect effects of socioeconomic background, as measured by father's education, on earnings via effects on the wage earner's educational attainment. In his work socioeconomic background affects the child's years of school completed by as much as 20 per cent. In another work Jencks (1972) found that socioeconomic background (as measured by parents' education and occupation) explains 11.1 per cent of the variance of educational attainment. In Duncan (1967) the corresponding figure is 33 per cent.

Although there exists a sizeable literature on the effects of ability on earnings, not much exists on the effects of ability on educational attainment (link 2). In Jencks' work, IQ independent from socioeconomic background explains 18.6 per cent of the variance in educational attainment. In Duncan (1968) the corresponding figure is 16.4 per cent.

Evidence on the strength of link 5 is even more scanty. Bowles (1972) found a standardized coefficient of socioeconomic background on childhood IQ equal to 0.2. Duncan (1968) and Sewell et al. (1969) found correlation coefficients between ability and socioeconomic background of the order of 0.21 to 0.27, and in Jencks (1972), family background explains 15.1 per cent of the variation of IQ at the age of eleven.

Turning to link 4, we note that we must go beyond the sequence in determining the *level* of earnings, as generated by links 1, 2, 3, and 5. In order to be able to talk about income *distribution* we must somehow bring into the analysis the numbers of people receiving a given level of earnings.

The classic work attempting to link the concept of equality of opportunity, schooling, and income distribution is Becker's. In his theoretical work (Becker, 1967), efficiency and equity do not necessarily contradict each other. Becker used a particular example of equality of opportunity, namely, the cost of financing educational expenditures. Equalizing opportunities in this sense means that all individuals, whether from a rich or a poor family, face an almost identical and very elastic supply curve of funds for education purposes. This elastic supply curve produces in turn almost equal rates of return to investment in education at all levels. In Becker's words (1967, p. 34), "if all supply curves have infinite elasticities, equalizing opportunities not only reduces the inequality in earnings and investments but also reduces the inequality in marginal rates, which means that the total investment in human capital is allocated more efficiently."

However, in a series of empirical works the link between schooling and income distribution becomes more ambiguous. Suppose that, because of equalization of opportunities, the level of schooling of the population increases. Will income distribution improve or not?

Several authors, Becker and Chiswick (1966), Chiswick (1969), Chiswick (1971), Chiswick and Mincer (1972), and Mincer (1972), have used in their empirical analyses an earnings-generating function where the logarithm of an individual's earnings depends upon the private rate of return to the average year of schooling and the total number of years of school completed. For the derivation of this earnings-generating function see Becker (1971) or Becker and Chiswick (1966). Considering all individuals, the variance of the logarithm of earnings measures income inequality:

the higher the variance of earnings, the more unequally income is distributed.

Using this income-generating function, Becker, Mincer, and Chiswick have expressed earnings inequality as a function of the variance and level of the rate of return to schooling and the years of school completed. This theory predicts a more unequal income distribution as the level of schooling of the population increases.

However, this result is obtained on the basis of a crucial simplifying assumption, namely, that the number of years of schooling and the returns to it are independent random variables. But as demonstrated (see Table 6), the level of schooling and the returns to it are negatively related. Given this fact, the prediction on income inequality as the level of schooling increases is reversed. Marin and Psacharopoulos (1973) have shown that when the exact formula for the variance of a product of correlated variables is used, income is distributed more equally as the level of schooling increases (see Goodman, 1960). This result was obtained by using roughly the same population as the one in the works of Becker, Mincer, and Chiswick —whites in the North of the United States.

The sensitivity test consisted of varying the level of schooling in the United States' actual situation and observing the change in income distribution. The test revealed that the current pessimistic prediction about income inequality and the level of schooling is reversed. In the United States, one extra year of schooling of the population is associated with a 10 per cent fall in the measure of income inequality (i.e., the variance of the log of earnings).

The encouraging policy implication of this finding is that in economic development an increase in the average level of schooling of the population is not only a socially profitable investment but also does not have the alleged bad side effect of worsening the income distribution.

Three propositions stem from the existing evidence on the various relationships presented. First, there exists a strong effect of education on earnings. Second, among the two prior independent variables, socioeconomic background and ability, background seems to be a stronger determinant of education, and subsequently earnings, than ability. Finally, increases of the average level of educational attainment are consistent with a more equal income distribution.

This last conclusion should be qualified further. In the first place, the distribution of the increased level of schooling in the population is not specified. Different results would be obtained if, for example, the average level of schooling of the population is increased by strengthening the lower levels of schooling rather than producing more doctorates. Second, the fifth equation deals with quantity of schooling—numbers of years of study. It says nothing about the quality of schooling. It might be, for example, that provision of better quality schooling to some groups of the population, without altering the total number of years of study, would result in a more equal distribution of income relative to extending the number of years of educational attainment. In other words, the whole analysis presented thus far deals exclusively with investing at the extensive margin. But what about the intensive margin?

Johnson and Stafford (1973) have estimated rates of return to either increasing the number of years of school completed or improving school quality. As Table 9 shows, the returns to schooling quality were found to be

TABLE 9
RETURNS TO EXPENDITURES ON THE QUANTITY AND QUALITY OF SCHOOLING

	Educational Level	Rate of Return (per cent)
Quantity	High school (vs. elementary)	11
	College (vs. high school)	9
Quality	Elementary	17
	High school	14
	College	12

SOURCE: Johnson and Stafford (1973).

NOTES: Rates of return to schooling quantity refer to schools of average quality ($300 per student expenditure). Rates of return to schooling quality refer to an increase of per student expenditure from $275 to $300.

superior to the returns to the quantity of schooling. This would suggest emphasis on expenditures in improving the quality of schooling, without necessarily lengthening the number of years the individual stays in school.

POLICY CONSIDERATIONS

Policy makers in every country, whether it is rich or poor, have to make decisions on these questions: how much of the country's resources to devote to education relative to other sectors of the economy; how much to spend on one level of education relative to another level; how to allocate the investment in education among individuals so as to equalize the distribution of income. The first two involve the efficiency considerations discussed in the first part of the chapter. Concern with the third is very recent and has not yet been fully treated in the literature.

Whether we call it "planning" or "policy making," every day around the world decisions are taken regarding the allocation of scarce resources between education and the rest of the economy and within the education sector itself. These resources are substantial; they amount to 5 per cent of GNP or 16 per cent of the budget in most countries (Edding and Berstecher, 1969). Moreover, expenditure on education grows three to four times as fast as the economy as a whole.

Such allocation is usually done on an ad hoc political basis, if not by administrative inertia following past investment decisions. Even in those countries where comprehensive planning at all levels is claimed to exist, much of the resource allocation to education is governed by political decisions.

If we exclude the political element, educational planning can essentially take place by means of these methodologies: (1) via estimating manpower requirements for the achievement of given production goals; (2) via a cost-benefit analysis of the type presented in the first part; (3) via the social demand approach, i.e., by providing as much education as people want or are able to take.

The choice among the three techniques depends upon factual and normative considerations. If the planner is after efficiency of some kind, he will choose either 1 or 2. If he is willing to sacrifice efficiency for what society wants, then he may use the social demand approach. Therefore, the choice of the technique depends to some extent on the planner's objective function.

The choice between 1 and 2, however, can become more objective. The two approaches use polar assumptions regarding the demand for skills (Blaug, 1967). The manpower requirements approach assumes zero substitution between skills, whereas the rate-of-return approach assumes infinite substitution. Empirical evidence indicates that the real world lies nearer to the rate-of-return end of the substitution continuum, as the elasticity of substitution is statistically higher than one but less than infinity (Dougherty, 1972; Psacharopoulos, 1973b).

But all approaches seem to abstract from equity considerations. Other, perhaps, than the elimination of rents by producing extra graduates of a skill that is temporarily in short supply, nothing in the manpower requirements approach would tell how income could be distributed more equally or unequally. On the other hand, the equality between rates of return stipulated by the cost-benefit method could take place at any level of distribution. On the surface, the social demand approach seems more equitable than the others, but this is not necessarily so. Children from favored socioeconomic backgrounds will always demand and acquire more education than children from adverse backgrounds. Therefore, by simply following the social demand approach, income distribution will get worse if no compensatory mechanism exists. So where do we stand?

We have examined a large number of theoretical and empirical issues centering around the efficiency and equity dimensions of education. In what follows I try to summarize the main points from the policy angle.

The educational policy maker first has to decide on his objective function in allocating resources to schools and to the rest of the economy. Neglecting social demand, political solutions, or administrative inertia, the two prevailing criteria are allocative efficiency and distributive justice. Even if today's policy maker does not have or cannot arrive at an explicit objective function, it would be useful for him to have information on the allocative and distributive effects of alternative courses of action. This might help him adopt an objective function tomorrow.

Among the two common educational planning methodologies that claim to be based on considerations of efficiency of some kind, the cost-benefit approach appears to be more meaningful and empirically relevant. Estimation of the exact number of required artists, photographers, and athletes (along with doctors and engineers, of course) for the year 2000 does not make much sense. It is my opinion that it makes more sense to estimate the relative costs and benefits of producing today one chemical engineer rather than one electrical engineer.

For the policy maker who knows his objective function, the first choice involves how much to invest in schools relative to investment in machines. Put in other words, the first question is what percentage of the GNP he should devote to education. The evidence presented in the first part of this chapter suggests that, in general, more should be invested in education relative to other sectors of the economy. However, this conclusion should be immediately qualified for two reasons. First, the percentage of GNP devoted to education is not an easily manipulated policy instrument. To be pragmatic, political considerations and administrative inertia override any efficiency consideration at this macro level in most countries. Second, even if the percentage of GNP devoted to education were a convenient policy instrument, one should go another step and ask how to allocate resources within education. The percentage of GNP or the budget devoted to education is cited by different countries around the world as a prestige statistic—the higher it is, the better the country's alleged standing relative to others. However, our earlier discussion suggests that this statistic is almost meaningless unless disaggregated by educational level. The fact that a country spends a lot on education does not necessarily imply a correct allocation of resources within the education sector.

On economic efficiency grounds, it is the lower levels of education, primary and secondary, that should receive increased budgetary expenditure relative to others. This is an almost universal, well-established, and well-documented fact. Note also that reshuffling of resources within the education sector is, in some sense, politically easier than affecting the total resources devoted to education relative to the rest of the economy.

On equity grounds, it is also the lower levels of education, primary and secondary, that should receive increased budgetary expenditures relative to others. Although this proposition has not been researched as much as the preceding one, it is supported by existing evidence. That higher education might be inequitable is also supported by the view that it helps those with higher abilities to obtain even higher incomes at the expense of the taxpayer (Staff and Tullock, 1973).

The form in which increased budgetary expenditure on education is utilized is crucial. Up to now, the main emphasis has been on lengthening the level of educational attainment of the population in terms of years of school completed. However, recent evidence indicates that improvements in the quality of schools might be more socially profitable than, say, raising the compulsory school leaving age. This proposition is particularly relevant in the case of advanced countries with nearly 100 per cent enrollment at the compulsory level. The most obvious place to put an increased budgetary allocation to primary and secondary education in these countries is in improving the quality of the education provided.

REFERENCES

Abramovitz, M. (1956). *Resources and output trends in the United States since 1870.* Occasional paper no. 52. New York: National Bureau of Economic Research.

Arrow, K. (1973). Higher education as a filter. *Journal of Public Economics*, July.

Ashenfelter, O., and Mooney, J. (1968). Graduate education, ability and earnings. *Review of Economics and Statistics*, February.

Bailey, D., and Schotta, C. (1972). Private and social rates of return to education of academicians. *American Economic Review*, March.

Becker, G. S. (1960). Underinvestment in college education. *American Economic Review*, May.

Becker, G. S. (1967). *Human capital and the personal distribution of income.* Woytinsky Lecture no. 1. Madison: University of Michigan, 1967.

Becker, G. S. (1971). *Economic theory.* New York: Knopf.

Becker, G. S., and Chiswick, B. R. (1966). Education and the distribution of earnings. *American Economic Review*, May.

Blandy, R., and Goldsworthy, T. (1972). Private returns to education in South Australia. The Flinders University of South Australia, Department of Economics, mimeo.

Blaug, M. (1967). Approaches to educational planning. *Economic Journal*, June.

Blaug, M. (1970). *An introduction to the economics of education.* Allen Lane, Penguin Press.

Psacharopoulos/61

Blaug, M. (1971). The rate of return to investment in education in Thailand. A report to the National Education Council on the Third Educational Development Plan. Bangkok: National Education Council.

Blaug, M. (1973). The rate of return on investment in education in the Philippines: by levels, fields and institutions. Higher Education Research Unit. London School of Economics, RS / 29, mimeo.

Bowles, S. (1972). Schooling and inequality from generation to generation. *Journal of Political Economy*, May–June, part 2.

Bowles, S. (1973). Understanding unequal economic opportunity. *American Economic Review*, May.

Carnoy, M. (1967). Earnings and schooling in Mexico. *Economic Development and Cultural Change*, July.

Chiswick, B. R. (1969). Minimum schooling legislation and the cross-sectional distribution of income. *Economic Journal*, September.

Chiswick, B. R. (1970). An inter-regional analysis of schooling and the skewness of income. In *Education, income and human capital*, ed. W. L. Hansen. National Bureau of Economic Research, Studies in Income and Wealth, no. 35.

Chiswick, B. R. (1971). Earnings inequality and economic development. *Quarterly Journal of Economics*, February.

Chiswick, B. R., and Mincer, J. (1972). Time-series changes in personal income inequality in the United States from 1939, with projections to 1985. *Journal of Political Economy*, May–June, part 2.

Corrazzini, A. J. (1972). Equality of employment opportunity in the federal white-collar civil service. *Journal of Human Resources*, fall.

Denison, E. F. (1962). *Sources of economic growth in the United States*. Committee for Economic Development.

Denison, E. F. (1964). Proportion of income differentials among education groups "due to" additional education: the evidence from the Wolffe-Smith survey. In *The residual factor and economic growth*. OECD.

Denison, E. F. (1967). *Why growth rates differ*. Washington: The Brookings Institution.

Dodge, D. A., and Stager, D. A. A. (1972). Economic returns to graduate study in science, engineering and business. *Canadian Journal of Economics*, May.

Dougherty, C. R. S. (1972). Estimates of labour aggregation functions. *Journal of Political Economy*, November–December.

Duncan, B. (1967). Education and social background. *American Journal of Sociology*, January.

Duncan, O. T. (1968). Ability and achievement. *Eugenics Quarterly*, March.

Eckaus, R. (1973). Estimation of the returns to education with hourly standardized incomes. *Quarterly Journal of Economics*, February.

Edding, F., and Berstecher, D. (1969). *International development of educational expenditure, 1950–1965*. UNESCO, Statistical Reports and Studies.

Gannicott, K. (1972). *Rates of return to education in Taiwan, Republic of China*. Planning Unit, Ministry of Education, Taiwan.

Goodman, L. A. (1960). On the exact variance of products. *Journal of the American Statistical Association*, December.

Griliches, Z. (1970). Notes on the role of education in production functions and growth accounting. In *Education, income and human capital*, ed. W. L. Hansen. National Bureau of Economic Research, Studies in Income and Wealth, no. 35.

Griliches, Z., and Mason, W. M. (1972). Education, income and ability. *Journal of Political Economy*, May–June, part 2.

Hanoch, G. (1965). Personal earnings and investment in schooling. Ph.D. dissertation, University of Chicago.

Hanoch, G. (1967). An economic analysis of earnings and schooling. *Journal of Human Resources*, summer.

Hansen, W. L. (1963). Total and private returns to investment in schooling. *Journal of Political Economy*, April.

62/Investment in Education and Equality of Opportunity

Hansen, W., Weisbrod, B., and Scanlon, W. (1970). Schooling and earnings of low achievers. *American Economic Review*, June.

Harberger, A. (1971). On measuring the social opportunity cost of labour. *International Labour Review*, June.

Hause, J. C. (1972). Earnings profile: ability and schooling. *Journal of Political Economy*, May–June, part 2.

Hines, F., Tweeten, L., and Redfer, M. (1970). Social and private rates of return to investment in schooling by race-sex groups and regions. *Journal of Human Resources*, summer.

Hirshleifer, J. (1958). On the theory of optimal investment decision. *Journal of Political Economy*, August.

Hirsch, Q. Z., and Segelhorst, E. W. (1965). Incremental income benefits of public education. *Review of Economics and Statistics*, November.

Hoerr, O. D. (1973). Education, income and equity in Malaysia. *Economic Development and Cultural Change*, January.

Hunt, S. (1963). Income determinants for college graduates and the return of educational investment. *Yale Economic Essays*, fall.

Jencks, C. (1972). *Inequality: a reassessment of the effect of family and schooling in America*. Basic Books.

Johnson, G. E., and Stafford, F. P. (1973). Social returns to quantity and quality of schooling. *Journal of Human Resources*, spring.

Jorgenson, D. W., and Griliches, F. (1967). The explanation of productivity change. *Review of Economic Studies*, July.

Klappholz, K. (1972). Equality of opportunity, fairness and efficiency. In *Essays in honour of Lionel Robbins*, ed. M. Peston and B. Corry. Weidenfeld and Nicolson.

Klevmarken, A. (1972). *Statistical methods for the analysis of earnings data*. Sweden.

Krueger, A. C. (1968). Factor endowments and per capita income differences among countries. *Economic Journal*, September.

Lassiter, R. L. (1966). *The association of income and educational achievement*. Gainesville: University of Florida Press.

Layard, P. R. G., and Psacharopoulos, G. (1974). The screening hypothesis and returns to education. *Journal of Political Economy*, September–October.

Layard, P. R. G., Sargan, J. D., Ager, M. E., and Jones, D. J. (1971). *Qualified manpower and economic performance*. Allen Lane: Penguin Press.

Marin, A., and Psacharopoulos, G. (1973). Schooling and income distribution. London School of Economics, mimeo.

Metcalf, D. (1973). The rate of return to investing in a doctorate: a case study. *Scottish Journal of Political Economy*, February.

Mincer, J. (1972). *Schooling, experience and earnings*. National Bureau of Economic Research.

Mingat, A., and Lévy-Garboua, L. (1973). Les taux de rendement privés de l'éducation en France. CREDCC–IREDU, mimeo.

Minhas, B. S. (1963). *An international comparison of factor costs and factor use*. North-Holland.

Morgernstern, R. D. (1973). Direct and indirect effects on earnings of schooling and socioeconomic background. *Review of Economics and Statistics*, May.

Morris, V., and Ziderman, A. (1971). The economic return on investment in higher education in England and Wales. *Economic Trends*, May.

O'Byrne, G. (1971). The application of the constrained optimisation model in planning investment in the New South Wales educational system, 1970–1980. Ph.D. dissertation, Macquarrie University, School of Education.

O'Donoghue, M. (1971). *Economic dimensions in education*. Gill and Macmillan.

Organization for Economic Cooperation and Development (OECD) (1971). *Occupational and educational structures of the labour force and levels of economic development: further analyses and statistical data*. Paris.

Psacharopoulos, G. (1970). Estimating shadow rates of return to investment in education. *Journal of Human Resources*, winter.

Psacharopoulos, G. (1972). Essai de détermination des priorités dans l'enseignement au Maroc. Direction du Plan, Rabat, mimeo.

Psacharopoulos, G. (1973a). *Returns to education—an international comparison*. Elsevier.

Psacharopoulos, G. (1973b). Substitution assumptions versus empirical evidence in manpower planning. *De Economist*, November–December.

Psacharopoulos, G., and Williams, G. (1973). Public sector earnings and educational planning. *International Labour Review*, July.

Rees, A., and Shultz, G. P. (1970). *Workers and wages in an urban labour market*. University of Chicago Press.

Ribich, T. (1972). The problem of equal opportunity: a review article. *Journal of Human Resources*, fall.

Rogers, D. (1969). Private rates of return to education in the U.S.: a case study. *Yale Economic Essays*, spring.

Schultz, T. P. (1968). Returns to education in Bogota, Colombia. Rand Corporation, memorandum RM–5645–RC / AID, September.

Schultz, T. W. (1961). Investment in human capital. *American Economic Review*, March.

Sewell, W. H., Haller, A. O., and Portes, A. (1969). The educational and early occupational attainment process. *American Sociological Review*, February.

Solmon, L. (1973). The definition and impact of schooling quality. In *Does College Matter? Some Evidence on the Impacts of Higher Education*, ed. L. C. Solmon and P. J. Taubman. Academic Press.

Staff, R. J., and Tullock, G. (1973). Education and equality. *Annals of the American Academy of Political and Social Science*. September.

Stroup, R. H., and Hargrove, M. B. (1969). Earnings and education in rural South Vietnam. *Journal of Human Resources*, spring.

Stoikov, V. (1973). The structure of earnings in Japanese industries. *Journal of Political Economy*, March–April.

Taubman, P., and Wales, T. (1973). Higher education, mental ability and screening. *Journal of Political Economy*, January–February.

Thias, H. H., and Carnoy, M. (1972). *Cost-benefit analysis in education: a case study of Kenya*. IBRD, occasional paper no. 14.

Weiss, R. D. (1970). The effect of education on the earnings of blacks and whites. *Review of Economics and Statistics*, May.

Weiss, Y. (1971). Investment in graduate education. *American Economic Review*, December.

Wiles, P. (1974). The external test not-content hypothesis. *Higher Education*, January.

Young, M. (1958). *The rise of the meritocracy, 1870–2033*. New York: Random House.

Ziderman, A. (1973). Rates of return on investment in education: recent results for Britain. *Journal of Human Resources*, winter.

The Public Economic Benefits of a
High School Education

Lillian D. Webb

In 1776 the economist Adam Smith wrote, "The expense of the institutions for education is . . . beneficial to the whole society and may therefore, without injustice, be defrayed by the general contribution of the whole society."[1] Although these views were expressed almost two centuries ago, until quite recently the economic significance of education to society has been largely ignored. Only in the past few years have economists recognized the significance of education to the rate of economic growth and prosperity of a nation. Now, however, the relationship between economics and education seems to be universally recognized. New terminology has come into existence; "investment in education" is employed as a substitute for "expenditures for education," and such terms as "the economics of human resources," "investment in human beings," and "human capital formation" have entered the literature.[2]

Most attempts to assess the economic role of education have explored the costs and returns of education in the realm of the returns to the individual that are derived from the investment in education. Benefits internal to the individual and his family are referred to as private benefits, and they may take the form of higher income, a larger number of vocational alternatives, increased productivity, opportunity for further education, or increased social and economic mobility. A large body of literature has developed which establishes the contribution of education to individual economic and social welfare.[3]

In comparison, minor emphasis has been placed on what are variously referred to as the "social benefits," "indirect benefits," or "externalities" of education. These consequences of education either confer benefits or impose costs on other members of the community, or on society as a whole, rather than just on the individual. As in the case of private benefits, these benefits may be economic or social in nature.

Social externalities generally represent less measurable benefits than those of an economic nature. For example, it is difficult to measure such social externalities as increased equality of opportunity or transmission of cultural heritage. For some social externalities, however, empirical evidence has been developed which attempts to show some of the benefits that accrue to society as a result of higher levels of educational achievement in its citizenry. For example, studies have shown a high correlation between educational attainment and political participation. Table 1 shows voter participation in the 1972 presidential election by the years of schooling completed. Participation is shown as rapidly increasing with higher levels of educational attainment.

TABLE 1
REPORTED VOTER PARTICIPATION IN THE 1972 PRESIDENTIAL ELECTION
BY YEARS OF SCHOOL COMPLETED

Years of School Completed	Per Cent Reported Voting
Elementary:	
0–4	33.0
5–7	44.3
8	55.2
High School:	
1–3	52.0
4	65.4
College:	
1–3	74.9
4	82.3
5 and over	85.6

SOURCE: U.S. Department of Commerce, Bureau of the Census, "Voting Participation in the Election of November 1972," *Current Population Reports*, series P-20, no. 253.

Persons with higher education are more able and more likely to become involved in politics and to influence the outcome of issues that affect them. Persons with lower levels of education are less knowledgeable not only of political issues, but also of political processes, and are consequently less able to make their views heard even when they are aware of relevant issues.[4] Thus, a lack of schooling restricts one's ability to exercise one's political rights, thereby weakening a basic democratic concept—the maximum political participation of an enlightened citizenry.

Some externalities might be considered both social and economic in effect. Weisbrod refers to them as "employment-related." The basic idea is that educating some workers raises the productivity of others.[5] Increased productivity of one worker may result from his emulating a co-worker and learning new skills, or his being influenced by psychological and motivational factors resulting from work association with more educated co-workers. Normally, workers with additional educational attainment have improved communication with management and co-workers, are more receptive to new ideas, and have greater flexibility and adaptability—qualities so important in a modern industrial society where production requires the coordination, cooperation, and interaction of workers.[6]

This chapter deals primarily with what are known as the public economic externalities of education. Economic externalities may be positive or negative in their effects. If they represent additional benefits to society as, for example, increased national income or increased tax revenues, they are considered positive. If, on the other hand, they affect expenditures on other services made necessary by a lack of education, such as the increased expenditures related to crime and welfare, they are considered costs and are thus negative in nature. First, consideration will be given to some of the negative (cost) economic externalities, then to a measurement of some of the positive benefits that might accrue to society as a result of increased levels of educational attainment.

Over the years, a substantial number of empirical studies have shown a high correlation between crime and inferior educational achievement. In 1940, the median grade of school completed by prisoners was found to be 7.4, as compared to 8.3 for others. More important, in proportion to their numbers, of persons in prison those with no schooling numbered four times those who had completed high school.[7] In 1951, Price Chenault estimated that between 10 and 30 per cent of all prisoners admitted to correctional institutions of all types throughout the country were illiterate.[8] A 1955 study found that of the 4,000 inmates over age 17 who were admitted to the Texas prison system, 5 per cent had not completed first grade, 44 per cent had not completed eighth grade, and 89 per cent had not completed high school. A parallel study in New Jersey yielded the comparable percentages of 3.6, 41, and 91. These percentages were much higher than those showing schooling of the general population.[9] A comparison of the educational attainment of persons aged 25–64 in correctional institutions to those in the general population in 1960 showed that more than four-fifths of the prison inmates had not completed high school as compared with about one-half of the general population of the same ages. In fact, more than one-half of the prisoners had not even reached secondary school, compared to about one-third of the general population.[10]

The more recent data included in Table 2 indicate that, while the median years of school completed of those in correctional institutions has continued to rise, it was still significantly lower than the median for the general population. Also, 75 per cent of those in prison had not received a high school education, compared to 45 per cent of those in the general population in the same year.

These differences do not, of course, prove that all crime is due to low educational attainment. The low educational level may be reflective or concomitant of low socioeconomic status. However, the fact that a person does have an inadequate education, with its limited occupational choices, low income and / or unemployment, and lower social status, seems to increase the likelihood of his turning to illegal means to fulfill his social and economic desires. Many scholars have accepted a figure of $25 billion as a

TABLE 2

A COMPARISON OF EDUCATIONAL ATTAINMENT OF PERSONS IN STATE AND FEDERAL PRISONS AND REFORMATORIES AND THE GENERAL POPULATION, 1970

Years of School Completed	Percentage of Inmates in Correctional Institutions	Percentage of the General Population
Elementary:		
1–4	6.4	5.3
5–7	17.6	9.1
8	16.2	13.4
High School:		
1–3	34.8	17.4
4	19.1	34.0
College:		
1–3	4.9	10.2
4 or more	1.0	11.0
Median years school completed	9.8	12.2

SOURCE: U.S. Department of Commerce, Bureau of the Census, "Persons in Institutions and Other Group Quarters" (July 1973), Table 24; *Statistical Abstract of the U.S.*, *94th Annual Edition* (1973), Table 175.

fair estimate of the economic loss to society resulting from crime.[11] Obviously, if any portion of this figure could be reduced by raising the educational attainment of the citizens to at least a high school level, a significant economic benefit would accrue to society.

In another problem area somewhat related to crime, educational attainment has also been shown to have a high correlation with civil riots and disorders. In a survey conducted by the National Advisory Commission on Civil Disorders in twenty cities where civil disorders had occurred, inadequate education and underemployment or unemployment, either of which is directly related to educational attainment, were included in the top four grievances of riot participants. Additionally, the typical ghetto riot participant was found to be a high school dropout. After an extensive study of self-reported rioters, counter-rioters, and those not involved, the commission reached the conclusion that "a high level of education . . . not only prevents rioting, but also is more likely to lead to active, responsible opposition to rioting."[12] It is impossible to measure the cost to society in terms of loss of life and property that resulted from the riots that at times have shaken this nation. However, since the rioters themselves considered inadequate education as one of their top grievances, this expression would seem to justify additional investments in education in terms of the possible benefits that would accrue to society if these disorders could be at least partially prevented.

Another economic cost to society that can be partially attributed to an inferior education is welfare expenditures. Although, of course, not all welfare costs are related to education, there are several categories which do seem to be directly related to educational attainment. These categories include Aid to Families with Dependent Children (AFDC), medical assistance payments, and unemployment compensation. Each of these can be said to be directly related to educational attainment because eligibility for benefits under each of them is dependent on income or employment, conditions proved to be related to educational attainment.

Studies by the U.S. Department of Health, Education, and Welfare have shown that the median levels of education of incapacitated and unemployed AFDC fathers were far below the national median, and that these men were "handicapped educationally in comparison with other men." About 76 per cent of the incapacitated fathers and 61.2 per cent of the unemployed fathers did not have a high school education. An additional 15.9 per cent in the first group and 22.8 per cent in the latter group whose educational level was unknown could presumably raise these amounts even higher.[13] Later figures indicate that 84 per cent of all AFDC unemployed fathers lacked a high school education.[14] Of the AFDC mothers, 82.5 per cent were also shown to be lacking a high school education; this was reported to be an important factor related to their employment potential.[15] The proportion of AFDC mothers known to have completed at least high school was 1.5 times greater for the employed than for the unemployed.[16] These empirical data support the obvious conclusion that AFDC recipients who did become self-supporting generally had more education than those who did not, regardless of race.

In 1972, $6.9 billion in public revenues went directly to AFDC recipients and another $2.1 billion in medical assistance to AFDC families. An additional $5.5 billion was paid in unemployment compensation.[17] This total of $14.5 billion of the nation's financial resources was being spent for public welfare programs that could be directly related to educational attainment. Needless to say, if raising the level of education of possible future welfare recipients to at least that of a high school education would result in the reduction of welfare rolls, a tremendous economic benefit to society would result, in addition to the psychological and sociological benefits that would accrue to the individual who could consider himself a contributing member of society rather than a recipient of its welfare.

The economic significance of a high school education has been considered in terms of the current costs to society resulting from the failure of a large number of individuals to complete at least a high school education. Now, attention will be turned to some of the positive public economic factors associated with high school completion. The specific benefits to be measured, and to which the body of this section has been devoted, are those which would accrue to society in the form of increased national income and increased tax revenues, were it not for the failure of a large number of its members to attain a high school education. In making these measurements, the basic procedure established by Levin will be followed in determining losses to society as measured by forgone national income and lost tax revenues.[18] Some variations have been introduced in establishing both the lower and upper levels of educational costs and by omitting Levin's procedure of adding years of income to the expected lifetime income of those not completing high school.

Procedurally, the first step consisted of a review of the incidence of dropping out among young males who were theoretically old enough to have completed their education. Second, the actual distribution of educational attainment of this sample was compared with the hypothetical distribution of educational attainment that would have resulted under a policy of high school completion for this group of males. Third, the contribution to national income under the actual distribution was compared with the contribution to national income under the hypothetical distribution. The difference between the two was the forgone national income attributed to the act of dropping out. Fourth, the loss in tax revenues to local, state, and federal governments resulting from this forgone income was estimated. Fifth, the forgone national income, together with the lost tax revenues, was compared to the costs of providing this age group of males with a minimum of a high school education.

INCIDENCE OF DROPPING OUT

The number of youths who have not completed high school has remained relatively stable in the past few years in contrast to the increases in the number who have graduated. This trend was broken, however, when the latest available census data were published, for the year 1972. In the period October 1971–October 1972, an estimated 730,000 persons 16–24 years old, who presumably could have entered the labor market, left school before graduation; an additional 112,000 persons who were 14 and 15 years old dropped out of school. This figure represented an increase of about 80,000 from the previous year in the number of dropouts. If this rate of increase were to continue, the problems related to inferior education would become even more important.[19]

In the total population, for males who were over 25 years of age, the age at which most would be assumed to have completed their education, the

TABLE 3
SCHOOL DROPOUTS, 1971–72 (TOTAL, 730,000)

	Number	Percentage
Men	371,000	50.8
Women	359,000	49.2
White	573,000	78.5
Nonwhite	157,000	21.5

incidence of failure to complete a minimum of a high school education was much higher, as shown in Table 4. The table also indicates that the dropout rate for nonwhite males was much higher than for white males. Furthermore, this rate was not improving for nonwhite males to any significant degree; the dropout rate for more recent high school male students (aged

TABLE 4
PERCENTAGE OF MALE POPULATION COMPLETING NO MORE THAN THREE YEARS OF HIGH SCHOOL, BY AGE (1972) AND BY RACE

	20–21	25–29	29+
Total	17.4	19.5	41.7
White	14.9	17.8	39.6
Nonwhite	34.7	34.9	59.2

SOURCE: U.S. Department of Commerce, Bureau of the Census, "Educational Attainment: March 1972," *Current Population Reports*, series P-20, no. 223 (February 1973), Table 1.

20–21 in 1972) was almost the same as that for earlier male students (aged 25–29 in 1972). This same trend was noted by Schweitzer who, in considering the census data related to educational attainment for 1968, concluded that there was actually a decrease in the marginal rates of graduation between these two age groups.[20]

For the purposes of this study, the scope of the population was narrowed to an age group that could be assumed to have completed formal educational training and to have many years left in work careers. Women were not included in the study because census data related to lifetime income, which is central to the calculations in this study, were not available for women. Therefore, this study utilized the 25–29 male age group with its attendant educational attainment. Table 5 gives the educational attainment and percentage distribution of the sample. In terms of percentages, the educational attainment for nonwhites was lower than that for whites. The total number of whites failing to attain a high school education was 1,128,000, and for nonwhites the total number of persons dropping out was 260,000. The level at which the closest percentage correlation existed was for four years of high school; 39.6 per cent of whites and 40.1 per cent of nonwhites made up this group.

As compared to the distribution in Table 5, if these same individuals were educated under a policy requiring high school completion as a minimum education, their hypothetical distribution of educational attainment would be that shown in Table 6. This was calculated by assuming that if all persons completed high school, a continuation of education beyond high school would follow the same pattern as that in the actual distribution for nonwhite males age 25–29. The use of the percentages of continuance of the nonwhite males was for the purpose of making as conservative an estimate of the rates of continuance as possible.

The estimated number of additional persons that would be educated at each level under a policy of universal high school completion is shown in Table 7. An additional 695,000 white males and 160,000 nonwhite males were projected to have completed high school before entering the labor market, and 433,000 additional white males and 99,000 additional nonwhite males were projected to have received some college training.

ESTIMATES OF FORGONE NATIONAL INCOME

Before presenting the calculations of the loss of income resulting from the reduced educational attainment for the sample population, an explanation is needed to justify the relationship between education and income that was referred to earlier. A large body of evidence has been developed which shows the correlation between education and income to be in a positive direction.[21] Even when other variables found to be correlated with income are considered, such as IQ, ability, and parental socioeconomic status, the effect of education on income has remained significant. In using 1960 census data for males by age, race, and region, even when holding constant socioeconomic background, Hanoch found a strong correlation between income and schooling.[22] Lassiter found regression coefficients for education explaining between 0.39 and 0.52 of the variance in middle age groups.

TABLE 5
Educational Attainment for Males 25–29 Years of Age, March 1972, by Race
(in thousands)

	Elementary		High School		College		
	Less than 8 Years	8 Years	1–3 Years	4 Years	1–3 Years	4 Years	5+ Years
Total males	263	229	895	2,822	1,341	893	673
Percentage	3.7	3.2	12.6	39.6	18.8	12.5	9.5
White males	207	190	731	2,534	1,246	845	630
Percentage	3.3	3.0	11.5	39.6	19.5	13.3	9.9
Nonwhite males	56	39	165	298	96	48	42
Percentage	7.5	5.2	22.2	40.1	12.9	6.4	5.7

SOURCE: U.S. Department of Commerce, Bureau of the Census, "Educational Attainment: March 1972," *Current Population Reports*, series P-20, no. 243 (November 1972), Table 1.

TABLE 6

HYPOTHETICAL DISTRIBUTION OF EDUCATIONAL ATTAINMENT FOR MALES 25–29 YEARS
OF AGE, MARCH 1972, UNDER A POLICY OF HIGH SCHOOL COMPLETION
(in thousands)

	High School	College		
		1–3 Years	4 Years	5+ Years
White males	3,219	1,469	956	729
Percentage	50.5	23.1	15.0	11.4
Nonwhite males	458	147	73	65
Percentage	61.6	19.8	9.8	8.7

TABLE 7

ESTIMATED NUMBERS OF ADDITIONAL MALES 25–29 YEARS OF AGE COMPLETING
EDUCATION AT EACH LEVEL UNDER A POLICY OF HIGH SCHOOL COMPLETION

	High School	College		
		1–3 Years	4 Years	5+ Years
White males	695,000	223,000	111,000	99,000
Nonwhite males	160,000	51,000	25,000	23,000
Total	855,000	274,000	136,000	122,000

TABLE 8

MEDIAN INCOME BY EDUCATIONAL ATTAINMENT OF MALES 25–34 YEARS OF AGE BY RACE

Years of School Completed	Median Income		Nonwhite Income as Per Cent of White Income
	Nonwhite	White	
Elementary			
8 years or less	$4,743	$ 6,618	72
High School			
1–3 years	5,749	7,910	73
4 years	6,789	8,613	79
College			
1–3 years	7,699	9,190	84
4 years	8,715	11,212	78
5 years or more	9,955	11,808	84

SOURCE: U.S. Department of Commerce, Bureau of the Census, "The Social and Economic Status of the Black Population in the U.S., 1972," Special Studies, *Current Population Reports*, series P-23, no. 46, p. 25.

Similarly, Wolfe and Smith found income to be significant even when IQ, grades, and family background were similar, but levels of education were different.[23] In spite of such evidence, the final income differentials associated with schooling (Table 10) were deflated by 25 per cent to compensate for such factors.

TABLE 9
ESTIMATED LIFETIME INCOMES FROM AGE 18 TO 64 FOR MALES
BY RACE AND EDUCATIONAL ATTAINMENT

Level of Schooling Completed	Lifetime Income		
	All Males	White	Nonwhite
Elementary			
Less than 8 years	$196,000	$208,400	$150,000
8 years	252,000	264,600	190,000
High School			
1–3 years	278,000	292,500	213,600
4 years	336,000	343,600	271,500
College			
1–3 years	378,000	382,400	322,000
4 years	489,000	495,000	386,000
5 or more years	544,000	549,500	461,600

SOURCE (for unweighted figures): U.S. Department of Commerce, *Current Population Reports*, ser. p-60, no. 74, Table 10 (1968).

NOTE: This table was based upon Levin's assumption that by not accounting for an expected annual productivity increase of 3 per cent, a 3 per cent discount rate is tacitly assumed. Thus, census data were used for expected lifetime income at a discount rate of 0 per cent with an annual productivity increase of 0 per cent. However, the additional earnings accrued by dropouts before the age of eighteen were not added to lifetime income in this table as they were in the Levin procedure.

The racial differences in income at the same level of educational attainment were also taken into consideration. Available census data on lifetime income by educational attainment were reported for males without regard for race. However, discrimination in the labor market evidently has resulted in differences in the average incomes of whites and nonwhites at the same educational level. Table 8 represents the latest available census figures comparing median income of whites and nonwhites.

Census figures related to lifetime income have been given only in terms of all males in the population. Thus, to estimate the separate income gains for whites and nonwhites according to educational level, the aggregate figure for all males was weighted according to the relative percentages of income reflected in Table 8 and according to the per cent nonwhites are of whites at each level (Appendix A). The calculated results are given in Table 9.

A difference of $58,000 in lifetime income existed between high school dropouts and high school graduates; between college dropouts and college graduates the difference was $111,000. A higher correlation for whites than for nonwhites also existed between income and educational attainment at all levels.

These data were then applied to the estimated number of additional males at each level under a policy of assumed high school completion to determine the income forgone to the nation as a result of high school dropouts. Table 10 reflects the gross forgone income as well as the forgone

TABLE 10
ESTIMATE OF INCOME FORGONE AS A RESULT OF MALES 25–29 YEARS OLD DROPPING OUT

	Gross Income Forgone (billions of dollars)	After 25 Per Cent Adjustment
White		
High school completion	80	60.00
College	46	34.50
Total whites	126	94.50
Nonwhites		
High school completion	19	14.25
College	10	7.50
Total nonwhites	29	21.75
Total all males	155	116.25

income after the 25 per cent reduction. Society forfeits a total of $116.25 billion in the form of forgone income loss over the lifetime of these males as a result of their failure to complete high school.

LOSS IN TAX REVENUES

Inherent in this loss of national income is a reduction of tax revenues at all levels of government. In 1971, total tax revenues represented 28.3 per cent of personal income. Of this, 16.5 per cent went to the federal government and 11.8 per cent to state and local governments.[24] Applying these percentages to our calculated figure of $116.25 billion in forgone income shows that, for the males of the 25–29 age group, $19.2 billion additional tax revenues were lost to the federal government and $13.7 billion to state and local governments as a result of their dropping out. This loss represents a second societal cost of $32.9 billion.

THE COST OF PROVIDING A HIGH SCHOOL EDUCATION FOR ALL MALES 25–29 YEARS OF AGE IN 1972

In the preceding discussion the costs to society have been considered in terms of forgone national income and loss in tax revenues. This section focuses on the costs for society to provide the same individuals with a minimum of a high school education, as well as the additional costs that would accrue as a result of a greater number of high school graduates continuing on to college.

The costs of providing additional education are of two main types. First, there are the direct expenditures for salaries, supplies, maintenance, capital outlay, and other current expense items. Second, there is the indirect, or opportunity, cost to the potential dropout in the form of earnings forgone as a result of his remaining in school. Since no addition was made to the expected lifetime income of our dropouts for the income that they accrued before reaching age eighteen, no comparable addition in the form of forgone income was made to the educational costs of providing these individuals with a high school education. There were, of course, other costs to the student in continuing his education, such as the loss of freedom one experiences in the classroom and the boredom of school for the unmotivated student.[25] However, since these costs were extremely difficult to measure in economic terms, no attempt was made to consider them as direct or indirect costs in this study.

Two basic methods may be used for determining direct educational costs. One is to assume that by maintaining present expenditure levels but changing their focus, schools would be able to increase their retention rate. The other method is to assume that it would take great increases in expenditures to meet the needs of these potential dropouts and keep them in school.[26] It is reasonable, therefore, to compute costs by both these methods and use the mean of the two to indicate the most representative national cost figure.

Lower Limits of Investment

Estimated total expenditures for all public school purposes in 1972–73 were $51.9 billion. The average estimated current expenditure per pupil in average daily membership (ADM) was $961 for all elementary and secondary pupils.[27] However, expenditures per pupil at the elementary level have been estimated to be only about 80 per cent of those at the secondary level.[28] The current average expenditure for secondary students, therefore, would be $1,040 and for elementary students $832. There is also a difference in capital outlay expenditures at the elementary and secondary level. Elementary capital outlay has been estimated to represent 66 per cent of secondary capital outlay costs.[29] If capital outlay costs of $138 at the secondary level and $90 at the elementary level are added to the current

TABLE 11
ESTIMATE OF INVESTMENT COST OF A POLICY PROVIDING A MINIMUM
OF HIGH SCHOOL COMPLETION AND COLLEGE CONTINUANCE

	Number of Additional Persons Completing Level (thousands)	Number of Years Additional Schooling Per Person	Cost Per Year	Total Cost Per Level (billions)
From elementary to high school completion				
Less than 8 years	263	3	$ 922	
		4	1178	$1.967
8 years	229	4	1178	1.079
1–3 years high school	896	2	1178	2.111
Total				$5.157
From high school completion to				
1–3 years college	274	2	$2623	$1.437
4 years college	136	4	2623	1.427
5 or more years college	122	6	2623	1.920
Total costs, college				$4.784
Total investment costs				$9.941

average expenditures, total annual expenditures are for a secondary student $1,178 and for an elementary student $922. These estimates were used to compute the costs of additional years of schooling to bring the potential dropouts up to high school completion.

The U.S. Office of Education also reported that the average expenditure per pupil in institutions of higher education in 1969–70 (the latest available data) is $2,623.[30] This figure was thus used as the annual cost for those continuing to college. Table 11 shows estimates of the lower limits of investment for obtaining a minimum of high school completion for all males 25–29 years of age, plus college continuance for a portion of the additional high school graduates.

The cost of providing a high school education for all males in the sample who would otherwise drop out was estimated to be $5.2 billion, and the cost of providing additional college training for those who might continue their education beyond high school was projected to about $4.8 billion. Thus, the lower limit of the cost of a public policy providing for a minimum of a high school education for this group of males was estimated to be about $10.0 billion. (This projection was for the combined number of white and nonwhite dropouts.) In contrast to the procedures used in calculating forgone income, no cost differentials were associated with race as far as expenses were concerned.

Upper Limits of Investment

To estimate the upper limit of investment, the assumption was made that schools would not be able to retain these potential dropouts by maintaining present expenditure levels and changing focus, but that instead they must make massive additional expenditures. At the present expenditure levels, yearly expenditures of $922 were established for elementary students and $1,178 for secondary students. The sum of these figures for the elementary and secondary years indicated that a total of $12,088 per pupil would be spent. According to the costs of compensatory and other special programs, the assumption was made that the sample would need additional expenditures equal to, or in excess of, that presently being spent on the average per pupil. Therefore, this figure of $12,088 was added for each of the potential dropouts, representing an additional $16.8 billion investment at the public school level over the $9.9 billion of our lower limit which must

TABLE 12
COST-BENEFIT ANALYSIS
(billions)

Benefits	
Increased national income	$116.25
Increased tax revenues	32.90
Total	149.15
Costs	
High school education for entire sample	13.54
College continuance for a portion of the sample	4.78
Total	18.32
Net gain to society	$130.83

be spent to prevent their dropping out. Thus a figure of $26.7 billion was considered to be the appropriate upper limit of the investment cost.

The mean of the upper and lower limits of investment was selected as the most reasonable estimate of costs. The cost to the nation to raise the educational attainment of the sample to a high school completion level and to provide college training for those of the group who might continue would then be $18.3 billion. The required investment to bring this group to a high school graduation level, without consideration of college continuance, would be the mean of the lower and upper limits of investment costs for high school only, a cost of $13.54 billion.

An analysis of the data derived in this study shows that society is paying dearly for its failure to retain its young people in schools until they attain a high school education. This limited sample indicated that the nation was losing $149 billion in forgone income and lost tax revenue, in contrast to an educational cost of $18 billion. This indicates a net loss of $131 billion over the lifetimes of these men. This figure is a very conservative estimate since lifetime income was based on 1968 data; however, educational costs were based on 1972 data, as were the costs for welfare expenditures that might eventually be attributed to the inferior education of some members of the sample. If all of these were included, the total societal cost would obviously be much higher.

CONCLUSIONS AND IMPLICATIONS

The data presented in this study suggest that the schools are not "economic parasites draining off national income into some nonproductive enterprise,"[31] as some would contend, but instead are one of the main factors in determining its growth. In spite of the high standard of living enjoyed by most Americans, a relatively large number of people are unemployed. Unemployment often leads to poverty and welfare. Each of these conditions is related to an inferior education. The $58,000 difference in lifetime income between the high school dropout and the high school graduate can represent the difference between owning one's own home or living in slum housing, between being able to provide for one's family or not being able to provide many of the necessities of life, or between providing one's children with a good education or committing them to an unequal educational opportunity. The findings imply that America's war on poverty can best be fought by greater attention to, and subsequent investment in, education.

Additionally, the impact of education in changing income distribution or providing equality of opportunity should not be overlooked. Education can be a great equalizing force. A comparison of whites' and nonwhites' incomes revealed that nonwhites' income as a per cent of whites' income seemed to increase as the level of educational attainment increased. Thus, one result of increasing investments could be to raise the educational attainment of the entire population, resulting in not only a reduction of forgone income, but also a reduction of the disparity between whites' and nonwhites' incomes.

The role of education as an instrument of social democracy can be carried further than just its importance as a determinant of differences in whites' and nonwhites' incomes. Education may have been a determining factor in participation in the racial riots that have shaken this nation in the last several years. As Joseph P. Lyford has said, "There is no question that racial tensions are going to make life impossible for all of us unless we develop an educational program that enables the Negro to enter our society and the white man to place a high value on his entry. It should be fairly obvious that education is the only method by which we can overcome our institutionalized system of cheating Negroes, halt the growth of a public welfare community, and slow down the emergence of a new group of aliens, the teen-age school dropouts. We are either going to broaden the boundaries of America to include the exiles, or most of us are going to join them."[32]

Recognizing the importance of education to American society is one thing; providing for it through adequate financing is another. This act requires that each citizen recognize that his personal, his community's, his state's, and his nation's educational expenditures are a sound investment in his and his nation's future growth and prosperity. Human losses have the same negative consequences as property losses. When educational expenditures are considered to be not so much a cost to society as an investment in its people, additional expenditures can be easily justified.

In the past the American people have exhibited what Lord Bryce called an almost religious faith in education. America's greatness today is seen by most historians to be largely a result of her successful experiment with universal free public education. As Commager stated, "No other people have demanded so much of education as has the American. None other was ever served so well by its schools and educators."[33] This faith and service should be rewarded with the expenditures necessary to ensure that the war against poverty, illiteracy, crime, and delinquency will be won.

Barring the outbreak of a major war or depression, the financing of education is likely to be this country's greatest fiscal problem for many years to come. Each year educational expenditures have set a new record. Because responsibility for education rests upon the fifty states through more than 16,000 local school districts, the problem of educational finance is often considered to be only a local one. Education's place in the national tax and expenditure picture is often overlooked.[34] However, in view of the struggle to obtain the necessary financing for education, the question may be fairly asked whether the nation can afford to put the major responsibility for public education on local governments, especially in view of the vast differences in their abilities and needs. The conclusion must logically be reached that substantially greater investment by the state and federal governments are needed to meet the challenges which face today's schools. As Walter Lippman expressed in a much quoted speech, "We have to do in the educational system something very like what we have done in the Military Establishment. . . . We have to make a breakthrough to a radically higher and broader conception of what is needed and of what can be done. Our educational effort today, what we think we can afford, what we think we can do . . . is still in approximately the same position as was the military effort of this country before Pearl Harbor."[35]

The nation cannot prudently wait for another Pearl Harbor or Sputnik to force it into making massive "catch-up" expenditures, but America should make the expenditures today that will insure prosperity tomorrow.

APPENDIX A.—NONWHITE MALES AS A PROPORTION OF ALL MALES 25–29 YEARS OF AGE

Educational Attainment	Nonwhite	White	Nonwhite as Per Cent of Total
	(thousands)		
Less than 8 years	56	207	21.3
8 years	39	190	17.0
1–3 years high school	165	731	18.4
4 years high school	298	2524	10.6
1–3 years college	96	1246	7.2
4 years college	48	845	5.4
5 or more years college	42	630	6.2

SOURCE (for numbers, not percentages): U.S. Department of Commerce, Bureau of the Census, "Educational Attainment: March 1972," *Current Population Reports*, series P-20, no. 223 (February 1973), Table 1.

APPENDIX B.—FEDERAL AND STATE-LOCAL TAX REVENUES AS PROPORTIONS OF PERSONAL INCOME, 1971 (in millions of dollars)

Type of Tax	Federal	State-Local
Personal income tax	89,517	17,334
Corporate profits	33,132	4,216
Indirect business	19,204	80,109
Total	141,853	101,659
Total Personal income	861,382	

SOURCE: U.S. Department of Commerce, Office of Business Economics, "National Income and Products Accounts," *Survey of Current Business* (July 1972), Tables 2–1, 3–1, and 3–3.

REFERENCES

1. *The Wealth of Nations* (New York: P. F. Collier & Son, 1905), p. 212.

2. Jesse Burkhead, *Public School Finance: Economics and Politics* (Syracuse: Syracuse University Press, 1969), p. 1.

3. Some examples: Gary Becker and Barry R. Chiswick, "Education and the Distribution of Earnings," *American Economic Review* 56 (May 1966):358–60; George Hanoch, "An Economic Analysis of Earnings and Schooling," *Journal of Human Resources* 2 (Summer 1967):310–29; George Johnson and Frank Stafford, "Social Returns to Quantity and Quality of Schooling," *Journal of Human Resources* 8 (Spring 1973):139–55; Randall Weiss, "The Effect of Education on the Earnings of Blacks and Whites," *Review of Economics and Statistics* 52 (May 1970):150–59.

4. James W. Guthrie, George B. Kleindorfer, Henry M. Levin, and Robert T. Stout, "School Achievement and Post-School Success: A Review," *Review of Educational Research* 41 (February 1971): 11.

5. Burton A. Weisbrod, *External Benefits of Public Education* (Princeton: Princeton University Press, 1964).

6. J. Ronnie Davis, "The Social and Economic Externalities of Education," in *Economic Factors Affecting the Financing of Education* (Gainesville, Fla.: National Educational Finance Project, 1970), pp. 65–66.

7. Joseph D. Lohman, Lloyd E. Ohlin, and Dietrich C. Reitzes, *Description of Convicted Felons as Manpower Resources in a National Emergency*, p. 24, as cited in Edwin H. Sutherland and Donald R. Cressey, *Principles of Criminology*, 7th ed. (New York: J. P. Lippincott Co., 1966), p. 251.

8. Price Chenault, "Education," in *Contemporary Corrections*, ed. Paul W. Tappan (New York: McGraw-Hill, 1951), p. 224.

9. Albert K. Cohen, "The Schools and Juvenile Delinquency," *Subcommittee to Investigate Juvenile Delinquency*, pp. 106, 110, as cited in Sutherland and Cressey.

10. Martin R. Haskell and Lewis Yablonsky, *Crime and Delinquency* (Chicago: Rand McNally and Co., 1970), pp. 389–90.

11. National Commission on the Causes and Prevention of Violence, *Crimes of Violence*, vol. 11 (Washington: U.S. Government Printing Office, 1968), p. 394.

12. National Advisory Commission on Civil Disorders, *Report* (Washington: U.S. Government Printing Office, March 1968), p. 75.

13. David B. Epply, "The AFDC Family in the 1960s," *Welfare in Review* 8 (September–October 1970):11–13.

14. Edward Prescott, William Tash, and William Usdane, "Training and Employability: The Effect of MDTA on AFDC Recipients," *Welfare in Review* 9 (January–February 1971):2.

15. Perry Levinson, "How Employable are AFDC Women," *Welfare in Review* 8 (July–August 1970):12–13.

16. Howard Oberhea, "AFDC Mothers: Employed and Not Employed," *Welfare in Review* 10 (May–June 1972):60–61.

17. *Social Security Bulletin*, vol. 36, no. 6 (U.S. Department of Health, Education, and Welfare, Social Security Administration, June 1973).

18. Henry M. Levin, *The Effects of Dropping Out*, A Report to the Select Committee on Equal Educational Opportunity of the United States Senate (Washington: U.S. Government Printing Office, 1972).

19. Howard Hayghe, "Employment of High School Graduates and Drop Outs," *Monthly Labor Review* 95 (May 1972):49–53; Anne Young, "Employment of High School Graduates and Drop Outs," *Monthly Labor Review* 96 (June 1973):25–29.

20. Stuart Schweitzer, "Occupational Choice, High School Graduation, and Investment in Human Capital," *Journal of Human Resources* 6 (Summer 1971):322–23.

21. See examples in note 3.

22. George Hanoch, "Personal Earnings and Investment in Schooling," *Journal of Human Resources* 2 (Summer 1967):310–29.

23. Schweitzer, p. 325.

24. See Appendix B.

25. Schweitzer, p. 332.

26. Levin, p. 27.

27. *Statistics of Public and Elementary and Secondary Day Schools* O.E.-73-11402 (Washington: U.S. Office of Education, 1973).

28. "Measuring Educational Needs and Costs," in *Alternative Programs for Financing Education* (Gainesville, Fla.: National Educational Finance Project, 1971), pp. 156–67.

29. "1973 Cost of Buildings Index," *School Management* 17 (June–July 1973):14.

30. *Financial Statistics of Institutions of Higher Education*, O.E.-74-11419 (Washington: U.S. Government Printing Office, 1973).

31. William E. Rosenstengel and Jefferson N. Eastmond, *School Finance, Its Theory and Practice* (New York: The Ronald Press, 1957), p. 6.

32. "Proposal for a Revolution: Part I," *Saturday Review*, October 19, 1963, p. 22, as cited in Burkhead, p. 366.

33. Henry S. Commager, "Our Schools Have Kept Us Free," *Life*, October 16, 1950, as cited in Rosenstengel and Eastmond, p. 3.

34. Roger A. Freeman, *School Needs in the Decade Ahead* (Washington: The Institute for Social Science Research, 1958), 1:46–47.

35. Walter Lippman, "The Shortage in Education," *Atlantic Monthly*, May 1954, p. 1, as cited in Freeman, p. 10.

Income Redistribution Effect of Public Schools on Low-Income Families

Kern Alexander
Thomas Melcher
Stephen Thomas

To obtain equality by redistributing income to the poorer segment of society has long been a goal professed by most Americans. Governmental policy for several generations has been directed toward obtaining greater equality of income and reducing poverty. Irving Kristol has said that the idea of equality itself is "indeed one of the most deeply rooted conventions of contemporary political thought."[1] A major justification for the enactment of the federal personal income tax originally was to bring about greater income redistribution among the classes in our society. This purpose is also found in the basic philosophy supporting the creation of the common school system of this country. Greater income redistribution is desirable not only for humanitarian reasons but also because it makes very good economic sense. Hugh Dalton of the University of London (later Chancellor of the Exchequer) made it very clear in 1920 that simple marginal utility spoke for positive redistribution when he said, "An unequal distribution of a given amount of purchasing power among a given number of people is, therefore, likely to be a wasteful distribution from the point of view of economic welfare, and the more unequal the distribution the greater the waste. This is merely an application of the economists' law of diminishing marginal utility . . . ."[2]

Whether or not redistribution policies in the United States have been successful is open to conjecture. Certainly, without the impact of the income tax and the public schools, the variation in income would be much greater. However, even with these positive influences, wide income disparities still persist from generation to generation. In 1950, the lowest fifth of the population's aggregate share of income was 4.5 per cent; by 1970, it had increased to 5.5 per cent.[3] The highest fifth of the population's share decreased from 42.6 to 41.6 per cent during the same period. Some would conclude that progress is being made although it is coming about very slowly; others dismally conclude that this little effect is really no progress at all. Increased funding of programs which have a positive redistributional

84

effect by both state and federal governments could undoubtedly bring about more rapid and equitable results.

Policies for the reduction of poverty and inequality may take several forms but may be conveniently classified in three categories. First, a direct income strategy is the most obvious, conceptually simple approach to redistributing income. Proponents argue that cash transfers redistribute the wealth quickly and efficiently, and no tendency exists for the funds to be siphoned off by the upper and middle classes before the benefits reach the poor. However, direct transfer systems have not been looked upon with favor by the public generally. In formulating the strategy for the War on Poverty, direct transfer policies were rejected because consensus apparently did not support the taking of income from one individual and simply giving it to another. Opposition to cash transfers also maintains that the recipients may not make proper use of the cash given them—they may expend money foolishly on cars or television sets while depriving their families of food and medical care.

A second redistribution mechanism is the in-kind transfer for essentials such as food, housing, medical care, and child care. The basic rationale for this approach is that government should ensure that everyone has a minimum amount of essential goods and services, that is, the necessities of life.

A third redistribution intervention policy suggests that a greater redistribution value is derived from a system which invests in human capital by increasing the knowledge of the poor, thereby increasing their productivity. Providing education and training for the poor is an investment in the future, increasing each person's productivity and ability to be self-sustaining. Manpower training, compensatory education, preschool training, and, in fact, general aid to public elementary and secondary education would fall into this category.

While the redistributive impact of expenditures for education is generally viewed as substantial, little is known of its magnitude or of variations in the redistributive impact of education among and within individual states. It is the problem of measuring the redistributive impact of the various state educational finance systems to which this chapter is directed.

REDISTRIBUTIONAL EFFECT OF EDUCATION

Little doubt exists today that the human capital approach to the distribution of resources has high returns. Schultz and others have documented the economic returns to investment in education well, justifying greater public investment in education, particularly at the elementary and secondary levels.[4] Investment in human capital, however, presents pervasive problems of measurement if one is to attempt to determine the redistributional effect of our taxation and allocation system and measure its effects on poverty and inequality. We can, though, presume that all persons do benefit from the system since public schools are free and participation is compulsory. The problems of measurement emanate largely from the fact that we have fifty state school systems and thousands of school districts in the United States. The benefits derived by the child vary widely among these systems, some instances finding high financial assistance, others finding low.

Because of the complexity of the many tax structures and allocation systems, studies of educational finance traditionally have not attempted to determine the income redistribution effect derived from governmental policies of investment in education. Generally, studies have been concerned with the equality of expenditures or the fiscal ability of local school districts to produce revenues for education. The school district itself has been the basic unit with which the data have been associated. Attempts to break down the clientele of the school districts as to contribution of the taxpayers and benefits received are uncommon. The paucity of redistributional studies may also be partially attributed to the belief that public education is free, indeed compulsory, and that the benefits are therefore the same to each if one avails oneself of the opportunity.

In viewing public schools as a redistributional tool to bring about greater equality, one must analyze the school fiscal structure from two aspects. One is the simple redistributive effect of the state tax structure and the school allocation system with regard to their impact on low-, middle-, and high-income families. If low-income families are receiving more educational benefits in terms of dollars for their education than they pay in taxes for education, there is a positive redistributional effect. On the other hand, the taxation and allocation system may be viewed from a position of equality both within and among income classes. The important question of "fiscal neutrality" among school districts may be addressed from the income redistribution point of view. It should be observed that this effect was generally ignored in litigation in recent years where the constitutionality of state school finance formulas was tested.

POLITICS AND REDISTRIBUTION

Redistribution of income is of vast political importance primarily because in a democratic society the "have-nots" are eligible to vote just as are the "haves." At least one theory of redistribution politics observes that the political efficacy of redistribution derives from self-interest political response to the wishes of the vast numbers of voting poor.[5] If votes are distributed and exercised equally among the people and income is distributed unequally, then the greater numbers of low-income voters will demand a system of redistribution to the poor. More specifically, should the low-income voters command 51 per cent of the votes, the political response would be to redistribute and equalize. This theory is, of course, not totally explanatory of the conditions which prevail in this country, for if it were, the progress toward redistribution of income would be much more definite and rapid.

Where education is concerned, the governmental response of providing better services to low-income families in low-wealth school districts has been very gradual. Expenditure variations among states and school districts were much greater thirty years ago, but wide differences still persist today. A theory of redistribution politics in education must recognize that, although each person has one vote, the significance and power of each vote is not equal, even after reapportionment. In analyzing the educational power structure, it quickly becomes apparent that redistribution of income through education probably is not the strategic basis on which most voters make fiscal decisions. The people who pay into the system and those who receive the benefits back may not be allied on the same economic base.[6] Low-income persons are not always *pro bono publico* where tax money for schools is in question. Families sending their children to parochial schools, or older persons who have very low incomes but see no benefit to be derived personally from voting for greater taxes to equalize resources among school districts, may generally reflect an adverse position to both redistribution and equalization. These voters may join the wealthy at the voting booths and generally retard a positive reallocation of resources to assist low-income children in poor school districts.

Another condition which tends to retard the egalitarian motive of public education is the lack of political power of those who find themselves both poor and living in poor school districts. With regard to legislative influence, it is certainly true that the more populous school districts in this country are also the ones with the greatest average wealth per pupil.[7] It is to their disadvantage to encourage state governments to fiscally equalize among school districts. Some argue quite rationally that for sheer numbers more poor persons are actually found in wealthier than in average or below-average school districts, thereby inducing a low-income voter response which may seek redistribution locally but retard similar stress at the state level. This problem is magnified by the unreasonably large number of school districts in many states, a variable in the redistribution discussion which holds vast implications for both inequality and politics generally.

Even where a majority of low-income voters exercise their franchise in poor school districts, the overall political power structure of the state responds to varying coalitions seeking divergent goals. Equality through redistribution becomes a cloudy objective. As Buchanan and Tullock have explained, over a series of issues the taxpayer/voter may respond differently.[8] In one situation he may find himself the beneficiary and be in the minority, but with another issue he may derive no benefits and yet find himself in the voting majority. Certain individuals may do very well with particular outcomes but badly with others.

The pattern of redistribution cannot therefore be specified under the present democratic method of financing public education. Many times considerations other than income form the basis for coalitions which naturally retard the progress toward the measurable ideal of income redistribution. The theory that by sheer numbers low-income voters will prevail in redistributing income obviously does not account for the complex political conditions which prevail in education. Redistribution through education requires a concerted political effort at the state or federal level to form coalitions having mutual interests encompassing the ideal of public education and advancing both the social and economic desirability of greater equality.

OTHER REDISTRIBUTION STUDIES

While several important studies have improved our understanding of the distributional impact of school finance programs, the movement toward more equitable alternatives has been hindered by a continued lack of reliable distributional information. Analysis of the equity of public investment in education centers on the distribution of benefits and costs. The costs of public investment in education are the taxes which support it, and the distribution of the costs is the incidence of these taxes. While private costs of education such as forgone income and tuition payments are of considerable importance, especially in higher education, only public costs, measured by the taxes supporting the program, are relevant in determining the redistributive effect of public investment.

The benefits of public investment in education are more complex, involving difficult conceptual problems. However, direct benefits may be defined as the subsidy allocated to each person participating in the program. Direct benefits are the difference between the per pupil cost of the program and the amount paid by each pupil in tuition and fees. Indirect benefits are both public and private. Public indirect benefits include a wide variety of intangible benefits to society as well as increased tax collections resulting from the greater earnings of the individual. Private indirect benefits include nonmonetary benefits to the student and his family as well as monetary benefits to the student in the form of increased lifetime earnings, discounted to present value. While the indirect benefits of public investment in education are of tremendous importance, conceptual and empirical problems have to date prevented reliable, accurate measurement of these benefits, and most distributional studies have considered only the direct benefits.

Most studies of the distributional effects of public investment in education have been concerned solely with the effects of higher education. Considerable controversy has arisen in this area, as some writers have concluded that present higher educational finance systems tend to redistribute wealth from low-income to high-income families, while others have concluded the reverse.

Hansen and Weisbrod compared the average subsidies received by families with children in the California public higher education system with the average total state-local tax burden levied on those families.[9] Subsidies were obtained by subtracting the tuition at each type of institution from the total per student costs in that institution, including capital as well as instructional costs. Average subsidies in 1964 ranged from nothing for families without children in California public higher education to $1,700 for families with children attending the University of California (see Table 1). Significantly, subsidies at the University of California campuses were substantially larger than those at the junior colleges. Estimates of tax burdens by income class were obtained, but no direct comparison was made between the tax burdens and benefits for each income class. Instead, the average family income for children attending each type of institution was computed, and the average state-local total tax burden associated with families of this income was subtracted from the average subsidy at each type of institution to obtain an average net transfer. Average family income was lowest among families with no children in college and highest among families with children attending the University of California. Families without children in California public higher education institutions received an average net loss of $650, while average net transfers to families with children attending California institutions of public higher education ranged from $40 in the junior colleges to $790 at the University of California. Hansen and Weisbrod concluded that "Some low-income persons have benefited handsomely from the availability of publicly subsidized higher education. But on the whole, the effect of these subsidies is to promote greater rather than less inequality among people of various social and economic backgrounds, by making available substantial subsidies that low-income families are either not eligible for or cannot make use of because of other conditions and constraints associated with their income position."

TABLE 1

AVERAGE FAMILY INCOMES, AVERAGE HIGHER EDUCATION SUBSIDIES, AND AVERAGE STATE AND LOCAL TAXES PAID BY FAMILIES, BY TYPE OF INSTITUTION, CALIFORNIA 1964

Item	All Families	Families without Children in California Public Higher Education	Family with Children in California Public Higher Education			
			Total	JC	SC	UC
1. Average family income	$8,000	$7,900	$9,560	$8,800	$10,000	$12,000
2. Average higher education subsidy per year		0	880	720	1,400	1,700
3. Average total state and local taxes paid	620	650	740	680	770	910
4. Net transfer (line 2 − line 3)		−650	+140	+ 40	+630	+790

SOURCE: Hansen and Weisbrod, *Benefits, Costs, and Finance of Public Higher Education*, Table IV-12.

NOTE: JC, junior colleges; SC, state colleges; UC, University of California.

The Hansen-Weisbrod conclusion that the California system for financing public higher education "leads to a sizeable redistribution of income from lower to higher income" families has been challenged by several writers, most notably by Joseph Pechman.[10] Pechman questioned the Hansen-Weisbrod methodology in five respects. First, while Hansen and Weisbrod utilized total state-local taxes paid by the family as the measure of costs, Pechman argued that only the portion of taxes actually allocated to public higher education should be considered. Second, Hansen and Weisbrod's failure to include the state's corporate income tax and estate and gift tax resulted in overly regressive estimates of family tax burdens. Third, Hansen and Weisbrod made no direct comparison of the benefits and costs for each income class. Fourth, the Hansen-Weisbrod data are limited to "parent-supported" students. Since the average income of families with self-supporting students is lower than that of families with parent-supported students, the subsidy to the lower income classes is underestimated. Finally, Pechman observed that the effects of public investment in higher education on the distribution of lifetime incomes of the recipients was not studied.

Re-analyzing the Hansen-Weisbrod data for California, Pechman made direct comparisons of the average net effect of the California system of public higher education finance on families in each income class (see Table 2). Contrary to Hansen and Weisbrod, Pechman concluded that the California public higher education finance system resulted in a redistribution of income from the upper-income classes to the low- and middle-income classes. Net subsidies ranged from $62 in the $4,000–5,999 income class to −$739 in the $25,000 and over income class.

While the conclusions of the Pechman re-analysis of the California data differ substantially from the conclusions drawn by Hansen and Weisbrod in the original California study, Hartman, reviewing the two studies, found enough common ground to draw three conclusions. Poor people pay taxes and very few of them use public higher education. Those who do, gain thereby; those who don't, don't. Middle-income people are heavy users of the system. Their taxes don't cover the costs. A few rich people use the system and gain handsomely thereby. The rest of the rich pay substantial taxes and get no direct return.

Windham estimated the distribution of costs and direct benefits of the Florida system of public higher education, concluding that the Florida system results in a redistribution of income from lower to higher income groups.[11] Unfortunately, his findings are of questionable validity due to the inadequacies of the data and procedures used in estimating the distribution of tax burdens. While the tax burden estimates in the California studies were made specifically for that state, Windham's tax burden estimates were based on extrapolations from national data.

To adjust these national estimates for conditions in Florida in 1967–68, Windham included only those taxes which represented potential sources of revenue for the Florida higher education system, excluding from consideration such taxes as the federal social security tax and the state personal income tax. The cost of the Florida public higher education system was apportioned among the various income classes on the basis of the national

TABLE 2
AVERAGE NET SUBSIDY OR TAX PAYMENT FOR THE HIGHER EDUCATION SYSTEM
BY INCOME CLASSES, CALIFORNIA 1965
(in dollars)

Adjusted Gross Income Class	Average Tax Payment Using Taxes Selected by Hansen-Weisbrod	Average Higher Education Subsidy	Net Subsidy (+) or Net Tax Payment (−)
0–3,999	66	83	+17
4,000–5,999	77	139	+62
6,000–7,999	88	143	+55
8,000–9,999	112	122	+10
10,000–11,999	142	160	+18
12,000–13,999	175	155	−20
14,000–19,999	229	181	−48
20,000–24,999	348	252	−96
25,000 and over	974	235	−739

SOURCE: Pechman, "The Distributional Effects of Public Higher Education in California," Table 3, p. 366.

incidence estimates for the remaining taxes. He relied on two studies, one by Irwin Gillespie at the Brookings Institution and the other by George Bishop at the Tax Foundation; they estimated the average tax burdens on selected income classes by major type of tax for the years 1960 and 1961, respectively. National collections of each major type of tax were allocated among the designated income classes in accordance with national consumption and expenditure patterns and the distribution of population among the income classes. Since the Tax Foundation estimated that the $0–2,999 income class paid 10.5 per cent of the general sales tax bill nationwide in 1961, Windham, in his estimates of the tax burdens in Florida in 1967–68, implicitly assumed that the $0–2,999 income class also paid 10.5 per cent of the general sales tax bill in Florida in 1967–68.

This assumption is clearly erroneous and results in an overestimation of the tax burden on the lower income classes in Florida for two major reasons. First, the distribution of population among income groups in Florida in 1967–68 was considerably different from the distribution of population among income groups in the entire country in 1960–61. Since the proportion of Florida population falling into the lowest income groups in 1967–68 was smaller than the national average proportion falling into those groups in 1960–61, the proportion of the tax burden assigned to this group is split among too few people, resulting in an overestimation of the burden on each. The fallacy of this method becomes quite clear when the approach is extended to other states. It would imply, for example, that the $0–2,999 income class would pay 10.5 per cent of the state general sales tax burden in both Mississippi and New York, despite the fact that a much higher proportion of Mississippi's population falls in this income class. As

TABLE 3

DISTRIBUTION OF COSTS AND BENEFITS OF PUBLIC HIGHER EDUCATION IN FLORIDA, 1967–68, AS ESTIMATED BY WINDHAM

	Income Class			
	$0–2,999	$3,000–4,999	$5,000–9,999	$10,000 and above
State and local costs	$12,895,590	$24,976,370	$68,821,760	$29,049,020
Federal costs	1,363,770	4,002,380	13,697,020	10,554,420
Total costs	$14,259,360	$28,978,750	$82,518,780	$39,603,440
Total benefits	10,419,600	20,296,320	70,395,980	64,278,490
Net Gain	−$ 3,839,760	−$ 8,682,430	−$12,122,800	+$24,675,050

SOURCE: Windham, *Education, Equality and Income Redistribution*, Table 5–7, pp. 42–3; incidence from Tax Foundation Study.

a result, the burden on this income class is underestimated for Mississippi and overestimated for New York. Second, Windham, in his approach, assumes that the entire burden of the taxes supporting the Florida system of higher education falls on Florida residents. Since Florida relies heavily on the tourist industry, the burden on Florida residents of taxes such as the sales tax is overestimated.

Hight and Pollack estimated the distributional effects of public higher education systems in three states—California, Florida, and Hawaii.[12] Approaching the distributional question by comparing percentage distributions rather than absolute dollar costs and benefits, this study provides interesting comparisons with the earlier studies of California and Florida. To obtain a measure of net transfer effects, the authors compared the percentage distribution of state-local tax payments by income class. Income classes for which the percentage of students contributed was greater than the percentage of taxes paid were classified as receiving positive net transfers. While the findings varied widely among the three states studied, the highest and lowest income classes in each state were net losers, while at least two of the middle-income classes in each state received net gains (see Table 4). With regard to the Florida system, they concluded that income groups between $4,000 and $20,000 received positive net transfers, while those below $4,000 or above $20,000 received negative net transfers. These findings differ considerably from those of Windham, primarily because of differing income class groupings and methods of allocating the distribution of tax burdens. Hight and Pollack's findings for California reflect to a considerable extent those of Pechman for that state, although significant differences of degree exist between the findings of the two studies.

Studies of this type have not been confined solely to the United States. Judy estimated the distribution of costs and benefits resulting from the Canadian system of public higher education, concluding that transfers among income groups were not appreciable. While the higher income groups were the main beneficiaries of the system, they also paid most of the taxes supporting it.[13]

While most existing research on the distributional effects of public investment in education has dealt solely with higher education, three notable studies have focused on the common school level. Holland and Grubb, in studies of the Oklahoma and Boston public schools, respectively, measured the distributional effects of these systems following procedures similar to those developed in the higher education studies.[14] Johns, in a National Educational Finance Project study, established procedures for evaluating state school finance programs in terms of the extent to which financial equalization of educational opportunity is provided, and the extent to which the taxes used to finance the programs are regressive or progressive. Each state school finance program was ranked according to these criteria.[15]

Holland found that the Oklahoma public school finance system resulted in a redistribution of income from the upper income classes to the lower income classes. As illustrated in Table 5, income classes below the $5,000 family income level received positive net transfers while income classes above the $5,000 family income level received negative net transfers. Estimates of tax burdens by income class were calculated, through the application of tax allocation bases similar to those of the Tax Foundation's nationwide study, to consumer expenditure and income data obtained largely from the southern region estimates of the Bureau of Labor Statistics' 1961 Survey of Consumer Expenditures. It was assumed that the expenditure and income patterns in Oklahoma were sufficiently similar to those of the southern region as a whole to use the Bureau of Labor Statistics' estimates for the southern region as representative of Oklahoma. Holland used expenditure as the benefit measure. The expenditure benefits of public primary and secondary education were allocated among

TABLE 4

DISTRIBUTION OF STATE AND LOCAL TAX PAYMENTS AND OF STUDENTS IN PUBLIC HIGHER EDUCATION IN THREE STATES WITH RESULTING TRANSFER EFFECTS

AGI Income Class (dollars)	California			Florida			Hawaii		
	Per Cent Net Gain or Loss	Per Cent of Students	Per Cent of Total State-Local Taxes	Per Cent Net Gain or Loss	Per Cent of Students	Per Cent of Total State-Local Taxes	Per Cent Net Gain or Loss	Per Cent of Students	Per Cent of Total State-Local Taxes
0–3,999	−1.9	9.7	11.6	−7.5	12.5	20.0	−2.3	6.2	8.5
4,000–5,999	+5.9	15.3	9.4	+1.3	16.1	14.8	−1.1	8.6	9.7
6,000–8,999	+10.9	28.4	17.5	+4.3	25.8	21.5	+6.1	22.2	16.1
9,000–14,999	−1.3	31.5	32.8	+4.3	31.0	26.7	+4.0	40.4	36.4
15,000–19,999	−3.1	8.0	11.1	+2.6	8.7	6.1	+0.1	13.0	12.9
20,000+	−10.7	6.9	17.6	−5.2	5.8	11.0	−6.9	9.6	16.5

SOURCE: Hight and Pollack, "Income Distribution Effects of Higher Education Expenditures in California, Florida, and Hawaii," Table 3, p. 324.

income groups as a function of the number of children under eighteen estimated to be enrolled in school. Using this basic study design, Holland
concluded that "a considerable public subsidy is being provided to
low-income families through public primary and secondary education."

TABLE 5
INCIDENCE OF FEDERAL, STATE, AND LOCAL TAXES AND EXPENDITURES FOR PUBLIC
EDUCATION IN OKLAHOMA IN 1961

	Income Class								
	Under $2,000	$2000– $2,999	$3000– $3,999	$4000– $4,999	$5000– $5,999	$6000– $7,499	$7500– $9,999	$10,000– $14,999	$15,000 and Above
1. Expenditure benefit per family	$ 119	$ 216	$ 232	$ 240	$ 287	$ 279	$ 283	$ 281	$ 233
2. Taxes per family	58	109	173	212	289	313	380	551	1571
Net Transfer (1–2)	61	107	59	28	−2	−34	−97	−270	−1338

SOURCE: Holland, "The Distribution of the Costs and Benefits of Public Schooling," Table
2, p. 75; and calculation of net transfer by the authors.

In a study of redistribution in one urban school system, Grubb analyzed
the redistribution effect of education for both whites and nonwhites. Grubb
sought to relate future earning power of the individual, as the determinant
of benefits, to education. The problem of showing the effect of education
on future earnings is a complex problem which has not yet been resolved
to anyone's satisfaction. Grubb's assumptions regarding future earnings
help very little and must be classified as unconvincing. A basic failure of
Grubb's study was his implicit assumption that school centers within the
urban system provided comparable services. Grubb, nevertheless, found
redistribution to low-income persons when using the more reliable expenditure per pupil as a measurable benefit.

General conclusions from these studies are fairly obvious. Regardless of
how the redistribution effect is calculated, aid to public elementary and
secondary schools has a powerful positive redistribution effect. This is true
whether the redistribution effect is determined from the benefits of present
common school expenditures or whether the benefits are presumed to
derive from increased lifetime earnings. Either measure supports governmental investment in the lower levels of education as a means of eradicat-
ing poverty and equalizing governmental benefits among the income
classes.

The evidence regarding the present system of higher education is less conclusive. A composite view may be found, however, where the high- and low-income families receive negative benefits, and the middle-income families receive neutral or slightly positive benefits.

It should be borne in mind that a major boost is given to the benefits to elementary and secondary education by the mere fact that compulsory attendance laws apply at this level. The poor thereby must attend school, usually public schools, and receive benefits whether they desire to do so or not. Also worthy of mention is that in many cases high-income families may send their children to public school at the elementary and secondary level but later send their children to private institutions of higher education. Thus, a tendency to skew the benefits is invoked by the exercise of parental choice. Another skewness is introduced by choice, probably with just economic consideration, whereby the children of poorer families tend to matriculate at state junior colleges or state teachers' colleges, while the higher income groups will migrate toward major state universities where the costs of instruction are higher and, therefore, benefits are presumably greater.

MEASURING THE REDISTRIBUTION

In order to determine the redistributional effect of public education and to examine equality among income classes and school districts, it was necessary to study both the tax structure and the school allocation system of several states. For this purpose sixty school districts in twelve states were selected. The twelve states represented a wide range of economic, social, and geographical conditions. The amount of funds for public schools varied substantially among states. In these twelve states (Arkansas, California, Delaware, Iowa, Kentucky, New Hampshire, New York, Oregon, South Dakota, Utah, Virginia, and Wisconsin) there was a great variety of tax structures as well as various types of school finance structures. New Hampshire and South Dakota were included because they represented states with the lowest percentages of state aid to support schools, relying to the greatest degree on local property taxes; Delaware was selected as one of the states with the highest percentages of state aid.

Within these states, local school districts were selected which broadly represented both the wealthy and the poor, along with the largest school district in each state. It was from this selection of both states and school districts that derivations of both income redistribution of public education and fiscal inequality among income classes of families and school districts were derived.

Procedurally, basic information was largely derived from two dissertations, one written by William P. Briley and the other by Stephen E. Lile.[16] Conducted as an element of the NEFP, Briley's described and analyzed the relationship between school district financial ability and school district revenue for the 1969 fiscal year for selected school districts in each of the forty-eight contiguous states and Alaska. School districts in each state were selected from a financial ability ranking of all districts which had a specified minimum size and which had K–12 or 1–12 instructional programs. Financial ability was expressed in per pupil units and represented the economic ability measure employed by the state for participation in the basic state school finance program. The minimum pupil size was set at 1,500 pupils in states which had seventeen or more K–12 or 1–12 school districts with 1,500 or more pupils and between 1,000 and 1,500 pupils for the remaining states. For selection purposes, first he chose the two largest districts in terms of number of pupils; then the remaining districts were ranked according to financial ability per pupil, and fifteen districts were chosen at determined intervals, from richest to poorest. The data in the Briley study, including financial ability, number of pupils, and revenue from local, state, and federal sources for each school district, were obtained by contacting the chief state school officer, or his designated representative, in each state.

For this study, five districts in each included state were selected from among the seventeen districts analyzed by Briley on these criteria: the largest district in terms of number of pupils, and the two wealthiest and two poorest school districts in terms of equalized assessed value of taxable property per pupil. For each selected district, 1968–69 data on equalized assessed valuation of taxable property, number of pupils,[17] revenue from local sources, and revenue from state sources were taken from the Briley study, or from unpublished NEFP data collected in connection with that study. Based on these data, state-local revenue per pupil and full value local school tax rates were calculated for each district in the sample. A basic and important assumption was that the revenue per pupil was indicative of the educational benefits received by all school children in that school district and that those benefits were uniform.[18]

Lile estimated the state and local tax burdens on a model family of four assumed to live in the largest city in each state for the following income levels: $3,500, $5,000, $7,500, $10,000, $17,500, $25,000, and $50,000. To separate those taxes whose incidence is primarily on the residents of the taxing state from those taxes whose incidence is widely diffused, state-local taxes were divided into group one taxes, the burden of which is primarily on in-state residents: sales and excise taxes, personal income taxes, taxes associated with the ownership and use of automobiles, and property taxes on owner-occupied homes; and group two taxes, the burden of which is diffused among the residents of many states: corporation income taxes, business property taxes, severance and other gross receipts taxes, and the unemployment insurance tax. Based on assumptions regarding level of income, house value, level of consumption expenditures, etc., the burden of group one taxes was estimated by applying the appropriate tax rates to the assumed tax base. Based on economic analysis of tax shifting patterns, group two taxes were allocated among both residents and nonresidents of the taxing state.

Several critical assumptions made in the Lile study are carried forward in this analysis:

1. Tax burdens were estimated for a hypothetical model family of four, assuming these income situations: $3,500, $10,000, and $25,000, all from wages and salaries.

2. The burden of the retail sales tax is on the buyer; estimates of burdens were based on the amounts allowed by the Internal Revenue Service for computing itemized deductions on the federal personal income tax.

3. The burden of excise and selective sales taxes is on the buyer; estimates of cigarette taxes were based on an assumed consumption of 400 packs annually per family and on state cigarette tax rates; estimates of gasoline taxes were based on a study by the U.S. Bureau of Public Roads; estimates of liquor tax burdens were not made because of inadequate expenditure data and because not all states are open license states.

4. Personal income tax burdens were estimated by applying the appropriate state and local effective tax rates to the assumed adjusted gross income for each model family.

5. Each model family was assumed to be living in its own home. Home values for each income level were estimated from data in the *Residential Finance Survey* of the 1960 Census of Housing and the *1965 Survey of Consumer Finances*. The model family income-home value pairings taken from Lile for this study are: $3,500 income—$9,000 home; $10,000 income—$16,300 home; $25,000 income—$37,500 home. Based on home values including these and estimates of full value property tax rates, Lile calculated the local property tax burden on each model family for the largest city in each state. While this study uses the Lile estimates of home values, local full value property tax rates for the public schools are taken from the Briley study.

6. Group two business taxes were allocated according to economic and tax incidence analysis. While several alternative allocation methods were considered, the assumption that group two taxes are shifted forward to consumers was actually used, making family tax burdens for these taxes dependent on consumption expenditure levels.

Lile's calculations were made only for the largest city in each state, and included all major state-local taxes paid by each model family. The purpose of this study was to estimate the tax burdens on model families in each of five selected school districts for each state included in the sample. Only those taxes attributable to elementary and secondary education were included. Since state tax rates are the same throughout a given state and since the characteristics of the model families are held constant, it was assumed in this study that Lile's estimates of the total state tax burden borne by each model family in the largest city of each state were also accurate for model families assumed to live in other parts of the same state. In other words, a model family with a given income living in a certain state was assumed to be paying the same amount of state personal income tax, state retail sales tax, and state excise taxes regardless of which school district it lived in. State taxes for elementary and secondary education were estimated by multiplying the total amount of state taxes paid by the family, from Lile, by the proportion of total state taxes in the particular state which were allocated to elementary and secondary education.[19] This "equiproportional allocation," while questioned by Hansen and Weisbrod, was employed by Pechman, Judy, Grubb, Hight and Pollack, and Holland in similar studies and was the most rational approach available.[20]

Since local property tax rates and assessment practices vary widely within states, the estimates of property tax burdens calculated by Lile for the largest city in each state could not plausibly be applied to taxpayers living in each of the five selected districts in each state examined in this study. However, reasonably accurate information on the full value school property tax rates in each district selected for this study was available in the data collected for the Briley study. Therefore, local property tax burdens for elementary and secondary education were estimated by applying the home value estimates made by Lile to the full value school property tax rates calculated from the Briley data. The total state-local tax burden on each model family was obtained by adding the local burden to the state burden.

STATE AND LOCAL TAX STRUCTURE

Tax burdens on families at each selected income level varied widely among both states and local school districts (Table 6). For example, the family in the $25,000 income category in Beverly Hills, California, paid $487.59 in state and local taxes for education, while the same income group in Alexis I. Du Pont, the wealthiest school district in Delaware, paid $886.35. A family of $25,000 income in Brookhaven, the wealthiest district among the selected districts in New York, paid $1,276.99, while the family of the same

TABLE 6
STATE AND LOCAL TAXES FOR ELEMENTARY AND SECONDARY
EDUCATION BY MODEL FAMILY INCOME (in dollars)

School District and State	Amount of Taxes		
	With $3,500 Income	With $10,000 Income	With $25,000 Income
Arkansas			
Crossett	160.05	306.62	623.80
Little Rock	188.19	354.90	734.87
Pulaski	198.72	372.98	776.45
Cabot	174.66	331.68	681.45
Gosnell	187.06	352.97	730.57
California			
Beverly Hills	120.77	223.71	487.59
Lake Tahoe	139.01	255.00	559.59
Los Angeles	150.44	274.61	604.71
Ceres	153.47	279.81	616.67
Travis	144.23	263.97	580.21
Delaware			
Alexis I. Du Pont	168.25	386.19	886.35
Wilmington	161.04	373.82	857.89
Mt. Pleasant	201.18	442.70	1,016.36
Woodbridge	141.80	340.81	781.94
Caesar Rodney	146.97	349.68	802.34
Iowa			
Pleasant Valley	148.39	325.45	557.99
Jefferson	157.00	340.21	591.95
Des Moines	205.42	423.30	783.11
Anamosa	187.63	392.77	712.87
Council Bluffs	225.19	457.22	861.14
Kentucky			
Bardstown	174.47	394.25	703.38
Franklin	174.60	394.47	703.88
Jefferson	206.71	449.56	803.63
Letcher	155.09	360.98	626.84
Breathitt	149.43	351.29	604.54
New Hampshire			
Gov. Wentworth	109.15	180.79	358.74
Berlin	130.03	216.61	441.15
Manchester	124.22	206.63	418.21
Fall Mountain	250.49	423.29	916.66
Merrimack Valley	271.95	460.12	1,001.37
New York			
Brookhaven 6	287.87	573.85	1,276.99
Hempstead 21	307.53	607.58	1,354.59
New York City	261.72	528.98	1,173.77
Salamanca	292.82	582.35	1,296.55
Fort Covington	239.97	491.67	1,087.94
Oregon			
Klamath	87.16	213.05	418.64
Reedsport	158.09	334.74	698.60
Portland	164.88	346.39	725.41

Continued

TABLE 6—*Continued*

School District and State	Amount of Taxes		
	With $3,500 Income	With $10,000 Income	With $25,000 Income
South Umpqua	256.03	502.79	1,085.22
David Douglas	310.16	595.67	1,298.89
South Dakota*			
Mitchell	203.19	345.55	731.85
Lake Central	205.81	350.04	742.19
Sioux Falls	201.61	342.83	725.60
Pierre	253.66	423.15	931.08
Utah			
San Juan	209.56	445.53	826.45
Iron	223.61	469.63	881.89
Grand	234.31	487.98	924.12
Weber	219.26	462.17	864.74
Davis	220.34	464.01	868.98
Virginia			
Arlington	205.98	416.78	868.19
Fluvanna	190.29	389.86	806.26
Fairfax	295.61	570.56	1,221.99
Smyth	243.26	480.74	1,015.35
Wise	271.20	528.69	1,125.65
Wisconsin			
West Allis	185.44	368.72	788.97
Madison	199.41	392.69	884.11
Milwaukee	223.39	433.83	938.76
Antigo	206.69	405.18	872.84
Tomah	229.40	444.14	962.49

*Douglas, a poor district in terms of assessed valuation of property, was excluded from the sample because of the possible effects on tax structure control by a large military base. The same rationale could possibly be applied to Travis, California.

income in the wealthiest district in Oregon paid only $418.64. These wide differentials are caused by a combination of regressive versus progressive tax systems and varying state and local effort for support of the public schools.[21] One may not be greatly disturbed by the variation in tax incidence among families in various states, but this phenomenon tends to exist within states as well. In Oregon, for example, the family in the $25,000 category paid only $418.64 in the wealthiest school district in our sample, while the same income family in the poorest district paid $1,298.89.

With regard to taxes paid by poor families, we see that a similar pattern of wide variations exists both among and within states. A low-income family ($3,500) paid $223.39 in taxes for education in Milwaukee, while a family with the same income in West Allis, the richest district in Wisconsin, paid

$185.44. The strong dependence on local taxation in New Hampshire, with its regressive tax structure, is illustrated by the fact that the poorest family in the poorest district in the state paid $271.95 in school taxes, and the wealthiest family in the wealthiest district paid only $358.74.

Since the relative progressivity of state-local systems for raising educational revenues is a key factor in this analysis, a progressivity index for each state's school tax system was calculated from the mean tax rates paid by the model families in each state for the $3,500 and $25,000 income levels. Defined as the percentage of income paid by the $25,000 income family divided by the percentage of income paid by the $3,500 income family, times 100 per cent, the progressivity index values for each state's school revenue system are shown in Table 7. A value of 100 on this index would

TABLE 7
PROGRESSIVITY OF STATE-LOCAL SCHOOL REVENUES, 1968–69

State	Index	Rank
Arkansas	54.6	9
California	56.3	7
Delaware	74.5	1
Iowa	53.1	10
Kentucky	56.5	6
New Hampshire	48.7	12
New York	62.4	2
Oregon	61.7	3
South Dakota	50.4	11
Utah	55.2	8
Virginia	58.5	5
Wisconsin	59.1	4

indicate that the state-local tax structure for education was exactly proportional. Values over 100 would indicate a progressive system, values under 100 a regressive system. As shown in Table 7 the state-local school revenue systems of every state included in this study were regressive in impact. Poor families paid a higher proportion of their incomes in taxes for elementary and secondary education than wealthy families. Of the twelve states in the sample, Delaware, with the highest percentage of revenues from state sources, had the least regressive tax structure. New Hampshire and South Dakota, with the lowest percentage of school funds from state sources, were the most regressive. In New Hampshire, poor families paid more than twice as great a percentage of their incomes in state-local school taxes as wealthy families.

As indicated in Table 7, states which relied on local property taxes to support the schools established a taxation pattern which effectively reduced the positive redistribution impact of the public schools. Reliance on local property taxes also appeared to make the incidence of tax payments fluctuate to a much greater degree within income classes, although with the interplay of local fiscal effort it is difficult to absolutely confirm this observation from the data presented.

From Table 6, it is quite obvious that the wealthy paid more taxes than the poor. But if one considers, for example, that in Arkansas the high-income group had 7.1 times the resources of the poorest but paid only 3.8 times the taxes for education, then the regressivity of the tax system is verified (see Table 7). The conclusion can quickly be drawn that the redistributional effect of the public schools is reduced by the regressiveness of the tax system to which it is attached. The traditional marriage of school finance and local property taxation requires strong equalization measures to overcome the impact of local property taxation. Where the percentage of local support for the schools is higher, the state should employ more stringent equalization standards from the state level.

In nine of the twelve states examined, the poor family in the poorest school district paid more state and local taxes to support the public schools than did its counterpart in the richest school district. This was equally true for the middle- and high-income groups. A citizen could generally look forward to paying higher taxes if he resided in a poor school district. As we will see later, the undesirability of living in a poor district was magnified when the benefits received were considered.

BENEFITS RECEIVED THROUGH PUBLIC SCHOOLS

Benefits received through the public schools are both direct and indirect. The direct benefits received can be easily quantified in terms of the amount of expenditures which government allocates for the education of each child. Indirect benefits are those long-range benefits an individual receives, primarily quantifiable as future earning power. Although either method may be used to determine redistribution benefits, we have chosen the former as more realistic in order to measure both redistributional effects and equality of treatment among income groups and school districts.

Table 8 shows the direct benefits from public schools as found in the richest and poorest school districts of over 1,500 average daily attendance in the twelve selected states. It is presumed that the benefits within the school districts flow equally to all the children regardless of their income level.

Only in Oregon did the wealthier of the school districts have a lower amount of state and local revenues. Wider disparities between the rich and

TABLE 8
DIRECT BENEFITS OF PUBLIC SCHOOL AS MEASURED BY STATE AND LOCAL REVENUES
PER ADA AND PER CENT OF POOR TO RICH DISTRICT
(in dollars)

School District and State	State and Local Revenue Per ADA	Per Cent Poor to Rich
Arkansas		
Crossett	450.59	$ 54.33
Little Rock	569.64	
Pulaski	385.69	
Cabot	312.78	
Gosnell	244.80	
California		
Beverly Hills	1,258.70	37.58
Lake Tahoe	941.42	
Los Angeles	674.29	
Ceres	605.02	
Travis	473.07	
Delaware		
Alexis I. Du Pont	934.26	39.47
Wilmington	785.63	
Mt. Pleasant	818.35	
Woodbridge	547.35	
Caesar Rodney	368.72	
Iowa		
Pleasant Valley	952.19	54.26
Jefferson	652.06	
Des Moines	708.20	
Anamosa	558.43	
Council Bluffs	516.67	
Kentucky		
Bardstown	641.75	68.71
Franklin	554.35	
Jefferson	603.41	
Letcher	413.93	
Breathitt	440.95	
New Hampshire		
Gov. Wentworth	873.17	77.76
Berlin	572.10	
Manchester	442.27	
Fall Mountain	691.08	
Merrimack Valley	678.92	
New York		
Brookhaven 6	$1,375.74	$ 86.14
Hempstead 21	1,442.92	
New York City	1,286.69	
Salamanca	1,017.94	
Fort Covington	1,185.00	
Oregon		
Klamath	591.67	113.38
Reedsport	774.17	
Portland	675.71	
South Umpqua	661.21	
David Douglas	670.85	

Continued

TABLE 8—*Continued*

School District and State	State and Local Revenue Per ADA	Per Cent Poor to Rich
South Dakota		
Mitchell	754.94	69.88
Lake Central	674.38	
Sioux Falls	605.26	
Pierre	527.31	
Utah		
San Juan	689.72	65.67
Iron	573.08	
Grand	484.54	
Weber	451.73	
Davis	452.91	
Virginia		
Arlington	1,026.22	47.09
Fluvanna	571.84	
Fairfax	720.75	
Smyth	500.93	
Wise	483.20	
Wisconsin		
West Allis	980.75	63.10
Madison	758.61	
Milwaukee	760.06	
Antigo	625.33	
Tomah	618.81	

NOTE: A word of caution is appropriate to remind the reader that these are 1969 data and conditions in allocation within certain states may have changed during the past few years. Also, it should be remembered that the revenue percentage of poor to rich may not be indicative of the true variation in each state, since only those school districts of at least 1,500 ADA were used in the sample.

poor school districts were found in California, where the wealthy district had 2.6 times the revenue of the poorest, and Virginia, where the richest had 2.1 times the poorest. The benefits available varied greatly among both states and school districts with the greatest per pupil benefit found in New York and the lowest in Arkansas.

REDISTRIBUTION OF INCOME

Public schools present a viable and attractive means by which government can redistribute income and generally advance vertical equalization. Families in the $3,500 income category in all states examined derived a substantial positive redistributional effect when taxation for education was compared with benefits received. As shown in Table 9 the redistributional effect for a low-income family was much greater on the average than for a middle- or high-income family. In Beverly Hills, California, a poor family received $10.42 in education benefits for every dollar paid for public school taxes at both state and local levels. A poor family in Governor Wentworth, the wealthiest school district in New Hampshire in our sample, received $8.00 worth of benefits for every dollar in taxes. The state with the lowest ratio for a poor family in the wealthy school district was Arkansas, where the benefit-tax ratio was 2.82.

The positive redistributional effect in the poor school districts of the public schools, while much less than in the rich districts, is substantial. In poor districts, the greatest redistribution for the low-income family was found in New York, where benefits received were $4.94 for every dollar of taxes. The lowest redistribution effect was found in Wise County, Virginia, where the poor family received benefits worth only 1.78 times as much as the taxes it paid.

Among the largest school districts in the states, New York City provided the poor family with the greatest redistribution benefits of 4.92, followed by Los Angeles with a 4.48 revenue-tax ratio. No particular pattern emerged when the largest school district in a state was compared with all the other sample school districts in the same state; however, it was obvious that the redistributional benefits were generally greater to the poor family living in the wealthy suburb than in the central city. For example, the benefit ratio for Beverly Hills was more than twice that of Los Angeles, and the ratio was also greater for the poor family in Alexis I. Du Pont than the poor family in Wilmington. The variation between New York City and other selected districts did not show such a wide difference in benefit ratios.

The redistributional effect of the public schools was uniformly positive when all three income levels were analyzed. In middle-income families ($10,000) the benefit-tax ratio was lower than for poor families. A middle-income family living in Beverly Hills, California, received $5.63 for every dollar paid, while the middle-income family in Travis, the poor district in California, received benefits at a 1.79 ratio. Wealthy families tended to receive a negative benefit return on the tax dollars they paid. A family with $25,000 income in Bardstown, Kentucky, received 91 per cent of its tax dollar in direct school benefits. As in the other income classes, the same family would receive much lower returns if it were located in a poor school district. The highest benefit-tax ratios for the wealthy were found in Beverly Hills, California, where $2.58 was derived for each tax dollar paid and in Governor Wentworth, New Hampshire, where $1.00 in taxes returned $2.43 in benefits. The lowest return to the highest income class was found in Gosnell, Arkansas, where only $0.34 on the dollar was returned in benefits. In that state, also, the benefit-tax ratio for the wealthiest family was negative even if the family lived in the wealthiest school district.

TABLE 9
REDISTRIBUTION EFFECT OF THE PUBLIC SCHOOL AS MEASURED BY THE REVENUE-TAX
RATIO FOR A MODEL FAMILY OF FOUR WITH ONE CHILD IN PUBLIC SCHOOL

School District and State	Benefit Ratio		
	Family with $3,500 Income	Family with $10,000 Income	Family with $25,000 Income
Arkansas			
Crossett	2.82	1.47	0.72
Little Rock	3.03	1.61	0.78
Pulaski	1.94	1.03	0.50
Cabot	1.79	0.94	0.46
Gosnell	1.31	0.69	0.34
California			
Beverly Hills	10.42	5.63	2.58
Lake Tahoe	6.77	3.69	1.68
Los Angeles	4.48	2.46	1.12
Ceres	3.94	2.16	0.98
Travis	3.28	1.79	0.82
Delaware			
Alexis I. Du Pont	5.55	2.42	1.05
Wilmington	4.88	2.10	0.92
Mt. Pleasant	4.07	1.85	0.81
Woodbridge	3.86	1.61	0.70
Caesar Rodney	2.51	1.05	0.46
Iowa			
Pleasant Valley	6.42	2.93	1.71
Jefferson	4.15	1.92	1.10
Des Moines	3.45	1.67	0.90
Anamosa	2.98	1.42	0.78
Council Bluffs	2.29	1.13	0.60
Kentucky			
Bardstown	3.68	1.62	0.91
Franklin	3.17	1.41	0.79
Jefferson	2.92	1.34	0.73
Letcher	2.67	1.15	0.66
Breathitt	2.96	1.26	0.73
New Hampshire			
Gov. Wentworth	8.00	4.83	2.43
Berlin	4.40	2.64	1.30
Manchester	3.56	2.14	1.06
Fall Mountain	2.76	1.63	0.75
Merrimack Valley	2.50	1.48	0.68
New York			
Brookhaven 6	4.78	2.40	1.08
Hempstead 21	4.69	2.37	1.07
New York City	4.92	2.43	1.10
Salamanca	3.48	1.75	0.79
Fort Covington	4.94	2.41	1.09
Oregon			
Klamath	6.79	2.78	1.41
Reedsport	4.90	2.31	1.11
Portland	4.10	1.95	0.93
South Umpqua	2.58	1.32	0.61
David Douglas	2.16	1.13	0.52

Continued

TABLE 9 — *Continued*

School District and State	Benefit Ratio		
	Family with $3,500 Income	Family with $10,000 Income	Family with $25,000 Income
South Dakota			
Mitchell	3.72	2.18	1.03
Lake Central	3.28	1.93	0.91
Sioux Falls	3.00	1.67	0.83
Pierre	2.08	1.22	0.57
Utah			
San Juan	3.29	1.55	0.83
Iron	2.56	1.22	0.65
Grand	2.07	0.99	0.52
Weber	2.06	0.98	0.52
Davis	2.06	0.98	0.52
Virginia			
Arlington	4.98	2.46	1.18
Fluvanna	3.01	1.47	0.71
Fairfax	2.44	1.26	0.59
Smyth	2.06	1.04	0.49
Wise	1.78	0.91	0.43
Wisconsin			
West Allis	5.29	2.66	1.24
Madison	3.80	1.93	0.90
Milwaukee	3.40	1.75	0.81
Antigo	3.03	1.54	0.72
Tomah	2.70	1.39	0.64

The implications of this redistribution analysis suggest that the public schools are a very effective vehicle for redistribution of income even if only the direct benefits are considered. A primary reason for this positive redistribution effect is the common and free nature of public schools wherein low-income classes participate as fully and equally as high-income groups. Compulsory attendance laws contribute to the positive income redistribution, since poor children must attend school and receive its benefits. The positive outcomes of governmental investment in public schools suggest that the state and federal governments should increase resources for public schools in order to provide poverty level families with a greater share of the income benefits.

EQUALITY OF BENEFITS

Equality as measured by redistribution of income presents a picture of fiscal inequality which is familiar in other studies, but it adds a new dimension.[22] Here we see an inequality of treatment within income classes created by location of residence—a horizontal inequality. With regard to taxation only, the incidence of taxation is greater on families living in poor school districts (Table 1). In addition, the benefits measured in terms of school revenues are much less. Combine this with an undue reliance on local property taxes and the net result is substantial inequality within income classes. A poor family in a poor district paid more taxes in nine of the twelve states studied; the benefit-tax ratio was nevertheless lower. In Arkansas, for example, poor families in the poor school district paid $187.06 in taxes for education while the poor family in a rich district paid only $160.05; the poor family in the rich district received $2.82 for each dollar in taxes, while the poor family in the poor district received only $1.31 for each of its tax dollars. This phenomenon was uniform, with one exception: New York, where the poor family in the poor district actually received a greater benefit ratio than did its counterpart in the rich school district.

The general pattern of inequality of benefits within income classes was also found in the middle- and high-income groups. It is easy to conclude that it is much better to be poor in a rich school district than to be poor in a poor school district, or one may conclude that it is simply better, from a redistributional point of view, to live in a rich school district regardless of income level. The implications of this within-class inequality are difficult to pinpoint; however, one may suspect that the despair which characterizes many of the nation's poor school districts emanates from this economic condition.

The remedy to the economic plight of taxpayers in low wealth school districts can be found in greater equalization of state resources for education. The school districts with low local fiscal ability must be buoyed up with greater state fiscal equalization.

Further, movement away from the local property tax would have a desirable twofold effect. First, it would create a more progressive tax structure whereby low-income families would use less of their income for taxes, and second, it would allow a more uniform distribution of benefits to local school districts whether they are rich or poor. The tendency would then be to have greater equality not only within income classes but also among income classes in all school districts.

REFERENCES

1. "Equality as an Ideal," *International Encyclopedia of the Social Sciences* (New York: Macmillan, 1968), pp. 108–11.

2. Hugh Dalton, *Some Aspects of the Inequality of Incomes in Modern Communities* (London: Routledge, 1920), p. 10.

3. Edward R. Fried, Alice M. Rivlin, Charles L. Schultze, and Nancy H. Teeters, *Setting National Priorities, The 1974 Budget* (Washington: Brookings Institution, 1973), p. 41.

4. See Theodore W. Schultz, *Investment in Human Capital* (New York: The Free Press, 1971), and George Psacharopoulos, *Returns to Education* (San Francisco: Jossey-Bass, 1973).

5. Anthony Downs, *An Economic Theory of Democracy* (New York: Harper and Row, 1957).

6. James D. Rodgers, "Explaining Income Redistribution," in *Redistribution through Public Choice*, ed. Hochman and Peterson (New York: Columbia University Press, 1974), p. 169.

7. Jack E. Fisher, "A Comparison between Central Cities and Suburbs on Local Ability to Support Public Education" (Ed.D. diss., University of Florida, 1972).

8. J. M. Buchanan and G. Tullock, *The Calculus of Consent* (Ann Arbor: University of Michigan, 1962).

9. W. Lee Hansen and Burton A. Weisbrod, *Benefits, Costs and Finance of Public Higher Education* (Chicago: Markham Publishing Co., 1969).

10. "The Distributional Effects of Public Higher Education in California," *Journal of Human Resources* 5 (Summer 1970):361–70.

11. Douglas M. Windham, *Education, Equality and Income Redistribution* (Lexington, Mass.: D. C. Heath, 1970).

12. Joseph E. Hight and Richard Pollack, "Income Distribution Effects of Higher Education Expenditures in California, Florida, and Hawaii," *Journal of Human Resources* 8 (Summer 1973).

13. Richard W. Judy, "The Income-Redistributive Effects of Aid to Higher Education," in *Canadian Economic Problems and Policies,* ed. Lawrence H. Officer and Lawrence B. Smith (New York: McGraw-Hill, 1970).

14. David W. Holland, "The Distribution of the Costs and Benefits of Public Schooling," *Southern Journal of Agricultural Economics* 5 (July 1973):71–79; W. Norton Grubb, "The Distribution of Costs and Benefits in an Urban Public School System," *National Tax Journal* 24 (1971):1–12.

15. R. L. Johns, "Criteria for Evaluating State Financing Plans for the Public Schools," vol. 5, *Alternative Programs for Financing Education* (Gainesville, Fla.: National Educational Finance Project, 1971), pp. 231–63.

16. William P. Briley, "An Analysis of the Variations between Revenue Receipts and Financial Ability for Selected School Districts in the Forty-Eight Contiguous States and Alaska" (Ed.D. diss., University of Florida, 1970); Stephen E. Lile, "Interstate Comparisons of Family Tax Burdens" (Ph.D. diss., University of Kentucky, 1969).

17. Number of pupils was measured in terms of average daily attendance (ADA) for all states except New Hampshire, which used average daily membership (ADM), and New York and Oregon, which used weighted average daily membership (WADM).

18. The lack of comparability among schools within a school district has been acknowledged in many instances; however, recent studies tend to indicate that the unevenness of revenues available to school centers may not be as disproportionate as once thought. See Douglas Forth, "Relationships between Economic Factors and Pupil Achievement in Selected Urban School Systems" (Ed.D. diss., University of Florida, 1974).

19. Proportion of state taxes allocated to elementary and secondary education for each state was obtained by dividing state revenue for elementary and secondary education by total state tax collections. State revenue for elementary and secondary education was taken from National Education Association, *Estimates of School Statistics, 1969–70*, Research Report 1969-R15 (NEA, 1969), Table 9. Total state tax collections in each state were taken from Tax Foundation, Inc., *Facts and Figures on Government Finance*, 13th biennial ed. (New York: Tax Foundation, Inc., 1969), Table 149.

20. W. Lee Hansen and Burton A. Weisbrod, "Who Pays for a Public Expenditure Program?" *National Tax Journal* 24 (December 1971):515–17; Pechman, pp. 361–70; Judy, "The Income-Redistributive Effects of Aid to Higher Education," pp. 302–17; Grubb, pp. 1–12; Hight and Pollack, pp. 318–30; Holland, pp. 71–79.

21. Muller, in studying the intra-district redistribution of the Delaware state school finance program, found that "substantial income redistribution at the intra-state level in Delaware results from the allocation of state educational grants despite the use of a flat 'nonequalizing' state formula, because the state provides a large share of total state revenues . . . . The level of income redistribution in Delaware is attributable to the progressive state income tax, the high share of state aid, and the concentration of high-income taxpayers in suburban districts." Thomas Muller, *Income Redistribution Impact of State Grants to Public Schools: A Case Study of Delaware* (Washington: Urban Institute, October 1973).

22. See Roe L. Johns, Kern Alexander, and Dewey Stollar, eds., vol. 4, *Status and Impact of Educational Finance Programs* (Gainesville, Fla.: National Educational Finance Project, 1971).

The Supply and Demand for Public Elementary and Secondary School Teachers

James A. Hale

The economics of education is rapidly becoming an area of specialized study in public sector economics, influenced not so much by the classical, neoclassical, and Keynesian positions as by the writings of Becker, Schultz, Hansen, Weisbrod, Bowman, and others relating to both qualitative and quantitative aspects of investment in "human capital."[1] Becker has suggested that major advances in economic theory and empirical work during the next decade will be in the application of human capital analysis to behavior in the nonmarket sector.[2] Schultz has enumerated an impressive array of research opportunities that would analyze the role of human capital in the economic system.[3]

Balogh and Streeten's treatment of the Cobb-Douglas production function, and their "accounting" for the unaccounted factors relating it to the Gross National Product, and Bowles' linear programming model of the education sector represent two of many recent studies that apply human resource notions to traditional studies of capital and to the utilization of contemporary econometrics.[4] This chapter will depart somewhat from those contemporary thrusts since it will draw upon neoclassical concepts of supply and demand as they may or may not relate to professional employment in the education industry.

The first part of this chapter contains some basic concepts of supply and demand that are utilized later in an application to professional employment. Then a critique is made of that application as it may or may not apply to the education industry. From that analysis, supply and demand functions are explicated, using a set of assumptions believed to be relevant to the education industry experience. In conclusion, I draw upon human capital concepts to analyze the current and projected employment market conditions for teachers and present several policy suggestions for federal and state governments.

DEMAND: SOME BASIC CONCEPTS

Demand for a good or service is the quantity that purchasers are willing to buy at a specified price and at a particular point in time or time period. Thus, three concepts are connected to form this definition: quantity, price, and time. While maintaining the integrity of those relationships, Rogers and Ruchlin expand the definition somewhat by saying demand is "a schedule indicating the amount of a particular good or service that consumers are willing and able to buy at each price in a set of possible prices during a specified time period."[5] That definition is both liberating and debilitating for our purposes but some prestructuring of our thinking can offset the debilitating effect and thereby provide some freedom in our use of the term "demand."

The use of the term demand to mean a "schedule" limits its utility if one insists that a schedule must contain two or more relationships. Since later in this chapter we will want to discuss demand as a particular price-quantity relationship, we must initially suggest that a schedule is a data array containing one or more established relationships. The liberating effect of the Rogers and Ruchlin definition is found in the phrase "willing and able" as it applies to consumers. The concept provides for both purchasers' propensities to consume and their ability to consume as it may or may not be constrained by income. The latter notion is extremely important for our analysis of the demand for public school teachers and is often referred to as "effective demand."

Generally, the quantity of goods or services that consumers will demand during a specified time period is affected by a number of individual or collective circumstances. Leftwich identifies the most important considerations to be the price of the good, consumers' tastes and preferences, the number of consumers under consideration, consumers' incomes, the prices of related goods, and the range of goods available to consumers.[6]

Price

The price-quantity relationship is the fundamental concept of demand. Consumers will purchase a certain quantity of goods or services based upon their prices. Under pure or quasi-pure competition several alternatives are normally available. In hypothetical schedule 1 three service stations offer three different brands of gasoline on a particular day. Part of the difference between the sales of brand A and brand B may be attributed to price effect since one was cheaper than the other. That is, some consumers chose brand A because of the price differences among brands.

Schedule 1. Hypothetical sales of 85.9 octane gasoline

Brand	Price ($/gal.)	Quantity Sold (gals.)
A	38.9	2,100
B	39.9	1,800
C	40.9	1,500

Consumers' Tastes and Preferences

Also related to demand for a specific quantity of goods and services are the individual tastes and preferences of consumers. In schedule 1, some consumers purchased their gasoline from the station offering brand C even though it had the highest price. Their preference may be based on several factors: advertising, use of credit cards, proximity of the station to home or work.

The Number of Consumers under Consideration

Obviously the amount of a certain good or service that will be demanded during a particular time period is related to the number of consumers who are willing and able to purchase it. The septuagenarian who rides an oversized tricycle rather than own an automobile does not require gasoline for automotive purposes and therefore reduces the number of consumers demanding that good. For most goods and services the number of consumers under consideration between time periods is variable. For example, more gasoline is sold for automotive purposes during summer vacation months than any other period during the year.

Consumers' Incomes

Consumers' incomes play an important role in demand for goods and services. If money (or credit, a real-time money substitute) is not available to the potential purchaser, consumption will be constrained. If he has an increase in disposable income, that condition also affects his consumption propensities for certain goods and services. The income effect upon demand is often measured by economists and is central to our analysis of the demand for public school teachers.

Prices of Related Goods

The prices of related goods affect demand when a good or service is used in conjunction with another good or service to yield the desired utility. It also affects demand if a substitute good or service will provide the same or nearly the same utility. This notion is termed the "substitution effect," especially when less desirable but cheaper items are purchased due to price increases or budgetary constraints. As in schedule 1, some consumers bought brand A gasoline even though they may have preferred to trade at the station selling brand C which also offers trading stamps, or they may have bought brand C because they wanted a car wash which was offered at a reduced rate with the purchase of gasoline. Both were substitutions made because of the prices of related goods.

The Range of Goods and Services Available to Consumers

If only one good or service is available to consumers, they have fewer options in their consumption propensities for related goods and services. A town with only one gas station does not allow the motorist an opportunity to exercise discretion when he needs automotive fuel. The concept goes beyond the limiting notion in that as more goods and services attract the consumer, one's propensity to consume a particular good or service is affected. For example, if a bowling alley opens in a community, one could expect that consumers' recreation expenditures will be partially shifted from past propensities to bowling. Therefore, a good or service need not be identical to compete with a particular good or service—it must only change consumer demand behavior. This is another case of the substitution effect, one that has been experienced widely in the education industry.

Demand Curves

The demand schedule may be transformed into a demand curve by plotting the price-quantity relationships on a graph (Figure 1). The vertical axis represents price, the horizontal axis quantity. The line connecting the plotted relationships is the demand curve for the hypothetical conditions. Although it is more often downward-sloping as in Figure 1, it may, under certain conditions, be horizontal, vertical, or even upward-sloping.

Changes in Demand and in Quantity Demanded

A change in the quantity demanded is simply a movement along the demand curve. For example, if we view Figure 1 as the demand curve for only one brand of gasoline at a particular station, then a change in price from 40.9 cents per gallon to 39.9 cents per gallon would produce an expected change in the quantity demanded from 1,500 gallons to 1,800 gallons. Further reductions in price would create corresponding increases in quantity demanded, assuming no changes in the habits of consumers or price changes by competitors.

A change in demand is different from a change in quantity demanded in that the propensities of all consumers cause a shift in the demand curve in

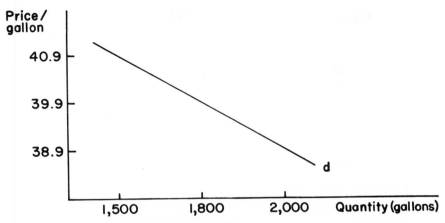

Fig. 1. Hypothetical demand curve for gasoline

the former case. For example, if all gasoline consumers suddenly bought economy cars, the total demand for gasoline would be reduced irrespective of price. That hypothetical condition is illustrated in Figure 2 where d' represents the new demand curve.

SUPPLY: SOME BASIC CONCEPTS

Supply of a good or service is the quantity that sellers will place on the market at a specified price at a particular point in time. The basic concepts of supply are, like demand, the relationship between price and quantity at a

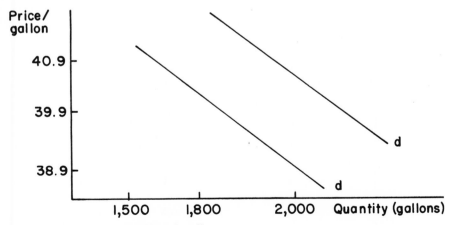

Fig. 2. Change in demand from d to d'

particular time, but in this instance they are viewed from the position of the seller rather than the purchaser. Rogers and Ruchlin define supply as "a schedule of various amounts of a good or service that producers are willing and able to sell at each specific price in a set of possible prices during a specified time period."[7] Recognizing that a schedule may present one or more price-quantity relationships, the foregoing definition is useful here.

The foremost decision-making condition facing a would-be supplier of a good or service is the market price for that good or service during a specific time period. If the market price reflects a reasonable rate of return to the supplier for his capital investments and labor, he will continue to supply the quantity demanded at that price. Changes in the quantity demanded or shifts in the demand curve will cause suppliers to reconsider their propensity to continue supplying an equal quantity in the long run. Therefore, changes in demand by consumers, for whatever reason, may create changes in prices which may further cause changes in supply.

Supply Curves

Supply curves are developed in a manner similar to the demand curve. The schedule from which the supply curve is established represents the various quantities a supplier is willing and able to put on the market at the associated prices. For example, assume that a producer of hula hoops has determined that his production costs vary so that he could supply hula hoops according to schedule 2.

Schedule 2. Hypothetical price-quantity relationship
for supplying hula hoops

Price	Quantity
$ 1.00	1,000
0.90	900
0.80	800
0.70	700

The supply curve for the hypothetical production period is established by plotting the price-quantity relationships on a graph. Figure 3 represents the supply curve developed from schedule 2.

The supply curve is, more often than not, upward-sloping, thus reflecting the notion that producers (singly or collectively) will increase the supply of a good or service as the price of that good or service increases within the analysis period. Shifts in the supply curve are brought about by increases or decreases in production by suppliers over two or more time periods. Finally, the supply curve may, under certain conditions, be horizontal (an infinite supply), vertical (a finite supply), or even downward-sloping (a short-run condition when large inventories are being sold off regardless of price).

Given the basic properties of price and quantity in a given time period for both supply and demand, we need only to put them together to establish market prices.

SUPPLY AND DEMAND RELATIONSHIP

Supply and demand curves may be plotted on the same set of axes to demonstrate the relationship between the willing and able sellers and the willing and able buyers. The intersection of the two curves represents the

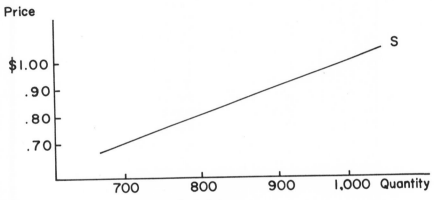

Fig. 3. Hypothetical supply curve for hula hoops

equilibrium price, or established market price. In Figure 4 the vertical axis represents price. Various prices are indicated by P_1, P_2, P_3, and so forth. The horizontal axis represents quantity, and the various quantities are indicated by q_1, q_2, q_3, and so forth. The S-curve represents the amounts that willing and able producers will supply at various prices. The D-curve represents the amounts that willing and able purchasers will demand at various prices. For example, at a price of P_4 suppliers are willing and able to offer quantity q_4, but purchasers are only willing and able to buy quantity q_2. The point of intersection of the supply curve and the demand curve is at P_3–q_3 and represents the equilibrium condition, i.e., the price that satisfies both sellers and buyers.

If, in the short run, suppliers offered only quantity q_2 and buyers demanded quantity q_4, then the market price would be P_4 and a short supply condition would exist in an amount equal to the difference between q_4 and

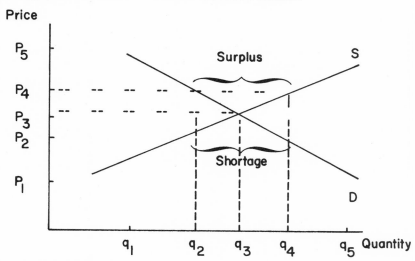

Fig. 4. Supply and demand curves

q_2. On the other hand, if suppliers offered quantity q_4 then buyers would only purchase that amount if the price dropped below P_2.

ELASTICITY OF SUPPLY AND DEMAND

The supply and demand curves in Figure 4 indicate that if prices change, quantities of goods or services supplied and quantities demanded will also change. Given the fluctuations experienced by suppliers in their capital and labor costs over time, they must adjust the market price to reflect their experience with costs. Suppliers are acutely aware that changes in prices may affect consumer demand and therefore attempt to predict the market effects of a price change through the concept of elasticity. Simply defined, elasticity of supply and demand is determined by the percentage change in quantity divided by the percentage change in price. That computation can lead to the three different results noted in these equations:

$$\frac{\% \Delta q}{\% \Delta p} > 1$$

$$\frac{\% \Delta q}{\% \Delta p} = 1$$

$$\frac{\% \Delta q}{\% \Delta p} < 1$$

The elasticities may be greater than, equal to, or less than 1. A condition such that the computation yields a result greater than 1 is said to be elastic; a condition such that the computation yields a result equal to 1 is said to be unitarily elastic; a condition such that the computation yields a result less than 1 is said to be inelastic. Under inelasticity of demand, a supplier is faced with a loss of total revenue since the percentage change in quantity is less than the percentage change in price.

Elasticities are also determined relative to changes in income. Income elasticity of demand is computed as the percentage change in quantity divided by the percentage change in income. McLoone found the income elasticity of demand for education between 1930 and 1958 to be 0.96 (inelastic), between 1944 and 1958 to be 1.45 (elastic), and between 1948 and 1958 to be 1.34 (elastic).[8] Hirsch found the income elasticity of demand for education between 1900 and 1958 to be 1.09 (elastic).[9] Together those analyses point to a highly elastic demand for education since World War II, which is another way of saying that willing and able consumers of educational services (either for themselves or for their children) have had a high propensity to spend their added income for education.

The price-quantity relationship is a fundamental concept of supply and demand theory. Both suppliers and purchasers attempt to maximize their economic positions at the market place through their esoteric propensities to buy and sell goods and services. We now turn our attention to the application of supply and demand theory to the employment of persons who are professionally trained. The focus is, therefore, upon the supply and demand for professional services and will be explicated through an analysis of two puzzles, the ''shortage'' of engineers and scientists during the 1950s, and the ''surplus'' of public school teachers.

THE ENGINEER-SCIENTIST SUPPLY AND DEMAND PUZZLE

Based upon data from the Blank and Stigler study, *The Supply and Demand of Scientific Personnel*, and the Beste case study of the chemical industry, Arrow and Capron have sought to explain the dynamics of the supply-demand relationship and the associated shortage of the trained engineer-scientist population in the United States during the 1950s.[10]

Drawing primarily from Marshallian analysis of the equilibrating process, the model builders first assumed stability of the market mechanism and then postulated that, in the classical sense, the shortage observed during the equilibrating process was transitory in nature and that it tended to disappear as the price approached an equilibrium position. That is to say, as in Figure 5, if P_1 represents the average salary of the engineer-scientist profession during a specified time period or point in time, then q_1 is the number of trained individuals who will be available for employment at that price. However, the market demands q_2 number of individuals at price P_1, and therefore the industry is experiencing a shortage of trained individuals in the amount of q_2 minus q_1. The obvious short-run equilibrium average salary is P_0 and the price differential of P_0 minus P_1 is seen as the causative factor of the shortage. Supply and demand theory suggests that when quasi-competitive conditions exist, market forces will operate to pressure average salary P_1 toward P_0. However, it is noted that if the demand curve is steadily shifting upward at the same time that a shortage in supply exists, then the short supply will persist and the price will continue to rise.

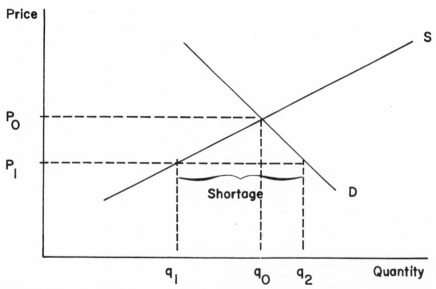

Fig. 5. Supply and demand for engineer-scientists (from Arrow and Capron, "Shortages in Salaries")

The latter condition is presented in Figure 6 where D_1 represents the original demand curve for engineers and scientists and D_2 represents the new demand arising from changes in external conditions. The equilibrium position attained through market forces in Figure 5 is now a position of short supply in Figure 6. Arrow and Capron suggest that this condition will also be accommodated through market forces as salaries are adjusted to attract more individuals to enter the field.[11] And, they seem to be aware of the training time lag constraining that adjustment as they proceed to model the dynamic shortages and price rises as functions of the elasticities of supply and demand.

It does not seem profitable for our purposes here to review the calculus of the Arrow-Capron model, but essentially they are computing the magnitude of the dynamic shortage as functions of the rate of increase in demand, the reaction speed of the market, and the elasticities of supply and demand. Finally, their argument that their computations of the interaction

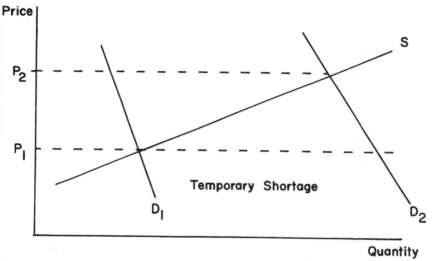

Fig. 6. Increase in demand for engineer-scientists due to external conditions (from Arrow and Capron)

of rising demand with price movements, which do not instantaneously equate supply and demand at a new equilibrium position, provides a plausible interpretation of the engineer-scientist shortage of the 1950s.

Critique

The Arrow-Capron model is attractive for its simplicity. One wonders whether or not their model would accommodate the surplus of engineer-scientists in the space industry resulting from NASA program cutbacks and cancellation of the SST if they were to look at more contemporary data. Certainly they could test the contrary case.

Those aspects of the model which attempt to explain the dynamics of the supply-demand relationship may have some application to the experience of the education industry. However, it is difficult to accept the model as it exists because of the competitive market assumption upon which the model is based. If one considers inter-school-district competition for teachers with certain specialties, one may give some weight to the competitive pricing function, although not much since it is not a pervasive practice for school districts to offer separate salary schedules for different teaching crafts. When one considers the whole education industry, as the model does, it seems that we must look for another model since we cannot meet the assumption that industry prices (salaries) are a function of the competitive market. The education industry has many individuals providing second or supplementary family incomes, and it offers an employment calendar that is attractive to individuals seeking limited-term job engagement. For those reasons alone one cannot assume individual job choice to be a function of price.

And, too, as Arrow and Capron point out, the price mechanism cannot be expected to function if indeed there is external interference with the mechanism, i.e., if prices are controlled. It is suggested here that in the education industry that is exactly what happens with regard to teachers' salaries, which therefore accentuates the need for a different set of assumptions to precede supply-demand analysis.

THE SCHOOL TEACHER SUPPLY AND DEMAND PUZZLE

The education industry is labor intensive. That is to say, personnel costs are the major input to the education production function. During the 1971–72 school year, teachers and other instructional staff salaries accounted for approximately 64 per cent of the funds expended for elementary and secondary education in South Dakota.[12] That statistic is not atypical of each of the states.[13] Further, Rossmiller and his associates found no statistically significant variation in the proportion of instructional expenditure per pupil in their discriminate function analysis of revenues and expenditures of different sizes of school districts in six states for 1962 and 1967.[14] Salaries for administrators, secretarial and clerical assistants, operation and maintenance workers, health services personnel, bus drivers, and other staff consume a significant proportion of the remaining educational expenditures of local school districts.

Local boards of education establish salary policies for teaching personnel, and generally those policies take the form of a salary schedule that provides teachers with added compensation as a function of added training and experience. More important, all beginning teachers (elementary and secondary) with a B.A. degree receive the same remuneration and all teachers who have earned a similar number of additional college-level course credits and have the same number of years' teaching experience receive the same remuneration. Thus, teacher salaries tend to discriminate only on two dimensions—additional college credits and teaching experience.[15]

The demand for teaching personnel is a function of the number of students to receive schooling and the nature of the educational program to be offered. The number of teachers demanded for basic instruction may be readily determined by establishing an average pupil-teacher ratio. Programs other than basic instructional programs require additional information. For example, programs for handicapped children have lower pupil-teacher ratios and often require itinerant services of teaching specialists.[16] The fact remains that staffing policy is established by the local board, and its judgment may not be congruent to the perceived staffing "need" articulated by the teachers' union or the administration. However, the school board's decision to employ a certain number of teachers for a particular year is what creates the *effective demand* for trained teaching personnel.

The facts are that teachers are faced with a predetermined salary schedule within a given community, and that salary schedules do not vary significantly enough to attract teachers to other communities. Since retirement and tenure policies inhibit teacher mobility, it appears evident that prospective teachers are not operating in a quasi-competitive market.[17]

The Oligopoly-Oligopsony Puzzle

Oligopoly describes those market situations in which there are few sellers of a particular product, such that the activities of one seller are of sufficient importance to other sellers. Although it may not have been true in the past century, we have sufficient evidence to suggest that public elementary and secondary education dominates the educational field today.

Leftwich has clearly articulated three classifications of oligopolistic industries: class 1, organized, collusive oligopoly; class 2, unorganized, collusive oligopoly; and class 3, unorganized, noncollusive oligopoly.[18] The underlying assumptions of each class will not be reviewed here, but the assumptions of class 3 seem to correlate highly to the *modus operandi* of the educational industry and its firms, the local private and public school districts.

The assumptions of the class 3 oligopoly are: (1) *The industry is unorganized and noncollusive.* That simply means there are no formal cartel-like arrangements as one would expect in class 1. This designation does not deny the national or state school boards associations because they do not transfer management decisions and functions of their individual districts to the central association. Although we prefer to parallel the public sector to the private sector, there is no reason for not developing a class 4 which would accommodate professional associations and thus become a quasi-organized, noncollusive class of oligopoly. (2) *Independent action of individual firms (school districts) is characteristic.* There is sufficient evidence of program and policy differentiation among school districts to accept this assumption without explication.

Given these definitions and assumptions, it is further suggested that the education industry is that special case of class 3 oligopoly characterized by price rigidity. Therefore, the industry must meet these assumptions.[19] (1) The industry is a mature one, either with or without product differentiation. (2) If one firm lowers price, others will follow. Although one does not see school districts cutting the total operational funds much, one does see them following each other relative to specific economy moves, e.g., closing their doors for part of the school year, or eliminating selected programs. We have some evidence of taxpayer revolt when we consider the number of bond and millage elections lost over the past six or seven years. (3) If one firm raises prices, other firms will not follow. Although Mort and his students significantly stimulated expenditures for education within school districts, there seems to be less acceptance today of the assumed cost-quality relationship. School boards are increasingly pressured to restrain product cost as evidenced by the thrusts toward accountability and millage election losses.

Technically speaking, public school districts do not compete with each other for product production (students), and, therefore, assumptions two and three may only be totally applicable to private education. However, the examples cited with each seem to be sufficient to meet the conditions.

Oligopsony is a resource market situation in which there are only a few buyers of a particular resource which may or may not be differentiated. That is, trained teachers may teach in either the private or public sector of the education industry. The market is further characterized by having one buyer taking such a large portion of the total supply of the resource that it is able to influence the market price of the resource. Certainly, public education does that.

Figure 7 illustrates the supply-demand relationship of the case 3 oligopolistic industry. The significant difference between this relationship and the competitive market relationship is the "kinked" demand curve. The kinked demand curve is an analytical way of interpreting the case 3 oligopoly assumptions. For example, if school districts are faced with a higher per teacher cost than P, they are likely to offer fewer new contracts than they would like. They may realign the district's programming by not initiating new programs, by closing marginal programs, by increasing pupil-teacher ratios, or by initiating other similar strategies.

The kinked demand curve further illustrates that if cost per teacher unit is less than P, the district may expand its professional teaching staff by initiating new programs, by providing more supplemental services, by lowering pupil-teacher ratios, etc.

Figure 8 represents an application of the oligopolistic concept to the supply and demand for public elementary teachers for the ten-year period 1960–70. The supply-demand relationship was determined by first plotting the long-run supply curve. Then the points of intersection along that curve were correlated with the average elementary teachers' salaries for various

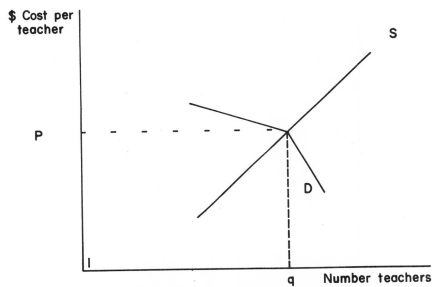

Fig. 7. Supply-demand relationship for public school teachers, an oligopolistic condition

years. The disconnected demand curves d_1, d_2, and d_3 illustrate the short supply conditions for those years. For example, the conditions at d_1 were such that, at the established price of approximately $5,100 average salary, the industry experienced a short supply of elementary teachers amounting to approximately 35,000. This does not mean that approximately 35,000 more elementary teachers were needed in the qualitative sense, only that the industry was seeking that number of trained individuals for declared positions.

Increasing elementary school enrollments and a lack of supply response did little to improve the conditions within the next four-year period, d_2. However, conditions improved somewhat by 1968, d_3, evidenced by the narrowing of the gap between supply and demand. The final two-year period closed, d_4, with conditions equilibrated.

The shifting kinked demand curve illustrated in Figure 8 parallels the Arrow-Capron analysis presented earlier, the significant difference being the set of assumptions underlying each model and especially the price control assumption of the oligopoly model. Wages in the education industry are overtly controlled where Arrow and Capron were suggesting that competitive market forces established the engineer-scientist wage rates. And, unlike the Arrow-Capron analysis to the effect that increases in beginning salaries tend to adjust salaries of all engineers in the long run, any increases in salaries of beginning teachers immediately adjust all teachers' salaries in the short run.

Demand for Inputs Puzzle

In its simplest form, the overriding constraint facing the production capability of the firm is the total dollars available for production as a function of output costs. That is to say,

$$C = f(O), \tag{1}$$

where C is total cost and O is output costs. Further, (O) is a function of associated production cost elements including wages, machines, plant, capital, and others. This relationship may be shown as

$$O = f(W, M, P, C, X), \tag{2}$$

where W = wages, M = machines, P = plant, C = capital, and X = other. Combining equations (1) and (2) yields

$$C = f(W, M, P, C, X). \tag{3}$$

Having developed the production function in this manner, the firm proceeds to vary its independent variables (cost elements) so that it maximizes production and minimizes costs within the constraints of its production budget.

A similar analysis may be made for the school district. The total dollars available for education (production) in any one time period is a function of federal, state, and local revenue sources, and the factors of production likewise include wages, machines, plant, capital, time, and others. Thus, at this conceptual level, although we may be considering total cost (C), the condition is equivalent to Thomas' output-oriented production function.[20]

It is not uncommon for school district budget builders to consider first the total dollars expected to be available before they initiate the often arduous task of programming those dollars toward the associated cost elements. Even those individuals who employ the zero based budgeting techniques have some notion about their expected total revenue throughout the fiscal programming process.

Although it is beyond the scope of this chapter to explore the functional relationships among sets of cost elements,[21] the *ceteris paribus* assumption is not being made. Indifference mapping is an example of cost variable

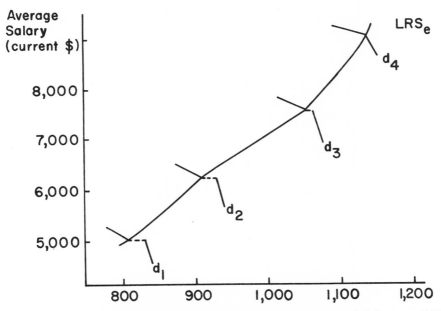

Fig. 8. Supply and demand curves for elementary teachers at four time periods between 1960 and 1970 (from NEA Research Publications 1971–R4 and 1973–R8)

relationships and trade-off matrices, but the purpose here is only to establish the context within which one may investigate factors affecting supply and demand for professional educational personnel. Therefore, it is conceded that total revenue dollars in any one time period determine the maximum number of dollars available for professional salaries which are then reduced as a function of decision makers' past and present propensities to allocate portions of those dollars to other production cost elements.

For purposes of example, let us assume that the cost elements of equation (3), for a particular time period, have been put into dollar terms so that we now have the relationship

$$C = I_w + Y, \tag{4}$$

where C = total cost of education, I_w = instructional wages, and Y = all other costs. Therefore, the total dollars available for instructional wages becomes

$$C - Y = I_w. \tag{5}$$

In this manner the total dollars available for instructional wages becomes fixed for any given time period. The issues surrounding the estab-

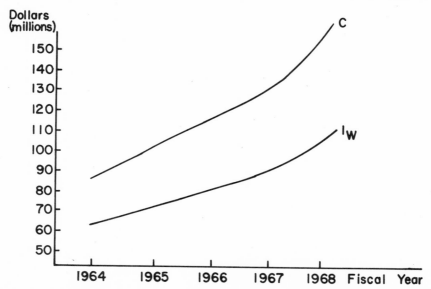

Fig. 9. Relationship between total cost and instructional wages of a particular school district, 1964–68

lishment of equation (5) and the analysis below are best illustrated by historical data. In this way we do not become entangled in the economics of collective bargaining and the decision-making rules applied to cost-element trade-off matrices.

Figure 9 illustrates the relationships established by a particular school district between total cost (C) and total instructional wages (I_w) for the period 1964–68. Included in instructional wages are teachers' wages (K–12), and teachers' wages for special education and vocational education. Wages for guidance and other instructional professionals, such as program coordinators, are also included in I_w. The difference between C and I_w is that C includes costs for instructional supplies, support personnel, capital outlay, debt service, and other expenses. The example district was allocating approximately $60 million for instructional teachers' salaries in 1964 and over $100 million for those salaries four years later.

At the time the school district was making its preliminary cost calculations for each of the cost elements, it was faced with the supply and demand relationship demonstrated in Figure 10. That is, for 1964 the district em-

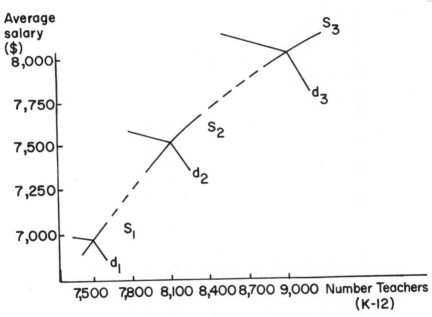

Fig. 10. Supply and demand for teachers (K–12) in a particular school district, 1964–68

ployed approximately 7,500 teachers for the K–12 regular program at an average cost of just under $7,000. For 1968 the district was employing almost 9,000 teachers in the K–12 program at an average cost of approximately $8,000. The kinked demand curve satisfies the market assumptions and further demonstrates the decision sets one would expect should the average price of teachers increase or decrease in the short run.

No data were available relative to the "shortages" of teachers in the K–12 program for the periods used. It is suspected that some shortages did exist for 1964 based upon the analysis of national data. If that suspicion is correct, the demand curve d₁ as presented in Figure 8 would be disjointed.

Supply: Market Conditions

One of the more direct approaches to assessing market conditions for a product is to determine how well the product is moving—that is, in our case, to what extent are the college graduates who hold teaching certificates gainfully employed within the education industry? Figure 11 represents several sets of data from a 1972 National Education Association study, "Teacher Supply and Demand in Public Schools." If one estab-

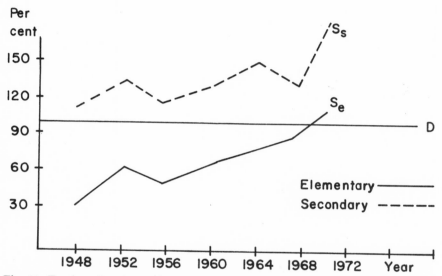

Fig. 11. Teacher education graduates as a per cent of new teachers employed in selected states

lishes demand as 100 per cent determined vacancies (as reported by school districts) and then plots the reported number of graduates of teacher education programs as a per cent of new teachers employed, one is immediately confronted by two facts. First, there has never been a shortage of secondary teachers for the years reported. That fact is readily conveyed when one considers that the graphs represent aggregated data. A closer inspection of the data reveals that we have consistently overproduced secondary teachers of agriculture, art, biology, physical education, and social studies, among others, while a short supply is evidenced for particular years in the areas of chemistry, mathematics, library science, and a few others. Currently, our deficient supply seems to be in the areas of mathematics and special education, although not critically so.

The second fact illustrated by the graph is that about 1970 the elementary teacher supply-demand relationship was equilibrated. Again, this does not mean some districts were not experiencing unfilled positions, but that industry-wide the supply was and continues to be sufficient to fulfill demand. This relationship is further demonstrated in Figure 12 which depicts differences in the supply and demand for elementary teachers in the long run. Note that until 1970 demand almost paralleled supply. However, we

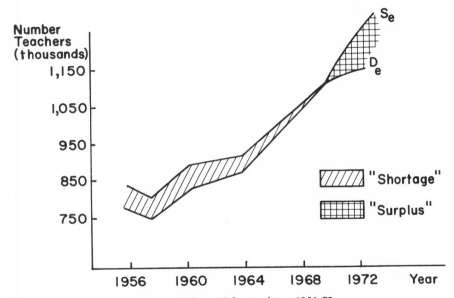

Fig. 12. Differences in supply and demand for teachers, 1956–72

are not relating supply and demand to price at this juncture, so one must be careful not to read more into Figure 12 than it represents.

The National Education Association repudiates the notion that there is an oversupply of teachers.[22] Through a calculation called the "Quality Criterion" the association contends that there is not an oversupply but indeed a demand for almost one million more teachers. Obviously the National Education Association is talking about "need" as they define it rather than the economic concept of demand.

Factors and Conditions that Affect Supply

Although it has been estimated that one out of six students who receive a B.A. degree and are qualified to teach in the public schools enters an M.A.

degree program, the fact remains that new graduates make the largest addition to teacher supply.[23] Qualified individuals who for various reasons return to teaching have been estimated to represent only about 3 or 4 per cent of the number seeking positions.[24] Further, it has been estimated by the U.S. Office of Education that approximately 8 per cent of the existing teacher force either retire or separate from teaching for other reasons each year.[25] Therefore, the three factors of supply are newly qualified graduates, returnees, and existing supply minus terminations. It is that set of factors which must be related to total demand discussed earlier, and it is that set of factors which contribute to the surplus demonstrated in Figure 12.

It should be recognized that teacher certification is often seen by college students as an employment hedge. That is to say, if fewer opportunities become available upon graduation they will seek employment as teachers. Historically, temporary teacher certification for individuals holding a B.A. degree in any field has been almost *pro forma*, although there is some evidence that conditions may be changing.

Also, one often loses sight of the notion that, just because colleges of education are professional schools, graduates need not be employed within the education profession. Certainly the private rate of return on a four-year investment (two years of which are in the professional school) would be marginal for those employed at a salary less than a beginning teacher, or even zero for one who did not choose to work following graduation. However, employment in a position other than teaching may provide a higher private rate of return. Personal qualities developed during the college years, such as one's ability to organize one's time and work space, to work effectively with people, and to communicate effectively, are attractive attributes to employers other than those representing the education industry.

Evidence suggests that a few boards of education engage in conspicuous consumption.[26] They report quite proudly that, compared to other school districts, a higher proportion of their teaching staff holds the M.A. degree, their pupil-teacher ratio is lower, and they employ more educational specialists per student. Each of the three conditions pressures colleges to produce instructional personnel.

Likewise, government action at the federal and state levels may change both the number employed and the composition of instructional staffs. The training of guidance personnel by the federal government during the early 1960s is a prime example, as is a state legislature's propensity to make early childhood programs mandatory or to expand vocational programs and programs for exceptional children. Quasi-governmental bodies, such as regional accrediting agencies, also influence the quantity of staff inputs through their evaluation guidelines.

Finally, factors and conditions that affect the supply of teachers facing the firm (local school district) are not necessarily industry-wide correlates. Preferences of individuals to live in warm climates, near a city, near a university, etc., create an additional resource distributional puzzle. Researchers at RAND Corporation have studied teacher mobility in both a school district and a state in an attempt to model elementary and secondary teachers' employment mobility behavior.[27] Both studies generate a series of testable hypotheses that, if adequately tested, should provide some directions for policy determination at both the local school district level and the state level of government.

Nothing has been said about manpower forecasting because it is inappropriate to relate manpower techniques to occupations that contain high substitution rates. This is not to say that educational planning should not make estimates of changing demand for certain teaching crafts, but it is to say that Blaug is probably right that "It should be obvious now that the manpower requirements approach is simply an illegimate extension of Leontief input-output models to periods so long that the assumption of fixed coefficients becomes an absurdity,"[28] and, further, "If educational planning is ever to grow up and to become integrated with economic planning, it must repudiate this modern form of crystal ball gazing."[29]

CURRENT AND PROJECTED MARKET CONDITIONS

The data are somewhat ambiguous with regard to whether the education industry is experiencing a *consumer surplus* or a *producer surplus*.[30] That is to say, it is unclear right now whether school districts are continuing to substitute larger than "quality" pupil-teacher ratios as charged by the National Education Association or whether colleges of education are indeed overproducing elementary and secondary teachers. The data indicate that given the effective demand of the oligopolist for elementary teachers, there is an industry-wide producer surplus. The effective demand for certain teacher crafts at the secondary level causes one to conclude that there is also an industry-wide producer surplus in some teaching areas.

Although I am inclined to agree in part with Blaug's critique that some of the most often listed spillover benefits of education are little more than old-fashioned sociology, we recognize that the point of diminishing returns for investment in elementary and secondary education has not yet been demonstrated.[31] Therefore, if additional teachers are employed, not only could one expect increased productivity within the industry, but investment would further stimulate full employment within the industry.[32] However, this latter notion moves us toward a labor surplus economy model, and it has not been conceded that those conditions exist.[33] What we have determined is this: under the assumptions of the oligopolistic model for the industry, budgeted demand for additional teachers is determined by the number that school districts can afford to hire, and local school district propensities to spend budget increments for teachers is approximately in the same proportion as currently provided, except where there is an added incentive to hire specialists.[34] (The income elasticity of demand for teachers is slightly greater than 1.) In that regard it might be argued that, given declining enrollments, the identified producer surpluses are in reality consumer surpluses brought about by underfunding the public education program.

RECOMMENDATIONS

Decisions by teacher training institutions concerning program offerings and pupil enrollment limits are rarely conditioned by research reflecting the value that society will place on the services of their graduates. Market information on a national and state level is needed to influence decision-making by all individuals, institutions, and agencies involved, including teachers, prospective teachers, teacher training institutions, and federal, state, and local education agencies. To develop and disseminate this information it is recommended that all colleges receiving federal program monies submit to the Office of Education, through the state education agency, an annual plan for keeping prospective teachers informed about employment opportunities in the industry. The state plan should include these elements: enrollments in all teacher training programs by craft for the preceding three years; the number of teachers employed by craft within geographical regions of the state; the number of teachers employed within the state during the previous three years; active current employment opportunities within the state, and the results of follow-up studies of graduates.

Further, these federal activities would be useful in establishing a fully developed market monitoring system: the stimulation of training through federally supported projects in crafts where measured shortages exist, i.e., where effective demand is greater than supply by a marginal deficiency in excess of 10 per cent for a projected time period (3–5 years maximum), and the simulation of research on the productive aspects of various economic inputs to the educational process, for example, the marginal product of lower pupil-teacher ratios.

REFERENCES

1. G. S. Becker, *Human Capital* (Princeton: Princeton University Press, 1964); T. W. Schultz, "Investment in Human Capital," *American Economic Review* 51 (1961); W. L. Hansen, "Total and Private Rates of Return to Investment in Schooling," *Journal of Political Economy* 81 (1963); B. A. Weisbrod, "Education and Investment in Human Capital," *Journal of Political Economy* 70 (1962); and M. J. Bowman, "The Human Investment Revolution in Economic Thought," *Sociology of Education* 39 (1966).

2. G. S. Becker, *Human Resources*, Fiftieth Anniversary Colloquium IV, National Bureau of Economic Research (New York: Columbia University Press, 1972), p. xviii.

3. T. W. Schultz, "Human Capital: Policy Issues and Research Opportunities," in Becker, *Human Resources*, pp. 67–73.

4. O. T. Balogh and P. P. Streeten, "The Planning of Education in Poor Countries," in *Economics of Education I*, ed. M. Blaug (Baltimore: Penguin Books, 1968); S. Bowles, "A Linear Programming Model of the Educational Sector," in *Economics of Education II*, ed. M. Blaug (Baltimore: Penguin Books, 1969).

5. D. C. Rogers and H. S. Ruchlin, *Economics and Education* (New York: The Free Press, 1971), pp. 35–36.

6. R. N. Leftwich, *The Price System and Resource Allocation* (New York: Rinehart & Co., 1955), p. 27.

7. Page 41.

8. E. P. McLoone, "Effects of Tax Elasticities on the Financial Support of Education" (Ph.D. diss., University of Illinois, 1961).

9. W. Z. Hirsch, "Analysis of Rising Costs of Education," Study Paper 4, Joint Economic Committee, Eighty-Sixth Congress of the United States (Washington: U.S. Government Printing Office, November 1959).

10. D. M. Blank and G. J. Stigler, *The Demand and Supply of Scientific Personnel* (New York: National Bureau of Economic Research, 1957); G. W. Beste, "A Case Study of the Shortages of Scientists and Engineers in the Chemical Industry" (Paper presented at the second meeting of the National Committee for the Development of Scientists and Engineers, June 21, 1956); K. J. Arrow and W. M. Capron, "Shortages in Salaries: The Engineer-Scientist Case in the United States," in *Economics of Education I*, pp. 318–37.

11. Actually, salaries are adjusted to attract trained individuals from one firm to another or to compete for newly trained individuals. The net result is that more individuals seek training and subsequent employment in the industry.

12. J. A. Hale, "Economic Status of Teaching Personnel," mimeographed (Pierre, S. Dak.: State Department of Education, 1973).

13. Expenditures for elementary and secondary teachers are approximately 60 per cent of the school district's budget nationally. Specialists in reading, education of the handicapped, guidance, etc., add approximately 10 per cent more to the district's institutional staff budget. For a regional analysis see S. J. Carroll, *Analysis of the Educational Personnel System, III. The Demand for Educational Professionals*, R-1308-HEW (Santa Monica, Calif.: RAND Corporation, 1973), p. 60.

14. R. A. Rossmiller, J. A. Hale, and L. E. Frohreich, *Fiscal Capacity and Educational Finance*, Special Study no. 10 (Gainesville, Fla.: National Educational Finance Project, 1970).

15. C. S. Benson, *The Economics of Education* (Boston: Houghton Mifflin Co., 1968), chap. 10.

16. R. A. Rossmiller, J. A. Hale, and L. E. Frohreich, *Resource Configurations and Costs in Educational Programs for Exceptional Children*, Special Study no. 2 (Gainesville, Fla.: National Educational Finance Project, 1970).

17. J. A. Kershaw and R. N. McKean, *Teacher Shortage and Salary Schedules* (New York: McGraw-Hill Book Co., Inc., 1962).

18. Pages 232 ff.

19. Ibid., p. 245.

20. A. J. Thomas, *The Productive School* (New York: John Wiley & Sons, 1971), p. 11.

21. Ibid., chap. 10.

22. *Teacher Supply and Demand in Public Schools, 1972*, NEA Research Publication 1973-R8 (Washington: National Education Association, 1973).

23. Comptroller General of the United States, "Supply and Demand Conditions for Teachers and Implications for Federal Programs," mimeographed draft copy (Washington: Office of Education, B-164031 [1], 1973), p. 20.

24. Ibid., p. 16.

25. Ibid., p. 18. Also see E. B. Keeler, *Analysis of the Educational Personnel System: IV Teacher Turnover*, R-1325-HEW (Santa Monica, Calif.: RAND Corporation, October 1973).

26. R. Perlman, *The Economics of Education: Conceptual Problems and Policy Issues* (New York: McGraw-Hill Book Co., Inc., 1973), pp. 104 ff.

27. D. Greenberg and J. McCall, *Analysis of the Educational Personnel System: I Teacher Mobility in San Diego*, R-1071-HEW (Santa Monica, Calif.: RAND Corporation, January 1973); D. Greenberg and J. McCall, *Analysis of the Educational Personnel System: VII Teacher Mobility in Michigan*, R-1343-HEW (Santa Monica, Calif.: RAND Corporation, forthcoming).

28. M. Blaug, *An Introduction to the Economics of Education* (Baltimore: Penguin Books, Inc., 1972), p. 167.

29. Ibid. Also see, H. P. Kraft, "Manpower Planning and Its Role in the Age of Automation," *Review of Educational Research* 40 (October 1972): 495–509.

30. Rogers and Ruchlin, p. 46.

31. Blaug, pp. 108–9.

32. W. G. Hack and F. O. Woodard, *Economic Dimension of Public School Finance: Concepts and Cases* (New York: McGraw-Hill Book Co., 1971), p. 43.

33. Rogers and Ruchlin, pp. 217 ff.

34. Comptroller General, p. 18; and S. J. Carroll, *Analysis of the Educational Personnel System: III The Demand for Educational Professionals*, R-1308-HEW (Santa Barbara, Calif.: RAND Corporation, October 1973).

Toward Greater Educational Productivity

Carol E. Hanes

Interest in increased educational productivity has spread among school districts and governing bodies throughout the nation. Since the mid-1960s the term "accountability" has been used in education to describe a growing concern with the effectiveness of educational institutions in meeting organizational goals. More than a program of financial accounting or cost reduction is involved, for the approach is concerned with the actual productivity of a system, that is, the relationships between the financial input for education purchases and educational output, or student development. The emphasis at the administrative and instructional levels has been on the development of more effective and efficient management and instructional practices; at the same time, educational and social science researchers have sought to develop means of measuring the productivity of schools. This chapter focuses on research attempts to establish a theory of educational production on which to base allocations. The earlier cost-quality research as well as more recent studies relating system inputs and outputs have been reviewed, and findings in several areas controlled by educational policy makers and administrators have been summarized. Recommendations for programs which, it is believed, would currently enhance educational productivity are offered for consideration in the concluding section.

BACKGROUND

Historically, the American system of public education has been widely viewed as a primary and effective method of promoting the achievement of the societal goals of social and economic mobility. This function evolved as a result of the wide variation in the backgrounds of early colonists. Established by immigrants without common religious, political, economic, or social traditions, the schools were delegated the responsibility of inculcating American social and philosophical values as well as instructing students in the traditional academic subjects. The schools were able to meet these societal needs rather well for a long time. During this period, however, American society was predominantly based on a rural pattern of life in which the majority of the goals of the schools were reinforcements and reflections of the family living experience of the students. A state of equilibrium was achieved in which there was little recognition of the failure of the system to meet the needs of individuals and groups which did not share this norm of experience.

During the 1950s the climate of support for education began to change. The politico-educational needs of the nation became explicit in the space age, changing the direction of American education dramatically. With this change in national priorities, it became useful to promote the idea that traditional American public education had failed by not anticipating the future needs of highly specialized technologists. Federal funds were appropriated for use in stimulating the development and implementation of revised programs in the sciences and mathematics. During the late fifties and the greater part of the sixties, federal funding programs were extended to compensatory education as the unmet educational requirements of minority groups became social and political issues of some importance for the first time in the nation's history. Thus, during a relatively short period of time diverse groups of people raised a great many questions about the goals of education, and there were no definitive answers.

The widespread cultural and economic developments of the first half of the twentieth century largely eliminated the supportive congruence of home life and destroyed the equilibrium of the educational system. As a result, the tasks of the public schools have been forcibly redefined by the pressures of large-scale urbanization, massive industrialization, technological development, and budgetary restraints. These factors have been compounded by the need to eliminate racial segregation and enable the full participation of all citizens in national life. The comprehensiveness of this new role led Henry Steele Commager to state recently that "if our educational enterprise is in disarray, it is because we have asked it to perform a miracle—to teach all the subjects necessary to enable the young to understand the world they are in and the one they shall live in in the future; to train them for all the skills required to run an immensely complicated economy and society; to all the ideals and values we ourselves do not observe."[1]

The complex socioeducational situation has been made the subject of many studies using the newly developed systems analytic research techniques. The widespread use of computers has made possible data processing and analysis which had heretofore been inaccessible to the social scientist. Further refinement and application of social science research techniques were encouraged by social and political developments. These, in various stages of development, have been used in countless studies which attempted to describe the causes of the perceived educational inefficiencies and social injustice. As the number of studies grew, it was discovered that the findings did not always agree, either with other studies or with the conventional wisdom.

In a less troubled period, theoretical development might have kept pace with the need for information, and the resultant research findings might have received a more considered reception. As it happens, however, the results of socioeducational studies receive wide publicity. Accustomed to accepting scientific research findings in the "hard" sciences without critical questioning, the American public has seized upon preliminary findings in a much "softer" and less well-developed area of inquiry with assurance.

Ironically, the work of many social researchers has not been used to create support for corrective action. By promoting or accepting this emphasis on the negative, the development of some public policy has been abandoned to whim and irrationality. Educational research establishing the basis for the optimal utilization of resources is still in a formative stage; however, it may provide great insight if this developmental stage is recognized. As the need to maximize the effectiveness of scarce public sector resources becomes more necessary, it is increasingly important that educators use the available information wisely to evaluate and support the need for educational funding.

EDUCATIONAL EXPENDITURE STUDIES

Philosophical Basis

During the first half of this century it was widely believed by the general public as well as by educators that increased expenditures for education provided educational opportunities of increased quality. Numerous empirical studies of the cost-quality relationship made by key figures in public school administration and finance supported this position. Educational expenditure studies made in the 1930s and 1940s were designed to show the relationship between expenditure, or cost, and quality, or "character," of the program provided.[2]

During this period the major tasks facing most communities were those of providing a school term of adequate length, providing materials and libraries, and developing the administrative function necessary to support the expanded program. It was obvious that providing an expanded program cost more than providing only a limited program; consequently, educators were interested in enumerating for the public those aspects of the program which increased expenditures made possible or enhanced. Research studies were designed to determine what quality indicators were associated with what expenditure level.

Major Studies

Largely patterned on work done by Paul R. Mort and his colleagues, these early studies of the cost-quality relationship were tremendously influential in generating public support for educational programs that more nearly met the needs of the nation in that period of rapid industrial growth and development. In addition, a large segment of the population was keenly aware of the advantages education had given them—or would have given them—in meeting personal goals. This broad base of support enabled the rapid growth and development of educational programs.

Underlying the early definitions of quality education was a strong concern for the welfare of the individual student. The encouragement of those characteristics in children which were judged to be good for the individual, and consequently for the nation, was treated as a major goal of public education. In his 1952 review of this early research, Mort wrote that the approach intended to show "how schools differ at different expenditure levels in what they do with children and young people—activities presumed to affect their individual strength and happiness and through them the economic and social well-being of the American people."[3]

Table 1 lists some of the major cost-quality studies. The director of the research, the state for which the study was performed, the date of publication, and the instruments used to measure school quality are included. The measurement instruments used in these studies are of great interest. Since the concern of educators at this time was that programs of greater scope be offered and that relatively new developments in educational and psychological theory and practice be implemented, a majority of studies rated school systems on the extent to which certain desirable practices were present.[4] According to Mort, the rating scales that evolved in the studies provided a "basis for judgment of relative degrees to which a given school approaches each objective within the range of the known invention or know-how. These instruments have as reference points the present understanding of psychology of learning on the one hand, and social and economic trends on the other."[5]

Most of the rating instruments were quite detailed, noting many of the observable characteristics of school programs. For example, the Mort-Cornell "Guide for Self-Appraisal of School Systems" contained 183 items. Many of these items were of a subjective nature. Of special interest

TABLE 1
Major Cost-Quality Studies

Research Director	Locale and Date	Rating Instrument
Paul R. Mort	New Jersey 1933	Adaptation of Mort and Hilleboe's "Rating Scale for Elementary School Organization" (1930)
Orrin E. Powell	New York 1933	Achievement tests
Paul R. Mort	Maine 1934	Adaptation of Mort and Hilleboe's "Rating Scale for Elementary School Organization"
D. T. Ferrell	Kentucky 1936	Ferrell's "Efficiency Index"
A. G. Grace and G. A. Moe	New York 1938	Achievement test results and observation
Lester R. Grimm	Illinois 1938	Achievement test results and extensive check lists
Paul R. Mort	Rhode Island 1941	Mort and Francis G. Cornell's "Guide for Self-Appraisal of School Systems" (1937)
Paul R. Mort and Francis G. Cornell	Pennsylvania 1941	Mort and Cornell's "Guide for Self-Appraisal of School Systems"
George D. Strayer	West Virginia 1945	Mort and Cornell's "Guide for Self-Appraisal of School Systems"
William S. Vincent	New York 1945	Adaptation of Mort, Arvid J. Burke, and Robert S. Fisk's "Guide for the Analysis and Description of Public School Services" (1942)
William P. McLure	Mississippi 1948	Adaptation of Mort and Cornell's "Guide for Self-Appraisal of School Systems"
Lorne H. Woollatt	New York and New Jersey 1949	Mort, William S. Vincent, and Clarence A. Newell's "The Growing Edge: An Instrument for Measuring the Adaptability of School Systems" (1946)

in this is the presence of items representing "good," progressive educational practices introduced into the schools since the turn of the century. This checklist was used to measure the "adaptability" of schools. An exception to this pattern was the six-item "Efficiency Index" developed by Ferrell for use in Kentucky. This instrument included pupil-teacher ratio, length of school term, holding power, and teacher training and experience. A later checklist, "The Growing Edge," developed by Mort, Vincent, and Newell (1946), was designed to "reflect those characteristics of schools which there was reason to believe from earlier studies differentiated schools in the higher expenditure brackets as a group from average American schools."[6]

A study made in Pennsylvania by Mort and Cornell in 1941 was part of a larger investigation to determine the degree of usage of innovative educational practices.[7] Expenditure was one of 183 items included in the "Guide for Self-Appraisal of School Systems" used in the survey. Expenditure data were for 1935 and ranged from $25 to $100 per weighted pupil. A correlation of 0.587 was reported between expenditure and the adoption of new practices.

In his study of Mississippi schools in 1948, McLure used an adaptation of Mort and Cornell's guide to investigate educational practices in a sample of school districts.[8] The sample was divided into three groups based on average expenditure level: $100, $80, and $50. Of the total of 156 items included in this checklist, 67 items showed a consistent relationship with expenditure; 35 showed better for the middle group than for the lower expenditure group but no higher for the top group; and 41 were consistently related in the top group only. This indicated that different improvements could be expected for different levels of increased expenditure.

The study performed by Woollatt in 1949 was one of a series of studies initiated by the Metropolitan School Study Council.[9] In it the relationship between expenditure level and quality as measured by the instrument "The Growing Edge" was investigated. Data for 1943–44 from thirty-three New York and New Jersey suburban communities were used, representing an expenditure range of from $101 to $263 per weighted pupil. The correlation found between expenditure level and the composite score measured by the instrument was 0.59. A replication of the Woollatt study made in the mid-1950s established a relationship of about 0.60 between expenditure level and quality. This figure was accepted at this time by key figures in public school finance as being "a most useful value for the relationship."[10]

The results of these and other similar studies consistently strengthened the presumption that the relationship between cost and quality was strong. Mort drew this conclusion in his 1952 summary: "That we can predict quality from expenditure to the extent indicated by a correlation some-where between .47 and .59 indicates that we can account for 22 per cent to 35 per cent of the variations in quality from expenditure alone, anywhere on the expenditure scale. This is of extremely great significance. Within certain minima and maxima the quality of a field crop can be predicted probably to no greater degree from moisture alone. This would not lead us to the conclusion that moisture is of no consequence. It is but one factor, and a crucial one, in predicting the extent and nature of the crop."[11]

The great impact which these studies had on the public is under-standable, for they presented convincing evidence that increased expendi-tures were making a difference in the "character" of programs available to public school students. Regardless of the measurement instrument used, a strong positive relationship was observed between the level of financial input and the quality of program provided.

EDUCATIONAL PRODUCTION FUNCTIONS

Theoretical Basis

A second phase in the development of a theoretical base for the allocation of funds for education began with the use of statistical analysis to relate system inputs and system products. First applied to industrial production following World War II, the use of input-output analysis is especially well suited for production processes which are clearly defined and quantifiable at many levels of production. In education, however, as in all experiential or brain-intensive industries, neither the processes nor the inputs are as susceptible to analysis as the production processes in an industry with a tangible product item made up of component elements. Consequently, the procedures useful for analysis in business and industry cannot be applied without substantial modification to education or many other public sector activities.[12]

The production function model specifies a relationship between a mea-sure of production, or the output variable, and some number of input variables that enter into the production process. In its most sophisticated form the educational production function is a formula, describing the educational process, that transforms selected resources allocated to an educational setting into the results of education. The most commonly used model is a linear regression equation in which the inputs may be either individual resource variables or composites of variables:

Production = f (Input A + Input B + . . . Input N).

A significant set of difficulties is encountered in the specification of a production model, for a generally accepted theory of the learning process that could be used as a basis in establishing the model is lacking. The theory of production function analysis assumes a known relationship among input resources which produce the outcome; that is, the production process can be expressed in terms of a specific set of inputs. Not only are the critical factors of the learning experience largely unspecified, but also the interactions between the in-school variables and a number of socioeconomic factors are undetermined.[13]

What constitutes an educational outcome? Because of the limited availability of data on students' activities in many noncognitive areas (degree of socialization, acquired skills, or employability), scores on achievement tests or other data items readily available from the central office of the school district, such as dropout rate, have been used predominantly as a measure of educational productivity. Despite the known limitations of both the testing process and the utilization of scores, this information is universally available and, therefore, has been attractive to researchers.[14]

The choice of input variables is, on the other hand, much wider. Indicators of student time spent in school, teacher quality, quality of school environment, and socioeconomic background usually have been sought. Although the ideal would be the selection of a set of variables explaining 100 per cent of the observed variance in production, the absence of a theory of learning makes this largely a matter of speculation. Thomas also noted that costs seldom have been considered in the production functions. "Since," he stated, "decisions must be partially based on cost, this omission needs correcting."[15] The matter has been further complicated by intercorrelation between input items and the difficulty in isolating in-school and nonschool contributors. Coleman raised the question of discrepancies between inputs as disbursed by the school system and the inputs actually received by children.[16] Consideration of this possibility is most important and is especially needed in studies where equality of educational opportunity is an issue. Increased use of program budgeting should make reliable data describing inputs to the educational system much more accessible to researchers.

These basic theoretical deficiencies necessarily result in the development of models which are based on the individual researcher's conception of the learning process and on the nature of the data available for analysis. Familiarity with statistical models that might be used also has had a limiting effect on the development of models with maximum explanatory power. Each statistical technique involves an attendant set of assumptions and limitations. The majority of educational production function research has used a simple linear regression function which specifies one outcome and a set of variables which are in effect additive. Some of the assumptions of this model are not particularly appropriate for analyzing the educational process; for example, the marginal effect of a unit of change in any variable is estimated at a constant level for all levels of input. The procedure also assumes that a desirable level of productivity could be reached by adding some determinable amount of any one of the input variables. An extreme example best illustrates the weakness of this position. If the number of library books held by a school is shown to be significantly related to a low dropout rate, the dropout problem could theoretically be eliminated through the provision of a large enough number of library books. This assumption, as well as others not mentioned here, would not seem substantiated by experience.

Many of the objections to the linear model can be mitigated through the use of a logarithmic form of the production function, which would allow the impact of inputs to vary according to size. Also, other types of models may be utilized. Simultaneous equations, for example, would take into account the existence of a set of production processes making up education. The use of canonical analysis, path coefficients, and cluster analysis has also been suggested. Such techniques are complex but promising.[17]

Major Production Function Studies

The following survey of the methodology and findings of several representative studies illustrates the state of development of the application of input-output analysis in education. It should be recalled that the results of each study were influenced by the available data and their manipulation in the analysis as well as by the relationships under study.

One of the best known investigations using the educational production function approach is the massive study directed by James S. Coleman for the Office of Education.[18] Carried out to fulfill a requirement of the Civil Rights Act of 1964, this study was designed to investigate the availability of equal educational opportunities for members of minority groups in public schools. As designed, the purposes of the Equality of Educational Opportunity Survey (EEOS) were to provide a description of resource inputs for six different racial and ethnic groups, a description of school achievement of these groups at grades 1, 3, 6, 9, and 12, and a basis for analysis of the effects of various inputs on achievement.[19]

A major impact of the EEOS was to shift the focus of attention of policy makers toward the effectiveness of inputs into the system from the traditional focus on simple quantification of resources. The EEOS found in the third purpose mentioned that although differences among schools were less important than socioeconomic factors in explaining differences in pupil achievement, variations in schools were important in their impact on minority students. That is, the achievement of minority pupils depended more on the school attended than did the achievement of white students. Variation in availability of science labs showed a consistent though small relationship to achievement; the quality of teachers was found to be more strongly related to achievement. The verbal ability of teachers and the educational background of teachers and their parents were found to be highly related. "Furthermore, it is progressively greater at higher grades, indicating a cumulative impact of the qualities of teachers in a school on the pupil's achievements."[20] It was also found that the educational background and aspirations of fellow students in a school were important in explaining variations in the achievement of minority students.

Burkhead, Fox, and Holland studied input-output relationships for Chicago and Atlanta high schools.[21] In each instance, output, or dependent, variables and input, or independent, variables were selected for correlation analysis preliminary to selection for use in the study. Stepwise multiple regression was then used to order the selected variables by importance of contribution, and an analysis of value added was made by predicting scores on the eleventh- and tenth-grade tests on the basis of ninth- and eighth-grade IQ scores.

Three dependent variables were used in the Atlanta study: tenth-grade school medians for verbal achievement test scores, per cent of male dropouts of male enrollment, and per cent of 1961 graduating class in school in 1961–62. Median family income, current expenditure per pupil, building age, library expenditure per pupil, average faculty salary, enrollment-faculty ratio, teacher turnover, and size of high school were selected as independent variables. The Atlanta study found that, when the dependent variable was postsecondary educational intentions, faculty salary was the only significant variable. Using dropouts as the dependent variable, family income, current expenditure, expenditure for libraries, and school size were found to be significant. Family income and enrollment-faculty ratio were significant in predicting verbal achievement. The only variable significantly related to verbal score residuals was teacher turnover. About 85 per cent of the variance in tenth-grade verbal scores was accounted for; the eight variables explained 91 per cent of the school dropout rates. Only 46 per cent of the variance in post–high school education was explained.

In the Chicago study, eleventh-grade IQ, eleventh-grade reading scores, number of dropouts, intentions for postsecondary education, eleventh-grade IQ residuals, and eleventh-grade reading residuals were used as dependent variables. Median family income, average daily membership, age of school building, textbook expenditure per pupil, expenditure per pupil for materials and supplies, median teacher experience, median per cent of teachers with M.A. or higher degree, teacher man-years per pupil, administrative man-years per pupil, and auxiliary man-years per pupil were used as independent variables. None of the independent variables proved statistically significant in predicting post–high school education intentions. However, family income, building age, and expenditures per pupil for materials and supplies were significantly related to dropout rates. Family income was the only variable significantly related to IQ and eleventh-grade reading scores. Only teaching experience was related to the reading residuals. About 86 per cent of the variance in both the eleventh-grade IQ scores and the eleventh-grade reading scores was accounted for. Seventy-four per cent of the variance in dropouts was explained; only 28 per cent of the variance in post–high school education was accounted for.

For Chicago, Fox used on these data a simultaneous equation model in which reading scores and dropout rates were jointly determined.[22] The explanatory power of the model was increased, and school variables, including teacher man-years, text and library book expenditures, and vocational class student hours, were found to be statistically related to reading scores.

In a study made for the RAND Corporation in 1969, Kiesling collected the scores of fourth-grade pupils in ninety-seven school districts in New York State.[23] Test scores were averaged by school district for sixth graders who were present in the fourth grade for gain from grade 4 to grade 6, and for pupils in five groups stratified according to occupation of the family head. A multiple regression model was fitted to average pupil performance in the five occupational groupings. Independent variables included an index of average occupation for breadwinners of pupils in grade 6, number of teachers per 1,000 pupils, expenditure per pupil on books and supplies, average salary of teachers at the top salary decile, value of school district–owned property per pupil, and expenditure per pupil on principals and supervisors.

The model lacked explanatory power in rural districts, and the models which used score level and those which used gain in score from the fourth grade to the sixth grade gave similar results. Teacher-pupil ratio was consistently related negatively to pupil performance. The most consistently important school variable was expenditure on supervision, although the salary variable was as important for the middle-class socioeconomic groups. Expenditure per pupil on books and supplies was found to be negatively related to pupil performance.

A study made by Eric Hanushek analyzed three student samples divided on the basis of ethnic background and occupation to determine whether there were differences among teachers in terms of their contribution to achievement gains.[24] The following independent variables were used in this study: raw scores on the Stanford Achievement Test for first and third grades, sex of student, per cent of time spent on discipline by third-grade teacher, scores of second- and third-grade teachers on the Quick Word Test, years since the most recent educational experience for second- and third-grade teachers, occupation of head of household (manual or non-manual), and years of experience with children of the particular socio-economic level taught for second- and third-grade teachers.

The effects of teachers and classroom composition appeared to be a significant factor in the achievement of white students but not for the Mexican-American students in this study. The teacher characteristics that appeared to be most important for the white manual sample were the verbal facility of the second- and third-grade teachers, the recentness of education for the second- and third-grade teachers, and the per cent of time spent in discipline by the third-grade teacher. The most important characteristics for white students from nonmanual occupational backgrounds differed. Verbal ability did not appear to be significant for this latter group, although recentness of education was again a significant factor. The number of years of experience of teachers with the socioeconomic group was also significant.

National Educational Finance Project Studies

Since 1968 the National Educational Finance Project has performed several studies using the educational production function approach in analyzing data from a total of seven states. In each of the studies the basic research design used included linear regression analysis, used to identify high and low productivity school districts by measuring the relationship between statistically selected input factors and a measure of student achievement, and discriminant analysis, used to determine which of several input variables measuring school and nonschool inputs were significantly associated with the classification of districts as high or low productivity units.

In a study using Florida data, average district SCAT-total scores for ninth graders in the sixty-seven school districts of the state were used as the dependent variable.[25] Per cent of nonwhite students and adult education level were statistically selected as the input variables for the classification of high and low productivity districts, explaining about 75 per cent of the variation in achievement among the districts. The cutoff point was established for this study at ±½ standard deviation; twelve districts were classified as low productivity units and twelve as high productivity units. The discriminant analysis of the data used four functions, composed of socioeconomic variables, in-school variables, community variables, and a composite function of all variables. Two variables were found to be significant in a positive direction in explaining the variance in productivity among districts: per cent of students involved in postsecondary education and per cent of teachers employed in the district from seven to fourteen years. A third item, per cent of teachers employed by the district for two years or less, was negatively significant, indicating the possible detrimental effect of high teacher employment turnover on students.

A study using Delaware data was made by Rose in 1972.[26] Applying the same technique used in the Florida study, four variables were found to be significant contributing variables in distinguishing between high and low productivity groups of school districts when fifth-grade reading achievement was used as the dependent variable: adult education level of the community, teacher experience and preparation, per cent of minority enrollment, and per cent of high school graduates pursuing further education. The multiple correlation coefficient between reading score and a set of in-school variables, including advanced preparation of teachers, average class size, teacher preparation, and teacher experience, was 0.8193, indicating that 67 per cent of the variance was associated with these variables.

A similar study made for Kentucky by DeRuzzo used fourth-grade reading achievement as the dependent variable for classification.[27] A composite function including these variables was found to be the best predictor: number of Title I eligibles (negative), average teacher salary, per cent of budget expended for instructional purposes, and expenses for transportation. Advanced teacher preparation accounted for more variation in production than any other in-school factor tested.

In a fourth study Rose analyzed data from two states.[28] Reading achievement scores were related to per pupil expenditures to differentiate between high and low productivity districts. Sixteen districts fell into the high and low classifications in the first state; ninety-three high productivity and ninety-seven low productivity districts were identified for study in the second state. Using only adult education level, number of ESEA Title I students, and attendance rate as independent variables in a composite discriminant function, 81 per cent of the districts were correctly classified in the first state, accounting for 72 per cent of the variability among districts. Ninety per cent of the districts were correctly classified in the second state, and 90 per cent of the variation was accounted for by using a discriminator function including these variables: income over $10,000, attendance, future training, teacher preparation, minority enrollment, average class size, advanced preparation, and pupil–support personnel ratio.

DeRuzzo studied data from two other states.[29] Expenditure per pupil and achievement test scores were used to identify high and low productivity districts. Twenty school districts in the first state and sixteen districts in the second state were identified as high productivity units; thirty-three districts in the first state and thirty-two districts in the second state were identified as low productivity districts. Twenty variables were grouped into socioeconomic, community, in-school, and composite discriminant functions. The results of this study suggested that the per cent of nonwhite student enrollment may account for most of the variation in productivity between school districts. In-school predictors reflected in the measures of teacher quality, such as beginning teacher salary and teacher certification level, appeared to be important predictors. Local fiscal effort, as measured by the extent to which a school district was using its capacity to raise revenue by taxation, appeared to be the best overall community variable that consistently improved the ability of the discriminant function to classify school districts.

The sixth study in the series, conducted by Daeufer, used achievement and expenditure data to select high and low productivity elementary schools in a large urban school district.[30] Fifteen schools were selected as high productivity school centers and fifteen were indicated as low productivity centers. Twenty-five independent variables were used to predict achievement in six different discriminant functions. These included one function using all factors, one function using student related variables, two functions dividing the factors into school and nonschool categories, and two functions developed by categorizing the factors as being either amenable to adjustment by administrative decision-making function or non-manipulatable. The predictors related to student socioeconomic and teacher preparation characteristics tended to be the maximal discriminating variables of school productivity. For the school-related function, the predictors related to staff sociocultural characteristics and to teacher preparation and experience were the maximal discriminators. For the nonschool-related function, the predictors related to pupil socioeconomic and sociocultural traits, pupil attendance, and voter patterns associated with passing a school tax levy tended to be the maximal discriminating variables. For the administrative nondecision-making-related function, the predictors related to pupil attendance and the income level of the residents of a geographical area served by an elementary school center tended to be the maximal discriminating variables of school productivity.

The representative studies reviewed and the studies made by the NEFP indicate the importance of some administratively controllable variables in the education process. Of these, teacher quality appears to be by far the most important factor. These studies are a natural extension of the earlier cost-quality studies in that they show, as Burkhead and his colleagues have so aptly stated, that "it is not enough simply to spend more—it is necessary to know how to spend it if school outputs are to be increased."[31]

FORENSIC SOCIAL SCIENCE

During recent years a form of scholarship, described by Alice Rivlin[32] as "forensic social science," has become popular. In the forensic mode, experts attempt to present as strong a case as possible to support a particular policy position. The form has distinct advantages over the traditional research report since it allows concentration on the clear and complete presentation of one view of a particular topic without the restrictions inherent in presenting a "balanced and objective" report. Readers no longer puzzle over the hidden agenda; however, a report using this approach has an aura of indisputable truth about it that may be quite misleading for the uncritical or less well-informed reader. The new mode demands that readers have sophisticated knowledge, critical thought processes, and skill in data manipulation. Because of the widespread publicity that such publications tend to receive, the public often reacts emotionally rather than intellectually, failing to consider alternative hypotheses. This is especially unfortunate in cases in which there is a question concerning the degree to which a study attains the high standards desirable for social science research.

The highly publicized study by Christopher Jencks and his associates presents just such a problem.[33] In the two years since the publication of *Inequality: A Reassessment of the Effect of Family and Schooling in America*, a veritable storm of protest has been raised by educators and social scientists against many aspects of the study.[34] Jencks stated recently that he was motivated to write the book because he felt that the "liberal social reforms of the 1960s had been seriously misdirected. I also felt that this could be at least partly traced to the fact that federal policy-makers and legislators had more or less accepted a series of plausible but erroneous assumptions about the nature of poverty and economic inequality in America."[35] The study was devoted to disproving these assumptions posited by Jencks as fundamental to the federal intervention in the sixties:[36] eliminating poverty is largely a matter of helping children born into poverty to escape it; the primary reason poor children do not escape poverty is that they do not acquire basic cognitive skills; the best mechanism for breaking this circle is educational reform. Thus, the aim of the book was to show that this supposedly widely held theory about the relationship between school reform and social reform was incorrect. Jencks summarized his findings: "The evidence presented in *Inequality* seems to me to show that variations in family background, IQ genotype, exposure to schooling, and quality of schooling cannot account for most of the variation in individual or family incomes. This means we must reject the conservative notion that income inequality is largely due to the fact that men are born with unequal abilities and raised in unequal home environments. We must also reject the liberal notion that equalizing educational opportunity will equalize people's incomes. The evidence in *Inequality* cannot carry us much further, even though its rhetoric sometimes tries."[37]

According to Thurow, *Inequality* may be summarized as "nothing affects anything, . . . or more accurately, as fifty to seventy per cent of what goes on does not seem to be explained by anything else that goes on."[38]

Inequality did not settle an issue. On the contrary, it has helped generate additional research and much popular interest in educational productivity. However, much of this publicity has been detrimental to the efforts of educators to implement reform programs. Because of the unusual exposure given to *Inequality* in the popular press, the report has had a negative impact on school funding. The results of other studies, such as the recently released report of a panel study of 5,000 families being conducted by the University of Michigan's Survey Research Center for the U. S. Office of Education, should be given equal dissemination.[39]

The Michigan study has amassed longitudinal information of 5,000 families, in an effort to identify the reasons for changes in the economic well-being of families. The data base represents five waves of full interviews with families over a five-year period. The primary goal was to see whether public policy did affect or was capable of affecting the economic fortunes of families. The interesting results of the study include these factors.

1. Income level presented only a partial picture of economic well-being—an individual with constant income was in a different welfare position than one whose income fluctuated unexpectedly. "The poor not only have low incomes, but they also have more unstable incomes."[40]

2. Education had a pervasive effect on the level of earnings of individuals. Persons with higher levels of education suffered less unemployment, worked more hours, and enjoyed more flexible working conditions.

3. The amount of education was primarily influenced by family background factors, family income levels, and certain need standards. The family background outweighed school expenditure levels and local labor market conditions as factors affecting amount of education.[41]

4. Quality of education as measured by expenditure per pupil and average salary of teachers did not enhance a young man's (under thirty) earning

power; that is, the increased economic returns of education did not show up until a man was over thirty and had overcome the experience deficit that was incurred by his attending school. Only parental family income made a significant difference in the young man's wage rate. It should be observed, however, that education paid off better at an earlier age level for women than for men.[42]

While these types of findings are of value, their relative importance must be viewed in light of other societal and more global measures of educational benefits. The Michigan study appears to be moving deliberately and objectively in this direction. This type of research shows great promise for providing answers to the problems of public policy development. Its value is enhanced by the absence of lopsided advocacy of a particular position.

UTILIZATION OF PRODUCTIVITY INFORMATION

The challenge facing educators at the present time is to discover ways of making schools more effective in achieving the goals and objectives established by their constituencies. Many different methods are being developed and implemented by educators in their attempts to move toward greater educational effectiveness. Productivity research indicates that increased value might accrue to students in educational programs which have certain characteristics. For example, a child with a learning disability can make progress in a specially designed program in which the teacher has had specialized training and has access to certain equipment, materials, and supplies. Similarly, each child in the "regular" program has abilities that could be enhanced by special programs, teacher abilities, supplies, materials, and equipment. Group dynamics research and psychology show that significant commonalities and differences may have important influences on perception, growth, and development. Educational programs that will be maximally effective for students must take all of these factors into consideration. Thus, the contribution of educational productivity studies is to provide increasingly detailed information which decision makers can use in combination with community values and professional judgment in allocating public resources. In the sections that follow I synthesize the primary findings of educational productivity studies to date which deal with aspects of the educational program over which the local board and superintendent have control.

Physical Facilities

The effect of the quality of physical facilities on student achievement has not been completely investigated; however, the indications are that learning is enhanced by higher levels of facility adequacy. Burkhead et al. found that school-building age was consistently and negatively related to dropout rate in Chicago—dropout rates were less in newer buildings.[43] In a re-analysis of EEOS data, Bowles found that science lab facilities were a significant contributor to verbal achievement scores of black male twelfth graders.[44] McPartland found that the regional inequality of southern blacks was primarily due to the quality of school facilities these students used.[45]

Materials and Supplies

Contributions to achievement made by materials and supplies are difficult to isolate. Adequate data for analysis are not usually available; also, the percentage of the school budget usually spent on materials and supplies is small.[46] Several studies, however, have shown the amount of materials and supplies to be an important predictor. Of particular interest was the association of a higher expenditure in this category with a lower dropout rate in Burkhead's Chicago study.[47] As more detailed data become available through program budgeting, more accurate estimations of the effect of materials and supplies on student achievement at different grade levels can be made.

Class Size

The ratio of instructional personnel to students has long been a source of controversy. Present research findings have not been very helpful, for the reported effects of class size on student achievement are mixed. Dunnell found that smaller classes were important in explaining achievement of seventh graders in suburban elementary schools in his model;[48] Burkhead et al. found the ratio of faculty to students to be of some importance in explaining tenth-grade verbal scores in Atlanta.[49] Class size appeared to be an important factor for students of low and high ability as measured by intelligence tests in Benson's California study.[50] Kiesling found a lower pupil-teacher ratio a significant predictor of academic achievement for students from the middle range of occupational background, i.e., "proprietors, managers, officials," and "clerks and kindred workers."[51] He also suggested that the explanation given by Vincent et al., that salary increases and reduction of the pupil-teacher ratio compete for funding, is correct. Political pressures are such that higher salaries are usually supported instead of additional personnel.[52]

Noninstructional Personnel

The contributions of noninstructional personnel to the production of specific educational outcomes has received little attention because of the difficulty of isolating data. However, available results indicate that the provision and caliber of supervisory and management personnel has been an important factor in effective operation. Kiesling found that expenditures per pupil on principals and supervisory personnel were highly related to performance of pupils from professional and skilled or semiskilled occupational backgrounds, that is, from the high and low ends of the occupational scale.[53] Hanushek found that the amount of time spent by third-grade teachers in disciplinary actions, time which could have been spent in instruction, was inversely related to class achievement. He suggested that efforts to reduce the amount of teacher time spent in discipline through the use of supervisory personnel might be profitable.[54] Benson found that administrative staffing was important for districts of certain types, for example, those in which there was a high rate of unemployment.[55]

Teacher Quality

Defined in terms of years of experience, educational qualifications, salary, or specific abilities, teacher quality has often been shown to be important in explaining achievement. In his California study Benson found a distinct relationship between quality of educational services and pupil performance. "We are led," he stated, "to the conclusion that caliber of teachers is the single most important factor."[56] Not only was teacher quality found to be a strong influence on pupil achievement in the EEOS, but it was also found to be "progressively greater at higher grades, indicating a cumulative impact of the qualities of teachers in a school on pupil achievement. Again, teacher quality seems more important to minority achievement than to that of the majority."[57] Burkhead et al. found that teacher experience was an important predictor in Chicago. In the companion Atlanta study, faculty salaries used as a proxy for teacher experience and higher degrees was a strong contributor to higher scores.[58]

Teacher verbal ability has been shown to be important in several studies, including those conducted by Coleman, Bowles, and Levin.[59] Hanushek found that teacher verbal ability and teacher experience were consistently related to the verbal scores of sixth graders.[60] He noted that the variable could be considered an indirect measure of overall intelligence as well as of communicative ability. Coleman's work provided similar evidence for minority students, and the productivity studies of the NEFP support these findings.

In a study combining evidence relating teacher characteristics to student achievement with data on the costs of obtaining teachers with different characteristics, Levin found that recruiting and retaining teachers with higher verbal scores was five to ten times as effective per dollar of teacher expenditure in raising achievement scores of students as the strategy of obtaining teachers with more experience.[61] In a study of the relationships of specific teacher-related educational inputs and reading performance of disadvantaged Title I pupils in California, Kiesling found that these elements were important resource-using variables: minutes of instruction by reading specialists (99.4 per cent probability level); hours of planning per week (98.0 per cent probability level); minutes of instruction by both reading specialists and assisting paraprofessionals (95.0 per cent probability level).[62]

CONTRIBUTING TO GREATER EDUCATIONAL PRODUCTIVITY

The results of the limited research utilizing the educational production function emphasize the centrality of importance of teacher quality to educational achievement. Although the elements of the relationship have not been fully explored at this time, an obvious conclusion to be drawn from the available research is that a greater investment in teachers would have substantial impact on the educational achievement, however measured, of the nation's children. Of the several elements of the educational program which may contribute to educational productivity, those related to the teachers themselves hold the greatest promise. Characteristics such as experience, training, and salary level all appear to be related to greater educational productivity. To facilitate increased financial support for teachers, two recommendations are presented: increase funds for teacher preparation and continuing, or in-service, education, and increase funds for teacher salaries.

Increased funds for professional development are needed to enable those persons already employed in the public school system to develop needed skills further and to stay abreast of developments in their areas of specialization. Not only should teacher training institutions provide stronger programs of preprofessional and beginning professional training, but teachers also need help from experienced professionals to solve problems and to encourage development of personal skills. Teacher centers such as those under consideration for establishment in Texas and Florida offer one method of providing the latter type of assistance.

Although the drive for increased teachers' salaries has taken on new perspective with the advent of collective bargaining, there is a very real need to provide for drastic restructuring of the salary schedules for instructional personnel. The realities of the economic marketplace remove teaching from consideration by innumerable capable people who find greater financial rewards in other fields. The relatively low salary levels for teachers ensure that the adage that "those who can't do, teach" is actualized. Competitive salaries would not immediately change those teachers already employed, but substantially higher salaries would ensure that more capable and more genuinely interested persons would be attracted to the profession. Federal monies should be made available to supplement salaries.

Additional funds are also needed to provide supplemental education for children of low-income or minority backgrounds, for all research indicates that pupil achievement is strongly influenced by socioeconomic background. The job of the school is to take the child's ability and use the appropriate pedagogical techniques to assist the child in developing his abilities. Research suggests that reduced class size and the use of teachers of the highest caliber would have a significant impact on the achievement of disadvantaged students. As Coleman, Benson, and others have noted, these students are rarely those who receive the attention of the best teachers or who have the use of the most stimulating materials or facilities. As the best prepared teachers move to schools or classes which serve students who are "easier" to teach, they take the initiative to generate a pupil-changing environment with them. Thus, it seems clear that unless the teaching of low-income and minority students is encouraged through changes in the resource allocations system, increased benefit by these students from school is unlikely. The availability of additional funds to provide an adequate quality and quantity of materials and facilities, teachers of increased caliber, and reduced class size would provide students needed assistance in overcoming environmental handicaps.

A goal of primary importance for educational systems is both to provide the educational programs needed by the nation and to optimize the effective use of educational resources. Heretofore, solutions have been obscured because of the complexity of the problem and the lack of alternative management processes. As systems for data analysis become available which can assist educational administrators in making sound judgments, the efficacy of the American educational system can be greatly increased.

REFERENCES

1. Henry Steele Commager, "American Education—A Historical Perspective" (Address presented to the annual convention of the American Association of School Administrators, February 22, 1974), reprinted in AASA's *The School Administrator* (April 1974), pp. 7–8, 17–18.

2. The cost-quality studies completed before 1950 are reviewed by P. R. Mort, W. C. Reusser, and J. W. Polley, *Public School Finance*, 2d ed. (1951), and by P. R. Mort in *Problems and Issues in Public School Finance*, ed. R. L. Johns and E. L. Morphet (1952). Studies completed between 1950 and 1960 are reviewed in the 3d ed. (1960) of *Public School*

Finance. W. E. Barron reviewed later studies in *The Theory and Practice of School Finance*, ed. W. E. Gauerke and J. Childress (1967).

3. Mort, p. 11.

4. Of the twenty-six studies referenced by Mort, Reusser, and Polley (1960), p. 80, in their discussion of cost-quality studies, seventeen used this type of quality standard. Five used achievement tests, and four used social and economic characteristics of the population.

5. Mort, p. 14.

6. Ibid., p. 15.

7. P. R. Mort and Francis G. Cornell, *American Schools in Transition* (New York: Teachers College, Columbia University, 1941).

8. This study is reported in William P. McLure, *Let Us Pay for the Kind of Education We Need: Report of a Study of State and Local Support of Mississippi's Schools* (Bureau of Educational Research, University of Mississippi, 1948).

9. Lorne H. Woollatt, *The Cost-Quality Relationship on the Growing Edge* (Teachers College, Columbia University, 1949).

10. Mort, Reusser, and Polley (1960), p. 86.

11. Mort, p. 52.

12. The application of systems analysis to educational institutions without adequate adaptation is a concern of proponents of the approach. See, for example, S. J. Knezevich, ed., *Administrative Technology & the School Executive*, p. 41, and J. Alan Thomas, *The Productive School: A Systems Analysis Approach to Educational Administration* (New York: John Wiley & Sons, Inc., 1971), pp. 6–8.

13. This aspect of production function modeling is widely treated in the literature. See Samuel Bowles, "Toward an Educational Production Function," *Education, Income, and Human Capital*, ed. W. Lee Hansen (New York: National Bureau of Economic Research and Columbia University Press, 1970); Thomas, p. 17; Henry M. Levin, "The Effect of Different Levels of Expenditure on Educational Output," *Economic Factors Affecting the Financing of Education* (National Educational Finance Project, 1970), pp. 173–206; Harvey Averch et al., *How Effective is Schooling?* (RAND Corporation, 1972), p. 32; and Jesse Burkhead, Thomas G. Fox, and John W. Holland, *Input and Output in Large-City High Schools* (Syracuse: Syracuse University Press, 1967), pp. 21–23.

14. Burkhead et al., pp. 24–26, provide a particularly lucid discussion of the alternatives available.

15. Thomas, p. 17. See also Elchanan Cohn, *The Economics of Education* (Lexington, Mass.: Lexington Books, 1972), pp. 243–44.

16. James S. Coleman, "The Evaluation of Equality of Educational Opportunity" (Washington: U.S. Office of Education, 1968), p. 10.

17. Cohn, p. 239, strongly encourages the use of simultaneous equation models: "It can be shown that under most circumstances only a simultaneous equation model would lead to unbiased estimates of the relevant coefficients." Bob N. Cage and Earl Blekking suggest alternatives in "Measuring Productivity in Education," *School Finance in Transition*, Proceedings of the 16th National Conference on School Finance (Gainesville, Fla.: National Educational Finance Project, 1973).

18. Coleman et al., *Equality of Educational Opportunity* (Washington: U.S. Office of Education, 1966).

19. Coleman, (1968), p. 4.

20. Coleman, (1966), p. 22 in Summary Report.

21. Burkhead et al.

22. Thomas G. Fox, "Joint Production and Cost Functions for a Big-City High School System" (Paper presented to the Joint National Meeting of the American Astronautical Society and the Operations Research Society, June 17–20, 1969), as reported in Cohn, p. 250. Levin uses a simultaneous model in "A New Model of School Effectiveness," *Do Teachers Make A Difference?* (Washington: U.S. Office of Education, 1970).

23. Herbert J. Kiesling, "The Relationship of School Inputs to Public School Performance in New York State" (prepared for RAND Corporation, 1969).

24. Eric Hanushek, "Teacher Characteristics and Gains in Student Achievement: Estimation Using Micro Data," *American Economic Review* 61:280–88.

25. Bob N. Cage and Earl Blekking, "The Assessment of School District Productivity in the State of Florida," *Financing the Public Schools of Florida*, prepared by the National Educational Finance Project for the Florida Department of Education (Gainesville, Fla.: National Educational Finance Project, 1973).

26. Scott N. Rose, "Variables Associated with Local School District Productivity in Delaware," *Financing the Public Schools of Delaware* (Gainesville, Fla.: National Educational Finance Project, 1973), pp. 265–316.

27. David DeRuzzo, "School District Productivity in Kentucky," *Financing the Public Schools of Kentucky* (Gainesville, Fla.: National Educational Finance Project, 1973), pp. 327–65.

28. Scott N. Rose, "A Study to Identify Variables to Predict Local School District Productivity in Two States" (Ed.D. diss., University of Florida, 1972).

29. David DeRuzzo, "Identification of Variables to Predict Local School District Productivity in Two States" (Ed.D. diss., University of Florida, 1972).

30. Carl J. Daeufer, "A Study to Identify Variables Which Predict Elementary School Productivity" (Ed.D. diss., University of Florida, 1972).

31. Burkhead et al., p. 44.

32. "Forensic Social Science," *Harvard Educational Review* 1 (February 1973): 61–75.

33. Christopher Jencks, Marshall Smith, Henry Acland, Mary Jo Bane, David Cohen, Herbert Gintis, Barbara Heyns, and Stephen Michelson, *Inequality: A Reassessment of the Effect of Family and Schooling in America* (New York: Basic Books, 1972).

34. See, for example, *Perspectives on Inequality*, Reprint Series no. 8, *Harvard Educational Review* (1973); *Rethinking Educational Equality*, ed. Andrew Kopan and Herbert Walberg, Contemporary Educational Issues (The National Society for the Study of Education, 1974); *Christopher Jencks in Perspective* (American Association of School Administrators, 1973).

35. Christopher Jencks, "Inequality in Retrospect," *Harvard Educational Review* 43 (February 1973):139.

36. Jencks et al., p. 7.

37. Jencks (1973), p. 164.

38. Lester C. Thurow, "Proving the Absence of Positive Associations," Perspectives on Inequality, *Harvard Educational Review* 43 (February 1973):106–12.

39. James N. Morgan, Katherine Dickinson, Jonathan Dickinson, Jacob Benus, and Greg Duncan, *Five Thousand Families—Patterns of Economic Progress* (Ann Arbor, Mich.: Survey Research Center, Institute of Social Research, 1974).

40. Ibid., 1:277–93.

41. Ibid., p. 377.

42. Ibid., pp. 150–53.

43. Burkhead et al., pp. 50–51.

44. Bowles (1970).

45. McPartland, pp. 8–12.

46. The average net current expenditure per pupil for 1973–74 is estimated in *School Management's* "Cost of Education Index 1968–74" at $1,017.67 and includes approximately $25, or 2.45 per cent, for library materials, audiovisuals, and teaching supplies. For details see *School Management* (January 1974), pp. 14–37.

47. Burkhead et al., pp. 50–51.

48. John P. Dunnell, "Input and Output Analysis of Suburban Elementary School Districts" (paper presented at the Annual Meeting of the American Educational Research Association, New York, February 4–7, 1971) (ED 047 366).

49. Burkhead et al., p. 93.

50. Charles S. Benson et al., *State and Local Fiscal Relationships in Public Education in California*, Report of the Senate Fact Finding Committee on Revenue and Taxation (Sacramento, 1965), p. 52.

51. Kiesling. Studies by Harvey Averch and Herbert J. Kiesling, "The Relationship of School and Environment to Student Performance: Some Simultaneous Models for the Project Talent High Schools" (RAND Corporation, 1971); William G. Mollenkopf, "A Study of Secondary School Characteristics as Related to Test Scores," Research Bulletin RB-56-6 (Educational Testing Service, 1956); and Samuel Bowles (1969) also support this finding.

52. William S. Vincent, Bernard H. McKenna, and Austin D. Swanson, "The Question of Class Size," *Research Bulletin* 1 (October 1960) (Institute of Administrative Research, Teachers College, Columbia University).

53. Kiesling, p. 24.

54. Hanushek, p. 286.

55. Benson, p. 52.

56. Ibid.

57. Coleman (1966), p. 22.

58. Burkhead, pp. 39–53, 68–72. This finding is supported by studies by James A. Thomas, "Efficiency in Education: A Study of the Relationship between Selected Inputs and Mean Test Scores in a Sample of Senior High Schools" (Ph.D. diss., Stanford University, 1962); M. T. Katzman, "Distribution and Production in a Big City Elementary School System" (Ph.D. diss., Yale University, 1967); Hanushek; and Henry M. Levin, "A New Model of School Effectiveness," in *Do Teachers Make a Difference?* Teacher salary, used as a proxy for experience and education, was found significant in explaining achievement by Elchanan Cohn, "Economies of Scale in Iowa High School Operations," *Journal of Human Resources* 3 (Fall 1968):422–34; Kiesling; Burkhead et al. (Atlanta).

59. Coleman (1966), p. 22; Samuel S. Bowles, *Education Production Function*, Final Report (Washington: U.S. Office of Education, 1969), p. 58; Levin, pp. 55–78.

60. Hanushek, p. 286.

61. Henry M. Levin, "A Cost-Effectiveness Analysis of Teacher Selection," *Journal of Human Resources* 5 (Winter 1970):24–33.

62. Herbert J. Kiesling, "Input and Output in California Compensatory Education Projects," R-781-CC / RC (RAND Corporation, 1971).

Projecting the Educational Needs and Costs of Elementary and Secondary Education

K. Forbis Jordan
James R. Stultz

Projecting educational costs has traditionally been a matter of assuming a standard expenditure increment based simply on numbers of children being served by the public schools coupled with an estimate of inflationary trends. This simplistic approach, however, does not lend itself to a justifiable projection of educational needs of children and the financing of programs necessary to meet those needs. Demand trends in recent years suggest an increasingly complex array of parental and judicial requirements for special treatment of certain children with various types of learning deficiencies and disorders. Great nationwide educational thrusts have been advocated which would bring to bear greater amounts of resources on such high cost educational programs as education of the handicapped, education of the culturally deprived, early childhood education, vocational education, and career education. Each of these represents an advance in educational thinking and is a reaction in large part to societal demands on the public educational system.

This phenomenon coupled with such problems as energy crises, monetary inflation at unprecedented rates, and corresponding demands for accountability in the entire public sector creates myriad problems of financing that must be borne by the legislator and educational policy maker.

The phenomenon of decreasing elementary and secondary public school enrollment is a new experience that increases the complexity of the issues, especially where it follows two decades of constant growth. The interplay of conditions that face public education certainly suggests the use of more adequate projection devices to deal more realistically with the needs of children and at the same time accommodate the accountability demands of the taxpayer. The basic goal of this study is to project more rationally the impact of enrollment predictions, educational needs, inflationary trends, and certain minimal equality requirements on educational funding to 1980.

163

GOALS OF STUDY

To accomplish this purpose it was necessary to fulfill several research objectives including a review of the recent related research designed to identify more precisely the incidence of varying educational needs of children and the relation of programmatic costs to these needs. From this review incidence rates of educational needs were developed and programmatic cost differentials were determined that, when applied to the need rates of each state in the United States, provided not only a composite estimate of numbers and types of children to be served but also the costs related to providing the necessary services.

Data utilized in this study were derived not only from a review of related research but also from state surveys of all fifty states, whereby each state reflected its own best professional estimates, and from kindred research performed during the past few years by the National Educational Finance Project (NEFP). Special and particular attention was given to the development of cost estimates for basic or regular educational programs, exceptional education for handicapped, compensatory education for the culturally deprived, vocational education, and kindergarten education. No attempt was made to project the costs of providing education at the postsecondary or adult levels and all cost projections were specifically exclusive of higher education expenditures. Further delimitations of the study exclude consideration of costs of elementary and secondary school transportation and the financing of school facilities, two important financing elements which are treated elsewhere in this book. It should be further observed that this study does not include response to such conditions as teacher supply and demand or to deviations in economic capacities of the fifty states, also issues which are of primary concern in other portions of this book. The projections of this study were based on 1973 data with projections to 1980.

MEASURING EDUCATIONAL NEED

Since the beginning of the twentieth century, educational finance theorists have expressed the necessity for objective measure of educational needs.[1] The principle in American educational philosophy that schools should provide equal opportunity to all youths regardless of social or economic background was firmly established by the early part of the twentieth century.[2] Equality of educational opportunity has more recently come to mean that every person should have the opportunity to obtain the kind and quality of education that will best meet his individual needs and the needs of society.[3]

The implementation of educational programs based on the needs of students requires the development of objective measures. Johns has stated that the allocation dimension of school finance models should use a single measure of need that relates programmatic costs to the needs of the target population being served. Establishment of an objective single measure of educational need that is equitable, practical, and relevant has been a primary goal of educational theorists in the pursuit of a state school support program to maximize educational opportunity.[4]

Necessity for the development of an objective measure of educational need was first expressed by Cubberley in 1905. Cubberley emphasized that the primary concern for an equitable system of school funding should deal with methods of distribution that enhance the common educational advantages of all students and that encourage the development by communities of new and desirable school programs.[5] After examining the various bases for apportionment of school funds, Cubberley identified the number of teachers actually employed as the best single distribution measure; however, he expressed reservations about using any single basis for distributing school funds.[6]

As a result of an extensive study of New York State rural schools in 1921, Updegraff introduced the concept of the teacher unit. Although he agreed with many of Cubberley's concepts, he suggested that, instead of using the number of teachers employed as a basis for the distribution of state funds, standard numbers of pupils per teacher should be established for different school levels, for urban and rural districts, and for different types of classes.[7]

Mort, using average practice in the New York State school system, estimated the number of pupils assigned to teachers in different grade levels, rural schools, and one-teacher schools. Using regression analysis, Mort concluded that average daily attendance could be used to estimate the number of teachers and therefrom advanced the idea of converting typical teacher units into weighted-pupil units.[8]

Mort later assessed the value of the weighted-pupil unit: "The weighted-pupil unit (or its mathematical equivalent—the weighted classroom) is the most systematically refined of all measures of educational need and has been in practical use for a quarter of a century in state-aid laws, in expenditure comparisons of various types of districts, and in comparisons of ability to support schools. During this period it has been subjected to continuous refinements. It still falls considerably short of the demands of a perfectly satisfactory measure of educational need but approaches these demands more closely than any other available measure."[9]

The importance of developing sound measures of educational need was emphasized in 1966 when Morphet noted that even though many advances had been made since the pioneering studies by Mort and others in the early 1920s, additional research was needed to determine adequately realistic methods of determining needs and costs of educational programs.[10] Among the purposes of the NEFP were the identification of dimensions of educational needs in the nation, target populations with special educational needs, cost accounting procedures to determine cost differentials among educational programs, and variations in educational needs as related to the ability of school districts, states, and the federal government to support education.[11] From this research by the NEFP, the cost differential approach for weighting pupils for the apportionment of public school funds was developed.[12]

After a comprehensive study of existing practices, the use of weighted-pupil units was recommended as a replacement for unweighted-pupil units in distributing school funds in the states of Delaware, Florida, Kentucky, and South Dakota.[13] Several states have adopted this measurement technique and adapted it to their particular situations.

Studies made subsequent to the NEFP recommendations have generally concluded that some scheme of need and cost weighting of educational allocations is indeed necessary.[14] Jordan has observed that efficiency is enhanced by the use of the cost differential method of distribution. The public may have the satisfaction of knowing that the state is at least allocating funds on rational need and cost rather than on a simple head count of pupils with the implied presumption that all children in all school districts are the same educationally. The gross presumption that all children are average or normal often results in abnormal distribution of funds creating inefficient use of the public dollar.[15]

PROGRAMMATIC COST DIFFERENTIAL METHODOLOGY

From the preceding section, the conclusion can be drawn that equality of educational opportunity demands the provision of educational programs suited to the unique needs of individual students and that such programs vary in cost. The majority of the educational cost studies conducted in the past either compared items of current expense among districts or over a time dimension, or compared the cost of public education to the cost of various municipal services. Generally, attempts to differentiate among expenditures for education have been made on the basis of elementary and secondary units, rather than on the basis of educational programs or target groups. The traditional structure of school accounting, while adequately serving the fiduciary function, has failed to provide information concerning the configuration of human and material resources being applied to various educational programs within the school.[16]

A major tenet of the cost differential studies of the NEFP was that the opportunity to obtain a public education should be substantially equal for all children and youths appropriate to individual needs.[17] The educational process was broken down into programs representing functional components related to the programmatic needs of pupils.[18]

The cost per pupil was extracted for both regular and special programs. The per pupil cost of each special program was then divided by the per pupil cost of the selected basic or regular program to obtain the cost index for the special program. Each special program index was then multiplied by the total number of pupils in the special program to derive the number of weighted pupils associated with the special program. The total number of weighted pupils for all programs, including pupils counted in the basic program, represented the number of pupils to be funded.[19]

A further refinement of the cost-index technique, identified as the pupil-cost unit, was found to be necessary in order to avoid duplication of funding where children were counted twice for weighting purposes if they happened to participate in more than one particular educational program.[20] The pupil-cost unit, the total cost of a special program per given school system, was expressed as the product of the weighted pupils in the special program and the basic program cost per full-time equivalent pupil (FTE). The cost formula may be expressed mathematically as the Number of Full-Time Equivalent Pupil Units (FTE) × Cost Differential Index × Basic Program Cost = Total Cost of the Program.[21]

The methodology for ascertaining cost indices consists of these six steps: identification of the existing program structure; determination of the number of full-time equivalent students in average daily membership during the regular school year for each selected program category; determination of the number of full-time equivalent teaching and nonteaching academic staff for each selected program category; collection and distribution of all directly chargeable current operating expenditures to each selected program category in proportion to the benefits received; distribution of all remaining educational expenditures not directly allocable to specific programs in proportion to services received, except expenditures for general transportation, capital outlay, debt service, and food service; calculation of the cost differentials and cost indices.[22]

The satellite studies conducted by the NEFP revealed conclusively that vocational, exceptional, and compensatory educational programs cost more per pupil than regular or basic educational programs.[23] The conclusion has been confirmed by studies completed by Aldrich, Embry, F. W. Sorensen, and W. W. Sorenson.[24]

QUANTIFYING PROGRAMMATIC COST DIFFERENTIALS

Original weights developed in NEFP special satellite studies, in conjunction with results of additional research shown in Table 1, were published in 1971. The weights were based primarily on current practice in selected public school districts reputed to offer good programs in certain program

TABLE 1
NEFP COST-INDEX SCALE FOR WEIGHTING PUPILS BY PROGRAM AREA

Educational Program	Weight
Early childhood	
Three-year-olds	1.40
Four-year-olds	1.40
Kindergarten	1.30
Basic elementary and secondary	
Grades 1–6	1.00
Grades 7–9	1.20
Grades 10–12	1.40
Exceptional education	
Mentally handicapped	1.90
Physically handicapped	3.25
Emotionally handicapped	2.89
Special learning disorder	2.40
Speech handicapped	1.20
Compensatory education	
Income under $4,000	2.06
Vocational-technical	
Average all programs	1.80

SOURCE: *NEFP Decision Process; A Computer Simulation* (Gainesville, Fla.: National Educational Finance Project, 1971), p. 48.

areas. The cost analysis for these differentials was limited to current operating expenditures for the fiscal year 1968–69, including payments from the school district budget for general control, instructional service, operation and maintenance of facilities, fixed charges, community services, and other school services. Expenditures for capital outlay and debt service were excluded.[25]

The average weights computed for the Texas instructional program by the Texas Education Agency staff with the assistance of the NEFP are shown in Table 2. The five-month study was based on actual program costs per participating pupil in a sample of twenty-eight "good practice" Texas school districts. The cost indices were based on 1970–71 current expenditures, excluding expenditures for capital outlay, debt service, transportation, and food service.[26]

The program cost differentials found in a special study designed to determine the actual differences in per pupil expenditures in Florida for different types of educational programs are set forth in Table 3. The study was conducted by William McLure for the Florida State Department of Education. A representative sample of twenty-five county school districts

TABLE 2

TEXAS PER PUPIL WEIGHTS FOR THE INSTRUCTIONAL PROGRAM

Basic Program	Cost Index		
Early childhood special education	1.26		
Kindergarten	1.05		
Elementary	1.00		
Middle school	1.12		
High school	1.28		
Special Programs	Elementary School	Middle* School	High* School
Speech handicapped	1.36	1.52	1.57
All other handicapped	2.21	2.30	2.71
Low income	1.37	1.38	1.51
Non-English-speaking	1.77	1.67	1.67
Migrant	1.07	1.51	1.81
Agriculture		1.37	1.56
Homemaking		1.21	1.38
Trades and industry		1.29	1.47
Office, D.E., health		1.24	1.42
Cooperative		1.23	1.41
Handicapped vocational		2.31	2.64
Coordinated vocational-academic education		1.59	1.82

SOURCE: Tish Newman Busselle, *The Texas Weighted Pupil Study* (Austin: Texas Education Agency, 1973), p. 32.

*Base cost for middle school and high school special programs was the middle school and high school regular programs, respectively.

was selected to include nine large districts, eight medium-size districts, and eight small districts.[27]

The cost differential analysis was based on 1971–72 current operating expenditures per full-time equivalent pupil.[28] Expenditures for transportation, food service, capital outlay, textbooks, and July and August payrolls were excluded. Also, teacher aides and paraprofessionals were identified only where assigned an estimated salary of $3,600 per full-time equivalent person.[29]

A summary of the average educational cost indices computed for the

Delaware public schools is shown in Table 4. The special NEFP study was conducted by Rossmiller and Moran for the Delaware State Board of Education. The study sample included twenty-three Delaware school districts. Costs were based on 1970–71 school year pupil, staff, and current operating expenditure data. September 1970 enrollment in day-school programs during the regular school year for each major category and subcategory of program by school were assumed to represent full-time equivalent pupils. Kindergarten enrollment and vocational-technical stu-

TABLE 3
FLORIDA PER PUPIL WEIGHTS FOR THE INSTRUCTIONAL PROGRAM

Educational Program	Average Cost Differential Index		
	Grades 1–6	Grades 7–12	Grades 9–12
Kindergarten	1.20		
Compensatory	1.58	1.88	
Basic	1.00	1.21	
Exceptional children—total	2.20	2.12	
Speech handicapped		2.76	
Educable mentally retarded	2.47	2.25	
Trainable mentally retarded	3.77	2.73	
Physically handicapped	4.73	2.11	
Homebound	1.57	1.61	
Deaf	3.79	3.16	
Visually handicapped	4.33	3.24	
Emotionally disturbed	3.98	3.85	
Specific learning disability	2.05	2.24	
Socially maladjusted		2.05	
Gifted	1.73		
Prevocational			1.61
Vocational—total			1.79
Agriculture			2.61
Business			1.95
Distributive			1.52
Diversified cooperative			1.71
Home economics cons			1.68
Home economics wage			1.61
Industrial			2.24
Technical			2.91
Health			2.67
Postsecondary and adult general education			1.71

SOURCE: *Financing the Public Schools of Florida* (Gainesville, Fla.: National Educational Finance Project, 1973), p. 20.

dents in Kent and Sussex counties were assumed to be one-half full-time equivalent enrollment.[30]

The average cost indices for Kentucky educational programs identified by an NEFP study conducted by Rossmiller and Moran for the Kentucky State Department of Education are given in Table 5. The Kentucky Department of Education selected a representative sample of twenty-eight Kentucky school districts for the study. A computer program was written to extract 1971–72 pupil, academic staff, and current expenditure data from

TABLE 4
DELAWARE PER PUPIL WEIGHTS FOR THE INSTRUCTIONAL PROGRAM

| | Sample Average Cost Differential Indices | |
| | Elementary Grades 1–8 | Secondary* Grades 9–12 |
Educational Program		
Regular programs (sec. / elem.)	1.00	1.11
Handicapped programs		
Educable mentally retarded	1.49	1.35
Trainable mentally retarded	1.67	1.24
Orthopedically handicapped	1.76	1.29
Blind or partially blind	1.83	2.48
Deaf or partially deaf	3.03	3.05
Socially and emotionally		
maladjusted	1.92	1.95
Learning disabilities	2.29	2.24
All programs for the		
handicapped	1.71	1.51
Vocational-technical programs		1.60

SOURCE: *Financing the Public Schools of Delaware* (Gainesville, Fla.: National Educational Finance Project, 1973).

*Base cost for the secondary special programs was the secondary regular program.

central storage files for each district and each program category. The data were analyzed separately for each school district and aggregated to obtain the cost for each full-time equivalent pupil in the basic and special educational program offering. Expenditures for food service, transportation, capital outlay, and debt service were excluded.[31]

Table 6 contains a summary of the average cost indices for the various special programs provided by thirteen South Dakota school districts included in the sample of an NEFP study conducted by Rossmiller and Moran for the South Dakota State Department of Education. The sample was selected with the assistance of the staff of the State Department of Education to include South Dakota school districts which provide a number of special educational programs for handicapped children. The sample included some of the largest districts in the state because only those districts provided programs for several categories of handicapped children.[32]

The cost analysis was based on 1971–72 school year pupil, staff, and net current operating expenditure data. Because current operating expense data were not available by category or subcategory of program, most current operating expenditures were allocated to programs according to

TABLE 5

KENTUCKY PER PUPIL WEIGHTS FOR THE INSTRUCTIONAL PROGRAM

Educational Program	Sample Average Cost Differential Indices	
	Elementary Grades 1–8	Secondary Grades 9–12*
Kindergarten	1.05**	
Regular programs (sec. / elem.)	1.00	1.11
Handicapped programs	1.76	1.80
Deaf	1.65	1.22
Educable mentally retarded	1.68	1.49
Emotionally disturbed	1.60	1.35
Hard of hearing	1.62	1.25
Neurologically impaired	1.61	1.51
Crippled (special class)	1.54	
Speech correction	1.62	1.91
Trainable mentally retarded	1.73	1.48
Partially seeing	1.79	1.70
Home instruction	2.58	2.27
Home and hospital instruction	2.36	2.07
Hospital instruction	2.32	2.34
Intellectually gifted	1.88	1.49
Learning disabilities	1.52	
Multihandicapped	1.65	
Compensatory programs	2.18	2.79
Reading program	2.23	2.74
Kindergarten	2.46	
Vocational technical	2.47	2.64
Special education	2.57	3.53
Other (miscellaneous)	2.22	1.91
Vocational technical programs	1.47	1.55
Business		1.39
Distributive		1.50
Trades and industries	1.14	1.65
Health occupations		1.60
Agriculture		2.13
Home economics	1.99	1.44
Special programs	1.21	1.64

SOURCE: *Financing the Public Schools of Kentucky* (Gainesville, Fla.: National Educational Finance Project, 1973), p. 6.

*Base cost for the secondary special programs was the secondary regular program.
**Base cost for the kindergarten program was the elementary regular program.

the number of academic staff. Exceptions were expenditure categories of district administration, attendance and health services, transportation, operation and maintenance of plant, fixed charges, and food service; these were applied equally to each student regardless of level. These allocation procedures resulted in an estimate of the cost per full-time equivalent student by category and subcategory of the program at both the elementary and secondary grade levels in each school district.[33]

The NEFP studies demonstrate that no one set of cost differentials will be descriptive of current financing practices in all states. State determination of special programs and local discretion in the allocation of resources

TABLE 6
SOUTH DAKOTA PER PUPIL WEIGHTS FOR SPECIAL EDUCATIONAL
PROGRAMS FOR HANDICAPPED STUDENTS

| | Sample Average Cost Differential Indices | |
Educational Program	Elementary Grades 1–8	Secondary Grades 9–12*
Regular programs (sec. / elem.)	1.00	1.13
Handicapped programs	2.55	2.41
Educable mentally retarded	2.43	1.72
Trainable mentally retarded	2.92	1.69**
Emotionally disturbed	3.36	3.96
Learning disabilities	2.47	
Physically handicapped	3.94	12.04**

SOURCE: *Financing the Public Schools of South Dakota* (Gainesville, Fla.: National Educational Finance Project, 1973), pp. 121–154.

*Base cost for the secondary special programs was the secondary regular program.
**Program reported in one district only.

among programs leads to a diversity which is difficult to compress or standardize.

The findings of NEFP cost differential studies to date and other cost analyses cited in the literature have indicated that, even though costs vary greatly among both programmatic areas and geographic regions, there is consistency in per pupil cost among some well-established categories of educational programs. Even though developmental programs and inconsistent fiscal accounting practices may complicate the data-gathering procedures, it is generally accepted that the cost differential analysis of educational programs is an objective and practical planning tool. The public policy receptivity for the concept is illustrated by the number of recent research studies which have been conducted and the legislative enactment of state school programs during the past two years which utilize the approach as the vehicle for allocating state funds to local school districts. With this in mind a review of these studies shows that much worthwhile information is to be found. First, it is evident that there are wide variations in costs of educational programs when the programs respond to either the physical and / or mental needs of children. For the states and the federal government to respond to financing problems by treating all children alike is to ignore reality. One interesting consequence of these studies is that they document what the federal courts have referred to as "judicially manageable standards." In 1969, federal courts in the Burruss and McInnis cases refused to establish judicial standards of constitutionality because of a general lack of definitive educational and cost data.[34] These studies obviously contribute to the solution of that dilemma, and, whether or not they may be termed "judicially" manageable standards or simply "legislatively" manageable, they will nevertheless be beneficial.

Second, these data, while showing substantial variations among costs of programs from state to state, do establish a pattern of costs of which one must be cognizant. For example, the category of physically handicapped consistently reflects a higher cost than do the categories of visually handicapped and emotionally disturbed. Those programs associated with compensatory education generally reflect much higher costs. It is also interesting to note that kindergarten and high school programs usually cost more to provide than regular elementary and junior high school programs.

Third, from an efficiency point of view, these studies allow the administrator to make a reasonable approximation of programmatic costs when establishing alternative programs. Support data for these studies exhibit the influence on costs of instructional arrangements and the importance of making wise instructional choices.

Finally, as pointed out before, the cost differentials provide a method which has not been present before for projecting educational fiscal needs at both the state and federal levels. By ascertaining the incidence of types of educational needs and applying the appropriate costs, rational governmental budgetary and allocation decisions are facilitated. It is this last benefit on which this chapter capitalizes to project education's fiscal needs for the future.

In order to synthesize the range of data results and to place them in a more usable context, a table of reasonable ranges is presented (see Table 7). This table is based on empirical data but also contains an element of judgmental intervention which the researchers feel reflects a realistic view of current practice.

PROJECTING EDUCATIONAL NEEDS AND COSTS

The basic plan for this study involved utilization of the incidence rates and cost differentials to estimate the needs and costs of providing educational programs in each state in the United States in 1980. To develop these estimates, current enrollment and cost data were collected from various sources for four target populations.

Relevant data for fiscal year 1972–73 were collected and compiled from these sources: Bureau of Census, U.S. Department of Commerce; Divi-

TABLE 7
NEFP REASONABLE RANGE COST DIFFERENTIAL SCALE FOR ESTABLISHING
PER PUPIL WEIGHTS FOR EDUCATIONAL PROGRAMS

Educational Program	Reasonable Range
Kindergarten	1.05–1.30
Grades 1–2	1.00–1.30
Grades 3–8	1.00
Grades 9–12	1.10–1.50
Special education	
Physically handicapped	2.50–4.00
Educable mentally handicapped	1.50–2.50
Trainable mentally handicapped	1.60–3.00
Emotionally disturbed	1.60–3.70
Learning disabilities	1.50–2.50
Homebound	2.40–2.60
Remedial reading	
(Grades 1–6)	1.60–2.40
Vocational-technical programs	
Business education	1.40–1.80
Distributive education	1.40–1.50
Trades and industries	1.50–2.90
Health occupations	1.40–2.70
Agriculture	1.60–2.60
Home economics	1.40–1.70

sion of Vocational and Technical Education, Bureau of Education for the Handicapped, National Center for Educational Statistics, and Division of Compensatory Education, U.S. Office of Education; Project Baseline; National Education Association; National Educational Finance Project; Institute for Educational Finance; *School Management*; National Planning Association; State Directors of Vocational-Technical Education; State Directors of Exceptional Education; and chief state school officers of the fifty states.

The population and cost estimates developed represent an attempt to forecast the needs of the target groups in each state in 1980. The NEFP incidence rates and cost differentials used in this study were based on comprehensive best practice and current educational expenditures in several sample states; therefore, the estimates should not be viewed as a comment on the efficacy or efficiency of a particular educational system. Inference of the *exact* educational resource input requirements for states or their educational subdivisions was *not* the purpose of this study. These estimates were developed for state and federal educational agency planning purposes.

The accuracy of these estimates was necessarily limited by the enrollment data reported by state and federal educational agencies and by the validity of the 1973 population estimates and 1980 population projections prepared from unpublished data furnished by the Bureau of the Census. Series I-E 1980 population projections were chosen because Series E assumes the most conservative fertility assumption, 2.11 children per woman, and Series I assumes the continuation of 1960–70 gross migration trends among the states.[35]

A further assumption was made that program category definitions and grade levels for the data reported by the state were consistent with the educational program typology selected for this study. In cases where differences were reported by the various educational agencies, uniform decisions were made in adjusting the data for these differences.

A further assumption was that there would be some duplication between the reported enrollments for the four target groups, but these duplications, where observed, were not significant in comparison with the overall estimate totals. The incorporation of the full-time equivalent factors adjusted many of the possible duplications.

An attempt was made to adjust the net current expenditure per pupil in average daily membership (ADM) for both regional economic differences among the states and the expense of educational programs already being provided in each state in fiscal year 1972–73. These adjustments should provide an appropriate estimate of the basic per pupil cost of high quality regular educational programs in each state.

The per cent increase in educational cost from the base year 1972–73 to 1979–80 was estimated by fitting a trend line to the reported educational cost from 1967–68 to 1973–74 and extending it to 1979–80. This estimate was assumed to be acceptable for predicting the cost of education in 1980. The predicted percentage increase of 62 per cent was assumed to include factors other than monetary inflation that influence educational costs, such as declining enrollments, expansion of educational programs, and increasing energy costs.

SPECIAL EDUCATIONAL PROGRAM POPULATION
AND COST PROJECTION PROCEDURES

The procedures used to estimate the needs and costs of providing high quality educational programs in each state in 1980 are explained in the following section. These procedures were applied uniformly and consistently to each state. State estimates were aggregated to provide a combined estimate for the United States.

Participating Pupil Population Projections

Estimates of the population of children requiring various educational programs were computed by multiplying the 1972–73 estimated program enrollments reported by each state by the ratio of the 1980 projected age 5–17 population (Series I-E) to the 1973 estimated age 5–17 population. The expected enrollment for compensatory programs was not calculated because data concerning compensatory program enrollments were not collected due both to the great diversity of program definitions and the variety of funding sources among the states. Table 8 shows the ratio of 1980 projected age 5–17 population to the 1973 estimated age 5–17 population and the corresponding percentage change.

Total need estimates of children requiring special education were computed by multiplying the estimated NEFP incidence rate for each program category by the applicable age group 1980 population projection. Table 9 has the estimated 1980 population projections for age 5–17, age 12–17, and age 5, which were applied to the estimated NEFP incidence rates for exceptional, compensatory, vocational, and kindergarten special educational programs, respectively. Table 10 shows the incidence rates for the six selected vocational education program categories which were computed by multiplying the state goal for 1980 by the percentage each program enrollment was of the total enrollment of all six programs reported by the states for 1972–73. The NEFP estimated incidence rates for the exceptional, kindergarten, and compensatory target groups are shown in column 1 of Table 11.

Estimates of the number of additional children needing service in 1980 were calculated by subtracting the expected enrollment from the total in need for each special educational program category in each target group.

Full-Time Equivalent Membership Estimates

The full-time equivalent membership of the participating pupil estimates were computed by multiplying each respective participating pupil estimate by the applicable educational program category full-time equivalent factor.

TABLE 8
ESTIMATED CHANGES OF POPULATION IN AGE 5–17
FOR EACH STATE IN 1980

State (1)	Ratio of Estimated Population Age 5–17 in 1980 to 1973 (2)	Per Cent Change in Age 5–17 Population from 1973 to 1980 (3)
Alabama	0.8613	−13.87
Alaska	0.9502	− 4.98
Arizona	0.9371	− 6.29
Arkansas	0.8863	−11.37
California	1.0449	4.49
Colorado	0.9435	− 5.65
Connecticut	0.9951	− 0.49
Delaware	0.9897	− 1.03
Florida	0.9438	− 5.62
Georgia	0.9591	− 4.09
Hawaii	0.9430	− 5.70
Idaho	0.8584	−14.16
Illinois	0.9486	− 5.14
Indiana	0.9293	− 7.07
Iowa	0.8375	−16.25
Kansas	0.8753	−12.47
Kentucky	0.8793	−12.07
Louisiana	0.9018	− 9.82
Maine	0.8604	−13.96
Maryland	1.0136	1.36
Massachusetts	0.9406	− 5.94
Michigan	0.9437	− 5.63
Minnesota	0.9217	− 7.83
Mississippi	0.8530	−14.70
Missouri	0.9730	− 8.27
Montana	0.8361	−16.39
Nebraska	0.8645	−13.55
Nevada	1.0809	8.09
New Hampshire	0.9850	− 1.50
New Jersey	0.9712	− 2.88
New Mexico	0.8547	−14.53
New York	0.9546	− 4.54
North Carolina	0.9143	− 8.57
North Dakota	0.7764	−22.36
Ohio	0.9236	− 7.64
Oklahoma	0.9229	− 7.71
Oregon	0.9388	− 6.12
Pennsylvania	0.8671	−13.29
Rhode Island	0.9374	− 6.26
South Carolina	0.8731	−12.69
South Dakota	0.8071	−19.29
Tennessee	0.8916	−10.84
Texas	0.9622	− 3.78
Utah	0.9535	− 4.65
Vermont	0.9438	− 5.62
Virginia	0.9465	− 5.35
Washington	0.9965	− 0.35
West Virginia	0.7716	−22.84

Continued

TABLE 8—*Continued*

State (1)	Ratio of Estimated Population Age 5–17 in 1980 to 1973 (2)	Per Cent Change in Age 5–17 Population from 1973 to 1980 (3)
Wisconsin	0.9141	− 8.59
Wyoming	0.8267	−17.33
United States	0.9381	− 6.19

SOURCE: U. S. Department of Commerce, Bureau of the Census, "Estimates of the Total Resident Population by Age for States: July 1, 1973," and "State Population Projection by Age and State, Series I-E" (Washington: prepared from unpublished data provided by the Office of the Director for research purposes only, 1973).

NOTE: Because of rounding, detail may not add to totals.

TABLE 9
ESTIMATED AGE 5–17, 12–17, AND 5
POPULATIONS FOR EACH STATE IN 1980

State (1)	Estimated Age 5–17 Population in 1980 (2)	Estimated Age 12–17 Population in 1980 (3)	Estimated Age 5 Population in 1980 (4)
Alabama	773,457	365,521	60,511
Alaska	90,266	39,318	7,978
Arizona	494,790	224,870	41,166
Arkansas	439,582	201,919	35,894
California	5,091,857	2,334,469	419,846
Colorado	573,651	267,852	46,313
Connecticut	748,318	342,915	61,359
Delaware	146,478	66,701	12,198
Florida	1,601,711	756,418	126,788
Georgia	1,165,265	538,069	94,458
Hawaii	197,091	91,931	15,782
Idaho	171,673	79,079	13,928
Illinois	2,624,694	1,199,036	217,458
Indiana	1,248,027	577,003	101,852
Iowa	608,870	283,945	49,169
Kansas	471,810	219,873	38,454
Kentucky	729,833	341,188	58,272
Louisiana	923,419	425,530	75,238
Maine	221,130	104,330	17,503
Maryland	1,050,133	479,805	87,102
Massachusetts	1,311,184	613,351	104,967
Michigan	2,227,154	1,025,813	181,621
Minnesota	936,440	429,768	77,477
Mississippi	521,182	244,455	41,322
Missouri	1,048,454	489,248	84,683
Montana	158,019	72,112	13,195

Continued

TABLE 9—*Continued*

State (1)	Estimated Age 5–17 Population in 1980 (2)	Estimated Age 12–17 Population in 1980 (3)	Estimated Age 5 Population in 1980 (4)
Nebraska	329,364	151,126	27,425
Nevada	148,086	65,453	12,821
New Hampshire	194,040	90,074	15,670
New Jersey	1,737,465	801,160	141,100
New Mexico	266,665	119,129	22,934
New York	4,056,854	1,883,373	325,719
North Carolina	1,177,669	554,818	92,900
North Dakota	130,432	59,510	10,944
Ohio	2,477,012	1,154,029	199,099
Oklahoma	573,112	266,893	46,236
Oregon	493,791	230,528	39,636
Pennsylvania	2,432,260	1,162,203	187,765
Rhode Island	210,916	99,041	16,803
South Carolina	617,265	290,889	48,818
South Dakota	142,861	65,400	11,973
Tennessee	887,116	417,670	70,276
Texas	2,845,307	1,299,632	235,614
Utah	300,356	134,621	25,292
Vermont	110,420	52,328	8,748
Virginia	1,119,654	522,305	90,431
Washington	833,092	389,784	66,478
West Virginia	326,404	156,711	24,752
Wisconsin	1,085,033	499,148	89,310
Wyoming	73,576	33,656	6,094
United States	48,143,237	22,314,000	3,901,472

SOURCE: U. S. Department of Commerce, Bureau of the Census, "State Populations by Age and State, Series I-E" (Washington: estimates prepared from unpublished 1970 census data provided by the Office of the Director for research purposes only, 1973).

NOTE: Because of rounding, detail may not add to totals.

These assumptions were based on NEFP data and experience and estimate the average amount of time a pupil spends in a special educational program during a specific school time period. Column 2 of Table 11 presents the full-time equivalent factors used in this study to compute the estimate of full-time equivalent membership of each special educational program category in each of the four target groups in each state.

Special Educational Program Cost Estimates

Estimates of the cost of providing various educational programs in 1980 at 1972–73 price levels for the expected enrollment, needing service, and total in need, respectively, were computed by multiplying the full-time equivalent membership of each educational program category in each target group of each state by the NEFP cost differential and the adjusted net current expenditure per pupil in ADM. Column 3 of Table 11 shows the NEFP cost differentials and column 5 of Table 12 the adjusted net current expenditure per pupil in ADM used in this study to estimate the cost of providing the selected educational programs in 1980.

The cost of providing the selected special educational programs in each target group in 1980 at 1972–73 price levels with an estimated 62 per cent increase in cost was computed by multiplying the cost for the total number

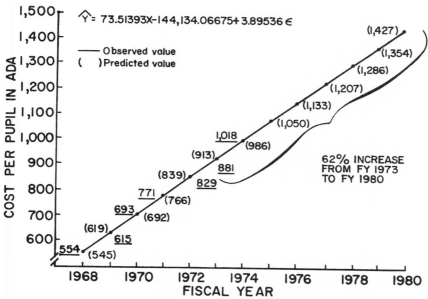

Fig. 1. Cost per pupil in average daily attendance for FY 1968 to FY 1974 with projection to FY 1980

of students in need of services in each educational program category at 1972–73 price levels by 1.62. The 1980 estimated increase in cost was based on an analysis of the trend in educational costs from 1967–68 to 1973–74, as shown in Figure 1 and Table 13. Column 4 of Table 13 shows the per cent change in total expenditures required to provide for the total number of students in need of each educational program category at 1972–73 price levels; an assumption was made that there would be a 62 per cent increase in cost by 1980. This estimate was calculated by dividing the difference between the cost for the total number of students in need of services with a 62 per cent increase in cost and the cost of the expected enrollment at

TABLE 10
STATE GOAL AND ESTIMATED INCIDENCE RATES FOR
VOCATIONAL EDUCATIONAL PROGRAMS BY STATE FOR 1980

State	State Goal (Total Incidence)	Agricultural Education	Distributive Education	Health Occupations	Home Economics (All Categories)	Office Occupations	Trades and Industries (Including Technical)
(1)	(2)	(3)	(4)	(5)	(6)	(7)	(8)
Alabama	0.5400	0.1403	0.0193	0.0044	0.2323	0.0560	0.0877
Alaska	0.3000	0.0017	0.0059	0.0045	0.0860	0.1438	0.0581
Arizona	0.2900	0.0189	0.0185	0.0038	0.1533	0.0545	0.0410
Arkansas	0.3400	0.0899	0.0126	0.0025	0.1789	0.0285	0.0276
California	0.3000	0.0239	0.0073	0.0036	0.1077	0.1043	0.0532
Colorado	0.4000	0.0252	0.0469	0.0045	0.1303	0.0992	0.0939
Connecticut	0.3300	0.0045	0.0094	0.0030	0.1494	0.1273	0.0364
Delaware	0.2800	0.0125	0.0112	0.0031	0.1076	0.0979	0.0477
Florida	0.5500	0.0491	0.0345	0.0097	0.2547	0.0593	0.1427
Georgia	0.5300	0.0799	0.0134	0.0029	0.2031	0.1720	0.0587
Hawaii	0.6000	0.0612	0.0200	0.0000	0.2507	0.2245	0.0436
Idaho	0.4300	0.0725	0.0184	0.0015	0.2485	0.0619	0.0272
Illinois	0.5000	0.0232	0.0233	0.0048	0.0722	0.2025	0.1740
Indiana	0.3100	0.0486	0.0164	0.0026	0.1693	0.0384	0.0347
Iowa	0.2300	0.0639	0.0075	0.0000	0.1401	0.0048	0.0137
Kansas	0.1800	0.0334	0.0091	0.0006	0.0939	0.0129	0.0301
Kentucky	0.5000	0.0874	0.0338	0.0040	0.2224	0.0845	0.0679
Louisiana	0.3500	0.0497	0.0131	0.0013	0.1487	0.1185	0.0187
Maine	0.3900	0.0165	0.0168	0.0047	0.0913	0.2054	0.0553
Maryland	0.4400	0.0099	0.0070	0.0025	0.2437	0.1171	0.0598
Massachusetts	0.2200	0.0023	0.0083	0.0023	0.0314	0.1290	0.0467
Michigan	0.4500	0.0342	0.0493	0.0144	0.2086	0.0581	0.0854
Minnesota	0.1900	0.0307	0.0105	0.0015	0.1206	0.0129	0.0138
Mississippi	0.3000	0.0641	0.0118	0.0008	0.1722	0.0066	0.0445
Missouri	0.3400	0.0556	0.0292	0.0105	0.1152	0.0572	0.0723

Montana	0.4000	0.0512	0.0248	0.0011	0.1827	0.0249	0.1153
Nebraska	0.3500	0.0644	0.0269	0.0014	0.1639	0.0505	0.0429
Nevada	0.4800	0.0319	0.0139	0.0140	0.0911	0.1523	0.1768
New Hampshire	0.2600	0.0108	0.0042	0.0007	0.1595	0.0690	0.0158
New Jersey	0.4800	0.0036	0.0161	0.0037	0.2104	0.1891	0.0571
New Mexico	0.2200	0.0248	0.0087	0.0035	0.0909	0.0722	0.0199
New York	0.4000	0.0074	0.0114	0.0076	0.1831	0.1238	0.0667
North Carolina	0.6800	0.0171	0.0452	0.0182	0.2689	0.0279	0.2127
North Dakota	0.3200	0.0861	0.0117	0.0035	0.1528	0.0461	0.0198
Ohio	0.3000	0.0305	0.0256	0.0034	0.1423	0.0380	0.0602
Oklahoma	0.3900	0.1083	0.0165	0.0064	0.1603	0.0219	0.0766
Oregon	0.4500	0.0197	0.0120	0.0072	0.2672	0.0946	0.0493
Pennsylvania	0.3000	0.0173	0.0146	0.0040	0.0817	0.0916	0.0908
Rhode Island	0.3400	0.0200	0.0187	0.0047	0.2318	0.0126	0.0522
South Carolina	0.5000	0.0301	0.0314	0.0038	0.2447	0.0718	0.1182
South Dakota	0.3500	0.0553	0.0227	0.0022	0.2379	0.0120	0.0199
Tennessee	0.3500	0.0714	0.0200	0.0042	0.1633	0.0246	0.0665
Texas	0.4000	0.0672	0.0251	0.0024	0.2235	0.0198	0.0620
Utah	0.7600	0.0603	0.0293	0.0065	0.2799	0.2311	0.1529
Vermont	0.3100	0.0302	0.0082	0.0068	0.1417	0.0623	0.0608
Virginia	0.5100	0.0475	0.0359	0.0046	0.2087	0.1543	0.0590
Washington	0.6400	0.0758	0.0270	0.0028	0.2744	0.2406	0.0194
West Virginia	0.3200	0.0339	0.0083	0.0037	0.0975	0.1035	0.0731
Wisconsin	0.2400	0.0418	0.0097	0.0014	0.0301	0.0905	0.0665
Wyoming	0.5000	0.0664	0.0303	0.0016	0.1636	0.1910	0.0471
United States	0.3908	0.0380	0.0184	0.0046	0.1616	0.0972	0.0710

SOURCES: (1): Erick L. Lindman, *Financing Vocational Education in the Public Schools*, National Educational Finance Project, Special Study No. 4 (Graduate School of Education, University of California, Los Angeles, 1970), pp. 30–31, Table 4.5, col. 4. (3–8): U. S. Office of Education form 3138, U. S. Department of Health, Education, and Welfare, Washington, FY 1973, Secondary Enrollments (grades 7–12). The incidence rates shown in columns 3 to 8 were computed by multiplying the ratio of each vocational educational program enrollment to the total enrollment of the six vocational programs reported on USOE Form 3138 by each state for 1972–73 by the state vocational education goal for secondary enrollment reported by E. L. Lindman in NEFP Special Study No. 2.

NOTE: Because of rounding, detail may not add to totals.

TABLE 11

NEFP INCIDENCE RATES, FTE FACTORS, AND COST DIFFERENTIALS FOR EXCEPTIONAL, VOCATIONAL, KINDERGARTEN, COMPENSATORY, AND BASIC EDUCATIONAL PROGRAMS IN THE UNITED STATES

Educational Program (1)	Incidence Rate (2)	F_TE Factor (3)	Cost Differential (4)
Exceptional education			
Gifted	0.0200	0.15	1.14[a]
Educable mentally retarded	0.0130	0.80	2.00[b]
Trainable mentally retarded	0.0024	1.00	2.30[b]
Auditorily handicapped	0.0010	0.90	2.99[a]
Visually handicapped	0.0005	0.45	2.97[a]
Speech handicapped	0.0360	0.05	1.40[c]
Physically handicapped	0.0021	0.95	2.75[b]
Special learning disorders	0.0112	0.50	2.00[b]
Emotionally disturbed	0.0200	0.70	2.65[b]
Multiple handicapped	0.0007	0.50	1.97[c]
Vocational education			
Agricultural education	—	0.30	2.10[b]
Distributive education	—	0.45	1.45[b]
Health occupations	—	0.40	2.05[b]
Home economics (all categories)	—	0.20	1.55[b]
Office occupations	—	0.40	1.60[b]
Trades and industries (including technical)	—	0.35	2.20[b]

Educational Program (1)	Incidence Rate (2)	FTE Factor (3)	Cost Differential (4)
Kindergarten education			
Half day programs	0.0000	0.50	1.18[b]
Full day programs	1.0000	1.00	1.18[b]
Compensatory education:			
All programs	0.2300	0.20	2.00[b]
Basic education:			
Grades 1–3	0.2447	1.00	1.15[b]
Grades 4–8	0.4339	1.00	1.00[b]
Grades 9–12	0.3214	1.00	1.30[b]

SOURCES: (2): Roe L. Johns, Kern Alexander, and K. Forbis Jordan, eds., *Planning to Finance Education*, vol. 3 (Gainesville, Fla.: NEFP, 1971), pp. 8–9, 61, 89. Basic program incidence rates were computed from col. 13 of Table 30 in *Digest of Educational Statistics: 1973 Edition*, by W. Vance Grant and C. George Lind (Washington: Government Printing Office, 1974), p. 31.

(3): Assumptions prepared from unpublished data and the experience of the staff of the Institute for Educational Finance, Gainesville, Florida, 1974.

(4): a. Richard A. Rossmiller, James A. Hale, and Lloyd E. Frohreich, *Educational Programs for Exceptional Children: Resource Configurations and Costs*, Special Study no. 2 (Gainesville, Fla.: NEFP, 1970), p. 127.

b. Kern Alexander, and K. Forbis Jordan, eds., *Financing the Public Schools of South Dakota* (Gainesville, Fla.: National Educational Finance Project, 1973), p. vii.

c. Kern Alexander and K. Forbis Jordan, eds., *Financing the Public Schools of Kentucky* (Gainesville, Fla.: National Educational Finance Project, 1973), p. 6. The cost differentials taken from the South Dakota and Kentucky studies represent the midpoint of the applicable reasonable range.

NOTE: Vocational incidence rates were computed separately from current practice data and NEFP reported state goals for each state in 1980.

TABLE 12
Adjusted Net Current Expenditure Per Pupil in ADM for 1972–73

School Management's Nine Geographical Regions in the United States (1)	Net Current Expense Per Pupil in ADM for 1972–73 (2)	Higher State or Region Average (3)	Weighted Average Cost Index (4)	Adjusted Net Current Expense Per Pupil in WADM (5)
Region 1: (average)	$ 1,010			
Maine	789	$ 1,010	1.1808	$ 855
New Hampshire	841	1,010	1.1749	860
Vermont	1,151	1,151	1.1939	964
Massachusetts	1,060	1,060	1.1882	892
Connecticut	1,141	1,141	1.2110	942
Rhode Island	1,075	1,075	1.1742	916
Region 2: (average)	1,246			
New York	1,424	1,424	1.1968	1,190
New Jersey	1,216	1,246	1.1922	1,045
Pennsylvania	1,100	1,246	1.1840	1,052
Region 3: (average)	992			
Ohio	883	992	1.1718	847
Indiana	833	992	1.1646	852
Illinois	1,058	1,058	1.2109	874
Michigan	1,115	1,115	1.1718	952
Wisconsin	1,071	1,071	1.1870	902
Region 4: (average)	876			
Minnesota	1,089	1,089	1.1863	918

Iowa	$ 1,007	$ 1,007	1.1841	$850
Missouri	837	876	1.1720	747
North Dakota	825	876	1.1848	739
South Dakota	803	876	1.1656	752
Nebraska	700	876	1.1888	737
Kansas	870	876	1.1726	747
Region 5: (average)	844			
Delaware	1,083	1,083	1.2202	888
Maryland	1,082	1,082	1.1832	914
Virginia	866	866	1.1964	724
West Virginia	702	844	1.1704	721
North Carolina	753	844	1.2022	702
South Carolina	702	844	1.1972	705
Georgia	722	844	1.9168	705
Florida	841	844	1.2154	694
Region 6: (average)	637			
Kentucky	649	649	1.1766	552
Tennessee	692	692	1.1936	580
Alabama	556	637	1.1869	537
Mississippi	651	651	1.1706	556
Region 7: (average)	778			
Arkansas	619	778	1.1877	655
Louisiana	855	855	1.1859	721
Oklahoma	663	778	1.1919	653
Texas	974	974	1.1848	822
Region 8: (average)	853			
Montana	895	895	1.1714	764
Idaho	704	853	1.1723	728

Continued

TABLE 12—*Continued*

School Management's Nine Geographical Regions in the United States (1)	Net Current Expense Per Pupil in ADM for 1972–73 (2)	Higher State or Region Average (3)	Weighted Average Cost Index (4)	Adjusted Net Current Expense Per Pupil in WADM (5)
Wyoming	$ 909	$ 909	1.1975	$ 759
Colorado	895	895	1.1761	761
New Mexico	799	853	1.1837	721
Arizona	1,022	1,022	1.1706	873
Utah	698	853	1.2191	700
Nevada	904	904	1.1978	755
Region 9: (average)	1,021			
Washington	861	1,021	1.1867	860
Oregon	939	1,021	1.1848	862
California	937	1,021	1.1721	871
Alaska	1,398	1,398	1.1873	1,177
Hawaii	970	1,021	1.1772	867
United States (averages)	966	960	1.1861	809

SOURCES: (1): "Cost of Education Index," *School Management* 18 (January 1974):16–21.

(2): *Ranking of the States: 1973* (Washington: National Education Association, 1973) Table I-15, p. 64. 1973 total current expenditure per pupil in ADM was not available for Idaho, Michigan, and Washington. These data were estimated by subtracting the national average cost per pupil in ADM from the national average cost per pupil in ADA, $68, from each state's missing 1972–73 expenditure per pupil in ADM.

(3): Higher of state or regional average net current expenditure per pupil listed in (2).

(4): FTE membership for selected special and basic programs for each state multiplied by the NEFP average cost differential divided by the ADM for 1972–73. *Ranking of the States: 1973* (Washington: National Education Association, 1973), Table B-9, p. 17. ADM for 1973 was not available for Idaho, Michigan, Missouri, Montana, and Washington. These data were estimated by multiplying the ratio of the 1973 ADM to the 1973 ADA for the United States by the reported 1973 ADA for each missing state.

(5): Adjusted net current expense per pupil in ADM for 1972–73, (3) divided by (4).

NOTE: Because of rounding, detail may not add to totals.

1972–73 prices by the cost of the expected enrollment at 1972–73 prices and multiplying by 100.

Analysis of Exceptional Education Estimates

Table 14 shows the variation in exceptional educational program mix provided by the fifty states. Columns 2 and 3 show the number of states that had FTE membership for 1973 either higher or lower than the highest need estimate in 1973. The data generated in this comparison indicate that there had been little development among the states of educational programs designed to meet the needs of gifted, speech handicapped, neurological and special learning disordered, physically handicapped, or emotionally disturbed exceptional program categories. The greatest development among the states appeared to have taken place in providing programs for educable mentally retarded, trainable mentally retarded, auditorily handicapped, visually handicapped, and multiple handicapped exceptional education pupils.

Table 15 provides a summary and comparison of exceptional educational

TABLE 13
ESTIMATED PERCENTAGE INCREASE IN NET CURRENT EXPENDITURE
PER PUPIL IN ADM FROM FY 1973 TO FY 1980

Fiscal Year (1)	Observed Value (2)	Predicted Value (3)	Percentage Increase from FY 73 (4)
1968	$ 553.95	$ 545.25	—
1969	615.23	618.75	—
1970	692.98	692.25	—
1971	770.53	765.75	—
1972	829.39	839.31	—
1973	880.64	912.81	3.65
1974	1,017.67	986.31	12.00
1975	—	1,059.84	20.35
1976	—	1,133.35	28.70
1977	—	1,206.87	37.04
1978	—	1,280.38	45.39
1979	—	1,353.90	53.74
1980	—	1,427.41	62.09

SOURCES: (1): "Cost of Education Index 1968–74, Average Cost Per Pupil (ADA)," *School Management* 18 (January 1974), p. 18.

(2): BMDO5R-Polynomial Regression on cols. 1 and 2, 1968–74. Predicted values computed from BMDO5R linear regression equation $Y = 73.51393X - 144134.06675 + 3.89536$ with a F-value significant at the 0.05 level.

(3): Percentage increases in the 1973–80 predicted values from the base 1973 observed value.

needs and the cost of programs to meet these needs in each state for the FTE pupils served in 1973 and the projected highest need in 1980. Column 6 shows that the increased expenditure required to fund exceptional programs at the 1980 highest need as compared to the 1973 enrollment level ranged from 84 per cent for Utah to 487 per cent for Montana. The increase in expenditure to meet the needs of all exceptional students by 1980 in the United States was 217 per cent or $4.5 billion.

Analysis of Vocational Education Estimates

Columns 2 and 3 of Table 16 show that six states had FTE membership for 1973 that exceeded the highest need estimate for that year in each vocational category. Since the incidence estimates were based on the current

TABLE 14
COMPARISON OF EXCEPTIONAL EDUCATIONAL PROGRAM
FTE MEMBERSHIP FOR 1973 ENROLLMENT AND 1973
NEFP INCIDENCE FOR THE UNITED STATES

Exceptional Education Program (1)	Number of States with FTE Membership Higher than NEFP Estimates in 1973 (2)	Number of States with FTE Membership Lower than NEFP Estimates in 1973 (3)
Gifted	1	49
Educable mentally retarded	21	29
Trainable mentally retarded	15	35
Auditorily handicapped	19	31
Visually handicapped	16	34
Speech handicapped	7	43
Physically handicapped	10	40
Neurological and special learning disorders	9	41
Emotionally disturbed	0	50
Multiple handicapped	14	36

SOURCE: James R. Stultz, "The Incidence of Educational Needs and the Cost of Meeting These Needs in the United States in 1980" (Institute for Educational Finance, 1974).

TABLE 15
Summary and Comparison of Students with Exceptional Educational Needs and Cost of Programs to Meet These Needs in Each State for Students Served in 1973 and Projected Highest Need in 1980
(in thousands)

State (1)	FTE Membership (in thousands)		Program Cost		
	1973 Enrollment (2)	1980 Highest Need (3)	1973 Enrollment (4)	1980 Highest Need (5)	Per Cent Change (6)
Alabama	23	39	$ 24,747	$ 73,922	199
Alaska	2	4	4,485	15,774	252
Arizona	9	20	16,456	64,113	290
Arkansas	12	22	17,016	51,118	200
California	83	216	138,453	662,982	379
Colorado	11	23	19,799	64,165	224
Connecticut	27	34	58,507	114,799	96
Delaware	4	7	8,217	22,212	170
Florida	45	72	66,931	181,163	171
Georgia	38	61	53,460	151,722	184
Hawaii	3	8	6,236	25,250	305
Idaho	3	7	4,507	18,586	312
Illinois	56	108	105,074	337,580	221
Indiana	20	51	34,018	155,704	358
Iowa	19	26	36,412	77,905	114
Kansas	10	19	14,971	51,606	245
Kentucky	13	31	15,376	60,313	292
Louisiana	22	41	33,245	105,959	219
Maine	6	10	11,167	30,039	169
Maryland	17	43	31,968	140,089	338
Massachusetts	34	59	64,974	190,081	193
Michigan	46	92	94,383	313,007	232
Minnesota	26	45	48,916	144,807	196
Mississippi	10	23	10,975	44,977	310
Missouri	25	49	37,478	129,339	245

Continued

TABLE 15—*Continued*

State (1)	FTE Membership (in thousands)		Program Cost		Per Cent Change (6)
	1973 Enrollment (2)	1980 Highest Need (3)	1973 Enrollment (4)	1980 Highest Need (5)	
Montana	2	6	$ 3,001	$ 17,620	487
Nebraska	9	15	14,092	39,784	182
Nevada	2	6	3,530	16,451	366
New Hampshire	3	8	4,881	24,514	402
New Jersey	42	71	94,406	267,719	184
New Mexico	7	11	10,241	28,803	181
New York	80	176	229,428	762,712	232
North Carolina	45	65	62,872	159,177	153
North Dakota	3	5	5,318	14,717	177
Ohio	56	114	94,780	342,536	261
Oklahoma	20	29	27,074	66,969	148
Oregon	13	21	23,838	66,217	178
Pennsylvania	70	113	155,823	426,049	173
Rhode Island	4	9	8,533	28,738	237
South Carolina	26	35	37,969	85,149	124
South Dakota	2	6	2,812	15,680	458
Tennessee	31	44	40,146	94,396	135
Texas	76	122	133,004	359,242	170
Utah	14	16	21,432	39,368	84
Vermont	3	5	7,448	17,245	132
Virginia	25	47	38,445	121,194	215
Washington	15	34	28,761	105,043	265
West Virginia	7	14	10,139	36,875	264
Wisconsin	19	44	36,569	142,845	291
Wyoming	3	3	4,424	9,536	116
United States	1,139	2,129	$2,056,674	$6,515,769	217

SOURCE: James R. Stultz, "The Incidence of Educational Needs and the Cost of Meeting These Needs in the United States in 1980" (Institute for Educational Finance, 1974).

practice program mix reported by each state for 1973, evidently six states were already serving in excess of their state goals for that year. The remaining forty-four states which did not exceed the 1973 highest need estimate would have had to provide for FTE membership increases of over 60 per cent to have met their state goals in 1973.

Column 6 of Table 17 shows that the additional expenditure required to provide for the highest vocational need in 1980 compared to the expenditure for the FTE pupils enrolled in 1973 ranged from 38 per cent for New Mexico to 335 per cent for Michigan. The increase in expenditure required to fund the highest need in 1980 from the 1973 FTE pupil enrollment was 124 per cent or $3.6 billion for the fifty states.

Analysis of Kindergarten Education Estimates

Table 18 shows a summary and comparison of kindergarten educational needs and the cost of programs to meet these needs in each state for the FTE pupils served in 1973 and the estimated population of 5-year-old children in 1980. Columns 2 and 3 reveal that all states but Iowa served fewer FTE pupils in 1973 than the NEFP estimate of highest need for 1980. Since Iowa's

TABLE 16
COMPARISON OF VOCATIONAL EDUCATIONAL PROGRAM
FTE MEMBERSHIP FOR 1973 ENROLLMENT AND 1973
NEFP INCIDENCE FOR THE UNITED STATES

Vocational Education Program (1)	Number of States with FTE Membership Higher than NEFP Estimates in 1973 (2)	Number of States with FTE Membership Lower than NEFP Estimates in 1973 (3)
Agricultural education	6	44
Distributive education	6	44
Health occupations	6	44
Home economics (all occupations)	6	44
Office occupations	6	44
Trades and industries (including technical)	6	44

SOURCE: James R. Stultz, "The Incidence of Educational Needs and the Cost of Meeting These Needs in the United States in 1980" (Institute for Educational Finance, 1974).

TABLE 17

SUMMARY AND COMPARISON OF STUDENTS WITH VOCATIONAL EDUCATIONAL NEEDS AND COST OF PROGRAMS TO MEET THESE NEEDS IN EACH STATE FOR STUDENTS SERVED IN 1973 AND PROJECTED HIGHEST NEED IN 1980

State (1)	FTE Membership (in thousands)		Program Cost		Per Cent Change (6)
	1973 Enrollment (2)	1980 Highest Need (3)	1973 Enrollment (4)	1980 Highest Need (5)	
Alabama	30	56	$ 29,701	$ 89,026	200
Alaska	5	4	9,179	14,130	54
Arizona	17	19	24,731	44,863	81
Arkansas	17	18	19,866	34,679	75
California	170	219	258,020	539,801	109
Colorado	17	35	22,779	74,744	228
Connecticut	38[a]	38[a]	59,260	95,531	61
Delaware	12[a]	12[a]	17,967	28,806	60
Florida	107	120	134,363	245,081	82
Georgia	59	87	72,653	171,882	137
Hawaii	7	17	10,389	39,585	281
Idaho	8	9	9,935	18,327	84
Illinois	171	211	271,991	542,780	100
Indiana	28	49	41,481	117,253	183
Iowa	13	16	20,252	39,960	97
Kansas	13[a]	11[a]	17,376	24,640	42
Kentucky	28	49	27,368	78,016	185
Louisiana	39	45	47,597	88,103	85
Maine	9	14	12,887	32,883	155
Maryland	51	59	79,208	148,759	88
Massachusetts	47	49	72,218	121,428	68
Michigan	51	136	84,810	368,823	335
Minnesota	39[a]	36[a]	62,100	92,726	49
Mississippi	16	19	16,154	30,960	92

Missouri	22	$ 29,627	51	$ 112,895	281
Montana	7	9,435	8	18,805	99
Nebraska	13	17,414	15	31,654	82
Nevada	8[a]	11,692	11	24,216	107
New Hampshire	8[a]	11,272	8[a]	17,987	60
New Jersey	72	125,741	118	333,676	165
New Mexico	13[a]	16,118	11[a]	22,318	38
New York	199	406,601	226	746,791	84
North Carolina	51	68,312	110	237,799	248
North Dakota	6	7,619	5	11,176	47
Ohio	62	93,620	100	243,056	160
Oklahoma	19	23,344	29	58,425	150
Oregon	19	28,323	28	66,792	136
Pennsylvania	69	131,417	114	351,712	168
Rhode Island	5	7,902	9	21,865	177
South Carolina	22	27,864	42	84,847	205
South Dakota	5	6,743	6	11,808	75
Tennessee	28	29,354	41	70,266	139
Texas	89	131,105	139	329,477	151
Utah	17	21,353	32	63,330	197
Vermont	4	6,937	5	13,121	89
Virginia	70	86,749	82	162,952	88
Washington	47	67,743	76	174,673	158
West Virginia	13	16,804	16	33,416	99
Wisconsin	44	73,036	41	111,060	52
Wyoming	4	5,513	5	11,262	104
United States	1,911	$2,883,907	2,655	$6,448,141	124

SOURCE: James R. Stultz, "The Incidence of Educational Needs and the Cost of Meeting These Needs in the United States in 1980" (Institute for Educational Finance, 1974).

NOTE: Because of rounding, detail may not add to totals.

[a]Total FTE pupils being served is in excess of NEFP incidence rate.

TABLE 18

SUMMARY AND COMPARISON OF STUDENTS WITH KINDERGARTEN EDUCATIONAL NEEDS
AND THE COST OF PROGRAMS TO MEET THESE NEEDS IN EACH STATE FOR THE
STUDENTS SERVED IN 1973 AND THE PROJECTED HIGHEST NEED IN 1980

| | FTE Membership (in thousands) | | Program Cost | | |
State (1)	1973 Enrollment (2)	1980 Highest Need (3)	1973 Enrollment (4)	1980 Highest Need (5)	Per Cent Change (6)
Alabama	0[a]	61	$ 152	$ 62,116	40,787
Alaska	3	8	3,732	17,950	381
Arizona	15	41	14,943	68,699	360
Arkansas	12	36	9,016	44,943	398
California	307	420	315,575	699,044	122
Colorado	18	46	16,452	67,373	310
Connecticut	23	61	25,639	110,491	331
Delaware	4	12	4,450	20,706	365
Florida	54	127	44,588	168,203	277
Georgia	8	94	6,347	127,299	1,906
Hawaii	12	16	12,154	26,156	115
Idaho	1	14	1,129	19,383	1,616
Illinois	83	217	85,195	363,315	326
Indiana	38	102	38,496	165,884	331
Iowa	59[b]	49	59,047	79,893	35
Kansas	16	38	14,531	54,911	278
Kentucky	2	58	1,096	61,489	5,512
Louisiana	30	75	25,358	103,698	309
Maine	9	18	8,958	28,607	219
Maryland	30	87	31,884	152,185	377
Massachusetts	40	105	42,578	178,984	320
Michigan	80	182	90,188	330,521	266
Minnesota	34	77	37,149	135,960	266
Mississippi	0[a]	41	251	43,919	17,416

Missouri	35	85	$ 31,291	$ 120,924	286
Montana	2	13	1,928	19,271	899
Nebraska	11	27	9,819	38,638	293
Nevada	4	13	3,786	18,504	389
New Hampshire	2	16	2,337	25,761	1,002
New Jersey	91	141	111,870	281,864	152
New Mexico	6	23	4,849	31,609	552
New York	133	326	186,678	740,946	297
North Carolina	31	93	25,552	124,666	388
North Dakota	1	11	955	15,460	1,519
Ohio	85	199	84,614	322,366	281
Oklahoma	17	46	13,288	57,715	334
Oregon	5	40	5,544	65,312	1,078
Pennsylvania	81	188	101,111	377,596	168
Rhode Island	7	17	7,295	29,422	303
South Carolina	10	49	8,132	65,791	709
South Dakota	9	12	8,188	17,211	110
Tennessee	19	70	13,036	77,917	498
Texas	83	236	80,942	370,228	357
Utah	11	25	9,161	33,844	269
Vermont	2	9	2,234	16,121	622
Virginia	40	90	34,510	125,156	263
Washington	25	67	25,225	109,452	334
West Virginia	13	25	10,650	34,155	220
Wisconsin	37	89	39,433	153,994	291
Wyoming	5	6	4,567	8,842	94
United States	1,645	3,901	$1,715,891	$6,414,431	274

SOURCE: James R. Stultz, "The Incidence of Educational Needs and the Cost of Meeting These Needs in the United States in 1980" (Institute for Educational Finance, 1974).

NOTE: Because of rounding, detail may not add to totals.

a. Less than 500 FTE pupils served in 1973.

b. Serving 100 per cent of the 5-year-old population in 1973 which is projected to decline 16.25 per cent by 1980.

TABLE 19
SUMMARY OF STUDENTS WITH COMPENSATORY EDUCATIONAL NEEDS
AND COST OF PROGRAMS TO MEET THESE NEEDS IN EACH
STATE FOR PROJECTED HIGHEST NEED IN 1980

State (1)	FTE Membership 1980 Highest Need (in thousands) (2)	Program Cost 1980 Highest Need (3)
Alabama	36	$ 61,903
Alaska	4	15,834
Arizona	23	64,378
Arkansas	20	42,912
California	234	660,992
Colorado	26	65,063
Connecticut	34	105,060
Delaware	7	19,386
Florida	74	165,671
Georgia	54	122,438
Hawaii	9	25,468
Idaho	8	18,627
Illinois	121	341,895
Indiana	57	158,477
Iowa	28	77,134
Kansas	22	52,528
Kentucky	34	60,043
Louisiana	42	99,229
Maine	10	28,178
Maryland	48	143,052
Massachusetts	60	174,314
Michigan	102	316,002
Minnesota	43	128,122
Mississippi	24	43,188
Missouri	48	116,727
Montana	7	17,993
Nebraska	15	36,178
Nevada	7	16,663
New Hampshire	9	24,871
New Jersey	80	270,604
New Mexico	12	28,655
New York	187	719,513
North Carolina	54	123,215
North Dakota	6	14,366
Ohio	114	312,690
Oklahoma	26	55,777
Oregon	23	63,438
Pennsylvania	112	381,354
Rhode Island	10	28,794
South Carolina	28	64,858
South Dakota	7	16,012
Tennessee	41	76,685
Texas	131	348,581
Utah	14	31,335
Vermont	5	15,865
Virginia	52	120,816

Continued

TABLE 19—*Continued*

State (1)	FTE Membership 1980 Highest Need (in thousands) (2)	Program Cost 1980 Highest Need (3)
Washington	38	$ 106,781
West Virginia	15	35,075
Wisconsin	50	145,865
Wyoming	3	8,323
United States	2,215	$6,170,909

SOURCE: James R. Stultz, "The Incidence of Educational Needs and the Cost of Meeting These Needs in the United States in 1980" (Institute for Educational Finance, 1974).

NOTE: Because of rounding, detail may not add to totals.

population aged 5–17 was projected to decline approximately 16 per cent from 1973 to 1980, this difference can probably be attributed to the increasing decline in the 5-year-old population or to a data error.

Column 6 of Table 18 shows that significant increases in expenditure are required to develop full day kindergarten educational programs by 1980 for most of the states. These additional expenditure requirements ranged from 35 per cent for Iowa to 40,787 per cent for Alabama. The increase in expenditure for the fifty states to fund the highest need by 1980 was 274 per cent or $4.7 billion.

Analysis of Compensatory Education Estimates

Table 19 provides a summary of compensatory educational needs and the cost of programs to meet these needs in each state for the projected highest need in 1980. According to the NEFP estimate of incidence for compensatory needs, the fifty states should provide compensatory programs for 2.2 million FTE pupils and plan to spend approximately $6.2 billion by 1980.

Since 1973 enrollment and cost data were not estimated for compensatory education, percentage of change comparisons could not be computed for FTE membership and costs among the states. However, the Division of Compensatory Education, U.S. Office of Education, reported that 6.7 million children participated in Elementary and Secondary Education Act (ESEA) Title I programs in the United States in 1973.[36] Since the ESEA Title I program was designed to provide supplemental aid to educationally deprived children, the number of children participating in 1973 was used as a rough estimate of the enrollment in compensatory programs for 1973.

Table 20 shows the summary and comparison of compensatory programs and costs from the ESEA Title I estimate for 1973 and the projected

TABLE 20

SUMMARY AND COMPARISON OF COMPENSATORY EDUCATIONAL NEEDS AND COST OF PROGRAMS TO MEET THESE NEEDS IN THE UNITED STATES FOR ESEA, TITLE I PUPILS SERVED IN 1973 AND PROJECTED HIGHEST NEED IN 1980

Total All Compensatory Programs (1)	FTE Membership (in thousands)		Program Cost		Per Cent Change (6)
	1973 ESEA, Title I Pupils Served (2)	1980 Highest Need (3)	1973 ESEA, Title I Pupils Served (4)	1980 Highest Need (5)	
United States	1,333	2,215	$ 2,157,354	$ 6,170,909	186

SOURCE: James R. Stultz, "The Incidence of Educational Needs and the Cost of Meeting These Needs in the United States in 1980" (Institute for Educational Finance, 1974).

highest need in 1980. According to this analysis, the fifty states should increase expenditures $4.0 billion or 186 per cent by 1980 to meet the compensatory needs estimate.

Analysis of Total Special Education Estimates

Table 21 has a summary and comparison of the needs and costs of providing exceptional, vocational, kindergarten, and compensatory educational programs in each state and for the students served in 1973 and the projected highest need for 1980; however, columns 2 and 4 did not include an estimate of the FTE membership or program cost for the 1973 enrollment in compensatory programs. Column 6 shows that the additional expenditure required to provide for the highest estimate of special need in 1980 compared to the expenditure required to provide for the FTE pupils enrolled in 1973 ranged from 138 per cent for Iowa to 495 per cent for Mississippi. Comparison of columns 2 and 3 shows that the states should make provision to serve 6.2 million or 132 per cent more FTE pupils by 1980. Column 6 shows a projected additional cost of $18.9 billion, or a 284 per cent increase, to meet the special needs of all children in the United States in 1980.

Analysis of Basic Education Estimates

Comparison of columns 2 and 3 of Table 22 shows that the FTE membership of basic pupils is expected to decline 9.0 million or 22 per cent from the 1973 enrollment to 1980 highest need estimate. This decline in FTE membership is the direct result of the increase in FTE membership for special educational programs in 1980. Special educational programs will increase by 6.3 million FTE pupils and basic educational programs will decrease 6.3 million pupils for the 1973 enrollment to the 1980 highest need estimates. Therefore, any increase in special program FTE membership will cause an equal decrease in FTE membership of basic programs for a given base year.

Column 6 shows that the additional expenditure required to provide for the highest need for basic programs in 1980 compared to the expenditure for the FTE pupils enrolled in 1973 ranged from 1 per cent for North Dakota to 46 per cent for Nevada.

An analysis of column 6 shows that the states will still need to spend an additional $10.5 billion or 27 per cent to provide high quality basic educational programs in 1980. The need for additional spending for basic educational programs in 1980 varied among the states according to the estimated change in population and additional special program needs in 1980.

TABLE 21
SUMMARY AND COMPARISON OF STUDENTS WITH SPECIAL EDUCATIONAL NEEDS AND COST OF PROGRAMS TO MEET THESE NEEDS IN EACH STATE FOR STUDENTS SERVED IN 1973 AND PROJECTED HIGHEST NEED IN 1980

State (1)	FTE Membership (in thousands)		Program Cost		
	1973 Enrollment (2)	1980 Highest Need (3)	1973 Enrollment (4)	1980 Highest Need (5)	Per Cent Change (6)
Alabama	53	191	$ 54,599	$ 286,968	426
Alaska	9	20	17,396	63,688	266
Arizona	40	103	56,130	242,053	331
Arkansas	41	96	45,899	173,652	278
California	600	1,089	712,047	2,562,819	260
Colorado	47	131	59,029	271,345	360
Connecticut	88	167	143,406	425,881	197
Delaware	20	38	30,633	91,110	197
Florida	206	393	245,881	760,117	209
Georgia	105	296	132,460	573,341	333
Hawaii	22	50	28,779	116,459	305
Idaho	12	38	15,571	74,923	381
Illinois	310	656	462,259	1,585,570	243
Indiana	86	259	113,995	597,318	424
Iowa	91	119	115,711	274,892	138
Kansas	39	91	46,879	183,685	292
Kentucky	43	172	43,840	259,861	493
Louisiana	91	204	106,201	396,988	274
Maine	24	51	33,012	119,707	263
Maryland	98	237	143,059	584,085	308
Massachusetts	121	273	179,770	664,807	270
Michigan	177	512	269,381	1,328,353	393
Minnesota	100	201	148,166	501,615	239

Mississippi	26	107	$ 27,380	$ 163,044	495
Missouri	82	233	98,397	479,885	388
Montana	11	35	14,365	73,689	413
Nebraska	33	73	41,325	146,254	254
Nevada	15	36	19,008	75,835	299
New Hampshire	13	40	18,490	93,134	404
New Jersey	205	411	332,017	1,153,863	248
New Mexico	25	58	31,208	111,385	257
New York	413	914	822,707	2,969,961	261
North Carolina	128	322	156,736	644,857	311
North Dakota	10	28	13,891	55,719	301
Ohio	203	527	273,014	1,220,647	347
Oklahoma	56	131	63,659	238,886	275
Oregon	38	112	57,704	261,759	354
Pennsylvania	220	527	388,352	1,536,710	296
Rhode Island	16	44	23,730	108,820	359
South Carolina	58	154	73,965	300,644	306
South Dakota	16	30	17,742	60,711	242
Tennessee	78	196	82,535	319,264	287
Texas	249	627	345,051	1,407,527	308
Utah	42	87	51,946	167,877	223
Vermont	9	23	16,619	62,351	275
Virginia	135	270	159,704	530,118	232
Washington	87	215	121,729	495,949	307
West Virginia	32	70	37,593	139,480	271
Wisconsin	101	225	149,037	553,763	272
Wyoming	12	18	14,505	37,963	162
United States	4,695	10,900	$6,656,491	$25,549,168	284

SOURCE: James R. Stultz, "The Incidence of Educational Needs and the Cost of Meeting These Needs in the United States in 1980" (Institute for Educational Finance, 1974).

NOTE: Because of rounding, detail may not add to totals. An estimate of 1973 enrollment for compensatory education was not included in cols. 2 and 4.

TABLE 22

SUMMARY AND COMPARISON OF STUDENTS WITH BASIC EDUCATIONAL NEEDS AND COST OF PROGRAMS TO MEET THESE NEEDS IN EACH STATE FOR STUDENTS SERVED IN 1973 AND PROJECTED HIGHEST NEED IN 1980

State (1)	FTE Membership (in thousands)		Program Cost		
	1973 Enrollment (2)	1980 Highest Need (3)	1973 Enrollment (4)	1980 Highest Need (5)	Per Cent Change (6)
Alabama	724	479	$ 440,827	$ 471,859	7
Alaska	76	60	101,106	130,542	29
Arizona	467	372	462,233	596,854	29
Arkansas	394	290	292,741	348,213	19
California	4,147	3,829	4,093,293	6,122,389	50
Colorado	526	410	453,814	572,591	26
Connecticut	587	504	626,234	871,286	39
Delaware	113	94	113,338	153,051	35
Florida	1,267	997	996,137	1,270,394	28
Georgia	986	750	787,593	970,345	23
Hawaii	157	119	153,911	189,512	23
Idaho	179	126	147,492	168,367	14
Illinois	1,973	1,509	1,953,819	2,421,305	24
Indiana	1,076	820	1,038,342	1,282,963	24
Iowa	557	424	536,487	661,009	23
Kansas	433	322	366,434	441,996	21
Kentucky	658	445	411,435	450,424	9
Louisiana	748	553	610,702	731,374	20
Maine	223	161	216,109	252,519	17
Maryland	819	692	848,200	1,160,461	37
Massachusetts	1,049	828	1,060,242	1,355,106	28
Michigan	1,963	1,507	2,117,938	2,634,220	24
Minnesota	813	640	845,462	1,077,817	27

Mississippi	494	337	$ 311,270	$ 343,851	10
Missouri	910	677	770,073	927,884	20
Montana	162	110	140,442	153,614	9
Nebraska	292	209	243,855	282,462	16
Nevada	115	104	98,552	144,378	46
New Hampshire	152	122	147,817	192,215	30
New Jersey	1,303	1,054	1,543,014	2,021,613	31
New Mexico	260	186	212,050	246,227	16
New York	3,103	2,442	4,183,772	5,333,663	27
North Carolina	1,012	720	805,334	927,821	15
North Dakota	131	82	110,049	111,524	1
Ohio	2,188	1,681	2,100,001	2,613,625	24
Oklahoma	524	405	387,986	485,222	25
Oregon	428	325	417,932	514,546	23
Pennsylvania	2,125	1,507	2,533,633	2,910,542	15
Rhode Island	171	132	177,393	221,136	25
South Carolina	562	388	449,320	501,848	12
South Dakota	144	100	123,040	137,470	12
Tennessee	813	598	534,313	636,673	19
Texas	2,420	1,940	2,253,606	2,927,946	30
Utah	262	203	207,911	261,413	26
Vermont	100	80	109,650	141,779	29
Virginia	925	733	758,579	974,401	28
Washington	706	576	688,393	910,065	32
West Virginia	380	248	310,204	328,162	6
Wisconsin	852	645	870,307	1,068,772	23
Wyoming	73	52	63,052	72,742	15
United States	40,542	31,586	$39,225,232	$49,725,904	27

SOURCE: James R. Stultz, "The Incidence of Educational Needs and the Cost of Meeting These Needs in the United States in 1980" (Institute for Educational Finance, 1974).

NOTE: Because of rounding, detail may not add to totals.

SUMMARY

Table 23 shows the total cost for all educational programs in each state developed in this study for the 1973 enrollment, 1973 highest need, and 1980 highest need.

Individual states varied in the need for additional spending according to the effect of the various fiscal and population factors used in this forecast, e.g., NEFP incidence rates and cost differentials, adjusted NCE per pupil in WADM, and projected population change by 1980. In column 5 of Table 23, a comparison of range in additional resource input needs from 1973 enrollment to 1980 highest need shows that the additional resource needs ranged from 35 per cent for North Dakota (which should experience a 22 per cent decline in the population aged 5–17 by 1980) to 87 per cent for Nevada (which should experience an 8 per cent increase in the population aged 5–17 by 1980). For the fifty states as a group, the estimated increase in expenditures was $29.4 billion or 64 per cent by 1980 to meet the educational needs developed in this study.

In Table 24 a summary and comparison of the 1973 enrollment, 1973 highest need, and 1980 highest cost estimates for the United States developed in this study have been compared to the estimated total NCE for public elementary and secondary day schools for the school year 1972–73. This analysis revealed that the use of NEFP incidence rates and cost differentials for the calculation of cost for 1973 enrollment, 1973 highest need, and 1980 highest need in comparison to the reported NCE for 1973 resulted in higher cost estimates of $2.4 billion or 5.49 per cent for 1973 enrollment, $5.9 billion or 13.54 per cent for 1973 highest need, and $31.8 billion or 73.07 per cent for 1980 highest need. Based on these data, state and federal educational agency planners should increase expenditures annually at the rate of $4.5 billion or over 10 per cent from 1973 to 1980 to meet the highest estimate of educational need.

The absence of adequate educational programs for all pupils dictates that increased funds be allocated for public elementary and secondary education to assure equality of educational opportunity for all children within each state. In this chapter ample evidence has been presented to justify the contention that additional funds are required to provide equal access to educational programs for all pupils. The state-by-state educational need and cost projections for the entire nation produce an accurate view of the level of financing necessary to support public education if enrollment, inflation, educational needs, program costs, and certain equalization standards are taken into account. The precision of this projection has been enhanced because full-time equivalent students were used to project costs, thus preventing duplication of pupil counting which unnecessarily inflates

TABLE 23
Summary of Total Cost of Providing All Educational Programs in Each State for 1973 Enrollment, 1973 Highest Need, and 1980 Highest Need
(in millions)

State (1)	Total Cost All Programs			
	1973 Enrollment (2)	1973 Highest Need (3)	1980 Highest Need (4)	Per Cent Change 1973–1980 (5)
Alabama	$ 495	$ 544	$ 759	53
Alaska	119	126	194	64
Arizona	518	553	839	62
Arkansas	339	364	522	54
California	4,805	5,135	8,685	81
Colorado	513	553	844	65
Connecticut	770	804	1,297	69
Delaware	144	152	244	70
Florida	1,242	1,329	2,031	63
Georgia	920	995	1,544	68
Hawaii	183	201	306	67
Idaho	163	175	243	49
Illinois	2,416	2,614	4,007	66
Indiana	1,152	1,250	1,880	63
Iowa	652	690	936	43
Kansas	413	441	626	51
Kentucky	455	499	710	56
Louisiana	717	773	1,128	57
Maine	249	267	372	49
Maryland	991	1,064	1,745	76
Massachusetts	1,240	1,326	2,020	63
Michigan	2,387	2,595	3,963	66
Minnesota	994	1,057	1,579	59
Mississippi	339	367	507	50
Missouri	868	948	1,408	62

Continued

TABLE 23—*Continued*

State (1)	1973 Enrollment (2)	Total Cost All Programs 1973 Highest Need (3)	1980 Highest Need (4)	Per Cent Change 1973–1980 (5)
Montana	$ 155	$ 168	$ 227	47
Nebraska	285	306	429	50
Nevada	118	126	220	87
New Hampshire	166	179	285	72
New Jersey	1,875	2,021	3,175	69
New Mexico	243	258	358	47
New York	5,006	5,374	8,304	66
North Carolina	962	1,063	1,573	63
North Dakota	124	133	167	35
Ohio	2,373	2,564	3,834	62
Oklahoma	452	485	724	60
Oregon	476	511	776	63
Pennsylvania	2,922	3,166	4,447	52
Rhode Island	201	217	330	64
South Carolina	523	568	802	53
South Dakota	141	152	198	41
Tennessee	617	662	956	55
Texas	2,599	2,785	4,335	67
Utah	260	279	429	65
Vermont	126	134	204	62
Virginia	918	982	1,505	64
Washington	810	872	1,406	74
West Virginia	348	374	468	34
Wisconsin	1,019	1,097	1,623	59
Wyoming	78	83	111	43
United States	$45,882	$49,380	$75,275	64

SOURCE: James R. Stultz, "The Incidence of Educational Needs and the Cost of Meeting These Needs in the United States in 1980" (Institute for Educational Finance, 1974).

TABLE 24

SUMMARY AND COMPARISON OF ADDITIONAL COST REQUIRED TO
PROVIDE PUBLIC ELEMENTARY AND SECONDARY EDUCATIONAL PROGRAMS
AT NEFP RATES IN THE UNITED STATES IN 1973 AND 1980
(in billions)

Study Cost Estimates (1)	Total Cost All Programs (2)	Estimated 1972–73 Expenditure (3)	Difference in Cost (4)	Per Cent Change (5)
1973 enrollment	$45.9	$43.5	$ 2.4	5.49
1973 highest need	49.4	43.5	5.9	13.54
1980 highest need	75.3	43.5	31.8	73.07

SOURCE: James R. Stultz, "The Incidence of Educational Needs and the Cost of Meeting These Needs in the United States in 1980" (Institute for Educational Finance, 1974).

NOTE: Percentages computed from expenditure data reported in thousands of dollars.

the total expenditure estimate. For all elementary and secondary pupils, the 1980 projected financial requirements have been estimated to be $75.3 billion, an increase of $29.8 billion over 1972–73.

The 1980 estimate for regular or basic programs is $49.7 billion, an increase of $10.5 billion over 1972–73. The remainder of the required additional funds are attributable to special programs, with kindergarten programs representing the greatest projected increase, from $1.7 billion in 1972–73 to $6.4 billion in 1980. For compensatory education the estimated required increase is from $2.2 billion in 1972–73 to $6.2 billion in 1980, for exceptional education programs from $2.1 billion in 1972–73 to $6.5 billion in 1980, and for vocational education programs from $2.8 billion in 1972–73 to $6.4 billion in 1980.

REFERENCES

1. Roe L. Johns and Edgar L. Morphet, *The Economics and Financing of Education: A Systems Approach* (Englewood Cliffs, N.J.: Prentice-Hall, Inc., 1969), p. 289.

2. Ellwood P. Cubberley, *Public Education in the United States* (Cambridge, Mass.: The Riverside Press, 1919), p. 491.

3. Johns and Morphet, p. 164.

4. Ibid., p. 289.

5. Ellwood P. Cubberley, *School Funds and Their Apportionment* (New York: Teachers College, Columbia University, 1905), p. 18.

6. Ibid., pp. 195–253.

7. Roe L. Johns, Kern Alexander, and K. Forbis Jordan, *Financing Education, Fiscal and Legal Alternatives* (Columbus, Ohio: Charles E. Merrill Publishing Company, 1972), p. 6.

8. Paul R. Mort, *The Measurement of Educational Need* (New York: Teachers College, Columbia University, 1924), p. 63.

9. Paul R. Mort and Walter C. Reusser, *Public School Finance* (New York: McGraw-Hill Book Company, Inc., 1951), p. 491.

10. Edgar L. Morphet, "Measurement of Educational Need," in *Partnership in School Finance* (Washington: National Education Association, 1966), p. 156.

11. Roe L. Johns and Kern Alexander, *Alternative Programs for Financing Education*, vol. 5 (Gainesville, Fla.: National Educational Finance Project, 1971), p. vii.

12. Kern Alexander and K. Forbis Jordan, *Financing the Public Schools of Kentucky* (Gainesville, Fla.: National Educational Finance Project, 1973).

13. *Financing the Public Schools of Delaware* (Gainesville, Fla.: National Educational Finance Project, 1973), p. 65; *Financing the Public Schools of Florida* (Gainesville, Fla.: National Educational Finance Project, 1973), pp. 66–69; *Financing the Public Schools of Kentucky*, pp. 3–8; and *Financing the Public Schools of South Dakota* (Gainesville, Fla.: National Educational Finance Project, 1973), p. vii.

14. Donald E. Embry, *Program Cost Differentials for State Financing of Indiana Public Schools* (Ball State University, 1973), pp. 96–99; Robert Clinton Craighead, *A Process Guide for the Development of an Equitable Distribution Formula for State Funds in Support of Public Education* (University of Alabama, 1972); K. Forbis Jordan, "School Support in the Future," *Compact* (April 1972), p. 11; K. Forbis Jordan, *The School Finance Reform Movement: Implications for School Business Administration* (October 1972, ERIC Microfiche ED 070 194), pp. 18–19; *Financing the Public Schools, A Search for Equality*, Phi Delta Kappa Commission of Alternative Designs for Funding Education (Bloomington, Ind.: Phi Delta Kappa, September 1973), pp. 29–32; and *Schools, People, and Money: The Need for Educational Reform, Final Report*, President's Commission on School Finance (Washington: United States Government Printing Office, 1972), p. xiii.

15. Jordan, *The School Finance Reform Movement*.

16. Richard A. Rossmiller et al., *Educational Programs for Exceptional Children: Resource Configurations and Costs*, Special Study no. 2 (Gainesville, Fla.: National Educational Finance Project, 1970), p. 28.

17. *Future Directions for School Financing* (Gainesville, Fla.: National Educational Finance Project, 1971), p. 2.

18. Johns and Alexander (1971), p. 134.

19. Ibid., pp. 270–75.

20. See Erick L. Lindman and Arthur Berchi, "Financing Vocational Education in Public Schools," *Planning to Finance Education*, vol. 3 (Gainesville, Fla.: National Educational Finance Project, 1971), p. 101–46.

21. *Financing the Public Schools of Kentucky*, p. 4.

22. "Educational Cost Differential Handbook," National Educational Finance Project (NEFP fellowship training material, 1973).

23. Johns and Alexander (1971), p. 271.

24. Daniel Gaskill Adlrich III, *An Analysis of Vocational Program Costs* (Ph.D. diss., University of California, Los Angeles, 1972); Embry, pp. 91–98; Francis William Sorensen, *A Cost Analysis of Selected Public School Special Education Systems in Illinois* (Ph.D. diss., University of Illinois, Urbana-Champaign, 1973); and Warren William Sorenson, *A Proposed System for Predicting Costs of Vocational Education Programs in The California Community Colleges* (Ph.D. diss., University of California, Los Angeles, 1972).

25. William P. McLure and Audra May Pence, *Early Childhood and Basic Elementary and Secondary Education: Needs, Programs, Demands, Costs*, Special Study no. 1 (Gainesville, Fla.: National Educational Finance Project, 1970), p. 83.

26. Busselle, pp. 11–33.

27. *Financing the Public Schools of Florida*, pp. 1–19.

28. School accounting practices did not identify and count pupils according to the proportion of time spent in the respective programs. However, according to "Dimensions of Educational Need and Program Cost Differentials," *Florida Study*, Appendix A, p. 163, these distinctions were made from various school records:

  (1) Kindergarten—1.0 pupil in ADA was counted as 1.0 FTE pupil.

(2) Exceptional child programs: full-time programs—1.0 pupil in ADA was counted as 1.0 FTE pupil; part-time programs—by definition these pupils were assumed to have spent more than half of their time in regular classes and in "special" or supplementary instruction less than half, hence they were counted as 1.0 FTE pupil for each 1.0 pupil in ADA. The "special" instruction was "added on."

(3) Compensatory programs—considered a supplement or "add-on" to the regular (basic) program, hence each 1.0 pupil in ADA equaled 1.0 FTE pupil.

(4) Vocational programs (high school: grade 7–12)—1.0 pupil in ADA taking a full-time credit load was counted as 1.0 FTE pupil. Pupils taking less than a full-time credit load were counted as fractions of full-time equivalents according to the proportion of their time spent in these programs.

29. Ibid., p. 138.

30. *Financing the Public Schools of Delaware*.

31. *Financing the Public Schools of Kentucky*, pp. 95–151.

32. *Financing the Public Schools of South Dakota*, pp. 121–22.

33. Ibid.

34. Burruss v. Wilkerson 310 F. Supp. 572 (1969) affd. mem, 397 U.S. 44, 90 S.Ct. 812 (1970); McInnis v. Shapiro, 293 F. Supp. 327, affd. mem. subnom. McInnis v. Oglivie, 394 U.S. 322, 89 S.Ct. 1197 (1969).

35. "Preliminary Projection of the Population of States: 1975 to 1990," *Current Population Reports: Population Estimates and Projections* (Washington: Government Printing Office, 1972), series P-25, no. 477, p. 1.

36. U.S. Department of Health, Education, and Welfare, Office of Education, Division of Compensatory Education, "Statistics for Title I of the Elementary and Secondary Education Act of 1965 for 1966–73 " (mimeographed).

Revenue Requirements for School Transportation Programs and School Facilities

C. M. Bernd

William K. Dickey

K. Forbis Jordan

The concepts of the weighted pupil and cost differentials discussed in other portions of this book are assumed to provide sufficient funds to support those programs and services which accrue uniformly among local school districts and are normally associated with the concept of net current expenditures, which excludes expenditures for transportation, food services, debt service, and capital outlay. Of the excluded items the two that are currently recognized as most important in assuring equality of educational opportunity and adequate funds for support of the ongoing instructional program are transportation and capital outlay or school construction.

PUPIL TRANSPORTATION

As an essential service to be provided by the schools, the need for transportation programs does not accrue evenly among all school districts within a given state. Size of the district, pupil density, and topographical features are among the factors which result in districts having to spend varying percentages of their budgets for school transportation programs.

Among the states there is a long history of transporting school children at public expense; such programs have been a part of American public education for over a century, the first program being initiated in Massachusetts in 1869. At that time towns in the state were given authority to raise money for the purpose of conveying children to and from school. Vermont followed in 1876 and Maine in 1880, and by 1900 transportation laws had been enacted in eighteen states with the rest following suit by 1919.[1] This development is outlined in Table 1.

The enactment of state educational transportation laws was accompanied by increased spending in the area. By 1920 the states were spending $14.5 million per year on pupil transportation.[2] Within the relatively short period of fifty years, a private, contractual business utilizing horse-drawn

212

wagons for conveyance grew to be a multimillion dollar public enterprise involving all the states.

How can public support and accompanying growth of pupil transportation be explained? "One of the criteria of whether an activity should be supported by public taxation or not is that, if that activity can be done more efficiently at public expense than private expense, it is a legitimate part of the community's tax program."[3] The difficulty of each family furnishing transportation to school for its children led to public transportation and its more efficient use of resources. Four additional factors have been related

TABLE 1
DATES OF FIRST TRANSPORTATION LAWS

Date	State	Date	State
1869	Massachusetts	1903	Virginia
1876	Vermont	1904	Maryland
1880	Maine	1905	Oklahoma
1885	New Hampshire	1905	Utah[a]
1889	Florida[a]	1907	Missouri
1893	Connecticut	1908	West Virginia
1894	Ohio	1909	Colorado
1895	New Jersey	1910	Mississippi
1896	New York	1911	Arkansas
1897	Iowa	1911	Georgia
1897	Nebraska	1911	Illinois
1897	Pennsylvania	1911	North Carolina
1897	Wisconsin	1912	Kentucky
1898	Rhode Island	1912	South Carolina
1899	Kansas	1912	Arizona
1899	North Dakota	1913	Idaho
1899	South Dakota	1913	Tennessee
1899	Indiana[b]	1915	Nevada
1901	California	1915	Alabama[c]
1901	Minnesota	1915	Texas[d]
1901	Washington	1916	Louisiana[e]
1903	Michigan	1917	New Mexico
1903	Montana	1919	Delaware
1903	Oregon	1919	Wyoming[g]

SOURCE: J. F. Abel, *Consolidation of Schools and Transportation of Pupils*, Bulletin no. 41 (Washington: U.S. Department of the Interior, Bureau of Education, 1923), p. 22.

a. Assumed under the powers of county boards.
b. Transportation was carried on in Indiana as early as 1888 under the general powers of township trustees.
c. Transportation was carried on in Mobile County earlier than 1915.
d. Transportation was carried on before 1915 under the general powers granted boards in 1905.
e. Dates to 1902 without specific legal authorization.
f. Assumed in the powers of county boards.
g. Carried on under a broad interpretation of the law.

to the growth of pupil transportation besides efficiency: compulsory attendance legislation, school district consolidation, widespread use of the motor vehicle, and the extension of paved roads throughout the country.

Compulsory attendance laws grew from the belief that society would benefit if the child received a minimum amount of education. The enactment of these laws meant that public schools would have to be built within walking distance of pupils or transportation would have to be furnished. Many schools were built within walking distance, but "factors were at work to decrease the number of schools; it gradually became evident that it would not be practicable to place educational opportunity within walking distance of all."[4]

The expense and inefficiency of the one-room school led to the consolidation of small school districts into larger ones with broader population and revenue bases. Consolidation led to a need to transport pupils to school because of longer distances between school and home. Consolidation is probably the most important single factor accounting for the use of public funds to transport school children in the United States. This movement began seriously in the middle 1800s. "From about 1840 to 1880 . . . the principle of centralization of schools was established in urban communities, extended to other independent districts and began in rural sections."[5]

As with transportation, consolidation began in New England. City districts were the first to consolidate, usually under special laws or acts of incorporation. After a state had two or three consolidated districts, the advantages became apparent, causing others to follow. The movement spread from the northeast to the rest of the country. Consolidation succeeded for a number of reasons related to educational quality and efficiency. State-wide educational surveys pointed out that "without exception one room and one teacher schools were the most ineffective in the United States." The growth of the high school hastened consolidation. "In 1890 there were 2,526 public high schools, enrolling 202,963 students; in 1920 there were 14,326, enrolling 1,857,155 students."[6] High school growth also increased demand for pupil transportation because of the relatively greater per pupil expense of providing these programs. A comprehensive high school within walking distance of every student was a fiscal impossibility.

Efficiency and quality factors, as well as citizen demand for better educational programs, gave consolidation and school transportation additional impetus through the late 1940s to the present. Pupil transportation has increased while the number of school districts has declined. "During 1968–69 more than 18,000,000 pupils were transported in 238,000 vehicles at a cost of over $900,000,000 excluding large sums for capital outlay."[7]

As the automobile became an established element in the American culture, negotiable roads became a necessity. Mileage of roads with an all-weather surface increased from 387,000 in 1921 to 2,557,000 in 1960. Numbers of pupils transported rose from 594,000 to 12,700,989.[8] The number of pupils being transported in the United States by 1969 was 18,467,944.[9]

A more recent change in American society which has affected the need for local school district transportation programs has been the rapid urbanization of the nation. Much of the original support for transportation at public expense can be traced to the school consolidation movement, and state aid programs for transportation have historically been rurally oriented. Minimum distances for state reimbursement have been determined on the basis of reasonable walking distances in rural areas along lightly traveled roads. These reimbursement regulations are grossly unrealistic for urban and suburban areas in which pupils must cross heavily traveled multilane traffic arteries serving urban areas. The problem has been furthered by the development of limited access highways which often split local school attendance areas. Most state aid programs for transportation do not contain recognition of problems confronted by urban and suburban districts which, in developing their transportation programs, must consider the safety of students going to and from school rather than an arbitrary distance between home and school.

Present Pupil Transportation Programs

A recent study of state programs for financing pupil transportation showed a great variety among states.[10] All but five states were assuming some financial responsibility for pupil transportation with eighteen including transportation expenses in their foundation program. Fifteen states were using flat grants in transportation finance plans while twelve paid 100 per cent of approved transportation costs. Allowable transportation expenses were paid by twenty-eight states by reimbursement. Different formulas for reimbursement were used by the states with seventeen including bus miles traveled in these formulas.

The use of the density factor for transportation cost calculation was fairly common among the states. Density was usually calculated by one of two methods—number of students transported divided by number of square miles in the district or number of students transported divided by bus miles to and from school.

Allowances for adverse road conditions have been de-emphasized in state plans for financing pupil transportation; only seven states were granting them. This was undoubtedly due to the general improvements in roads throughout the country.

Minimum distance requirements were found in forty states, with a 1.5-mile average for elementary students and a 2-mile limit for secondary pupils. Some states considered hazardous conditions in setting minimum distance requirements for transporting pupils.

In twenty-eight states, state bids or similar purchasing procedures assisted school districts in the purchase of buses.

These provisions for funding transportation give the impression that states were bearing the main burden of pupil transportation cost; however,

TABLE 2
PUPIL TRANSPORTATION, PUBLIC ELEMENTARY AND SECONDARY SCHOOLS, 1930–70

Year	Number Transported[a]	Per Cent Transported	Total Expenditure[b]	Cost Per Pupil Transported
1930	1,903,000	7.4	$ 54,823,000	$28.81
1940	4,144,000	16.3	83,283,000	20.10
1950	6,947,000	27.7	214,504,000	30.88
1960	12,225,000	37.6	486,338,000	39.78
1970	18,199,000	43.4	1,218,755,000	66.96

SOURCE: U.S. Office of Education, *Digest of Educational Statistics*, annual.

a. At public expense; figures are for enrollment prior to 1960. Figures for 1960 and 1970 refer to average daily attendance.
b. Excludes capital outlay.

more than one-half of local district transportation expenditures were being paid out of local funds if all states were considered.[11]

Expenditures for Pupil Transportation

Expenditures for pupil transportation have increased steadily since 1930, as have the number and percentage of pupils transported. The data in Table 2 show an increase in expenditure from $54,823,000 in 1930 to $1,218,755,000 in 1970 (excluding capital outlay). This is over a 2,000 per cent increase.

The number of pupils transported has risen from 1,903,000 to 18,199,000 over the same forty-year span. This represents a 956 per cent increase. Per cent of enrollment transported has risen from 7.4 per cent to 43.4 per cent. Cost per pupil has risen 232 per cent, from $28.81 to $66.96. Much of the growth in per pupil and total expenditures can be traced to inflation.

Table 3 contains more detail on the growth of pupil transportation from 1954–55 to 1968–69. (Data in tables may not agree because of inclusion or exclusion of capital outlay in expenditures, rounding, or different attendance measures.) The number of pupils transported increased from

9,509,699 in 1954–55 to 18,467,944 in 1968–69, a 94 per cent increase in that fourteen-year span. Per pupil expenditures rose from $34.60 to $48.81, or 41 per cent. Total expenditures, excluding capital outlay, rose from $329,035,047 to $901,353,107 in the fourteen years, a 174 per cent increase. These increases are not as striking if the impact of inflation is considered. The use of 1957–59 dollars as a basis for comparison reduces the increase in per pupil cost during the time period to 7 per cent.[12] At the same time,

TABLE 3

GROWTH OF SCHOOL TRANSPORTATION IN THE UNITED STATES, 1954–59

Year	Number of Pupils Transported	Cost Per Pupil	Expenditure (excluding capital outlay)
1968–69	18,467,944	$48.81	$901,353,107
1967–68	17,271,718	47.63	822,595,699
1966–67	16,684,922	45.77	763,600,617
1965–66	16,423,396	42.40	696,325,421
1964–65	15,413,000	41.69	642,627,000
1963–64	15,559,524	39.35	612,310,333
1962–63	14,247,753	40.57	578,017,634
1961–62	13,687,547	39.46	540,017,634
1960–61	13,106,779	38.59	505,754,515
1959–60	12,700,989	37.34	474,202,128
1958–59	12,021,372	36.72	441,402,595
1957–58	11,343,132	36.99	419,539,863
1956–57	10,683,643	25.83	382,751,973
1955–56	10,199,276	34.94	356,349,783
1954–55	9,509,699	34.60	329,035,047

SOURCE: Dewey H. Stollar, "Pupil Transportation," in *Planning to Finance Education*, vol. 3, eds. R. L. Johns, Kern Alexander, and K. Forbis Jordan (Gainesville, Fla.: National Educational Finance Project, 1971), p. 340.

1954–55 expenditures are increased by 6 per cent, and 1968–69 expenditures are reduced by 19 per cent.

Transportation costs have not risen drastically in relation to other educational expenditures. During the two decades from 1950 to 1970, total pupil transportation expenditures have risen 129 per cent less than total educational expenditures and 179 per cent less than instructional costs.[13]

Transportation figures for 1971–72 are given in Table 4. Number of pupils transported at public expense rose to 20,047,589, an increase of 9 per cent from 1970. Total expenditures rose 8 per cent from 1970 to $1,324,740,407, while 1971–72 cost per pupil averaged $65.75 (Tables 3 and 4). In 1971–72, Wyoming and Alaska spent the most per pupil on transportation, $150.47 and $169.96, while North Carolina spent the least, $33.78.

TABLE 4
PUPIL TRANSPORTATION SUMMARY BY STATES, 1971–72

	Number of Pupils Transported	Total Expenditure Including Capital Outlay	Expenditure Per Pupil Transported
Totals	20,047,589	$1,324,740,407	$65.76
Alabama	410,252	18,400,000	44.85
Alaska	32,303	5,490,150	169.96
Arizona	159,098	10,799,297	67.88
Arkansas	254,264	9,557,513	37.59
California	928,972	76,663,647	82.53
Colorado	180,747	13,760,705	76.13
Connecticut	395,000	27,600,000	69.87
Delaware	79,837	5,739,213	71.89
District of Columbia	3,796	112,209	29.56
Florida	632,478	28,819,900	45.57
Georgia	596,991	30,800,000	51.59
Hawaii	28,158	3,200,000	113.64
Idaho	89,562	6,014,657	67.16
Illinois	760,049	54,258,727	71.39
Indiana	638,250	42,665,945	66.85
Iowa	286,921	25,282,858	88.12[c]
Kansas	167,104	16,696,716	99.92[c]
Kentucky	429,461	20,242,695	47.14
Louisiana	562,045	40,078,675	71.31
Maine	151,235	9,854,623	65.16
Maryland	497,094	33,256,521	66.90
Massachusetts	559,381	50,516,474	90.31
Michigan	900,000	52,500,000	58.33[a]
Minnesota	536,199	34,973,864	65.23[c]
Mississippi	295,359	16,165,841	54.73
Missouri	506,907	35,415,513	69.87[c]
Montana	54,626	7,510,715	137.49[b]
Nebraska	60,643	8,338,474	137.50
Nevada	51,064	3,217,188	63.00
New Hampshire	94,415	6,317,789	66.92
New Jersey	605,000	58,026,314	92.61
New Mexico	125,976	8,866,762	70.38
New York	1,524,351	134,771,460	88.41
North Carolina	722,714	24,410,659	33.78
North Dakota	59,493	7,995,579	134.40
Ohio	1,247,110	65,720,930	52.70
Oklahoma	238,167	16,817,598	70.61
Oregon	249,966	13,404,837	53.63
Pennsylvania	1,356,351	85,979,858	63.39
Rhode Island	82,483	3,630,619	44.02[b]
South Carolina	378,000	14,000,000	37.04
South Dakota	54,797	6,795,585	124.01
Tennessee	447,993	21,340,228	47.64
Texas	611,721	27,515,533	44.98
Utah	92,506	5,604,374	60.58
Vermont	68,053	5,104,886	75.01
Virginia	660,207	30,967,378	46.91

Continued

TABLE 4—*Continued*

	Number of Pupils Transported	Total Expenditure Including Capital Outlay	Expenditure Per Pupil Transported
Washington	376,519	$31,570,419	$ 83.85
West Virginia	272,447	18,194,516	66.78
Wisconsin	504,753	47,744,704	94.59
Wyoming	26,771	4,028,288	150.47

SOURCE: National Association of State Directors of Pupil Transportation Services, Washington, 1972.

a. All figures estimated.
b. Information for 1970–71 was used.
c. Does not include capital outlay.

(The District of Columbia was excluded.) Alaska spent over five times as much per pupil as North Carolina (Table 4).

In general, states with greater number of pupils per vehicle spend less per pupil than states with fewer pupils per vehicle. Sparsely populated states also tend to spend more per pupil on transportation. In many cases, low expenditures for instruction are accompanied by high expenditures for transportation.

Future Status

Predictions of school transportation needs for the 1980s, if based on K–12 enrollment figures alone, would show a decreasing need for this service. Table 5 has the predicted K–12 average daily membership (ADM) for 1980. Also shown is predicted number of students to be transported for the same year. These are relatively conservative predictions in that they use percentage of students transported in 1970, exclude preschool children,

TABLE 5
PROJECTED ADM, NUMBER OF PUPILS TO BE TRANSPORTED,
AND TRANSPORTATION COSTS, 1973 AND 1980

Year	ADM	Transported	Cost Per Pupil	Total Cost
1973	45,237,282	19,632,038	$68.06	$1,336,220,639
1980	42,485,859	18,438,862	86.59	1,596,621,129

SOURCE: Bureau of Census unpublished population projections; U.S. Office of Education, *Digest of Educational Statistics*, annual.

NOTE: Total number transported based on 1970 U.S. average per cent transported. Base for per student cost was 1971–72 data with calculations based on an annual increase in per student cost of 3.5 per cent.

and are not weighted to include those increases which will accrue from increased busing to achieve racial balance.

The number of children in preschool in 1965 was 3,407,000, which was 27.1 per cent of the three- to five-year-old population. This had increased to 4,104,000, or 37.5 per cent, of this population by 1970. A further increase is shown by 1972 figures at 4,231,000, or 41 per cent, of this population.[14] By 1980 this population will have increased by 10,347,000.[15] Involvement by the public schools in early childhood education will increase transportation need in areas where these programs are least developed.

Cost for pupil transportation will increase through the 1980s. Table 5 shows predicted total and per pupil transportation costs through 1980. The number of pupils transported was derived from projected K–12 ADM for public school children. Using the percentage transported in 1970, it was projected that approximately 19.6 million pupils were transported in 1972–73 and that 18.4 million would be transported in 1979–80. A review of the pattern of expenditures for the previous years indicated that the cost per transported pupil had been increasing at the rate of 3.5 per cent per year, an amount somewhat lower than would have been expected. Using these two rather conservative estimates, the cost for pupil transportation was projected to be slightly less than $1.6 billion in 1980, an increase of $260 million over the 1973 estimate. If present inflationary trends continue, the costs could be considerably higher. In addition, the pattern of school transportation programs could be changed drastically by various social changes, technological developments, court decisions, and state legislation.

Program Cost Elements

Several state programs for financing pupil transportation have been rooted, at least indirectly, in the work of Mort, Burns, and Johns. These researchers sought to use population density as an independent variable for the assessment of transportation need and cost.

Mort introduced the idea of density into the problem of determining the need for school transportation in his *Measurement of Educational Need*. The cornerstone of his analysis of educational costs was a two-group scheme. Group one consisted of costs that were equal for all classrooms or teacher units of all communities. Group two included the costs of special provisions, such as transportation, which were not required of all communities.[16]

"Mort attempted no fundamental solution for the problem of measuring transportation costs"; nevertheless, his work was instructive.[17] Two suggestions were given for the funding of transportation. One was to ". . .

consider all rural school population as if it were attending one teacher schools, assuming that the extra allotment to consolidated schools on the basis of the one teacher schools that they supplant would take care of transportation."[18] The assumption was that consolidated schools incurred a larger transportation expense than one-room schools. On the other hand, one-room schools were deemed by Mort as having greater need so they were allotted greater weight in relation to financial entitlement. The result of his plan was to provide more state funds to consolidated rural schools to take care of transportation costs.

Mort's alternate suggestion was to "measure educational need represented by transportation" on the basis of actual previous expenditures. These expenditures were transformed into relative cost measures by subtracting total group-two costs from total cost of the minimum program, and then dividing total educational need by the result and multiplying by transportation cost. Density was introduced into the computation indirectly by Mort's linking of transportation to group-one costs based on density. Typical transportation costs were preferred because funding on actual cost "would favor a consistently high cost for transportation in the state aid program." Mort called for an index capable of measuring pupil transportation costs.[19]

Burns attempted to develop such an index. His ideas were based on the contention that a great many factors involved in transportation cost could be summarized by an index. A variable was sought which was not susceptible to local manipulation. Burns considered such factors as the number of pupils transported divided by the ADA, the area of the county divided by the number of school buildings, and the population density of the district. Certain deficiencies in Burns' work were subsequently identified by Johns. Chief among these was Burns' reliance on an "undiscovered relationship between cost variances and area per school building."[20] Johns contended that it was "unsafe to use any weighting factor for cost whose influence is not known."[21] Another criticism was that Burns' plan did not lend itself to effective administrative control over funds distributed for local school district transportation programs.

In attempting to remedy the deficiencies of Burns' work, Johns used data from five states and found that density of school population was predictive of per pupil transportation cost. This relationship could be used in a state formula for funding transportation programs. Both Burns and Johns sought to measure transportation need and cost by using factors beyond the control of the local district. Johns originated the curve of best fit to determine the state-recognized transportation cost per pupil.[22]

The National Educational Finance Project has carried forward the earlier work which contributed to the development of an efficiency oriented transportation support formula.[23] This basic method has been recommended:

    1. Determine the average transportation cost per pupil per day on an individual district basis.

    2. Determine the density of transported pupils per linear route mile in each district.

    3. Generate an equation giving the line of best fit in the form of $Y = aX^b$ using all districts' density in cost per pupil, with Y equaling formula adjusted cost and X reflecting the density of each school district.

    4. Determine the formula adjusted cost for each district by substituting the density of that district for X in the equation $Y = aX^b$.

    5. Compute the allowable transportation cost per pupil on the basis of the formula adjusted cost (Y) times number of days transported.

    6. Include a special weight of 5.0 for exceptional or physically handicapped children, who require special high cost equipment.

Criteria for Evaluating State Transportation Aid Formulas

The most important criterion for a state aid formula for funding pupil transportation is that recognition be given to the legitimate factors affecting transportation cost. The main objective of the formula should be to eliminate economic, social, or geographical inequalities which hinder a school district in the transportation of its students. However, caution should be exercised to provide assurances that the formula does not discourage desirable reorganization of local units and attendance areas.

States have attempted to mitigate factors causing variations in the cost of service by funding on the basis of formulas which recognize sparsity of population, road conditions, depreciation, and similar factors. These factors are essentially beyond the control of the local district. Three primary expenditure categories which constitute a major portion of school transportation costs are capital outlay expenditures, maintenance and operation expenditures, and drivers' salaries. State funds for capital outlay will encourage districts to purchase buses and equipment that meet state specifications and also to utilize various kinds of safety equipment.

A second criterion for the state aid formula is that it should be simple while retaining accuracy. A simple formula allows local administrators to estimate the state entitlement with greater ease while eliminating complicated recordkeeping or extensive statistical work at the district level. Clerical requirements at the state level are also reduced by a simple formula.

Simplicity, while important, should not outrank accuracy in the state formula. The simpler the formula, the more likely will be the prospect of inaccurate measurement of some extremes of need at the local level. The ideal formula combines simplicity with the ability to recognize local variations in need. The goal of the formula is to provide sufficient funds to enable the local unit, with reasonable local effort, to operate a safe, economical, efficient, sound, and practical system of transportation for all pupils who should be transported. The formula should also stimulate the attainment of desirable standards for school bus equipment, maintenance and operation, and employment of qualified personnel. In the earlier discussions of transportation funding, stress was placed on the desirability of eliminating extensive records; however, sufficient accounting records and reports should be maintained to provide the basic data needed for computation of the state formula. There is also general agreement that local districts should maintain sufficient maintenance records to assure safe and economical performance of equipment.

The third criterion for a state formula for funding pupil transportation is that it not be susceptible to local manipulation. If the school district can control the factors which affect its own funding for transportation, it may alter those factors to suit its advantage at the cost of reduced efficiency. An example of this would be the operation of inefficient routes when mileage is reimbursed by the state. A district also might purchase unneeded equipment with state funds. If the state uses factors in its formula which are susceptible to local manipulation, it must exercise sufficient control and review to prevent abuses.

Fourth, certain aspects of the state funding program must be based on past experience. One may theorize as to what some elements of the transportation program should cost, but a tremendous amount of evidence would be required to determine a defensible method for computing such costs as salaries. On the other hand, past experience may reflect inefficient operations which will inflate costs unnecessarily. In general, the use of the state average cost in some aspects of the funding will serve to promote efficiency.

The fifth criterion is that the state plan for funding pupil transportation should be as objective as possible in the determination of local need. State standards should be applied to local districts equally unless extreme hardship is a consequence. In some cases local needs may be so different from state requirements that subjective judgments will be necessary to achieve equality of educational opportunity for the students of the affected district. A state plan should cover such contingencies with workable policies.

The basic purpose of a pupil transportation funding formula is to compensate for the additional burden that falls upon school districts which provide pupil transportation. A sixth criterion related to the development of the formula is that the formula recognize additional costs incurred through the transportation of special groups such as handicapped or vocational students. Another matter of concern is the degree to which the state formula encourages schools to broaden and extend the school program through the use of school buses for field trips and related instructional activities.

Seventh, the state pupil transportation plan should promote efficiency at the local level. This can be done through the application of state average cost to funding programs where appropriate. Efficiency can also be promoted by state approval and monitoring of local programs. Special caution should be exercised to provide flexibility at the local district level which will permit adjustments in the transportation program so that the overall quality of the program will not suffer because of increases in the number of pupils, school district reorganization, or school consolidation, which require, in most instances, additional transportation services.

SCHOOL FACILITIES' NEEDS AND COSTS

The relationship between school facilities and instructional programs has long been recognized, but is of even greater importance in current educational programs which are so dependent upon laboratory facilities and various electronic equipment as supporting elements for the instructional program. Since the end of World War II the need for school facilities has been a constant problem confronting American public education. During the forties school construction was deferred because of the war effort, and the baby boom of the postwar period merely added to the magnitude of the problem.

In his 1950 budget message the president recognized the shortage of school facilities throughout the nation and expressed concern over the overall extent of the shortage, the particular areas in which it existed, and the capacity of state and local governments to alleviate the problem without federal assistance.[24] This expressed concern was largely responsible for the enactment of Public Law 815 which authorized the first comprehensive survey of the nation's public elementary and secondary school facilities. Over a period of four years, $3 million was allocated to the states for making inventories of public elementary and secondary school facilities, surveying the need for construction programs, and studying the adequacy of state and local resources available to meet school facility requirements.

Results of the Office of Education's *Report of the Long-Range Planning Phase of the School Facilities Survey* indicated a need to provide 476,000 additional classrooms by the fall of 1959 if the public elementary and secondary students in the United States were to be adequately housed.[25] The findings of this survey provide a reference point from which to review the progress states made during the late 1950s toward meeting facility needs.

In 1954, the Office of Education began collecting and publishing information pertaining to public school classrooms in the nation. Table 6 presents historical data of fall statistics in school housing for 1954–55 through 1959–60. As indicated in the table some progress was made in alleviating the classroom shortage between 1954 and 1959 with the construction of 333,556 classrooms and the abandonment of 76,738, representing a net gain of 256,818 classrooms. The discrepancy between the projected need from the earlier study was attributable to the high population projections in the study. In the *Report of the Long-Range Planning Phase of the School Facilities Survey*, the number of elementary and secondary pupils was projected to be 37,363,000; however, actual enrollment was 36,087,000, or 1,276,000 fewer students (3.5 per cent).[26]

The combination of available classrooms in 1954–55 plus the projected need for additional classrooms in 1959–60 would have required the availability of 1,472,246 classrooms at the start of the 1959–60 school year. Reducing the total number by the 3.5 per cent, representing the over-projection, would suggest an adjusted need for 1,420,717 classrooms in the fall of 1959. When this figure is compared with the number of classrooms available in 1959, the data indicate that a shortage of 185,286 classrooms existed.

The next major survey of school facility needs was conducted in 1962 by the Office of Education.[27] During the years since 1954 the Office of Education had been publishing data related to the status of school facilities, but the information was collected using the principle of local and / or state determination for the count of crowded or unsatisfactory classrooms. Under these conditions data were not comparable from year to year or from state to state.

The *National Inventory of School Facilities and Personnel, Spring 1962* stimulated a demand for more detailed information on school housing. During the 1964–65 school year, a survey was conducted by the Office of Education's Bureau of Educational Research and Development and the National Center for Educational Statistics to provide factual information on the need for additional classrooms and the physical condition of existing classrooms in the nation.[28] This survey was based on a sample of 18,000

TABLE 6

HISTORICAL SUMMARY OF FALL SURVEY STATISTICS ON ENROLLMENT, TEACHERS, AND SCHOOL HOUSING

Item	1954–55	1955–56	1956–57	1957–58	1958–59	1959–60
Number of publicly owned instruction rooms at beginning of school year[c]	*996,246	1,043,246	1,105,433	1,184,104	1,231,952	1,286,960
Number of instruction rooms completed during school year	60,000	63,283	68,660	72,070	69,543	69,400
Number of rooms abandoned for instructional purposes during school year	13,000	14,114	15,851	17,399	16,374	17,800
Total number of additional instruction rooms needed for housing pupils enrolled at beginning of school year	a	a	159,800	143,200	141,900	135,264
To accommodate pupils in excess of normal capacity	a	a	80,300	65,100	65,800	62,543
To replace unsatisfactory facilities	a	a	79,500	78,100	76,100	72,721
Per cent of additional instruction rooms needed						
To accommodate pupils in excess of normal capacity	a	a	50.3	45.5	46.4	46.2
To replace unsatisfactory facilities	a	a	49.7	54.5	53.6	53.8
Total number of instruction rooms scheduled for completion during school year	60,132[b]	62,429	69,609	70,960	68,930	61,727

SOURCE: Office of Education, *Statistics on Enrollment, Teachers, and School Housing in Full-Time Public Elementary and Secondary Day Schools* (Washington, 1962).

* Estimate.
a. Data not available; item not included in annual survey.
b. Excludes Hawaii.
c. Incomplete; total for states reporting.
d. Because of changes in school plant inventories, the number of instruction rooms at the beginning of a particular school year is not always the sum of the number of rooms available at the beginning of the previous year, plus rooms completed, and minus rooms abandoned during the previous school year.

school plants which at the time represented approximately 20 per cent of all school plants in the nation. With regard to the number of schoolrooms, the survey reported a median number of students per schoolroom of 27.5 and determined that 107,000 additional classrooms would have brought all school facilities to the national mean. An additional 78,000 classrooms were identified as makeshift, nonpermanent, and offsite; if school officials were to have ceased using these facilities, 78,000 classrooms would have been needed to replace them.

Information reported by *Conditions of Public School Plants* was based on at least three measures of need:

1. A pupil / classroom median of 27.5 for the nation and replacement of makeshift, nonpermanent, and offsite classrooms would have required 185,000 additional classrooms.

2. A pupil / classroom ratio of 25.0 pupils per room in elementary and 20.0 pupils in secondary school plants and replacements of makeshift, nonpermanent, and offsite classrooms would have required 376,000 more classrooms.

3. Appraisals of local officials as to their classroom needs and replacement of makeshift, nonpermanent, and offsite classrooms revealed a need for 187,000 classrooms.

No comparison can be made of the measures of need identified by *Conditions of Public School Plants* and information supplied by the U.S. Office of Education. Data reported by the U.S. Office of Education on classrooms needed to accommodate pupils in excess of normal building capacity and to replace unsatisfactory facilities were not collected after the 1963–64 school year when the need was reported to be 124,300 classrooms.[29] Regardless of the measure chosen, it was evident that a need for additional school facilities existed in 1964–65 and the classroom gap identified in 1954 was not closing.

Current Facility Needs

The most recent assessment of the need for school facilities was a projection from 1968–69 through 1972–73 released by the Office of Education in May 1968.[30] Projected needs were reported for preschool through the junior community college level by population distribution (urban, suburban, and rural), educational level (preschool, elementary, and secondary), and educational program (disadvantaged, handicapped, vocational, and general). The survey relied extensively on the previous survey, *Conditions of Public School Plants*, with respect to the number of new classrooms required to eliminate makeshift classrooms, replace facilities that have four or more site or building defects, and improve pupil / room ratios from those existing at the time of the survey.

Several assumptions which were made in projecting school facility needs for 1972–73 were standards for gross square footage and pupil / room ratios. The gross square footage needs for elementary and secondary students were considered to be 70 and 115, respectively. Pupil / room ratios for various instructional programs were established for both the elementary and secondary levels. Further assumptions were made in the projection of future enrollment trends for total public school population and the percentage of the total population enrolled in each of the instructional programs. Estimates were made for preschool enrollments as well as for disadvantaged, handicapped, and vocational students. Total enrollments were expected to increase between 1967–72 at the same rate as between 1960–67.

The findings of this projection indicated that a public elementary and secondary classroom backlog of 519,300 existed during the 1967–68 school year and 251,200 additional classrooms would have to be constructed by 1972–73 if students were to be adequately housed. The progress which had been made toward meeting the school facility needs identified in 1967–68 was difficult to measure, although the use of *Projections of Public School Facilities Needs* and U.S. Office of Education information on instructional rooms available and in use during the 1971–72 school year provided an estimate.

The Projections of Public School Facilities Needs indicated that 1,709,000 classrooms were available in 1967–68. At this time, the backlog of classroom need was estimated to be 519,300. In projecting the needs for 1971–72, the study assumed a population of 48,679,000 students in 1971–72. This estimate proved to be excessive, for the actual enrollment was 46,081,000, representing a difference of 2,598,000 pupils, or 5.3 per cent. The combination of the 1967–68 backlog and the facilities required to house the actual enrollment increase dictated a need for 2,315,000 public elementary and secondary classrooms in the fall of 1971. The Office of Education reported that 1,918,000 classrooms were available in the fall of 1971,[31] indicating a shortage of 397,000 classrooms. At the beginning of the 1971–72 school year, the 1959 school facility needs of 185,286 classrooms had increased by 114 per cent to 397,000 classrooms.

NEFP Survey of School Facility Needs and Costs

The documentation of school facility needs in the United States has become more difficult within the last ten years. Prior to the 1964–65 school year the Office of Education discontinued collecting data on the number of classrooms needed to accommodate pupils in excess of normal capacity and to replace unsatisfactory facilities. Scarcity of information became more acute when the Office of Education discontinued collection of data on the number of classrooms constructed and abandoned during the school year 1971–72. Most recently, the Office of Education has discontinued the collection of all information on school facilities.

As a result of the lack of current information on the number of classrooms presently being used to house the public elementary and secondary student population in the nation and the need for additional classrooms, the NEFP conducted the National School Facilities Survey. The purpose of the survey was to arrive at a school facility needs measure from data supplied by the state education agencies. Information requested from the states included public elementary and secondary school enrollments, classrooms presently being used to house enrollments, and classrooms which could be described as makeshift, improvised, temporary, or obsolete.

Table 7 has a summary of 1972–73 public elementary and secondary enrollments, classrooms, and pupil / classroom ratios for kindergarten, grades 1–8, and grades 9–12 for the nation. Enrollments were secured from state education agencies, with the exception of Georgia and Texas. Enrollment data for these states were obtained from the U.S. Office of Education. Enrollment information obtained indicated that 46,849,722 students were enrolled in public elementary and secondary schools in 1972–73. In arriving at this figure, the kindergarten enrollments, reported as full-time equivalents in Table 7, were doubled to reflect the number of students attending kindergarten programs. In comparison, enrollment reported by the U.S. Office of Education for the same period was 45,754,000 students or 2.3 per cent less.[32]

Information on classrooms used to house public elementary and secondary students during the 1972–73 school year was requested for kindergarten, grades 1–8, and grades 9–12. Many states supplied information on total classrooms, but few kept facility inventories by grade level. In these cases, classrooms were assigned to kindergarten, grades 1–8, or grades 9–12 in proportion to the respective enrollments at these grade levels. Nine states were unable to provide information on the number of classrooms being used to house public school students in their states. The available classrooms in these states were estimated by securing the most recent school facility information the state had reported to the U.S. Office of Education and calculating the expected 1972–73 classrooms based upon enrollment increases. In estimating the expected 1972–73 classrooms for the nine states involved, it was not necessary to use U.S. Office of Education information before the 1969–70 school year.

TABLE 7
Enrollment, Classrooms, and Pupil Classroom Ratios for Kindergarten, Grades 1–8, and 9–12—United States and District of Columbia, 1972–73

State	Enrollment Kindergarten	Classrooms Kindergarten	Pupil / Class-Room Ratio Kindergarten	Enrollment 1–8	Classrooms 1–8	Pupil / Class-Room Ratio 1–8	Enrollment 9–12	Classrooms 9–12	Pupil / Class-Room Ratio 9–12
Alabama	4,139	207	20.0	563,320	20,528	27.4	245,081	11,169	21.9
Alaska	5,417	A 215	25.2	55,991	A 2,227	25.1	20,171	A 803	25.1
Arizona	30,565	A 1,308	23.4	309,368	13,235	23.4	126,259	A 5,402	23.4
Arkansas	2,010	84	23.9	322,148	14,558	22.1	136,904	6,187	22.1
California	310,143	F 12,243	25.3	2,813,711	F 108,438	25.9	1,377,124	F 54,219	25.4
Colorado	36,614	A 1,455	25.2	358,439	15,525	23.1	162,275	A 7,277	22.3
Connecticut	47,704	G 2,056	23.2	473,516	G 19,684	24.1	188,120	G 7,638	24.6
Delaware	4,256	A 193	22.1	84,217	A 3,816	22.1	41,589	A 1,885	22.1
District of Columbia	11,167	A 463	24.1	105,518	A 4,374	24.1	25,828	A 1,071	24.1
Florida	D 54,444	1,314	41.1	1,092,572	27,460	39.8	483,382	12,637	38.3
Georgia	7,587	E 458	16.6	D 769,506	E 32,517	23.7	305,599	E 12,824	23.8
Hawaii	12,372	496	24.9	116,003	4,308	26.9	D 53,178	1,905	27.9
Idaho	0	0	0.0	124,549	B 5,206	23.9	60,114	B 2,828	21.3
Illinois	82,610	3,755	22.0	1,478,351	59,122	25.0	704,056	35,203	20.0
Indiana	76,609	1,771	21.6	775,319	29,977	25.9	367,542	12,803	28.7
Iowa	45,803	A 2,160	21.2	403,479	A 19,032	21.2	196,663	A 9,276	21.2
Kansas	32,969	A 1,413	23.3	297,564	A 12,722	23.4	152,959	11,826	12.9
Kentucky	5,582	A 224	24.9	510,167	A 20,436	25.0	219,056	A 8,774	25.0
Louisiana	34,065	A 1,232	27.7	595,031	A 23,418	25.4	243,670	14,172	17.2
Maine	17,568	633	27.8	170,110	6,398	26.6	77,604	3,500	22.2
Maryland	30,271	E 931	28.8	583,124	E 23,138	25.2	275,282	E 10,868	25.3
Massachusetts	66,193	E 2,859	23.2	760,057	E 30,502	24.9	356,602	E 14,298	24.9
Michigan	79,567	3,183	25.0	1,312,807	48,885	26.9	651,556	29,148	22.4
Minnesota	31,325	1,846	17.0	560,584	17,505	32.0	285,710	25,591	11.2
Mississippi	764	37	20.6	376,696	12,816	29.4	148,435	9,738	15.2
Missouri	73,677	A 2,877	25.6	692,726	27,050	25.6	316,341	A 12,353	25.6
Montana	3,288	165	19.9	113,880	A 5,740	19.8	55,168	A 3,077	17.9
Nebraska	22,583	A 1,326	17.0	203,430	A 11,948	17.0	102,363	A 6,013	17.0

Nevada	4,185	B 175	23.9	63,499	B 2,500	25.4	56,985	B 2,400	23.7
New Hampshire	4,606	A 160	28.8	115,135	A 3,845	29.9	48,353	A 3,037	15.9
New Jersey	106,723	A 4,337	24.6	970,836	A 39,455	24.6	525,342	A 21,351	24.6
New Mexico	7,666	A 382	20.0	191,726	A 9,552	20.1	88,688	A 4,418	20.1
New York	132,983	6,497	20.5	2,163,440	90,803	23.8	1,088,537	39,773	27.4
North Carolina	13,731	566	24.3	820,222	33,646	24.4	365,202	14,978	24.4
North Dakota	1,095	A 58	18.9	92,129	A 4,877	18.9	47,216	A 2,499	18.9
Ohio	83,003	3,721	22.3	1,493,205	59,538	25.1	756,513	29,769	25.4
Oklahoma	19,833	G 863	23.0	404,149	G 16,207	24.9	193,000	G 10,013	19.3
Oregon	10,972	B 323	34.0	327,471	B 13,391	24.5	160,265	B 10,287	15.6
Pennsylvania	82,870	A 4,184	19.8	A 1,445,884	A 50,911	28.4	A 757,552	A 40,380	18.8
Rhode Island	6,729	299	22.5	103,941	3,957	26.3	70,439	2,815	25.0
South Carolina	10,624	376	28.3	401,347	17,604	22.8	241,777	11,270	21.5
South Dakota	9,236	A 440	21.0	101,125	A 4,817	21.0	52,037	A 2,479	21.0
Tennessee	26,822	1,493	18.0	618,701	21,068	29.4	265,090	13,610	19.5
Texas	D 93,881	3,609	26.0	D 1,861,169	81,809	22.8	D 783,081	34,889	22.4
Utah	11,530	473	24.4	192,128	7,794	24.7	95,616	4,394	21.8
Vermont	3,928	A 218	18.0	72,089	A 4,004	18.0	30,500	A 1,694	18.0
Virginia	27,720	E 1,225	22.6	711,438	E 31,435	22.6	311,052	E 13,743	22.6
Washington	24,553	A 1,117	22.0	492,973	A 22,430	22.0	247,589	A 11,265	22.0
West Virginia	23,843	A 984	24.2	232,596	A 9,598	24.2	161,522	A 6,665	24.2
Wisconsin	74,097	A 3,195	23.2	594,221	A 25,622	23.2	326,291	A 14,069	23.2
Wyoming	2,504	G 136	18.4	52,927	G 2,911	18.2	26,691	G 1,501	17.8
TOTALS	1,912,426	79,735	H 24.0	H 28,946,901	1,178,339	H 24.6	H 14,077,969	629,784	H 22.3

SOURCE: NEFP National School Facilities Survey.

A. Prorated from state total.
B. State estimate.
D. Source: *Statistics of Public Elementary and Secondary Day Schools—Fall 1972* (Washington, D.C.: U.S. Office of Education), 1972.
E. Estimated from 1971-72 data—Source: *Statistics of Public Elementary and Secondary Day Schools—Fall 1971* (Washington, D.C.: U.S. Office of Education), 1971.
F. Estimated from 1970-71 data—Source: *Statistics of Public Schools—Fall 1970* (Washington, D.C.: U.S. Office of Education), 1970.
G. Estimated from 1969-70 data—Source: *Statistics of Public Schools—Fall 1969* (Washington, D.C.: U.S. Office of Education), 1970.
H. Average Pupil / Classroom Ratio for the nation.

The information provided by the state education agencies and estimates for those states without school facility inventories indicated the availability of 1,887,858 classrooms during the 1972–73 school year to house the public school students in the nation. This figure can only be compared with the U.S. Office of Education information on available classrooms for the 1971–72 school year, when the total availability was reported to be 1,918,000 classrooms.[33] The difference between classrooms reported to the U.S. Office of Education for 1971–72 and reported to the National Educational Finance Project for 1972–73 was 30,142 classrooms, or 1.6 per cent.

Pupil / classroom ratios reported in Table 7 for kindergarten, grades 1–8, and grades 9–12 reflect the actual, prorated, or estimated ratio of total enrollment to total classrooms in each of the three categories. These figures represent state average pupil / classroom ratios; however, within a state, pupil / classroom ratios could vary considerably among districts depending on student population trends or population mobility.

In reviewing the pupil / classroom ratios for an individual state, the following procedures were observed. If the state education agency furnished both enrollment and classrooms by grade level, the pupil / classroom ratios were average ratios for the respective grade categories. However, if the state agency furnished only the total classrooms in the state or, in the absence of state facility inventories, classrooms were estimated, classrooms were prorated to the grade levels based upon enrollment. In this case, the pupil / classroom ratios reported were not as representative as the ratios for states which reported classrooms by grade level.

The national pupil / classroom ratios for kindergarten, grades 1–8, and grades 9–12 were 24.0, 24.6, and 22.3, respectively. Florida was high in all three categories with a pupil / classroom ratio of 41.1 for kindergarten, 39.8 for grades 1–8, and 38.3 for grades 9–12. Georgia was the lowest state in the kindergarten level with a pupil / classroom ratio of 16.6; Nebraska was the lowest in grades 1–8 (17.0); and Minnesota was the lowest in grades 9–12 (11.2).

The descriptors used by the NEFP to measure the need for additional public elementary and secondary facilities in the nation were temporary, obsolete, and overcrowded classrooms. Need in these classifications was subsequently related to the cost of providing educational facilities in each of the states.

The cost of providing educational facilities and the quality of school construction varied widely among the states. Differences in regional construction costs, local school district wealth, level of state participation in financing school construction, and the public's willingness to provide educational facilities accounted for such variations. With the existence of these variations, it would be impossible to design a model classroom costing $X which could be used as the unit cost in determining the total cost of alleviating the school building needs of the nation. The model classroom would not cost the same in every state, and every state could not be expected to provide the model classroom for its students.

An alternative was to use the average cost per classroom by state as the unit cost in determining the school facility needs for each of the states. The cost per classroom for each of the fifty states and Washington, D.C., was obtained from the *School Management* "1973 Cost of Building Index" (Table 8). These figures represented the average cost per classroom of constructing elementary and secondary school facilities during 1972. The cost of constructing an elementary classroom ranged from a high of $114,000 in the District of Columbia to a low of $18,000 in Mississippi. The corresponding cost of constructing a secondary classroom was $191,000 in the District of Columbia and $31,000 in New Mexico. In determining the cost of meeting the school facility needs of each of the states, the average cost per elementary and secondary classroom from Table 8 was used.

Temporary Classrooms

One data element which reflected a need for additional school buildings was the number of temporary facilities used to house students. These facilities were used by local school districts to relieve overcrowded conditions in permanent facilities until new facilities were constructed. Facilities which were considered temporary in nature included makeshift rooms, rooms in nonpermanent buildings, or offsite rooms in churches, vacant stores, or houses.

The state education agencies were asked to report the number of temporary classrooms used to house students in their state during the 1972–73 school year for grades K–8 and 9–12 (Table 9). In states where an inventory of temporary classroom by grade level was not kept, a state total was reported and subsequently prorated between the educational levels in proportion to enrollment. As was found with classroom information, many states did not keep an inventory of temporary classrooms used by local school districts in their states. In the absence of this information, data secured from *Condition of Public School Plants—1964–65* were used to provide a best estimate. This survey reported the number and per cent of instructional rooms housed in nonpermanent buildings and offsite facilities for each state during the 1964–65 school year. The percentage figure from this survey was applied to the 1972–73 classroom data for each state unable

TABLE 8
CONSTRUCTION COST PER PUBLIC ELEMENTARY AND SECONDARY CLASSROOM, UNITED STATES AND DISTRICT OF COLUMBIA, 1972

State	Cost Per Elementary Classroom	Cost Per Secondary Classroom
Alabama	$ 34,000	$ 39,000
Alaska	79,000	148,000
Arizona	39,000	74,000
Arkansas	32,000	42,000
California	56,000	64,000
Colorado	50,000	79,000
Connecticut	90,000	153,000
Delaware	108,000	95,000
District of Columbia	114,000	191,000
Florida	50,000	80,000
Georgia	37,000	51,000
Hawaii	99,000	103,000
Idaho	40,000	62,000
Illinois	49,000	68,000
Indiana	62,000	96,000
Iowa	45,000	67,000
Kansas	45,000	88,000
Kentucky	44,000	60,000
Louisiana	42,000	55,000
Maine	74,000	72,000
Maryland	69,000	95,000
Massachusetts	99,000	103,000
Michigan	72,000	93,000
Minnesota	55,000	91,000
Mississippi	18,000	75,000
Missouri	37,000	53,000
Montana	46,000	75,000
Nebraska	53,000	65,000
Nevada	40,000	66,000
New Hampshire	50,000	60,000
New Jersey	83,000	102,000
New Mexico	51,000	31,000
New York	107,000	127,000
North Carolina	40,000	56,000
North Dakota	44,000	107,000
Ohio	51,000	80,000
Oklahoma	42,000	57,000
Oregon	53,000	72,000
Pennsylvania	94,000	120,000
Rhode Island	69,000	95,000
South Carolina	41,000	57,000
South Dakota	51,000	56,000
Tennessee	45,000	60,000
Texas	35,000	47,000
Utah	50,000	37,000
Vermont	67,000	87,000
Virginia	47,000	73,000
Washington	51,000	80,000
West Virginia	50,000	85,000
Wisconsin	40,000	76,000
Wyoming	36,000	74,000

SOURCE: *School Management*, "1973 Cost of Building Index" (July 1973).

to provide information on the number of temporary classrooms used during the 1972–73 school year. Although the enrollment increases during the late 60s and early 70s would suggest that temporary classrooms as a percentage of total classrooms would have increased, these estimates reflected neither progress in the elimination of temporary classrooms nor an increase in their percentage of total classrooms from 1964–65 levels.

The number of temporary classrooms (Table 9) used to house the nation's students during the 1972–73 school year was 66,461, or 3.5 per cent of all classrooms. Grades K–8 accounted for 45,877 classrooms, and grades 9–12 contributed the remaining 20,584. California was estimated to have 17,840 temporary classrooms, the highest number reported for any state. Alabama reported the highest percentage of temporary classrooms, 14.6 per cent. The lowest incidence of temporary classrooms was found in the state of Kentucky which reported 0.04 per cent of its classrooms temporary. Thirty-five temporary classrooms were reported by the state of Delaware, the fewest for any state.

The average cost per elementary and secondary classroom by state, obtained from *School Management*'s "1973 Cost of Building Index," was used to estimate the cost to replace the nation's 66,461 temporary classrooms. This cost was estimated to be $3.7 billion, ranging from a high of $1.04 billion in California to a low of $2.66 million in Wyoming.

Obsolete Classrooms

School facilities should, above all, complement and enhance the educational program housed within their walls and on their grounds. If facilities are inadequate, they consume staff and administrative time which could better be spent educating children. Therefore, the number of substandard and obsolete facilities provides another measure of the need for school buildings in the nation.

In gathering information from the state education agencies on the number of obsolete classrooms used to house students in their states, the concept of state determination was used. No attempt was made to develop a standard of obsolescence which could be applied in every state to measure the number of obsolete classrooms. Furthermore, it can be expected that states and local school districts will replace only those facilities which they consider to be obsolete regardless of imposed obsolescence standards.

Again, the number of obsolete classrooms was requested from the state education agencies for grades K–8 and 9–12 and prorated between the elementary and secondary level on the basis of enrollment if grade level inventories were not kept. If the state education agency did not inventory obsolete facilities, *Condition of Public School Plants—1964–65* was again used to provide a best estimate. This 1965 survey reported informa-

TABLE 9
TEMPORARY CLASSROOMS: NUMBER, COST TO REPLACE, AND PERCENTAGE OF TOTAL CLASSROOMS, UNITED STATES AND DISTRICT OF COLUMBIA, 1972–73

State	Number of K–8 Temporary Classrooms		Cost to Replace K–8 Temporary Classrooms (in thousands)	Number of 9–12 Temporary Classrooms		Cost to Replace 9–12 Temporary Classrooms (in thousands)	Total K–12 Temporary Classrooms	Per Cent of Classrooms Temporary	Cost to Replace K–12 Temporary Classrooms (in thousands)
Alabama	A	3,270	$ 111,180	A	1,392	$ 54,288	4,662	14.6	$ 165,468
Alaska	C	78	6,162	C	26	3,848	104	3.2	10,010
Arizona	A	979	38,181	A	363	26,862	1,342	6.7	65,043
Arkansas		1,610	51,520		681	28,602	2,291	11.0	80,122
California	C	12,310	689,360	C	5,530	353,920	17,840	10.2	1,043,280
Colorado	A	579	28,950	A	248	19,592	827	3.4	48,542
Connecticut	C	239	21,510	C	84	12,852	323	1.1	34,362
Delaware		25	2,700		10	950	35	0.6	3,650
District of Columbia	A	410	46,740	A	0	0	410	6.9	46,740
Florida		3,042	152,100		1,555	124,400	4,597	11.1	276,500
Georgia	C	495	18,315	C	192	9,792	687	1.5	28,107
Hawaii	C	211	20,889	C	84	8,652	295	4.4	29,541
Idaho	B	120	4,800	B	65	4,030	185	2.3	8,830
Illinois		380	18,620		110	7,480	490	0.5	26,100
Indiana	A	444	27,528	A	192	18,432	636	1.4	45,960
Iowa	C	317	14,265	C	139	9,313	456	1.5	23,578
Kansas	I			I					
Kentucky	A	86	3,784	A	37	2,220	123	0.4	6,004
Louisiana	A	298	12,516		182	10,010	480	1.2	22,526
Maine	C	105	7,770	C	52	3,744	157	1.5	11,514
Maryland	C	580	40,020	C	261	24,795	841	2.4	64,815
Massachusetts	C	433	42,867	C	186	19,158	619	1.3	62,025
Michigan		698	50,256		384	35,712	1,082	1.3	85,968
Minnesota	B	150	8,250	B	75	6,825	225	0.5	15,075
Mississippi	C	283	5,094	C	214	16,050	497	2.2	21,144
Missouri	C	569	21,053	C	235	12,455	804	1.9	33,508

Montana	C	147	6,762	C	77	5,775	224	2.5	12,537
Nebraska	C	159	8,427	C	72	4,680	231	1.2	13,107
Nevada	B	110	4,400	B	90	5,940	200	3.9	10,340
New Hampshire	C	36	1,800	C	27	1,620	63	0.9	3,420
New Jersey	C	263	30,129	C	128	13,056	391	0.6	43,185
New Mexico	A	833	42,483	A	371	11,501	1,204	8.4	53,984
New York	C	1,556	166,492	C	636	80,772	2,192	1.6	247,264
North Carolina		4,527	181,080		1,982	110,992	6,509	13.2	292,072
North Dakota	C	113	4,972	C	57	6,099	170	2.3	11,071
Ohio	C	949	48,399	C	446	35,680	1,395	1.5	84,079
Oklahoma	C	734	30,828	C	430	24,510	1,164	4.3	55,338
Oregon	B	110	5,830	B	50	3,600	160	0.7	9,430
Pennsylvania	A	465	43,710	A	202	24,240	667	0.7	67,950
Rhode Island		38	2,622		6	570	44	0.6	3,192
South Carolina	C	1,508	61,828		823	46,911	2,331	8.0	108,739
South Dakota	I	105	5,355	I	49	2,744	154	2.0	8,099
Tennessee	C	3,416	119,560	C	1,395	65,565	4,811	4.0	185,125
Utah	C	80	5,360	C	32	2,784	112	1.9	8,144
Vermont	A	1,077	50,619	A	453	33,069	1,530	3.3	83,688
Virginia	A	1,280	65,280	A	612	48,960	1,892	5.4	114,240
Washington	C	191	9,550	C	120	10,200	311	1.8	19,750
West Virginia	C	432	17,280	C	211	16,036	643	1.5	33,316
Wyoming	C	37	1,332	C	18	1,332	55	1.2	2,664
Totals		45,877	$2,358,528		20,584	$1,370,618	66,461	H 3.5%	$3,729,146

SOURCE: NEFP National School Facilities Survey.

A. Prorated from state total.
B. State estimate.
C. Estimated from 1964–65 data. Source: Condition of Public School Plants—1964–65 (Washington: U.S. Office of Education, 1965).
H. Average for the nation.
I. Reported in Table 5.

tion about the physical condition of school facilities on nine specific building characteristics. The percentage of classrooms in facilities which were
deficient in four or more characteristics in 1964–65 was applied to 1972–73
classroom totals to estimate obsolete classrooms. However, the number of
obsolete classrooms reported for those states for which estimation was
necessary assumes the incidence of classroom obsolescence has remained
at the 1964–65 level.

The states reported 86,189 obsolete classrooms in use in 1972–73 to
house the nation's elementary and secondary students (Table 10). New
York reported 10,687 classrooms in this category, the most reported for
any state. It was estimated from 1964–65 information that Connecticut had
no obsolete classrooms used to house students. Incidence of classroom
obsolescence was highest in Arkansas which reported 32 per cent of its
classrooms obsolete. Excluding Connecticut, for which no obsolete classrooms were estimated, Delaware reported the lowest obsolescence rate
(0.6 per cent). It is estimated that the cost to replace the nation's obsolete
school buildings would be more than $5.4 billion. New York would need
$1.17 billion to replace its substandard facilities; Delaware's needs would
only approach $4 million.

Overcrowded Classrooms

The final variable considered by the NEFP in surveying school facility
needs and costs was the number of overcrowded classrooms used to house
the public elementary and secondary school population in the nation. High
pupil / classroom ratios or double session use of school buildings result
when local school districts are unable to provide new facilities to accommodate increased enrollments. In 1971 a study conducted for the
President's Commission on School Finance showed that presently little
need is seen for classrooms to house enrollment increases, except in
specific localities as a result of population shifts.[34] If the conclusion can be
drawn from the report of the President's Commission that local school
districts will not be required to provide additional facilities in the near
future to house enrollment increases, progress may be made toward alleviating overcrowded conditions which exist at present enrollment levels.

Ideally, square footage per pupil would be the best method of measuring
the incidence of overcrowded facilities; however, lack of information on
this factor precluded its use in this survey. Instead, pupil / classroom
ratios were used to determine the number of additional classrooms which
would be needed if the nation's students were to be housed at optimal
pupil / classroom levels. The ratio of twenty-five elementary and twenty
secondary pupils per instructional room is one widely used measure of the

adequacy of school facilities. This ratio was used by both *Condition of Public School Plants—1964–65* and *Projections of Public School Facilities Needs, 1968–69 through 1972–73* as one criterion of effective facility utilization.

State average pupil / classroom ratios (Table 7) were computed by dividing the classrooms available to house students in kindergarten, grades 1–8, and grades 9–12 by enrollment at these grade levels. Again, these pupil / classroom ratios represent state averages and would be expected to vary substantially among local school districts in a state. Substitution was made of state average pupil / classroom ratios for a ratio of twenty-five and twenty pupils per elementary (K–8) and secondary (9–12) classroom. State enrollments were divided by these classroom utilization ratios to determine optimal classroom requirements. If the state average pupil / classroom ratio for either elementary or secondary grade levels was below the optimal ratio of twenty-five or twenty pupils per classroom it was assumed that classroom needs were being met. However, if available classrooms for either elementary or secondary levels were less than optimal, the difference was considered the number of additional classrooms needed to relieve overcrowded conditions in a state. Unfortunately, the use of state mean pupil / classroom ratios to determine optimal classroom requirements fails to reflect the need of many school districts with overcrowded facilities in states where a low average pupil / classroom ratio suggests none exists.

The results of the NEFP school facility survey indicate the national mean pupil / classroom ratio for grades K–8 and 9–12 was 25.2 and 22.4, respectively, during 1972–73. As an alternative measure of the need for classrooms to relieve overcrowded school plants, it is estimated that 89,934 additional classrooms would reduce the maximum class size to the mean elementary and secondary pupil / classroom ratio for the nation (Table 11). This would require the construction of 43,199 elementary and 46,735 secondary classrooms at an estimated cost approaching $6.6 billion. When the national mean elementary and secondary pupil / classroom ratios were used as the criteria for effective facility utilization, Florida's needs were greatest in both absolute and relative terms. Housing Florida's elementary and secondary students at the national mean pupil / classroom ratio would require 25,757 additional classrooms at a cost of $1.55 billion. Nineteen states had classroom utilization ratios below the national mean and were meeting their school facility requirements.

During 1972–73, estimates indicated that 148,751 additional classrooms were needed to bring all states to an average classroom utilization ratio of twenty-five students per elementary classroom and twenty students per secondary classroom (Table 12). Of this total, 47,047 classrooms were

TABLE 10

OBSOLETE CLASSROOMS: NUMBER, COST TO REPLACE, AND PERCENTAGE OF TOTAL CLASSROOMS, UNITED STATES AND DISTRICT OF COLUMBIA, 1972–73

State		Number of K-8 Obsolete Classrooms	Cost to Replace K-8 Obsolete Classrooms (in thousands)		Number of 9-12 Obsolete Classrooms	Cost to Replace 9-12 Obsolete Classrooms (in thousands)	Total K-12 Obsolete Classrooms	Per Cent of Classrooms Obsolete	Cost to Replace K-12 Obsolete Classrooms (in thousands)
Alabama	A	1,827	$ 62,118	A	789	$ 30,771	2,616	8.2	$ 92,889
Alaska	C	177	13,983	C	59	8,732	236	7.3	22,715
Arizona	A	352	13,728	A	131	9,694	483	2.4	23,422
Arkansas		4,686	149,952		1,980	83,160	6,666	32.0	233,112
California	C	2,293	128,408	C	1,030	65,920	3,323	1.9	194,328
Colorado	A	547	27,350	A	235	18,565	782	3.2	45,915
Connecticut		0	0	C	0	0	0	—	0
Delaware		36	3,888		0	0	36	0.6	3,888
District of Columbia	C	144	16,416	C	32	6,112	176	3.0	22,528
Florida		2,624	131,200		1,029	82,320	3,653	8.8	213,520
Georgia	C	1,847	68,339	C	718	36,618	2,565	5.6	104,957
Hawaii		209	20,691		97	9,991	306	4.6	30,682
Idaho	B	211	8,440	B	126	7,812	337	4.1	16,252
Illinois		3,062	150,038		1,714	116,552	4,776	4.8	266,590
Indiana	C	1,651	102,362	C	666	63,936	2,317	5.2	166,298
Iowa	A	347	15,615	A	153	10,251	500	1.6	25,866
Kansas	A	786	35,370		1,106	97,328	1,892	7.3	132,698
Kentucky	C	595	26,180	A	253	15,180	848	2.9	41,360
Louisiana		1,084	45,528	C	623	34,265	1,707	4.4	79,793
Maine	A	242	17,908		43	3,096	285	2.7	21,004
Maryland	C	508	35,052	C	228	21,660	736	2.1	56,712
Massachusetts	C	767	75,933	C	329	33,887	1,096	2.3	109,820
Michigan		2,826	203,472		2,390	222,270	5,216	6.4	425,742
Minnesota	B	1,000	55,000	B	750	68,250	1,750	3.9	123,250
Mississippi	C	462	8,316	C	350	26,250	812	3.6	34,566

Missouri	C	2,754	101,898	C	1,136	60,208	3,890	9.2	162,106
Montana	A	175	8,050	A	66	4,950	241	2.7	13,000
Nebraska	C	319	16,907	C	144	9,360	463	2.4	26,267
Nevada	B	168	6,720	B	140	9,240	308	6.1	15,960
New Hampshire	C	112	5,600	C	85	5,100	197	2.8	10,700
New Jersey	C	569	47,227	C	277	28,254	846	1.3	75,481
New Mexico	A	993	50,643	A	442	13,702	1,435	10.0	64,345
New York		9,301	996,170		1,386	176,022	10,687	7.8	1,172,192
North Carolina		451	18,040		198	11,088	649	1.3	29,128
North Dakota	C	365	16,060	C	185	19,795	550	7.4	35,855
Ohio	C	1,265	64,515	C	595	47,600	1,860	2.0	112,115
Oklahoma	C	1,177	49,434	C	691	39,387	1,868	6.9	88,821
Oregon	B	2,510	133,030	B	1,500	108,000	4,010	16.7	241,030
Pennsylvania	A	1,379	129,626	A	249	29,880	1,628	1.7	159,506
Rhode Island		207	14,283		39	3,705	246	3.5	17,988
South Carolina	C	288	11,808	C	180	10,260	468	1.6	22,068
South Dakota	C	342	17,442	C	161	9,016	503	6.5	26,458
Tennessee		589	26,505		336	20,160	925	2.5	46,665
Texas	C	2,562	89,670	C	1,047	49,209	3,609	3.0	138,879
Utah	A	702	35,100	A	884	32,708	1,586	12.5	67,808
Vermont	C	363	24,321	C	146	12,702	509	8.6	37,023
Virginia	C	1,111	52,217	C	467	34,091	1,578	3.4	86,308
Washington	A	1,360	69,360	A	650	52,000	2,010	5.8	121,360
West Virginia	C	773	38,650	C	486	41,310	1,259	7.3	79,960
Wisconsin	C	922	36,880	C	450	34,200	1,372	3.2	71,080
Wyoming	C	253	9,108	C	125	9,250	378	8.3	18,358
Totals		59,293	$3,484,551		26,896	$1,943,817	86,189	H 4.6%	$5,428,368

Source: NEFP National School Facilities Survey.

A. Prorated from state total.
B. State estimate.
C. Estimated from 1964–65 data. Source: *Condition of Public School Plants—1964-65* (Washington: U.S. Office of Education, 1965).
H. Average for the nation.

TABLE 11

Classrooms Needed and Cost to Achieve Mean Pupil Classroom Ratio (PCR) of 25.2 (K-8) and 22.4 (9-12), United States and District of Columbia, 1972-73

State	Classrooms to Achieve PCR 25.2, K-8	Cost to Achieve PCR 25.2, K-8 (in thousands)	Classrooms to Achieve PCR 22.4, 9-12	Cost to Achieve PCR 22.4, 9-12 (in thousands)	Total Classrooms to Achieve Mean PCR K-8 and 9-12 for Nation	Per Cent of Existing Classrooms	Total Cost to Achieve Mean PCR K-8 and 9-12 for Nation (in thousands)
Alabama	1,797	$ 61,089	—	$ —	1,797	5.6	$ 61,089
Alaska	—	—	99	14,705	99	3.1	14,705
Arizona	—	—	246	18,222	246	1.2	18,222
Arkansas	—	—	—	—	—	—	—
California	3,281	183,762	7,260	464,624	10,541	6.0	648,386
Colorado	—	—	—	—	—	—	—
Connecticut	—	—	778	118,977	778	2.6	118,977
Delaware	—	—	—	—	—	—	—
District of Columbia	—	—	84	16,126	84	1.4	16,126
Florida	16,770	838,493	8,987	718,984	25,757	62.2	1,557,477
Georgia	—	—	—	—	—	—	—
Hawaii	—	—	847	43,202	847	1.8	43,202
Idaho	293	29,037	474	48,816	767	11.4	77,853
Illinois	—	—	—	—	—	—	—
Indiana	558	34,598	3,639	349,359	4,197	9.4	383,957
Iowa	—	—	—	—	—	—	—
Kansas	—	—	—	—	—	—	—
Kentucky	329	13,824	—	—	329	3.5	13,824
Louisiana	—	—	1,026	61,534	1,026	0.8	61,534
Maine	421	31,155	—	—	421	4.0	31,155
Maryland	166	11,434	1,447	137,452	1,613	4.6	148,886
Massachusetts	—	—	1,655	170,439	1,655	3.5	170,439
Michigan	3,218	231,707	—	—	3,218	4.0	231,707

Minnesota	4,152	228,336	—	—	4,152	9.2	228,336
Mississippi	2,135	38,422	—	—	2,135	9.5	38,422
Missouri	504	18,652	1,799	95,329	2,303	5.4	113,981
Montana	—	—	—	—	—	—	—
Nebraska	—	—	—	—	—	—	—
Nevada	12	500	149	9,850	161	3.2	10,350
New Hampshire	749	37,474	—	—	749	10.6	37,474
New Jersey	—	—	2,150	219,341	2,150	3.3	219,341
New Mexico	—	—	—	—	—	—	—
New York	—	—	8,923	1,133,245	8,923	6.5	1,133,245
North Carolina	—	—	1,359	76,130	1,359	2.8	76,130
North Dakota	—	—	—	—	—	—	—
Ohio	—	—	4,074	325,915	4,074	4.4	325,915
Oklahoma	—	—	—	—	—	—	—
Oregon	—	—	—	—	—	—	—
Pennsylvania	5,606	528,993	—	—	5,606	5.9	526,993
Rhode Island	138	9,543	336	31,931	474	6.7	41,474
South Carolina	—	—	—	—	—	—	—
South Dakota	—	—	—	—	—	—	—
Tennessee	3,070	138,168	—	—	3,070	8.5	138,168
Texas	—	—	142	6,696	142	0.1	6,696
Utah	—	—	—	—	—	—	—
Vermont	—	—	—	—	—	—	—
Virginia	—	—	172	12,559	172	0.4	12,559
Washington	—	—	—	—	—	—	—
West Virginia	—	—	561	47,664	561	3.3	47,664
Wisconsin	—	—	528	40,111	528	1.2	40,111
Wyoming	—	—	—	—	—	—	—
Totals	43,199	$2,433,187	46,735	$4,161,211	89,934	H 4.8%	$6,594,398

Source: NEFP National School Facilities Survey.

H. Average for the nation.

TABLE 12
Classrooms Needed and Cost to Achieve Pupil Classroom Ratio (PCR) of 25(K–8) and 20(9–12), United States and District of Columbia, 1972–73

State	Classrooms to Achieve PCR 25,K–8	Cost to Achieve PCR 25,K–8 (in thousands)	Classrooms to Achieve PCR 20,9–12	Cost to Achieve PCR 20,9–12 (in thousands)	Total Classrooms to Achieve PCR 25,K–8;20,9–12	Per Cent of Existing Classrooms	Total Cost to Achieve PCR 25,K–8;20,9–12 (in thousands)
Alabama	1,963	$ 66,754	1,085	$ 42,317	3,048	9.5	$ 109,071
Alaska	11	875	206	30,421	217	6.7	31,296
Arizona	—	—	911	67,410	911	4.6	67,410
Arkansas	—	—	658	27,644	658	3.2	27,644
California	4,273	239,297	14,637	936,781	18,910	10.8	1,176,078
Colorado	—	—	837	66,103	837	3.5	66,103
Connecticut	—	—	1,768	270,504	1,768	6.0	270,504
Delaware	—	—	194	18,473	194	3.3	18,473
District of Columbia	—	—	220	42,096	220	3.7	42,096
Florida	17,107	855,332	11,532	922,568	28,639	69.2	1,777,900
Georgia	—	—	2,456	125,253	2,456	5.4	125,253
Hawaii	331	32,769	754	77,652	1,085	16.2	110,421
Idaho	—	—	178	11,017	178	2.2	11,017
Illinois	—	—	—	—	—	—	—
Indiana	797	49,409	5,574	535,113	6,371	14.3	584,522
Iowa	—	—	557	37,329	557	1.8	37,329
Kansas	—	—	—	—	—	—	—
Kentucky	—	—	2,179	130,728	2,179	7.4	130,728
Louisiana	514	21,581	—	—	514	1.8	21,581
Maine	476	35,233	380	27,374	856	8.1	62,607
Maryland	346	23,860	2,896	275,129	3,242	9.2	298,989
Massachusetts	—	—	3,532	363,806	3,532	7.4	363,806
Michigan	3,627	261,141	3,430	318,971	7,057	8.7	580,112
Minnesota	4,325	237,895	—	—	4,325	9.6	237,895
Mississippi	2,245	40,417	—	—	2,245	9.9	40,417

						%	
Missouri	729	26,977	3,464	183,594	4,193	9.9	210,571
Montana	—	—	—	—	—	—	—
Nebraska	32	1,294	—	—	—	—	—
Nevada	785	39,232	449	29,650	481	9.5	30,944
New Hampshire	—	—	—	—	785	11.1	39,232
New Jersey	—	—	4,916	501,442	4,916	7.5	501,442
New Mexico	—	—	16	508	16	0.1	508
New York	—	—	14,654	1,861,039	14,654	10.7	1,861,039
North Carolina	—	—	3,282	183,797	3,282	6.7	183,797
North Dakota	—	—	—	—	—	—	—
Ohio	—	—	8,057	644,532	8,057	8.7	644,532
Oklahoma	—	—	—	—	—	—	—
Oregon	6,055	569,185	—	—	—	—	—
Pennsylvania	171	11,785	—	—	6,055	6.3	569,185
Rhode Island	—	—	707	67,160	878	12.4	78,945
South Carolina	—	—	819	46,674	819	2.8	46,674
South Dakota	3,260	146,696	123	6,880	123	1.6	6,880
Tennessee	—	—	—	—	3,260	9.0	146,696
Texas	—	—	4,265	200,457	4,265	3.5	200,457
Utah	—	—	387	14,311	387	3.1	14,311
Vermont	—	—	—	—	—	—	—
Virginia	—	—	1,810	132,101	1,810	3.9	132,101
Washington	—	—	1,114	89,156	1,114	3.2	89,156
West Virginia	—	—	1,411	119,943	1,411	8.2	119,943
Wisconsin	—	—	2,246	170,662	2,246	5.2	170,662
Wyoming	—	—	—	—	—	—	—
Totals	47,047	$2,659,732	101,704	$8,578,595	148,751	H 7.9	$11,238,327

SOURCE: NEFP National School Facilities Survey.

H. Average for the nation.

needed at the elementary level and 101,704 at the secondary level. Florida had the greatest absolute and relative need of any state. Construction of 28,639 additional classrooms in Florida, an increase in present classrooms of 69.2 per cent, would provide for optimal facility utilization. Nine states were below the elementary and secondary mean pupil / classroom ratios of twenty-five and twenty and were meeting school facility utilization requirements. Nationally, the average classroom need, as a percentage of existing classrooms, was 7.9 per cent. The estimated cost of relieving the overcrowded conditions which existed in many of the nation's classrooms was more than $11.2 billion. Of this total, the combined cost to the states of California, Florida, and New York was $4.8 billion, with the $1.86 billion cost to the state of New York being the greatest of any state.

Comparing the National Educational Finance Project's estimated need for 148,751 additional classrooms to relieve overcrowded conditions in the nation's schools with the results of *Condition of Public School Plants—1964–65* would suggest that some progress had been made in the decade. The 1964–65 survey estimated 285,900 classrooms or 18.6 per cent of the 1,536,500 available classrooms were needed to reduce maximum class size to twenty-five elementary pupils per room and twenty secondary pupils per room. However, the sampling techniques used in this earlier survey resulted in the development of median rather than mean pupil / classroom ratios, which may have more accurately measured the number of overcrowded classrooms. It can also be argued that, in the face of rising enrollments during the late 60s, school districts concentrated their efforts on relieving overcrowded facilities by constructing new school plants, increasing the use of temporary classrooms, and postponing the renovation of obsolete school buildings. This would explain the decrease in classrooms needed to relieve overcrowding and the increase in the incidence of temporary and obsolete facilities.

Results of the NEFP survey of school facility needs and costs indicated 301,401 additional classrooms were needed during 1972–73 to replace the temporary and obsolete classrooms and to reduce overcrowded conditions in the nation's public elementary and secondary schools (Table 13). These classrooms represent 16.0 per cent of the 1.9 million available classrooms in the nation in 1972–73 and would cost $20.4 billion at 1972–73 construction price levels. The use of mean pupil / classroom ratios to determine the number of additional classrooms needed to relieve overcrowded conditions in school plants would suggest that the actual need was much greater than the 148,751 classrooms this survey reports. Lack of current information on obsolete and temporary classrooms by many states and the subsequent reliance on earlier school building surveys for this information would

TABLE 13

CLASSROOMS NEEDED AND COST TO REPLACE TEMPORARY AND OBSOLETE FACILITIES TO
ACHIEVE MEAN PUPIL / CLASSROOM RATIO OF 25 (K–8) AND 20 (9–12),
UNITED STATES AND DISTRICT OF COLUMBIA, 1972–73

Classroom Category	Classrooms	Per Cent of Existing Classrooms	Cost (in thousands)
Temporary	66,461	3.5	$3,729,146
Obsolete	86,189	4.6	5,428,368
Overcrowded	148,751	7.9	11,238,327
Total	301,401	16.0	20,395,841

SOURCE: NEFP National School Facilities Survey.

indicate that the number of additional facilities needed to replace the 66,461 temporary and 86,189 obsolete classrooms was also understated.

The data in Table 13 reflect the level of expenditures which would have been required in 1972–73 if immediate action were taken to resolve the problems related to providing adequate housing for all school children. Recognizing that expenditures of that magnitude, in all probability, will not be made in a single year, further projections were made of the level of funding which would be needed between 1973–74 and 1979–80 if the backlog of building needs were to be met and if normal replacement of school facilities were to take place over that period of time.

Fiscal projections in Table 14 were computed with the following assumptions. First, the backlog of building needs in 1972–73 would be met on an equal basis during each year between 1973–74 and 1979–80. Second,

TABLE 14

LEVEL OF ANNUAL EXPENDITURES BETWEEN 1973–74 AND 1979–80 REQUIRED TO MEET
THE BACKLOG OF SCHOOL BUILDING NEEDS IN 1972–73 AND TO PROVIDE FOR
NORMAL REPLACEMENT OF CLASSROOMS DURING THAT PERIOD

Year	Amount of Funds (in thousands)		
	K–8 Classrooms	9–12 Classrooms	Total
1973–74	$ 2,907,738	$ 3,002,795	$ 5,910,533
1974–75	3,096,741	3,197,977	6,294,718
1975–76	3,298,029	3,405,845	6,703,874
1976–77	3,512,401	3,627,225	7,139,626
1977–78	3,740,707	3,862,995	7,603,702
1978–79	3,983,853	4,114,089	8,097,942
1979–80	4,242,803	4,381,505	8,624,308
Total	$24,782,272	$25,592,431	$50,374,703

SOURCE: NEFP National School Facilities Survey.

beyond the backlog, an additional 2 per cent of existing classrooms in 1972–73 would be replaced each year, assuming a normal life of fifty years for school facilities. Third, 1973–74 national average classroom costs from *School Management*[35] were used with an annual inflation factor of 6.5 per cent. Fourth, allowance was not made for the expected decline in school enrollments, for data were not available concerning the possible impact of pupil migration within and among school districts. Further, allowances were not made for the shifts in percentages of pupils who would be attending various grade levels, e.g., elementary and secondary grades.

As shown in Table 13, over $20 billion would have been required to provide adequate facilities in 1972–73; however, the projected cost increased to over $50 billion when the schedule for constructing the required facilities was extended evenly from 1973–74 through 1979–80 and additional needs for normal replacement were projected.

Present Capital Outlay Financing

Providing funds for school facilities is not a problem of identifying the needs, but rather one of determining the best method for financing school construction projects. Various alternatives are available to local districts in most states; however, the principal methods have been to use local funds, either through reserve funds, the issuance of general obligation bonds or revenue bonds, or a pay-as-you-go system.

The primary method for financing school construction has been through the issuance of general obligation bonds. School districts have chosen this method over pay-as-you-go for a variety of reasons. The most obvious has been to reduce the impact on the local community of a one-time tax levy or extremely high property taxes for a limited period of time. Local districts have instead elected to spread the payment for facilities over a number of years at additional cost and thereby to maintain a more stable tax rate. This practice also enables those who use the facilities to assume the burden of paying for them. In periods of inflation and rising prices, borrowing can be a further advantage to the school district. By financing construction with borrowed funds, the school district may obtain the facility at today's prices and repay the principal and interest on the debt with cheaper dollars.

Although forty-one states reported utilization of building reserve funds for construction in 1969–70, several distinct disadvantages have been associated with this method of financing. As is the case with using current revenues to pay for facilities, reserve funds result in present or past taxpayers bearing the full burden of the cost of capital outlay projects which will be used by future generations. Critics of the reserve fund approach also have been concerned about the control and security of the funds, for they fear that funds may be diverted and used to support current school operating costs or misapplied by irresponsible local school officials. Even though the funds may be invested under controlled conditions, the interest yield on the investment and the subsequent growth of the total amount may not be sufficient to keep pace with the rate of inflation. Shifts may take place in the tax base, or the population mobility pattern may result in significant inequities.

A recent device used to facilitate school construction in several states has been the school building authority. This financing arrangement may ɔperate at either the state or local district level. School building authorities finance and construct, but they do not operate the facility. Since the authority is not a governmental agency, state and local debt limits need not apply. The authority obtains its funds through the sale of revenue bonds, and the guarantee for the revenue bond is the contract between the authority and the local school district using the facility.

Authorities and similar agencies have proved to be flexible fiscal devices. Funds for authorities have been obtained from legislative and local appropriations, state permanent and retirement funds, and sales of stock, debentures, and revenue bonds. Lease and lease-purchase contracts with local school districts have provided the revenues from which the authority or similar agencies have met repayment and interest requirements.

State participation in the financing of school facilities is a relatively new development; state funds for facilities were not provided to any extent until after World War II. The inability of local districts to construct buildings during the Depression, the lack of civilian construction during World War II, and enrollment increases attributable to the "baby boom" following World War II have compounded the need for school facilities. Various studies revealed that many local school districts simply have not had the quantity of financial resources required to construct the needed facilities.[36]

The usual form for state aid to local school district construction projects has been through a loan or a grant. In a recent study,[37] fourteen states were making loans to local districts for capital outlay projects or debt service payments. Rather than being available to all local districts, the loans have normally been limited to those local districts which have reached or are approaching their legal debt limits. Loans offer a type of immediate relief to districts with the need for additional facilities, but the problem is only delayed for the loan must eventually be repaid from local revenue sources.

State grant programs for capital outlay and debt service vary widely in appropriation and method of computing the allocation to local district. Of the twenty-six states which provided state grants for capital outlay or debt service, fourteen were recently providing funds in a manner which was fiscally equalizing, e.g., proportionately more funds were being provided to local school districts with low taxpaying ability. The remaining twelve states were allocating funds on a flat grant basis. The essential difference in the grant programs was whether funds were being allocated on the basis of some predetermined measure of unit costs or a percentage of locally determined expenditures.[38]

Even though states appear to have been somewhat hesitant to assume responsibility for providing adequate housing for school children in local school districts, attention has been directed toward the desirability of state participation in this area in the recent series of court cases concerned with fiscal neutrality in the state school support program.[39] The importance of adequate facilities to the teaching and learning environment can be supported from a variety of perspectives. The basic question is the degree to which the state should participate in this area and the latitude in facility planning which should be left to the discretion of local school officials.

A most interesting example of state participation in the financing of local school district capital outlay projects has been the system utilized by the state of Maryland.[40] In 1971, the state initiated a program under which the state assumed the complete cost of school construction projects with the local district only being responsible for the purchase of the school site. Under this arrangement long-range planning has become vital, and local districts have lost some of their options in the type of facilities to be constructed and the schedule for construction. However, the problem of financing capital outlay projects no longer is dependent upon the availability of local revenue and bonding power or the whims of the voters in each local school district.

Elements of a Fiscal Model

In the design of a state program for financing public school facilities, certain essential components should be included to serve as a skeletal framework for the program. In earlier research efforts of the NEFP, determination of needs, allocation procedures, use of proceeds, and source of funds were identified as key components.[41]

Determination of needs.—Formal programs for granting or loaning funds normally identify elements of need which can be objectively determined and quantified. If the state is to provide significant portions of the funds for the local project, it is only logical that the state also must have a local project approval process as a prerequisite for allocating state grants or loans. In the process of approving a project, a determination would be made of the "approved project cost" based on the number of pupils to be served and the program to be housed. This projection would then be used in computing the amount of funds that the state would grant or loan to the local district. Factors related to this allocation should be based on standardized space and facility requirements and the dollar costs based on state or regional construction indices.

Another alternative would be to determine the cost of the total "approved project," including construction costs, engineering and architectural fees, site costs, and other costs related to construction, such as sewage treatment plants, site development, and equipment. Various items might be excluded through state statutes or regulations; however, such limitations and exclusions should be clearly defined and not subject to administrative interpretation.

If the state program for supporting capital outlay and debt service is to be in the form of a grant program, the units of need—whether pupil, classroom, or instructional unit—should be expressed in the same form as in the basic state aid program for current operation. This will facilitate administration of the program and development of understanding on the part of legislators and local school officials. Various special conditions, such as rapid enrollment increases, may also be recognized in the calculation of a local district's eligibility. Underlying this entire discussion has been the assumption that an objective process will be used in determining the quantity of needs in each local school district.

Allocation procedures.—Depending upon the objectives of the program in a specific state, grants may be for uniform amounts, may vary inversely with local fiscal ability, or may be allocated on a percentage basis. Funds may be allocated on a one-time basis or may be spread over a period of years. The latter procedure is most appropriate when the purpose of the program is to allocate funds on the basis of assumed depreciation or for payment of debt service.

If the state funds are in the form of loans or advances to local districts, interest savings will normally be realized; the funds can usually be secured at a lower interest rate if the state is the guarantor of the securities. In contrast to grants, loans through state appropriations or from state authorities result in debt which is payable in the future. If responsibility for repayment of the loan must be assumed by the local school district and if no "forgiveness" features are included, the burden of repayment will fall on the local property taxpayers, with all of the resultant inequities.

Development of allocation procedures will normally be dependent upon the availability of funds to meet the level of need that has been identified. If the magnitude of the need is too great for immediate resolution, an effective mix of local and state funds and of current appropriations and borrowed funds will often be required to stabilize the revenue requirements and enable governmental units to secure the desired quantity of funds.

Use of proceeds.—Several alternatives for use of grants or loans are feasible. Funds may be transferred immediately into construction accounts in local districts, or they may be invested as reserve funds until contracts require payment. If an immediate need for funds does not exist in the local district, the funds may be held in escrow at the state level until the local district has a project underway or has incurred debt that is scheduled for repayment.

The state may elect to base its allocation on a depreciation allowance basis and distribute a standard amount on a unit basis. In these instances, funds may be utilized for construction or debt service payments, or accumulated in construction reserve funds. An additional alternative is for the local district to use the funds for capital outlay or debt service until that need no longer exists, and then to use the allocation to meet current operating costs. This choice may be in direct conflict with legislative intent, but districts which have made prior effort and have no current or projected need can put the funds to effective use through this alternative.

Source of funds.—The most obvious source of state funds for state aid to local districts for capital outlay and debt service is through direct appropriation from current revenues. This alternative is the most economical and provides the funds on a current basis. Other options are for the state to issue bonds on the full faith and credit of the state or to establish an authority for the purpose of raising revenue to provide local districts with funds for capital outlay projects or debt service payments. In the latter choice, the state must provide some security for the bonds through either subsequent legislative appropriations, proceeds from a designated tax, or repayments from local school districts.

State funding for local district capital outlay projects and debt service payments will broaden the available tax base and tend to equalize the tax rates among districts within the state. Obvious advantages accrue through the use of current appropriations; however, this approach may result in fluctuating revenue requirements which will be misunderstood by taxpayers.

Criteria for Evaluating Capital Outlay and Debt Service Support Programs

Legal responsibility for all aspects of education resides with the state; therefore, the state through the legislature and other state agencies has the responsibility to provide adequate school facilities for educational programs, fiscal and technical support for the design of school facilities, quality control in the construction of school facilities, and fiscal accountability in the use of funds for school facilities. Each function does not have to be performed by a state agency, but the state does have the responsibility to assure that each function is performed by a state or local agency.

The first criterion is that the state take steps to assure that facilities throughout the state are adequate in terms of their capacity to house and support a sound educational program and to meet accepted standards of safety and efficient operation. Achievement of this criterion suggests the desirability of the state developing and maintaining a facility inventory system which will provide the information required to indicate the level of need for additional or replacement facilities in each local school district in the state.

A second criterion is that the state, through its state aid program, provide funds or funding mechanisms which will assure that each district has adequate funds to meet its capital outlay and debt service requirements. The disparity in fiscal ability among school districts within a state suggests that state funds either be distributed on a fiscally equalized basis or be of sufficient amount to meet all of the capital outlay and debt service needs in each local district. Achievement of this criterion may require that varying amounts be allocated to individual districts on the basis of enrollment growth or inadequacies of existing facilities.

The third criterion, quality control, can be achieved through state review of facility plans and requirements that local districts conduct periodic inspections during the progress of the construction project. A more subjectively oriented facet of the quality control criterion is that the state assume a leadership role in assuring that the facility's design will accommodate both present and projected educational programs which may be offered in the local district. Consideration should also be given to assuring that adequate and enforceable requirements will provide sound standards related to space, site, environment, and building materials for construction and rehabilitation.

The fourth criterion relates to fiscal accountability procedures in local school districts. Funds should be expended in accordance with legislative intent, and adequate records should be maintained for reporting purposes. In addition to fiscal disbursement records, attention should also be given to various cost data elements which will be of value in analyzing the current program and planning for revisions which should be incorporated into future funding proposals.

CONCLUSIONS

School transportation programs have become an integral part of American public education and are expected to maintain their present level or possibly increase as a result of various public policy decisions. Even with the decline in pupil population, the level of expenditure required to support pupil transportation programs has been projected to increase by $260 million between 1973 and 1980. States and localities will have little choice in making these expenditures, for the precedent of providing school transportation has become an expected part of the American educational scene.

Strong evidence can be found to support state aid for local school district transportation programs. Districts vary in the percentage of their enrollment which is transported and the average number of miles of travel to transport each pupil. The best technique which has been developed to recognize these differences is the efficiency oriented transportation formula discussed in an earlier portion of this chapter. Through this formula, recognition can be given to the differences among districts, and the calculation process encourages and rewards those districts which operate efficient programs. Rather than being static, the technique has a dynamic quality which permits recalculation and adjustments on an annual basis. This responsive characteristic keeps the formula current and encourages local districts to seek optimum levels of efficiency in the operation of their transportation programs.

The magnitude of the school facility problem is much more complex than that of transportation. The expected life of a classroom is forty to fifty years; a school bus is used eight to twelve years. The difference in cost per unit is even greater. Also, buses are mobile and classrooms are fixed, often resulting in a greater hesitancy on the part of local school boards to make a decision. This is evidenced in the relatively slow pace at which the problem of providing adequate housing has been resolved at the local level.

If the school facility needs existing in 1972–73 had been met immediately, slightly over $20 billion would have been required. If the backlog of need at that date is projected to be filled on an equal basis during each year from 1973–74 until 1979–80, and if additional allowance is made for normal "retirement" of school facilities, the sum of the revenue requirements for school construction is slightly over $50 billion.

As school enrollments stabilize, and even decline in some instances, the necessity for states to seek different ways to fund capital outlay and debt service programs becomes more evident. The past patterns of uniform depreciation allowances on a pupil or classroom unit basis are no longer adequate because some districts will have a stable pupil population, others will have a declining population, and still others will have increasing enrollments.

Structural and educational obsolescence of school facilities occurs irrespective of the increase or decline in pupil population; for this reason, merit can be found in a state depreciation allowance on a unit basis to provide sufficient funds for renovation and updating of facilities. However, this approach will not be sufficient for those districts which are confronted with enrollment increases. This latter problem suggests the desirability of providing discretionary funds at the state level which can be allocated to local districts on the basis of demonstrated need for new facilities. The state board of education, through the department of education, should develop a system for maintaining a current inventory of school facilities. These data would then serve as indicators of the level of need in local districts and would be invaluable for projecting the amount of revenue required to provide adequate facilities for all pupils in a given state. Either through direct appropriation or the issuance of bonds guaranteed by the state, the legislature should appropriate sufficient funds to provide the required facilities. The state board of education, through the department of education, should then be charged with responsibility for administering the program and allocating funds to local districts on the basis of objective standards and criteria.

Traditional uniform grants for transportation programs and capital outlay and debt service are no longer adequate as techniques for state support of these areas. Differences among districts dictate that formulas and allocation procedures be based on factors which reflect the variation in level of need among individual school districts. Only through this process can a state be assured that sufficient funds are provided to transport and house its school children.

REFERENCES

1. E. Glenn Featherston and D. P. Culp, *Pupil Transportation* (New York: Harper and Row, 1965), p. 2.
2. J. F. Abel, *Consolidation of Schools and Transportation of Pupils*, U.S. Bureau of Education Bulletin no. 41 (Washington: U.S. Government Printing Office, 1923), p. 58.
3. R. L. Johns, *State and Local Administration of School Transportation* (New York: Columbia University Teachers College, Bureau of Publications, 1928), p. 2.
4. Featherston and Culp, p. 2.
5. Abel, p. 5.
6. Ibid., pp. 22–23, 26.
7. Dewey H. Stollar, "Pupil Transportation," in *Planning to Finance Education*, vol. 3, ed. R. L. Johns, Kern Alexander, and K. Forbis Jordan (Gainesville, Fla.: National Educational Finance Project, 1971), p. 340.
8. Featherston and Culp, p. 4.
9. Stollar, p. 340.
10. Ibid.
11. Ibid.
12. Ibid., p. 341.
13. United States Department of Commerce, *Statistical Abstract of the United States* (1973), p. 127.
14. Ibid., pp. 113–14.

15. William P. McLure and Audra May Pence, *Early Childhood and Basic Elementary and Secondary Education* (Urbana: University of Illinois, 1970), p. 18.

16. Paul R. Mort, *The Measurement of Educational Need* (New York: Columbia University Teachers College, Bureau of Publications, 1924), p. 8.

17. Asael C. Lambert, *School Transportation* (Palo Alto: Stanford University Press, 1938), p. 52.

18. Mort, p. 61.

19. Ibid.

20. Robert L. Burns, *Measurement of the Need for Transporting Pupils* (New York: Columbia University Teachers College, Bureau of Publications, 1927), p. 11.

21. Johns, p. 25.

22. Lambert, p. 59.

23. Kern Alexander and K. Forbis Jordan, *Financing the Public Schools of Kentucky* (Gainesville, Fla.: National Educational Finance Project, 1973), p. 277.

24. Office of Education, *First Progress Report of the School Facilities Survey* (Washington: United States Government Printing Office, 1952), p.1.

25. U.S. Department of Health, Education and Welfare, *Report of the Long Range Planning Phase of the School Facilities Survey* (Washington: United States Government Printing Office, 1955), p. 18.

26. Office of Education, *Digest of Educational Statistics*, OE-10024-63 (Washington, 1963).

27. George J. Collins, *National Inventory of School Facilities and Personnel, Spring, 1962*, OE-21026 (U. S. Department of Health, Education and Welfare, U.S. Office of Education, 1964).

28. George J. Collins and William L. Stormer, *Condition of Public School Plants*, 1964–65 (U.S. Department of Health, Education and Welfare, U.S. Office of Education, 1965).

29. Office of Education, *Digest*.

30. Task Force on Public School Facilities Needs, Office of Education, *Projections of Public School Facilities Needs, 1968–69 through 1972–73*, *Congressional Record* (May 1968).

31. Office of Education, *Statistics of Public Elementary and Secondary Day Schools—Fall 1971* (Washington, 1971), p. 32.

32. Office of Education, *Statistics of Public Elementary and Secondary Day Schools—Fall 1972* (Washington, 1972).

33. Office of Education, *Statistics . . . 1971*.

34. Cresap, McCormick, and Paget, Inc., Report of the President's Commission on School Finance, *Economics in Education*, *Part D* (New York, 1971).

35. "1974 Cost of Building Index," *School Management* (May 1974), pp. 19–20.

36. R. L. Johns and Edgar L. Morphet, *The Economics and Financing of Education* (Englewood Cliffs, N.J.: Prentice-Hall, Inc., 1969), p. 380.

37. W. M. Barr, K. F. Jordan, C. C. Hudson, W. J. Peterson, and W. R. Wilkerson, *Financing Public Elementary and Secondary School Facilities in the United States*, Special Study no. 7 (Gainesville, Fla.: National Educational Finance Project, 1970), p. 137.

38. Johns and Morphet, p. 392.

39. Clarence Hollins et al. v. W. P. Shofstall et al., Superior Court of the State of Arizona, Maricopa County, No. C-253652 (June 6, 1972).

40. Alfred R. Carey, "The Maryland Experience: Full State Funding and Capital Outlay," *School Finance in Transition*, Proceedings of the 16th Annual National School Finance Conference (Gainesville, Fla.: National Educational Finance Project, 1973), pp. 145–49.

41. Barr et al., pp. 231–37.

Alternative State and Local Tax Sources for Education

John Due

The financing of education in the coming decade must compete for funds with other growing activities of government—for example, control of air and water pollution and elimination of poverty—which are likely to receive high priority. It is my purpose to consider various alternative state and local tax sources for additional funds and possible improvements in present sources that will make them more acceptable.[1]

SUMMARY OF CRITERIA FOR EVALUATION OF TAXES

Several criteria have come to be generally accepted for use in evaluating tax structures. These criteria are not derived by scientific analysis, but merely reflect widespread popular attitudes in conformity with generally accepted objectives of contemporary society. While consensus on the criteria is strong, interpretations of their meaning in particular circumstances vary widely.

Economic Distortions

A major criterion is the establishment of tax structures in such a fashion as to minimize distorting effects upon the functioning of the economy—that is, effects that cause persons to alter economic behavior in a fashion contrary to the objectives of the society. Such alterations in behavior result in "excess burdens"—in the sense of reduced real income of society not offset by governmental output.

Distortions take several forms. First, taxes may reduce the output of some commodities relative to others and cause a loss in satisfaction on the part of those persons with high preferences for the goods whose relative output is reduced. Deliberate changes—sought, for example, because excessive use of the product (e.g., liquor) causes losses for society—may be defended. It is the unintended type of change that reduces the economic well-being of the society. Second, taxes may interfere with efficiency in the conduct of production and physical distribution of goods by altering decisions about the selection of methods of organization and operation utilized. If taxes cause a firm to use a method of production other than the most efficient, output from given resources is reduced below the potential level and society suffers a loss; total real income is less than the potential.

A specific type of distortion important in the sphere of state and local taxation involves decisions relative to location. Tax differentials among areas may cause firms to select locations other than those that are optimal from the standpoint of efficiency.

A further type of distortion is interference, in an undesired fashion, with decisions about work; taxes may cause some persons to drop out of the labor market or seek to work fewer hours. Similar considerations apply to owners of other resources used in production and particularly the willingness to undertake risk. If taxes reduce the willingness of persons to work, to accept more responsible positions, to gain education necessary for professional work, or to take risks, society suffers a loss in the form of reduced output.

Finally, distortions that reduce the rate of economic growth are regarded as objectionable. Not only do distortions reduce the extent to which the economy attains the goals of society, but they also reduce governmental revenue from a given tax structure and require higher overall tax rates. Any tax that causes persons to change behavior to escape it will produce less revenue than could be obtained from the given tax rates if behavior were not altered.

Equity

Taxes are compulsory payments imposed upon individuals by government to distribute the costs of governmental activities among the various members of society. The rule that governmental costs be distributed in a fashion regarded by contemporary society as equitable is generally accepted. What constitutes equity, however, is strictly a value judgment, and there are wide differences of opinion. Usually equity is considered to require: (1) equal treatment of equals—persons regarded as being in the same circumstances should be taxed the same amount; (2) distribution of tax burden on the basis of ability to pay as measured by income, wealth, consumption, or other criteria; (3) exclusion from tax of persons in the lowest income groups on the grounds that they have no taxpaying capacity; (4) a progressive overall distribution of tax relative to income on the basis that tax capacity rises more rapidly than income. This last requirement is less generally accepted than the others. There is general agreement that the structure should be at least proportional to income.

Unless a tax structure meets to an acceptable degree the current attitudes on equity, it will not attain general tolerance. If many persons regard a particular tax as inequitable, there will be continuous complaint and political pressure to modify the structure.

Compliance and Administration

Attainment of the objectives of society requires that taxes be collectible to a high degree of effectiveness with minimum real costs (money and nuisance) to the taxpayers and reasonable cost to the government for collection. Inability to enforce a tax effectively at tolerable cost will cause loss of both revenue and equity. If some persons are meeting their liabilities while others are not, discrimination results and economic distortion will arise from the efforts of others to escape tax. Easy compliance is important if taxpayers are to accept the tax and to meet their obligations with minimum use of resources for the purpose. Expenditures on collections reduce the net yield from the tax and utilize resources that would otherwise be available for productive purposes.

Revenue Elasticity

Governmental expenditures tend to rise at least in proportion to national income even if programs are not increased and in inflationary periods to rise even faster, given the labor intensivity of governmental activity. If tax revenues do not keep pace at given tax rates, constant rate changes are required. Experience suggests that legislative bodies are slow to make these changes and the changes may have disruptive effects on the economy. As a consequence, revenues tend to lag behind expenditures.

THE PROPERTY TAX

The traditional support for financing education and other local government activities in the United States has been the property tax. In the 1973 fiscal year, local governments received about $44 billion or 84 per cent[2] of their tax revenue from the property tax despite expansion of local nonproperty taxes in recent years, and the school districts received 99 per cent of their tax revenue from this source. Property tax revenue receipts for the states totaled $1.3 billion, or 2 per cent of their total tax revenues. Property tax yields expressed as a percentage of the Gross National Product (GNP) have risen slowly over the last decade from 3.4 per cent (1962) to 4.0 per cent (1973). Current percentages are lower than they were in the twenties and thirties and not much higher than they were throughout the period 1870–1914.[3]

The property tax applies to a variety of types of property but to an increasing extent to real property, now the source of 88 per cent of the revenue. In 1972, about 50 per cent of the tax was collected from households in the form of tax on real property and some personal property, 42 per cent from nonfarm business (including public utilities) property, and about 8 per cent from farm property.[4]

Shifting and Distributional Impact of the Tax

Under traditional assumptions the burden of the tax is borne primarily in relation to housing expenditures—by the homeowner directly with owner-occupied housing, by the tenant with rental housing. The portion on business property is assumed to be borne primarily by the consumers of the products produced or handled, and thus represents an uneven sales tax (with a relatively heavier burden on products that have disproportionate amounts of taxable property involved in their production). The portion of farm land and vacant land (and perhaps other land, to some extent) is assumed to capitalize, reducing the selling price by the capitalized sum of the tax. This assumption about shifting has been questioned in recent years by persons who argue that the tax is distributed in relation to the ownership of wealth as it reduces the overall return to capital.[5] But this conclusion is not generally accepted as yet, partly because of the realization that it depends on highly simplified assumptions about perfect competition and perfect mobility of capital.

General Evaluation

The dominance of the property tax in local finance is a product primarily of the limited potential of other local tax revenues. School districts usually have no other taxing powers, and those of other local units are severely limited. As subsequently explained, even if the local governments had broader powers, there would be significant administrative and economic obstacles to collecting large sums of money from these other sources. Most property cannot escape from local jurisdictions and can be discovered by local authorities—to a greater extent than other tax bases. In part, admittedly, the dominance of the property tax is a matter of tradition rather than necessity. Local governments were given the power to levy the tax when income and sales taxes were virtually unknown. They came to rely highly on them; other levels of government came to dominate sales and income tax fields.

In addition to revenue productivity there are certain specific advantages to the property tax. Some local government expenditures directly benefit property owners, and thus the taxes are regarded in part as a form of user charge. This reasoning, however, does not apply to education finance. A portion of the tax rests upon land, an ideal base for taxation since the supply is fixed and since landowners benefit from economic growth whether they make a contribution to it or not. A large portion of the tax rests upon business property. Business taxation is always politically popular, even if it has little support on more rational grounds. This is particularly true with large corporate holdings whose stockholders live outside the taxing jurisdiction. Especially in earlier years of the country's development, ownership or rental of expensive homes was a reasonably good measure of taxpaying ability not then reached directly by income taxation.

The property tax, however, suffers from several inherent limitations —economic and equity—that restrict its ability to finance additional expenditures for education or other local activities. These limitations are reflected in part in political resistance to further property tax increases. The Advisory Commission on Intergovernmental Relations' (ACIR) survey of attitudes toward taxes showed that the property tax is by far the most unpopular tax politically. Forty-five per cent of those surveyed thought that the property tax was the worst (least fair) tax; only 7 per cent thought it the fairest tax.[6]

Economic Effects

It is difficult to quantify the economic effects of the property tax. But studies suggest three areas in which there are almost certain to be some adverse effects, one of which is related to the most pressing current economic and social problems of the nation. In the first place, under usual assumptions about shifting, the tax constitutes a very heavy "excise" tax on housing. Nearly half of the tax rests directly upon housing facilities and is likely to be borne by those owning or renting the facilities.[7] While the precise elasticity of demand for housing is not known, it is certainly not zero, and the property tax inevitably creates excess burden by deterring expenditures on improved housing. From the viewpoint of social policy it may be argued that this is a particularly undesirable consequence; modern society is relatively short of quality housing compared to other goods. In the higher income levels this effect is offset by the favorable treatment given homeowners under the federal income tax, but there is no comparable offset for the lower income group where housing deficiencies are the most severe.

Much more serious—given the concerns of contemporary society—is the adverse effect the property tax has upon rehabilitation of the deteriorating central-city portions of metropolitan areas. Part of the impact is direct and immediate. If property is improved by replacing slum dwellings or old store buildings by modern facilities, the property tax may rise so drastically as to render the change unprofitable. But also important is the common tax differential pattern in metropolitan areas—the tax rates in the central city are often higher than those in portions of the surrounding areas.[8] Thus investors have incentive to locate outside the central city—whether for apartment or office buildings, industrial or other developments—instead of in the older areas. Therefore, the depressed areas become more depressed.

Apart from the central city, property tax differentials can affect other location decisions within metropolitan areas—although they are unlikely to have much effect on decisions among widely dispersed locations.[9] Since other locational factors may be comparable within a metropolitan area, property tax rate differentials may be the key element in the decision. Particularly attractive are "industrial enclaves," cities with a large industrial property base and few people to serve and few children to educate. Vernon in Los Angeles County and Emeryville in the San Francisco–Oakland area are classic examples.

Finally, the property tax places a relatively heavier burden, per dollar of sales, on industries that use disproportionate amounts of real property relative to total sales. To the extent that the tax reflects higher costs of local government for which the particular industries are responsible (e.g., fire protection), the differential burden may be regarded as warranted. But for financing education the differential is not acceptable, relative to most efficient use of resources. Netzer in his study of the property tax concludes that of all industries the railroads are most seriously affected by the property tax, because their ability to compete with motor transport not subject to equivalent burdens is reduced.[10]

Equity

The property tax fails to meet accepted standards of equity on several counts.

Unequal treatment of equals.—Because of uneven assessment, lack of uniformity of valuation results in different tax burdens on persons owning equivalent amounts of property. Innumerable studies have shown the dispersion in assessments even when efforts are made by assessors to do a careful job.[11] The difficulty is in part inherent with the tax. Other levies are imposed on flows—on income or sales. Since the property tax is imposed on the value as of a particular time, constructive valuation is required. This is not difficult with some property but is very troublesome with others. In addition, as is well known, the approach to assessment has often been unscientific. This defect can be corrected, but the inherent difficulty of the task will remain.

Inequity from varying ratios of taxable property to total wealth and total income.—Income is typically regarded as the best measure of taxable capacity with total net wealth as a secondary acceptable measure. But the property tax is not closely correlated with either. The portion of the property tax on homes distributes the tax burden on the basis of the gross value of one particular kind of property. Since there is a wide dispersion in ratios of such property to income or net wealth, there is substantial departure from accepted criteria of equity. Specifically, the tax places a disproportionate burden on persons owning their homes but having little current income and on those having relatively high portions of their total wealth in taxable form. The effect is a severe burden on older persons owning their homes, on families with incomes temporarily reduced, and on persons who prefer to spend relatively high percentages of their incomes on housing. As noted later, recent reforms have lessened this effect.

Much of the remainder of the tax has direct impact on business property. Under usual assumptions there will be a tendency for this portion to shift forward to the consumers of the products—but in uneven fashion, since the ratio of tax to selling prices will vary. Any firm having high property tax relative to sales volume will find complete shifting impossible, and the owners will bear a portion of the cost for a time. Farmers selling in perfectly competitive markets will be unable to shift until market supply falls in response to the higher cost, and presumably they cannot shift tax on land at all. The distributional pattern of the shifted portion is similar to that of a sales tax, but with uneven burden on various goods arising from the varying ratios of real property to sales in different lines of production. Thus persons with relatively strong preferences for high-tax goods will bear disproportionate amounts of the overall tax burden.

Regressive distribution of burden.—The property tax is usually characterized as being highly regressive relative to income under the assumption that the tax is borne by homeowners, tenants, and consumers (for the part on business property). This tendency is illustrated in column A of Table 1, reproduced from a recent ACIR study. These figures, however, as well as those of other studies, show that the tax is close to being proportional in the range of $10,000 to $50,000 income—a range that includes a substantial portion of the population. The overall regressivity is due primarily to the fact that housing expenditures do not rise in proportion to income and constitute a particularly high percentage of the incomes of the lowest income groups. The regressivity may be aggravated in some jurisdictions by a common but not universal tendency to assess lower value homes but not more expensive homes closer to their sale value.

If the assumption is made that the property tax is borne in relation to ownership of wealth, the tax is still regressive in the lower income brackets, as shown in column B of Table 1, because the lowest income groups (many of them elderly retired persons) own disproportionate amounts of wealth compared to their current incomes. If the distribution of burden is considered in relation to lifetime income rather than annual income, the tax is much less regressive and may even be progressive, but the appropriateness of this comparison is open to question since tax must be paid out of

TABLE 1
DISTRIBUTION OF PROPERTY TAX BURDEN BY INCOME CLASS, 1972

| Income | Property Tax Burden as Per Cent of Income | |
	Assumption of Burden on Renters and Consumers (A)	Assumption of Burden on Wealth (B)
0–2,999	13.0%	7.2%
3,000–4,999	8.0	5.4
5,000–9,999	5.9	3.6
10,000–14,999	4.9	2.6
15,000–19,999	4.7	2.9
20,000–24,999	4.4	3.7
25,000–49,999	4.4	5.7
50,000–99,999	3.7	14.1
100,000–499,999	3.5	22.4
500,000–999,999	3.0	24.5
1,000,000 and over	2.1	18.2
All incomes	5.0	5.0

SOURCE: Advisory Commission on Intergovernmental Relations, *Financing Schools* (Washington, 1973), p. 34.

current income or liquid assets. Regardless of the assumptions made about shifting, the heavy absolute burden on the lowest income groups constitutes a serious indictment of the tax, one only partially alleviated by recent reforms to be noted later.

Revenue Elasticity

The elasticity of property tax revenue at a given tax rate is dependent upon the relationship of increases in property values to increases in national income and the relationship of changes in assessed values to changes in sale values. The former relationship is undoubtedly high although uneven. The behavior of assessed valuation is controlled by the reassessment patterns. Unlike other taxes, the base does not rise automatically with expansion of business activity since increase depends upon action by assessors. The time lag is often very substantial, particularly in states in which actual reappraisal takes place at intervals as long as ten years or more. The overall behavior of actual property tax yields in recent years relative to national income has not been bad: Netzer concludes that a 0.8 relationship is a reasonable estimate; that is, if national income rises 1 per cent, property tax revenues rise 0.8 per cent. Some estimates show a figure as high as 1.4, others as low as 0.34,[12] but the record is not nearly as good as that of other major taxes and in some jurisdictions the record has been very poor.

Reforms

Reform of the property tax has been a subject of discussion for at least a century, and some changes have been made. One set of proposals relates to administrative changes made possible with greater state aid; the purpose of these changes was to professionalize and improve assessment, and thus improve equity as well as revenue. The most important change, however, relates to the burden on the poor. In the last five years major changes have been made to lessen the burden on the lowest income groups, particularly the elderly poor, who are often the ones squeezed the most severely.[13] The principal approach is called the "circuit breaker"—persons with income less than a specified figure are granted a credit against income tax (or cash refund) for property tax payments, up to a maximum figure. Some states provide credits or rebates to tenants as well as homeowners. Most limit the systems to the elderly, but others give it to all low income persons. A few states do not phase out the assistance as income exceeds a certain figure. Others use the old "homestead exemption" system, exempting owner-occupied housing under a certain figure. This is grossly inequitable against tenants compared to homeowners and in usual form places the burden of the relief on the local government. The circuit breaker systems are state financed.

All of these programs do, of course, reduce property tax revenue, especially if all low income persons are granted relief, but they materially lessen the complaints of the poor against the tax and the resistance to rate increases.

Other changes, such as exemption of certain types of new construction and placing of a greater relative burden on land than on improvements, would lessen adverse effects, but are not likely in the immediate future. The property tax is certain to continue to play a major role in the financing of education. But it does not offer potentialities for significant increases in revenue, except to some southern states with very low income. The objectionable features are sufficiently serious that the case for increased use is difficult to defend. The objections voiced by many groups make continued increases progressively more difficult politically. Other fields of taxation offer much greater potentiality for additional revenue for education.

THE SALES TAX

Although, with minor exceptions, sales taxes are not used directly by school districts, the sales tax has indirectly become a major source of funds for the financing of education through state grants to school districts and offers potential for still greater support.

Present Use

As of July 1, 1974, the sales tax was being used by forty-five states containing 98 per cent of the population of the United States. The tax was also used extensively by the local governments in Alaska. In only four states (Montana, New Hampshire, Delaware, and Oregon), three of which had populations of less than a million, was the sales tax not employed. The sales tax yielded 29 per cent of total state tax revenue and about 5 per cent of local government tax revenue (1973 fiscal year). The states collected $19.7 billion from sales taxes in 1973, and the local governments collected about $2.8 billion.[14] In that year the sales tax yielded 40 per cent or more of the total tax revenues of Connecticut, Florida, Hawaii, Mississippi, New Mexico, South Dakota, Tennessee, Texas, Washington, and Wyoming. Hawaii, at 49 per cent, was the highest; on the other hand, the tax yielded only 14 per cent in Massachusetts. The tax collections ranged downward from 5.7 per cent of total personal income in Hawaii to 1.1 per cent in Massachusetts. These figures are shown in Table 2.

Summarization of the use of the tax at the local level, usually city and / or county, is more difficult. In 1974, in nine states (California, Illinois, Missouri, Oklahoma, Tennessee, Texas, Utah, Virginia, and Washington) the municipal tax is universal or almost so (in terms of population) and is state collected. Most of these use 1 per cent rates. State collected county taxes cover much of the state in North Carolina. A universal mandatory county tax in Nevada is regarded as a state levy. In Alaska, with no state levy, the tax is widely used at the local level, with rates as high as 5 per cent. In seven states local sales taxes are widespread but less universal with purely local collection (Arizona, Louisiana), partly state, partly local collection (Alabama, Colorado), or entirely state collection (Nevada, New York, Ohio). The rates are less uniform, ranging from 1 per cent to 3 per cent. Limited use of the tax is made in seven states; in a few of these it is used only in one local jurisdiction. Collection may be state (Arkansas, Georgia, Kansas, New Mexico, Nebraska, South Dakota) or local (Minnesota).

TABLE 2
SALES TAX REVENUES AS PERCENTAGE OF TOTAL STATE TAX REVENUE
AND TOTAL PERSONAL INCOME, 1973

State	State Sales Tax Revenue 1973 Fiscal Year	Sales Tax Revenue as a Percentage of Total Tax Revenue	Sales Tax Revenue as a Percentage of Personal Income
Alabama	301	32	2.8
Alaska	0	—	—
Arizona	257	38	3.5
Arkansas	168	32	2.8
California	2,189	30	2.3
Colorado	220	33	2.3
Connecticut	447	40	2.9
Delaware	0	—	—
Florida	1,041	42	3.8
Georgia	477	35	2.8
Hawaii	211	49	5.7
Idaho	61	27	2.4
Illinois	1,209	33	2.3
Indiana	275	23	1.3
Iowa	244	29	2.2
Kansas	200	33	2.1
Kentucky	372	37	3.4
Louisiana	288	25	2.4
Maine	118	39	3.4
Maryland	394	27	2.2
Massachusetts	282	14	1.1
Michigan	1,092	31	2.7
Minnesota	351	21	2.3
Mississippi	316	48	5.0
Missouri	359	30	1.9
Montana	0	—	—
Nebraska	109	29	1.8
Nevada	70	34	2.8
New Hampshire	0	—	—
New Jersey	682	36	1.9
New Mexico	162	42	4.7
New York	1,734	21	1.9
North Carolina	370	22	2.1
North Dakota	70	39	3.2
Ohio	808	30	1.8
Oklahoma	150	22	1.6
Oregon	0	—	—
Pennsylvania	1,109	25	2.2
Rhode Island	96	30	2.4
South Carolina	286	35	3.5
South Dakota	72	48	3.1
Tennessee	403	40	3.1
Texas	1,133	40	2.7
Utah	136	38	3.6
Vermont	38	22	2.3
Virginia	338	24	1.8
Washington	532	41	3.7
West Virginia	123	22	2.1
Wisconsin	432	23	2.5
Wyoming	44	42	3.3
Total	19,769	29	

SOURCE: U.S. Bureau of the Census, *State Tax Collections in 1973.*

Local taxes differ in one very important respect. In some states, such as Illinois, liability for tax depends upon location of the vendor; in others liability is determined by place of delivery and thus, typically, place of residence on delivery sales.

The median state sales tax rate was 4 per cent (July 1, 1973), ranging from 2 per cent in three states to 7 per cent in Connecticut (reduced to 6 per cent by May 1, 1974). Eighteen states have figures of 4 or 4.5 per cent, and five had 5 per cent figures; two were above this figure. If the maximum local rates are added to the state rates, the range is changed only slightly (high of 7), and the median remains 4 per cent, with 6 per cent or above in three and 5 per cent in thirteen. The sixteen states with rates of 5 per cent to 7 per cent contain about half of the population of the country.[15]

The exemptions vary somewhat among the states. Nineteen states, primarily ones introducing the tax since 1948, exempt all food (as of July 1, 1974). Most states exempt prescription drugs, and five exempt some or all clothing. Five states provide credit against income tax liability for sales tax paid on prescribed minimum necessary expenditures, and a sixth (Idaho) does to a restricted extent.

Evaluation—Equity

Despite the importance that sales taxes now play in state-local tax structures, virtually never have they been introduced as measures to reform the structures; they have been established as emergency financial measures to meet expenditure needs in the face of lagging yields from other taxes. The reluctance of legislators to enact them or voters to approve them, coupled with their tendency to remain once they have been introduced, and the fact that, according to the ACIR study, they are regarded as the least fair tax by only a small percentage of the population, suggest that there are significant arguments on both sides.

Sales taxes may meet equity requirements more satisfactorily than property taxes do. Under the assumption that they are shifted forward, they are distributed in relation to consumer spending on taxed goods rather than to outlay on housing, and thus on a much broader and presumably more equitable base. Nevertheless, most of the opposition to them has been based on equity grounds. First, if they apply to all goods, they place a substantial absolute burden on the lowest income groups, persons who may be considered to have no tax capacity. Second, the overall distribution of burden tends to be regressive relative to income if all goods are taxed. This has been demonstrated empirically in a number of studies.[16] Expenditures on nontaxable services and savings tend to rise as a percentage of income as income rises, and therefore expenditures on taxable goods tend to fall. Third, the tax affects various families in a somewhat haphazard way, placing a heavier burden on those families whose circumstances (such as number of children) compel them to spend relatively high percentages of their incomes. Likewise, no adjustment of tax burden on the basis of circumstances affecting taxpaying ability (e.g., heavy medical expenses) is possible.

The first two basic defects and, in large measure, the third as well, can be eliminated much more easily than equivalent ones of the property tax. One alternative, the most widely used, is the exemption of food from the base of the sales tax. Much of the burden (but not all) is removed from the lowest income groups, which concentrate their expenditures very heavily for food, and the tax is, according to various empirical studies, made more or less proportional instead of regressive.[17] Much of the penalty on large families is removed. Food exemption, however, suffers from several defects, and a more satisfactory alternative approach is the provision of a credit against income tax liability for sales tax paid on minimum necessary purchases.

With this type of adjustment the sales tax may be regarded as reasonably in accord with usually accepted standards of equity. It cannot effectively be made progressive, however. Accordingly, under the assumption that progression is desired in the tax structure as a whole, the role of the sales tax must be restricted relative to that of income taxation.

Economic Distortions

The most significant potential distortions of state and local sales taxes are those affecting location, especially of retailing. With rates of any magnitude, shoppers have an incentive to shop in a low-tax area, and shopping centers and other large store developments have incentive to locate in the low-tax areas. The importance of effects is difficult to assess. Since stores must be located close to their customers, the effect is only on the precise site within a metropolitan area, and local sales taxes therefore offer much greater potential hazard than do state sales taxes. The danger from the state levies has become less serious as the levies have spread, since now the opportunity to buy tax-free over-the-counter is limited to a very few areas. With many purchases it is not worthwhile to have the goods shipped across a state line to escape tax.

Empirical studies in recent years have concluded that there are measurable effects on sales when a jurisdiction using a sales tax has populated areas close to a border of a jurisdiction not using the tax. Harry McAllister discovered significant effects on sales in border cities in Washington state,[18] and W. Hamovitch concluded that New York City retailers lost substantial revenue to nearby states when the latter did not have sales taxes.[19] On the other hand he concluded that Alabama, with little of its population located close to borders and with taxes in the neighboring states, suffered little loss. An econometric study by John Mikesell concluded that municipal sales taxes cause significant loss of sales to nontax areas.[20] On the whole the dangers of locational influences are most significant for local sales taxes that are not uniform throughout a trading area.

A second type of distortion with a retail sales tax arises from the application of the tax to some producer goods, such as industrial machinery and equipment, building materials, office supplies, fuel, etc. A few states make a strong effort to exclude major classes of producer goods, but most do not, except for sales for resale, including goods becoming physical ingredients of articles produced for sale. Taxation of producer goods may affect location decisions of business firms and may affect choice of methods of production since some methods will result in a greater tax burden than others. As sales taxes increase in rate, exclusion of producer goods becomes increasingly important, but this type of change in the tax structure has little political appeal and reduces revenue. Administrative considerations make complete exclusion of all producer goods difficult since all purchases for business use cannot be identified at time of sale, but major classes can be excluded from tax.

A third type of distortion arises from nonuniform coverage. If some goods are exempted or, as is customary, few services are taxed, consumers are encouraged to buy more of the exempt goods and fewer taxable goods, thus distorting choice away from the optimum and potentially producing excess burden. Taxation of producer goods has some effect of this type also since this portion of the tax will be more significant relative to final selling prices for some consumer goods than for others.

Despite these effects, the overall distorting effects of a sales tax appear to be minor compared to those of property taxes, and they can be minimized by avoiding consumer goods exemptions except when there is strong justification, excluding major categories of producer goods from tax, and avoiding geographic rate differentials within metropolitan areas.

Administration and Compliance

The sales tax is basically an easier tax to operate than a property tax since no constructive valuations are needed (with minor exceptions), the tax rate being applied to actual sales figures. As long as the tax structure is kept simple, the task of the retailer is not a difficult one, requiring merely the addition of the tax at the cash register and determination of tax liability each month by applying the tax rate to the figure of taxable sales. An audit program involving examination of vendors' accounts is necessary, but the cost of audit is seldom in excess of 1 per cent of revenue gained from the tax. The task of the retailer is made unnecessarily difficult in some states by the nature of the tax. A number of exemptions, with fine lines of distinction between taxable and exempt goods, is perhaps the major source of difficulty. Incorrect application of tax by clerks results, and the task of record-keeping is complicated with a new avenue opened for evasion. Audit is made more difficult and costly. Minor provisions of the acts sometimes cause retailers unnecessary headaches, such as the rule that the retailer pay the state the exact sum collected in tax from customers.

The chief administrative difficulty arises with interstate sales. A state cannot tax sales made for delivery outside the state; the state of the purchaser can apply the use tax but cannot effectively reach the purchaser except on automobiles and a few other goods. Only by requiring the out-of-state vendor to collect and remit tax can the states be assured of their revenue. But the courts have restricted the powers of the states to enforce collection from out-of-state vendors, and proposed federal legislation would restrict the powers still more drastically. Even if the states had the power, they would not be able to enforce tax effectively against out-of-state firms selling only by mail to numerous customers in the state.

Serious complications are created for compliance and enforcement when local sales taxes are applied on the basis of location of the purchaser with local use taxes imposed on purchases made in other local jurisdictions in the state. The vendor must collect tax on the basis of place of delivery; the task of applying and reporting tax is greatly complicated. With local collection, many local units are not actually able to enforce tax against outside vendors selling into the area. Record-keeping and audit are greatly complicated. When local sales taxes are locally collected, as in a few states, complications for the vendor are multiplied still further, particularly if the bases of the tax in the various jurisdictions are different. Unnecessarily, nuisance is created through the need for filing more than one tax return. Audit, if any, by the local governments duplicates state audit. Probably no greater mistake was ever made by the states in the tax field than allowing local governments to impose and collect their own sales taxes with liability dependent upon place of delivery and a tax base different from that of the state levy.

Revenue Elasticity

While presumably consumption of taxable goods rises less rapidly than income, the differential does not appear to be great. Estimates of elasticity of the tax (the response of the tax to increases in personal income) range from 18 to 1.3.[21]

Additional Revenue from the Sales Tax

There are several ways in which the states can gain additional revenue for education from the sales tax:

Introduction of the tax in the five states not using it.—This change has little impact on the national picture but is of great importance for the five states. Introduction in Alaska, except to replace the present local taxes by a simpler statewide tax, is less important as substantial revenues are already being obtained from the tax at the local level.

Rate increases.—The experience of states with 5 per cent and 6 per cent rates suggests that these figures cause no measurable economic disturbances (except minor ones arising out of interstate complications) and, with proper adjustment of the tax cause, no serious inequity. Table 3 indicates the additional revenue available to the states from raising the state rate to 6 per cent subject to the constraint that the combined state-local rate does not exceed 6 per cent.

Increasing the sales tax rate to 6 per cent in all states would increase the yield from the tax by about $8.2 billion a year, with the assumption that the rate elasticity is 93 per cent.[22] Each additional 1 per cent increase beyond 5 per cent would bring in an additional $5 billion, or, with the broader base noted below, $6.7 billion—again with the given assumption about demand elasticity. Figures by state are given in Table 3 and in summary fashion in Table 6. These figures are based upon 1973 tax rates, exemptions, and sales volumes. The actual figures would be greater for 1975 except where rates had already been increased or other changes made since July 1, 1973.

There is justification for restricting the combined state-local rate to 6 per cent, at least in the immediate future, in view of the interstate problem, the difficulty of complete exclusion of producer goods from tax, and failure of the sales tax to contribute toward progressivity.

Some states sacrifice revenue needlessly by applying lower rates to automobiles. For example, the rate in Alabama is 1.5 per cent on motor vehicles, compared to a basic 4 per cent rate (July 1, 1973). This differentiation makes no sense whatever, given the relationship of automobile purchases to incomes; it makes the taxes more regressive and sacrifices substantial revenue.

The suggestion is sometimes made that higher than basic rates might be applied to luxury goods. Such a system is hard to implement because of the tasks created for vendors in applying more than one rate, and it discriminates among consumers on the basis of individual preferences. Uniformity of rate, with progression provided by income taxes, is greatly preferable.

Improved structure of the taxes.—The structures of the sales taxes have often been designed without careful attention to criteria. There are several ways in which redesign could increase revenue and simplify operations.

Exemptions.—Exemptions of various classes of consumption goods from sales taxes are objectionable in several ways. Revenue is sacrificed; exemption of food, for example, reduces the yield by 20–25 per cent. Some exemptions pave the way for demand for additional ones. All exemptions complicate the application of the tax. Merchants must distinguish between exempt and taxable sales; questions of interpretations arise; additional opportunities are created for evasion; record-keeping is complicated; audit by the state is made much more difficult. Any exemption inevitably favors those persons whose preferences for the taxed goods are relatively high.

The most common of the major exemptions is food, provided now in nineteen states.[23] This exemption does reduce both the absolute burden on the poor and the regressivity; a sales tax with food exempt is more or less proportional except at high-income levels. But food exemption is far less satisfactory in accomplishing the objectives than is the system of providing a credit against income tax representing sales tax paid on a minimum necessary level of expenditures with cash refund to those having no income tax liability. This system removes the tax burden completely from the lowest income groups, whereas food exemption does not. At the same time it avoids a large unnecessary loss in revenue on food purchases in the middle- and high-income groups. Since food expenditures rise with income the exemption is greater at the higher income levels. Many food expenditures are in no sense necessary; the exemption favors those families concentrating luxury spending on expensive and exotic foods. Food exemption significantly complicates the tasks of the retailers in applying the tax and keeping records, makes audit more difficult, and increases evasion. The income tax credit increases somewhat the number of no-tax income tax returns, but these can be handled easily and inexpensively with modern computer equipment as demonstrated by the experience of states that use the system. Elimination of food exemption in the states now providing it would increase tax yields by about $3 billion—whereas a $10 tax credit per person limited to those in the low income levels would cost no more than $500 million. Unfortunately, however, the food exemption has much more political appeal than the credit.

TABLE 3
PRESENT AND POTENTIAL SALES TAX REVENUES FROM CHANGING RATES AND STRUCTURES BY STATE, 1973 FISCAL YEAR
(in millions of dollars)

State	State Tax Rate July 1, 1973	Revenue 1973 Fiscal Year	Revenue Per 1% of Tax Rate Present Taxes	Additional Revenue From Raising Rates to 6%[6]	Food At Present Rate	Food At 6% Rate	Clothing At Present Rate	Clothing At 6% Rate	Commercial Services At Present Rate	Commercial Services At 6% Rate	Motor Fuel At Present Rate	Motor Fuel At 6% Rate	Cigarettes At Present Rate	Cigarettes At 6% Rate	Total from Rate Increase and Broader Coverage
Alabama	4	$ 301	$ 75	$ 70					$ 30	$ 37	$ 15	$ 19			$ 126
Alaska		0	11	31						7		3			41
Arizona	3	257	86	120					26	38	13	19			177
Arkansas	3	168	56	156					12	23	3	16			200
California	3.75[1]	2,189	461	536	$ 547	$ 681			219	341	11[5]	14	$ 3	$ 5	1,572
Colorado	3	220	44	41					22	26	11	13	4	5	85
Connecticut	7[1]	447	64		112	112	14	14	57	57	29	29	11	11	223
Delaware			19	106						11		6			123
Florida	4	1,041	260	484	260	381			91	133	65	97			1,095
Georgia	3	477	159	444					48	92					536
Hawaii	4	211	53	99											99
Idaho	3	61	20	56					6	12		6			74
Illinois	4	1,209	302	281					121	149					430
Indiana	2[1]	275	137	510	6	16			34	98					624
Iowa	3	244	81	226					7	14	12	24			264
Kansas	3	200	67	156					14	25	10	18			199
Kentucky	5	372	74	69	62[3]	73			43	51	22	26			219
Louisiana	3	288	96	179	72[4]	117			11	18	15	29			343
Maine	5	118	24	22	30	35			15	18	7	9	3	4	88
Maryland	4	394	98	182	99	144			49	73	25	36			435
Massachusetts	3	282	94	262	71	136	35	68	39	75	19	37	8	15	593
Michigan	4	1,092	273	508					109	160					668
Minnesota	4	351	88	164	88	129	44	64	48	71	24	35	10	14	477
Mississippi	5	316	63	59					32	38					97

Missouri	3	$ 359	$ 120	$ 223					$ 36	$ 58	$ 18	$ 29			$ 310
Montana			21	117						13		6			136
Nebraska	2.5	109	44	123					11	23	5	12			158
Nevada	3	70	23	54					7	12	4	6			72
New Hampshire			24	134						14		7			155
New Jersey	5	682	136	126	$ 171	$ 202	$ 85	$101	94	111	47	56	$ 19	$ 22	618
New Mexico	4	162	40	74							8	12			86
New York	4	1,734	433		434	434			217	217					651
North Carolina	3	370	123	229					26	60	19	30			319
North Dakota	4	70	17	32	4	6[2]			7	11	4	6			55
Ohio	4	808	202	376	202	296			101	148	51	74			894
Oklahoma	2	150	75	209					15	36	8	18	3	7	270
Oregon			70	391						42		21			454
Pennsylvania	6	1,109	185		333	333	144	144	79	79	79	79	32	32	667
Rhode Island	5	96	19	18	24	29			12	14	6	7	2	3	71
South Carolina	4	286	71	132					28	42	14	21			195
South Dakota	4	72	18	25							4	5	1	2	32
Tennessee	3.5	403	115	161					12	17	20	28			206
Texas	4	1,133	283	263	283	349			142	175	71	87	28	35	909
Utah	4	136	34	47					4	18	7	9			74
Vermont	3	38	13	36	10	19			5	9	2	5	1	2	71
Virginia	3	338	113	210					34	55	17	27			292
Washington	4.5	532	118	110					37	64	27	32			206
West Virginia	3	123	41	114					4	7	6	12			133
Wisconsin	4	432	108	201	108	158			16	24	27	40	11	16	439
Wyoming	3	44	15	42					1	3	2	4	1	2	51
Total		19,709	5,166	8,208	2,916	3,650	322	391	1,921	2,819	738	1,069	137	175	16,312

SOURCE: U.S. Bureau of the Census, *State Tax Collection in 1973*; adjusted to exclude Washington and West Virginia gross receipts business taxes and Indiana gross income tax, and include separately imposed taxes on hotel-motel service and sale of automobiles that are essentially portions of sales tax structures.

1. Rates changed as follows: California, 3.75% (July 1, 1972) to 4.75% (April 1, 1974); Connecticut, 6.5% (July 1, 1973) to 6% (May 1, 1974); Indiana, rate to 4% (May 1, 1973) and food exempted.
2. All food exempt as of July 1, 1973.
3. All food exempt as of October 1, 1972.
4. All food exempt as of January 1, 1974.
5. California repealed the exemption of motor fuel on July 1, 1972.
6. Combined state and local rates not exceeding 6%. A rate elasticity figure of 93% is assumed, except for states not having the tax.

Similar reasoning applies to exemption of drugs and medicine although with less force; there is greater justification for allowing specific exemption of prescription drugs than food because expenditures on drugs are unevenly distributed among families at given income levels. By their nature these drugs do not attract voluntary luxury spending. Exemption should, for control purposes, be confined to items sold on prescription.

The argument applied to food exemption is valid with even greater strength for other exemptions, such as clothing, as provided by five states. Recent studies show that a clothing exemption does not lessen regressivity.[24] All of these exemptions complicate the tax and reduce rather than increase equity in many respects. Likewise, the exemption of cigarettes and motor fuel is objectionable; it is far simpler to apply tax to these goods than to exclude them, even though separate excises are also applied. Motor fuel tax revenue is almost always restricted to highway finance, although there is no reason why consumers of motor fuel should not also make a contribution to financing of education and other state activities as well.

Estimates of additional revenue to be gained from eliminating these exemptions are given in Table 3.

The same arguments do not apply to exclusion from tax of various producer goods—although these exclusions do complicate operation of the tax.

Services.—The sales taxes initially applied only to sales of tangible personal property. It has long been recognized that there is no logic in taxing commodities alone, and gradually a number of states have applied the tax to a limited range of services. If the tax is confined to those of a type typically rendered by commercial (as distinguished from professional or personal service) establishments to individual consumers, there is a strong case for taxation. Most of these firms, such as repair shops, are already registered taxpaying vendors, and it is far simpler to tax them on their entire charges than on charges for materials only. Broadening the base in this fashion would increase revenue—although by no more than 10 per cent. The principal activities covered would be fabrication and installation of all forms of tangible personal property in real property (but not real property contracts), repair, cleaning, and all related activity; laundry and dry cleaning; hotel and motel service; rental of tangible personal property; and similar activities. Barber shop and beauty parlor service can justifiably be included, but doing so adds to administrative costs since there are large numbers of small barber shops, many of which are not now registered vendors, and control is somewhat difficult.

Some states have considered much broader coverage of services, including all professional services, transport, and other activities.[25] Such proposals, however, encounter serious difficulties and objections and are not recommended. Many of these professional services are of such character that taxation is not regarded as desirable on the grounds of equity and social policy. Medical, dental, hospital, and educational services are examples. Many of the other services are rendered primarily to business firms, and taxation of them is objectionable on the same basis as is taxation of any producer goods. Taxation of these services offers strong incentive to firms to produce the services within the firm. For example, firms are encouraged to ship goods on their own trucks rather than by public carrier if freight is taxed.

Gross receipts taxes.—The gross receipts taxes of the Hawaii, West Virginia, and Washington varieties are not desirable as an expanded revenue source. They apply in part to nonretail businesses, thus discouraging the location of wholesaling and manufacturing in the states. Frequently they have multiple-application features, applying to the receipts from each transaction through which a commodity passes, encouraging integration in production and distribution channels, and discriminating against the small, nonintegrated firms. As sales taxes they are highly objectionable on economic distortion and equity grounds; as business occupation levies they are inferior to net income taxes or value-added taxes subsequently noted. Some elements in these structures, such as severance taxes, may be justified in particular instances.

Revenue gain from improved sales tax administration.—While there is little mass evasion of state sales taxes, especially on in-state sales, examination of state sales tax administration suggests that substantial revenue is being lost, primarily through inadequate audit programs. Audit coverage varies widely, as shown in Table 4. On the basis of audit coverage and other aspects of effective operation, the states were rated and classified according to the estimated additional revenue that could be attained if administration were optimized, as shown in Table 5. The figures range from 1 per cent for California to 5 per cent in the states with the least effective administration. No claim is made that the evaluation of the effectiveness of administration in the various states or the estimated revenue loss is scientifically accurate, but there is reason to believe that the estimates are reasonable. The point must be stressed that ineffective administration is primarily the result of legislative and state executive action rather than the fault of the tax administrators themselves, whose hands are tied by inadequate staffing and staff salaries and by defective legislation.

Vendor discounts.—Another source of substantial revenue is elimi-

TABLE 4
AUDIT STAFFS RELATIVE TO NUMBER OF REGISTERED VENDORS, 1970

State	Number of Accounts	Number of Accounts per Auditor
Alabama	45,789	458
Arizona	53,500	1,783
Arkansas	47,000	2,350
California	385,919	551
Colorado	42,000	2,100
Connecticut	51,000	1,135
Florida	208,748	2,087
Georgia	75,000	882
Hawaii	50,000	1,250
Idaho	22,379	2,034
Illinois	177,539	949
Indiana	135,000	1,350
Iowa	93,019	1,368
Kansas	53,000	2,944
Kentucky	66,705	2,667
Louisiana	60,000	2,000
Maine	30,000	1,072
Maryland	50,000	589
Massachusetts	120,000	2,667
Michigan	127,500	1,275
Minnesota	90,180	722
Mississippi	57,496	1,044
Missouri	78,526	981
Nebraska	55,285	4,601
Nevada	13,000	591
New Jersey	198,709	4,967
New Mexico	36,000	800
New York	430,000	716
North Carolina	95,461	1,110
North Dakota	19,732	1,973
Ohio	211,000	1,206
Oklahoma	49,199	1,366
Pennsylvania	214,538	1,308
Rhode Island	18,000	514
South Carolina	53,532	1,115
South Dakota	21,000	2,625
Tennessee	75,000	937
Texas	225,000	1,830
Utah	19,000	760
Vermont	11,841	1,316
Virginia	73,423	992
Washington	62,000	826
West Virginia	31,200	1,155
Wisconsin	87,050	2,638
Wyoming	15,000	7,500

SOURCE: J. F. Due, *State and Local Sales Taxation* (Chicago: Public Administration Service, 1971), p. 127.

TABLE 5
ADDITIONAL SALES TAX REVENUE FROM IMPROVED ADMINISTRATION
AND ELIMINATION OF VENDOR COMPENSATION, 1973
(millions of dollars)

	Additional Revenue from	
State	Improved Administration	Elimination of Vendor Compensation
Alabama	9	8
Alaska		
Arizona	8	
Arkansas	8	3
California	22	
Colorado	4	7
Connecticut	13	
Delaware		
Florida	31	31
Georgia	14	14
Hawaii	11	
Idaho	2	
Illinois	30	24
Indiana	12	
Iowa	7	
Kansas	7	
Kentucky	9	7
Louisiana	12	6
Maine	2	
Maryland	10	6
Massachusetts	11	
Michigan	22	
Minnesota	9	
Mississippi	9	3
Missouri	18	7
Montana		
Nebraska	3	3
Nevada	1	1
New Hampshire		
New Jersey	27	
New Mexico	3	
New York	43	
North Carolina	9	11
North Dakota	2	
Ohio	32	8
Oklahoma	7	5
Oregon		
Pennsylvania	39	11
Rhode Island	2	
South Carolina	7	6
South Dakota	3	
Tennessee	12	8
Texas	45	11
Utah	4	

Continued

TABLE 5—*Continued*

State	Additional Revenue from	
	Improved Administration	Elimination of Vendor Compensation
Vermont	1	
Virginia	8	10
Washington	11	
West Virginia	4	
Wisconsin	9	9
Wyoming	2	
Total	554	199

NOTE: The figures are based upon 1973 rates and coverage. The figures would be increased by an estimated 88 per cent with a 6 per cent tax rate and broad coverage.

nation of vendor discounts, allowed in twenty-two states. Vendors receive a specified percentage of the amount of tax collected. Traditionally, firms are not compensated for costs incurred in tax compliance, and there is no particular need to do so with the sales tax. The arbitrary percentages in no way compensate firms for actual costs of compliance; some firms undoubtedly experience greater costs and others much less. Without compensation, the expenses of compliance become an expense of doing business and ultimately are passed on to the consumer, as is appropriate. The province of Ontario has recently taken the initiative in eliminating long-established vendor discounts. Table 5 shows the potential gain from elimination of vendor discounts.

Interstate sales.—The weak link in operation of state sales taxes is the control of interstate transactions. Legally the states can require the in-state purchaser to pay use tax, but this power is effective only on automobiles and a few other expensive items, and on purchases by registered vendors whose accounts are audited. Tax cannot be collected from individuals making small purchases. Effective collection requires the ability to require the out-of-state vendor to collect and remit use tax. The states can do this if the out-of-state firm has a place of business in the state, as do the large mail-order houses. The mere making of delivery into the state or solicitation of business by catalogs does not enable the state to enforce collection, and federal legislation pending now for ten years would weaken the powers of the states still more. There is urgent need for effective federal legislation that would enable the states to enforce payment without placing an intolerable burden on firms making large numbers of small sales into a number of states. The most effective approach is one that would require the vendor to remit tax either to his home state or to the customer state on interstate sales. This is not a perfect solution, but it would eliminate most of the present leakage without injury to interstate sellers.

Local, State, and Federal Use of the Sales Tax

The sales tax is most appropriately employed at the state level. As noted, local sales taxes have caused several difficulties. If they are universal throughout the state at a uniform rate and are state collected, they are tolerable, at least from standpoints of administration and location effects. But disproportionate revenue goes to the local units that have extensive sales volume relative to population and inadequate amounts to ones with large population and little retailing. For example, in Los Angeles County, local sales tax per capita ranged from .04 cents in Hidden Hills to the fantastic figure of $12,051.78 in Vernon; the Los Angeles city figure was $20.55.[26] A much more satisfactory alternative is an increase in the state

TABLE 6

SUMMARY OF ESTIMATED ADDITIONAL REVENUE FROM SALES TAXES
(in millions of dollars)

Total sales tax revenue, 1973 fiscal year		$19,709
Additional revenue from rate and structure changes		
From increases in state rates to 6%	8,208	
From extension of tax to consumer services	2,819	
From elimination of food and clothing exemptions	4,041	
From elimination of motor fuel and cigarettes exemptions	1,244	
Total		16,312
Additional revenue from		
Improved administration, existing rates, and coverage	554	
Elimination of vendor discount, existing rates, and coverage	199	
Total	753	
Total, at 6 per cent rate and broader base		1,416
Grand total, rate, structure, and administrative changes		17,728
Possible offset, credit for sales tax on minimum purchases		500
Elimination of gross receipts taxes		500
Net total of additional sales tax revenue		$16,728

(Note: "At 6% rate" brace applies to the four rate and structure change items.)

rate with the funds returned to the local governments on some basis other than point of collection. By this means, also, there is much greater chance that the funds will be available, in part, for education rather than exclusively for other purposes. In 1969, Mississippi and New Mexico took the step of eliminating (except for county taxes) local taxes and increasing the state rate.

If local taxes are not uniform, the tasks of the vendors are greatly complicated and local decisions may be influenced. In some states, such as New York, Alabama, and, to a lesser extent, Colorado, the tasks for all concerned have been increased unnecessarily by the variety of local taxes. These states would particularly benefit from a shift toward a uniform state rate with distribution of funds to local governments.

At the other extreme, it may be argued that federal use of the tax in lieu of the states would be advantageous in eliminating the interstate enforcement problem and avoiding adverse locational effects. However, this is true of virtually all taxes. The complications arising out of state rather than federal use of the taxes are not of great overall significance and could be alleviated by federal legislation relating to interstate commerce. If the federal system is to be preserved the states must retain autonomous revenue sources—this is the most productive levy that they can operate with minimum difficulty.

The addition of a federal sales tax, whether of the value-added or other form, on top of the state levies would seriously impair ability of the states to raise revenue from the tax and would lessen their financial autonomy; it would also create all of the evils noted (sharp increases in the state taxes) and lessen the total amount of money available for education. Since the federal government can easily raise its required revenue via the income tax, there is no need for it to infringe upon the major state revenue source. Some writers in recent years have stressed the value-added tax as the appropriate form of tax for use at the federal level. Actually, this form of sales tax has no significant advantages in a country such as the United States over the usual retail sales tax and would complicate the tax structure unnecessarily.

EXCISE TAXES

State excise taxes are confined, with minor exceptions, to three categories—motor fuel, liquor, and tobacco products. Taxes on motor fuel are appropriately assigned for highway purposes and are not suitable as levies for financing education (although sales tax should logically apply to the sale of motor fuel). During the 1972–73 fiscal year taxes on cigarettes plus minor levies on other tobacco products yielded $3.1 billion, or 4.7 per cent of state tax revenue, while levies on alcoholic beverages yielded $1.8

billion, or 2.8 per cent of total tax revenues. The tax on cigarettes ranged from 2 cents to 21 cents a package, with a median figure of 12 cents in contrast to a median of 3 cents in 1950. Taxes on distilled spirits ranged from $1.50 to $3.50 per gallon, with a median of $2.50 (1973).

Liquor and tobacco taxes offer the advantage of substantial productivity, widespread popular acceptance, and minimal danger to economic development. They have, however, limited justification beyond some compensation for social costs for which use of the products may be responsible and the principle that use can appropriately be penalized. The tax on cigarettes is highly regressive, more so than any other major levy. Declining cigarette consumption may likewise limit future productivity of the tax. States that are well below the median could gain additional revenue with little harm by moving upward. The elasticity of these taxes is particularly low—estimated to be 0.6 for liquor, 0.4 for cigarettes.[27]

Estimated potential additional revenue is shown in Table 7, based on the assumption of a 20 cents per package rate on cigarettes and a price elasticity of demand of 0.9 (arbitrarily assumed). The liquor tax yields are adjusted on the basis of per capita revenue in each state compared to that in Vermont, the highest per capita yield state. The states could gain an additional $1.8 billion from cigarettes if they all went to a 20 cent per package rate; they could gain an additional $3.6 billion from beer, wine, and liquor if the per capita yield was as high in all states as it is in Vermont.

The additional revenue potential is based on the assumption that all states make the increase; the additional revenue gain to one state from a sharp increase, when neighboring states do not make similar increases, will be much less. The point must also be stressed that the increases suggested have somewhat questionable support on the basis of usually accepted principles of taxation; about the best that can be said for them is that they are not likely to do much harm.

PERSONAL INCOME TAXES

The inherent advantages of personal income taxation are so well known that only a brief summary is required. Income taxes alone are directly related to the most generally accepted measure of tax capacity and are adjustable on the basis of circumstances affecting tax capacity at given income levels, such as numbers of dependents, medical expenses, and the like. Only the income tax can provide effective progression in the overall tax structure. A properly designed income tax should have minimum distorting effect on the economy, provided all income is treated in a uniform fashion. While progression increases the danger of distortions,

TABLE 7
CIGARETTE AND LIQUOR TAX REVENUES AND POTENTIALS

State	Cigarettes			Beer, Wine, Liquor		
	Revenue[2] 1973 Fiscal Year	Rate per Package (cents)	Additional Revenue at 20 Cent Rate	Revenue	Additional Revenue Potential	Total Potential Revenue
Alabama	42	12	25	59	31	56
Alaska	3	8	4	5	4	8
Arizona	25	10	22	13	35	57
Arkansas	38	17¾	4	15	34	38
California	251	10	226	115	383	609
Colorado	15	10	13	15	41	54
Connecticut	70	21		24	54	54
Delaware	12	14	4	5	9	13
Florida	159	17	25	155	37	62
Georgia	67	12	40	74	46	86
Hawaii	7	8	10	10	12	22
Idaho	7	9	8	5	14	22
Illinois	163	12	98	74	201	299
Indiana	48	6	101	21	116	217
Iowa	41	13	20	12	66	86
Kansas	28	11	21	14	47	68
Kentucky	19	3	97	14	77	174
Louisiana	50	11	37	41	56	93
Maine	19	14	7	19	8	15
Maryland	32	6	67	25	83	150
Massachusetts	111	16	25	61	98	123
Michigan	132	11	97	73	164	261
Minnesota	75	18	7	47	55	62
Mississippi	23	9[1]	25	14	47	72
Missouri	56	9	61	23	97	158
Montana	10	12	6	7	11	17
Nebraska	20	13	10	9	30	40
Nevada	10	10	9	8	6	15
New Hampshire	24	11	18	3	17	35
New Jersey	166	19	8	52	141	149
New Mexico	12	12	7	6	20	27
New York	323	15	97	155	349	446
North Carolina	20	2	162	75	64	226
North Dakota	7	11	5	5	20	25
Ohio	187	15	56	67	223	279
Oklahoma	44	13	22	29	40	62
Oregon	30	9	33	3	75	108
Pennsylvania	231	18	23	98	221	244
Rhode Island	18	13	9	7	19	28
South Carolina	21	6	44	54	16	60
South Dakota	8	12	4	6	11	15
Tennessee	58	13	28	29	79	107
Texas	244	18.5	18	97	218	236
Utah	6	8	8	4	22	30
Vermont	8	12	4	12	0	4
Virginia	16	2.5	101	41	77	178

Continued

TABLE 7—*Continued*

State	Cigarettes			Beer, Wine, Liquor		Total Potential Revenue
	Revenue[2] 1973 Fiscal Year	Rate per Package (cents)	Additional Revenue at 20 Cent Rate	Revenue	Additional Revenue Potential	
Washington	51	16	12	58	31	43
West Virginia	24	12	14	19	26	40
Wisconsin	77	16	17	38	86	103
Wyoming	4	8	5	1	8	13
Total	3,112		1,764	1,817	3,625	5,389

SOURCE: U. S. Bureau of the Census, *State Tax Collections in 1973*. Revenue potential for cigarettes is based on the assumption of a 20 cent package rate. The potential for alcoholic beverages is the difference between the per capita liquor tax revenue in the state and what the figure would be if the burden were as heavy as that in Vermont, the highest liquor revenue state.

1. 11 cents as of July 1, 1973.
2. All tobacco products.

particularly of factor supplies, the federal income tax rates of the last two decades have produced little evidence of significant adverse effects upon the economy.[28] Treasury studies of the late sixties showed that the overall progression was much less than the tax rate table suggests, with a substantial degree of inequality of treatment. But these consequences resulted from defects in the federal income tax structure, not from the use of the income basis for taxation. Responses of revenue to increases in national income is greater than that of any other tax, estimated in the range of 1.3 to 2.4 at the state level.[29]

The personal income tax, by its inherent nature, is of course the mainstay of the federal tax structure with very good justification, partly because of its potential use as an instrument of fiscal policy. Unlike most other taxes the rates can be varied from time to time in light of changing business conditions and inflationary pressures.

State-Local Use

At the state level, the income tax offers the general advantages of income taxation: providing greater equity for the state tax structures, lessening the absolute burden on the lowest income groups encountered with other taxes, providing at least a limited degree of progression, and ensuring greater response of state revenue to increases in personal income. Given the resistance to other taxes, a state can gain greater revenue with an income tax in the tax structure than otherwise. Table 8 summarizes the

TABLE 8

STATE INCOME TAX REVENUES AND POTENTIALS, 1973

State	Personal Tax Revenue 1973 (millions of $)	July 1, 1973 Range of Tax Rates	Exemption, Family of 4 ($)	Potential Additional Revenue (millions of $)	Corporate Income Tax Yield (millions of $)	Corporate Income Tax Rate, July 1, 1973	Potential Additional Corporate Income Tax Revenue, at 8% Rate (millions of $)
Alabama	142.2	1.5–5	3,600	235	41.9	5[4]	25
Alaska	43.4	16% of Fed.	3,000	12	7.0	5.4–9.36	1
Arizona	108.6	2–8	3,200	156	37.4	2–8[4]	5
Arkansas	89.3	1–7	[3]	123	37.8	1–6	38
California	1,886.4	1–11	[3]	1,417	866.3	7.6	46
Colorado	185.8	3–8	4,500	154	39.0	5	23
Connecticut	50.6	6[1]		484	138.6	8	
Delaware	110.3	1.5–8	2,400		19.1	7.2	2
Florida					147.7	5	89
Georgia	284.9	1–6	4,400	992	114.1	6	38
Hawaii	134.9	2.25–11	3,000	306	12.9	5.85–6.435	4
Idaho	57.7	2.0–7.5	3,000		16.0	6.5	4
Illinois	894.7	2.5	4,000	32	229.1	4	229
Indiana	284.9	2.0	3,000	974	10.1	3[8]	17
Iowa	242.9	.75–7	[3]	456	47.3	6–10[5]	
Kansas	114.3	2–6.5	2,400	146	53.8	4.5	42
Kentucky	179.2	2–6	[3]	215	69.3	4–5.8	42
Louisiana	100.2	2–6	[3]	200	88.0	4	88
Maine	31.3	1–6	4,000	321	10.0	4–6[7]	6
Maryland	515.9	2–5	3,200	90	80.0	7	11
Massachusetts	876.4		3,800–5,800	122	259.4	7.5	17
Michigan	925.3	3.9	4,800[8]	44	364.4	7.8	9
Minnesota	586.2	1.6–15	[3]	474	170.7	12	
Mississippi	70.0	3–4	8,000	149	26.1	3–4	26
Missouri	314.1	1.5–6	3,200	337	62.7	5[4]	38

Montana	77.1	2–11	2,400	14	12.1	6.75	2
Nebraska	85.1	13% of fed.	3,000	129	14.0	3.25	20
Nevada				88			24
New Hampshire	7.6	4.25[2]	600	94	19.1	7	3
New Jersey	25.5	2–15	2,600	1,206	170.6	5.5	78
New Mexico	49.5	1–9	3,000	72	15.1	5	9
New York	3,211.9	2–15	2,600		874.6	9	
North Carolina	431.2	3–7	3,200	190	139.2	6	46
North Dakota	27.3	1–10	3,300	51	10.1	3–6[4]	6
Ohio	373.5	.5–3.5	2,000	1,192	168.0	4–8	56
Oklahoma	105.1	.5–6	3,000	217	35.4	4	35
Oregon	300.6	4–10	2,700		51.1	6	17
Pennsylvania	1,010.8	2.3		709	497.2	11	
Rhode Island	67.7	15% of fed.	3,000	74	30.9	8	21
South Carolina	183.2	2–7	3,200	108	63.6	6	16
South Dakota				81			34
Tennessee	15.1	6[2]		448	103.0	6	34
Texas				1,510			364
Utah	88.5	2.5–7.25	3,000	89	29.6	6[4]	10
Vermont	49.7	25% of fed.	3,000	54	7.9	6	3
Virginia	441.9	2–5.75	2,400	204	96.6	6	32
Washington				495			47
West Virginia	88.5	2.1–9.6	2,400	20	12.2	6	4
Wisconsin	727.5	3.1–11.4	[3]		136.1	2.3–7.9[4]	58
Wyoming				47			9
Total	15,597.5			14,531	5,435.1		1,694

SOURCE: U.S. Bureau of the Census, *State Tax Collections in 1973*; ACIR, Federal-State-Local Finances, 1973. The potential additional personal income tax revenue is based upon the yield in Oregon converted to other s ites on the basis of total personal income.

1. Tax only on capital gains.
2. Interest and dividends.
3. Tax credit in lieu of exemption.
4. Federal tax deductible from income.
5. Limited to 5 per cent of federal income taxes paid or accrued during the taxable year.
6. Tax on adjusted gross income.
7. Effective January 1, 1974, rates changed; now range from 5–7 per cent.
8. $6,000, as of 1974.

income tax picture by state, with yields for the 1973 fiscal year and rates and exemptions as of July 1, 1973. As of January 1, 1974, thirty-nine states used a general personal income tax. Tennessee, New Hampshire, and Massachusetts taxed income from intangibles only; Connecticut taxed capital gains only; New Jersey taxed income of commuters only. Florida, Nevada, Pennsylvania, Texas, Washington, and Wyoming had no personal income tax. In 1973, the tax yield was $15.6 billion, or 23 per cent of state tax revenue.

Unlike sales taxes, which are basically very similar, income taxes vary widely. The Mississippi levy, for example, applies only to married persons with incomes in excess of $6,500, whereas in some states the figure is $1,000. Initial rates range from 0.5 per cent to 4 per cent, top rates from 2.3 per cent to 15 per cent. Four states with general levies have proportional rates (Illinois, Indiana, Michigan, and Pennsylvania). Five states base their liability on that of the federal tax; the Rhode Island tax, for example, is 15 per cent of the federal tax liability. One of the best measures of the height of the taxes is the ratio of state income tax to total adjusted gross income as reported for federal income tax; these range for a family of four with $10,000 income from 0.5 per cent (California) to 3.9 per cent (Wisconsin).[30] Table 9 gives some indication of the degree of diversity.

Local income taxes are used, as of 1974, in ten states. These taxes are summarized in Table 9. Most of these taxes are locally collected; the Indiana and Maryland levies are piggybacked on the state taxes and state collected. The older local income taxes, such as those of Ohio and Pennsylvania, apply only to wage and salary income and a few other types rather than to all income.

Evaluation

State use of income taxation is strongly justified for reasons already suggested. Interstate problems with personal income taxes are not serious. Since the state of residence normally allows credit for tax paid the state where the income is earned, there is little double taxation. Likewise, there is little escape from taxation. States rely heavily on Internal Revenue Service information and audit for control of income taxes. There are practical limits, however, to the potential revenue given the federal income tax rates and the fear of loss of economic activity to other states. To the taxpayer the combined rate is the significant element, and the federal tax is—as it should be—sufficiently high that the margins for the states are limited. A number of the taxes are extremely low, however. If the Oregon levy is taken as a model, with rates from 4 to 10 per cent and exemption of $675 per person, the states as a whole would obtain $31.5 billion from the tax (1973) instead of the present $15.6 billion, on the basis of rough expansion of total personal income. Estimates by state are given in Table 8. Because of variations in per capita incomes by state, these estimates are only very rough. Low income states will not be able to raise as much as indicated and high income states can raise more.

A few features of the structure warrant attention. Progression in rates is much less important than might be expected because of the deductibility of state income tax liability in determining federal income tax. The exemption provides a considerable degree of progression. On the other hand, the

TABLE 9

LOCAL INCOME TAXES, 1973

Alabama	1%; 2% local	5 cities, includes Birmingham
Delaware	1.25%	Wilmington only
Indiana	0.5%; 1%	34 counties
Kentucky	0.5%–2%	30 cities, including large ones, plus 3 counties
Maryland	20% to 50% of state tax	Baltimore county, plus 23 counties
Michigan	1%; Detroit 2%	6 cities
Missouri	1%	St. Louis, Kansas City
New York	0.7%–3.5%	New York City only
Ohio	0.25%–2%	335 cities and villages, large and small
Pennsylvania	0.5%–2%; many 1%	About 3,800 local governments, including 1,000 school districts

federal experience of recent years suggests the need for a broad definition of income at the state level including full taxation of capital gains (in view of the limited progression) and minimization or perhaps complete elimination of all personal deductions except the exemption for the taxpayer and each dependent. Theoretically, deductions should improve the equity of the tax, but the federal experience has not been encouraging. The practice in five states of defining tax liability as a percentage of federal liability has the merit of simplicity but opens the state levies to the defects of the federal and makes the state yield vary with changes in federal rates unless offset by state legislation. Using the federal adjusted gross income figure with deduction of a specified personal exemption for each taxpayer is a preferable alternative.

Use of the income tax at the local level is much more questionable. Separate collection of a local income tax—as is the common policy —compounds the nuisance to the taxpayer. A large portion of income is interjurisdictional, earned in one local area by a resident of another. As a consequence, opportunities for multiple taxation are substantial and control is made much more difficult. Local governments are not in a position to audit income tax returns independently; all that they can do is rely on information in state and federal returns. But these returns do not localize income sufficiently for local income tax purposes. In practice most of the local income taxes are confined to wage and salary income, thus discriminating against this form relative to others. Given the small size of local units, distortion of location may be significant. If liability depends upon residence, persons have incentive to select those cities in a metropolitan area that do not use the tax. With liability on the basis of place of earning and withholding, business firms are given an incentive to locate plants in jurisdictions not having the tax. But regardless of locational impact, the nuisance factor alone suggests the need to avoid local income taxes except in unusual circumstances and for the states to distribute a portion of their income tax yield to local governments, including school districts.

So far as the federal government is concerned, given the usually accepted criteria of taxation and the importance of sales taxation at the state level, there is strong justification for primary federal reliance on the income tax. There is obvious need for further reform of the federal tax beyond that provided by 1969 legislation if the tax is to accomplish its objectives in the desired fashion.

GENERAL LEVY ON CORPORATIONS

Most states have some form of general levy on corporations. In part these are regarded as supplements to the personal income tax (although four states[31] have a corporate tax but no general coverage personal tax). Primarily the taxes are a means for ensuring that the state in which the business operates makes some contribution to the expenses of the state from whose services it is benefiting.

Currently, the general levy takes the form of corporation income tax in forty-five states and partially in another (Indiana). Washington and Indiana, in part, use gross receipts taxes as general business taxes, distinct from their sales taxes, and West Virginia does so in addition to the corporate income tax. One state (Texas) has a corporate franchise tax based on capital stock that is productive of revenue. The other three states (Nevada, South Dakota, and Wyoming) have no effective general corporate levy. The median rate of the corporate income tax is 6 per cent (July 1974), with a range from 3.25 per cent (Nebraska) to 12 per cent (Minnesota). Ten of the taxes have a limited amount of progression; the remainder use proportional rates. Interstate income is usually allocated on the basis of a formula. The corporate income tax currently yields $5.4 billion, 8.0 per cent of state tax collections (1973 fiscal year), as shown in Table 8.

A state corporate income tax can be justified as a desirable element in the tax structure on the bases suggested above. The tax provides a means on a current basis of reaching income earned by corporations and an effective means of obtaining revenue from corporations owned outside of the state yet benefiting from state services. Income elasticity, estimates of which range from 0.7 to 1.4 per cent, is higher than that of other levies except the personal income tax.[32]

Although the final distributional effects of the taxes are not clear, they appear to accord reasonably well with accepted standards of equity. Administration is simple because of the ability to rely on federal returns and federal audits as the primary basis of control. Interstate problems are minor so long as uniform formulas are employed for allocation of interstate income, although some nonuniformity still exists. The taxes are not likely to have distorting effects upon location decisions so long as they are more or less uniform among states. Even with the nonuniformity that has prevailed (three major midwest industrial states—Ohio, Illinois, and Michigan—have introduced the tax only in the last decade), there is no measurable effect on location of industry. If the differentials became too great, however, particularly within metropolitan areas extending over state lines, there would inevitably be some influence. A state cannot safely go too far out of line from its neighbors.[33] As a political matter, corporate income taxes are usually essential if voters are to accept personal income taxes. The chief obstacle to substantial increases in the state corporate income taxes—apart from interstate differentials—is the high level of the federal tax. With federal rates in the neighborhood of 50 per cent, there is a limit to the amount the states can impose without strong resistance by business groups and possible adverse effects upon economic development. If all states used an 8 per cent rate, however, total yield would be about $7.1 billion instead of the present $5.4 billion.

The gross receipts basis used for general business levies by a few states (and as supplements to the retail sales tax in a few others) is objectionable on many grounds. To the extent that these taxes are shifted they have distributional effects comparable to those of sales taxes. In practice, shifting is likely to be difficult for many firms because of interstate competition, and the taxes rest on the owners in a highly capricious fashion. Because of their cumulative nature they distort business methods, encouraging integration and leading firms to produce goods and services themselves instead of acquiring them from other firms. Under no circumstances should states not now employing them turn to them. Capital stock taxes are equally capricious in their effects, being tolerable only because the rates are low.

In some states a proposal has been advanced to replace gross receipts taxes or corporate income taxes by a tax on value added, and Michigan used this form of tax for its general business levy for a time. The primary argument is along benefit lines: corporations benefit from state services and should pay accordingly for this "input" into the production process. The best measure of the benefits received by any firm is the value it adds to the materials and other goods it buys—the difference between its receipts and the cost of goods it purchases from other firms. This approach ensures that all firms pay for the inputs of state services whether the firms are profitable or not, whereas the corporate income tax does not. Value added is a much better measure of benefits received than gross receipts, and the value-added tax avoids the economic distortions created by a gross receipts tax.

It is obvious that a value-added tax is preferable on several grounds to a gross receipts tax, but its advantage over a corporate income tax is not clear. The latter complements the personal tax much more effectively than a value-added tax. There are fewer interstate complications, and it may be argued that net earnings are a better basis for taxation than value added, certainly in terms of distributional effects. At any rate, given the widespread use of the corporate income basis, it is more satisfactory from the standpoint of any one state than the value-added tax, and widespread change to the latter is most unlikely.

In general, therefore, the most suitable approach for additional revenue in this field includes these elements: establishment of the corporate income tax in those states not now using it, replacing capital stock and gross receipts taxes where these are used; use of a rate of perhaps 8 per cent in those states now using lower figures (these two changes would add about $1.7 billion to state tax revenue); and greater uniformity in allocation of interstate income to minimize the compliance tasks, the danger of double taxation, and restrictive federal legislation.

At the federal level the corporate income tax is the second most productive tax, yielding $36 billion in the 1972–73 fiscal year, or 15 per cent of total tax revenue. It is certain to remain a major source of federal revenue despite serious questions about distributional effects. The question of whether the corporate income tax is reflected in higher prices or not has been subject to extensive debate and to a number of empirical studies which show conflicting results. It is impossible at present to be certain about the shifting of the tax. Further exploration of the tax and of possible reforms is beyond the scope of this paper.

OTHER POSSIBLE SOURCES OF REVENUE

At the state level there are no major potentials for tax revenues beyond those noted. A few states are able to gain substantial revenue from severance taxes on the output of petroleum and minerals, and others could undoubtedly gain additional money from this source. Estate and inheritance taxes are not productive of substantial amounts. They could be made more effective than they are, but the overall potential is not great relative to other major sources. Other state levies, such as those on public utility or insurance companies, are essentially supplements to sales or income taxes. There is no major tax avenue to which the local governments and the states can turn for large sums of revenue. State lotteries, now used in several states, are not proving to be major sources of revenue and are questionable on equity grounds.

The same considerations apply at the federal level; there are no new, major, untapped taxes. The argument for a federal value-added tax is merely a disguised argument for a federal sales tax. The federal government can raise all revenue needed from the current pattern of income taxes with some modifications in structure; the sales tax can be left to the states as the major source of state finance for education and other purposes.

CONCLUSIONS

By generally accepted standards of taxation, additional funds for the financing of education cannot be found, on any significant scale, in the local property tax or in expansion of local nonproperty taxes, but will need to come from expanded state use of sales and income taxes plus reliance on federal income taxation for federal grants. There are specific examples of additional revenues.

Most states can make more effective use of sales taxation by increasing the rate to 6 per cent and ultimately beyond and by broadening the structure to eliminate most exemptions of consumption goods and to include some services. At the same time, to alleviate the burden on the lowest income groups and lessen opposition to the tax, credit should be given against state income tax for an amount representing sales tax payments on basic necessary expenditures with cash refund when the person has no income tax liability. Net revenue can also be gained by improving administration and eliminating vendor discounts.

Cigarette and liquor taxes, while lacking strong justification, can yield additional revenue with little harm.

Most states can make more effective use of income taxation—in some states by lowering exemptions, in many by broadening the coverage of the tax by reducing deductions and including tax-free income, and by the use of higher rates.

The corporate income tax should be the primary general business levy, replacing gross receipts and capital stock taxes where these are still used. Many states can gain substantial revenue by raising the rate to perhaps 9 per cent.

Local sales taxes, and to an even greater extent local income taxes, are objectionable in a number of respects and should be integrated into the state levies, except in unusual circumstances when one or a few cities require much more revenue than others.

Table 10 contains a summary of the total additional revenue by state and indicates, for comparative purposes, the untapped revenue potential as estimated by ACIR. There are two major differences: the ACIR data relate to 1971, and they include local as well as state levies. The ACIR data were derived in a very different fashion. It was ascertained that New York State was the state making maximum use of its revenue potential. For the other states the potential is the gap between actual tax revenues and those that would be obtained if the state makes as good use of its potential (as calculated on the basis of personal income, tourist travel, and other determinants) as New York. The figures for many states are very similar to those derived in this study; the southern states, with their low property taxes, show greater potential under the ACIR approach than under that employed in this chapter. If the total for all states is adjusted upward from 1971 to 1973 on the basis of the actual increases in tax yield over the two years, the ACIR figure becomes $43,456 million, the excess over the total in this study being easily accounted for by the property tax gap in the southern states.

Against the figures in this study two deductions are necessary—$500 million to provide credit against income tax for lower income groups to lessen regressivity of the sales tax and $500 million revenue loss by eliminating the gross receipts taxes of several states. The remaining potential, however, of $37.7 billion on a 1973 base is very substantial.

TABLE 10

SUMMARY: POTENTIAL ADDITIONAL REVENUE BY STATES, 1973

State	Sales Tax Rate and Structure	Sales Tax Administration and Vendor Discount	Cigarettes, Liquor	Personal Income Tax	Corporate Income Tax	Total	ACIR Estimate of Untapped Tax Capacity 1970–71
Alabama	126	17	56	235	25	459	665
Alaska	41	—	8	12	1	62	45
Arizona	177	8	57	156	5	403	302
Arkansas	200	11	38	123	38	410	485
California	1,572	22	609	1,417	46	3,666	3,004
Colorado	85	11	54	154	23	327	453
Connecticut	223	13	54	484	0	774	569
Delaware	123		13	0	2	138	131
Florida	1,095	62	62	992	89	2,300	2,094
Georgia	536	28	86	306	38	994	942
Hawaii	99	11	22	0	4	136	49
Idaho	74	2	22	32	4	134	132
Illinois	430	54	299	974	229	1,986	1,976
Indiana	624	12	217	456	17	1,326	940
Iowa	264	7	86	146	0	503	479
Kansas	199	7	68	215	42	531	598
Kentucky	219	16	174	200	42	651	660
Louisiana	343	18	93	321	88	863	825
Maine	88	2	15	90	6	201	95
Maryland	435	16	150	122	11	734	492
Massachusetts	593	11	123	44	17	788	401
Michigan	668	22	261	474	9	1,434	1,594
Minnesota	477	9	62	0	0	548	396
Mississippi	97	12	72	149	26	356	306
Missouri	310	25	158	337	38	868	1,159

Continued

TABLE 10—Continued

State	Sales Tax Rate and Structure	Sales Tax Administration and Vendor Discount	Cigarettes, Liquor	Personal Income Tax	Corporate Income Tax	Total	ACIR Estimate of Untapped Tax Capacity 1970–71
Montana	136	—	17	14	2	169	153
Nebraska	158	6	40	129	20	353	360
Nevada	72	2	15	88	24	201	236
New Hampshire	155	—	35	94	3	287	216
New Jersey	618	27	149	1,206	78	2,078	1,261
New Mexico	86	3	27	72	9	197	209
New York	651	43	446	0	0	1,140	0
North Carolina	319	20	226	190	46	801	948
North Dakota	55	2	25	51	6	139	81
Ohio	894	40	279	1,192	56	2,461	2,677
Oklahoma	270	12	62	217	35	596	857
Oregon	454		108	0	17	579	453
Pennsylvania	667	50	244	709	0	1,670	1,563
Rhode Island	71	2	28	74	0	175	84
South Carolina	195	13	60	108	21	397	359
South Dakota	32	3	15	81	16	147	81
Tennessee	206	20	107	448	34	815	825
Texas	909	56	236	1,510	364	3,075	3,381
Utah	74	4	30	89	10	207	150
Vermont	71	1	4	54	3	133	19
Virginia	292	18	178	204	32	724	923
Washington	206	11	43	495	47	802	597
West Virginia	133	4	40	20	4	201	293
Wisconsin	439	18	103	0	58	618	102
Wyoming	51	2	13	47	9	122	136
Total	16,312	753	5,389	14,531	1,694	38,679	34,758

Source: ACIR. *Federal-State-Local Finances* (1973–74), pp. 61–62.

REFERENCES

1. Invaluable assistance on this chapter has been provided by Miss Carolyn King and Mrs. Elaine Knudson.

2. Fiscal year 1972 percentage.

3. Yield data from U.S. Bureau of the Census, *Quarterly Summary of State and Local Tax Revenue* (October–December 1973); *State Tax Collections in 1973*; D. Netzer, *Economics of the Property Tax* (Washington: Brookings Institution, 1966).

4. *Federal-State-Local Finances* (Washington: Advisory Commission on Intergovernmental Relations, 1974), p. 173.

5. For example, H. Aaron, "A View of Property Tax Incidence," *Proceedings of the American Economic Association* (1973), pp. 212–21.

6. Of the state levies, the state sales and income taxes were each held to be the most uniform by 13 per cent: *Public Opinion and Taxes* (Washington: Advisory Commission on Intergovernmental Relations, 1972).

7. Even if the property tax is viewed as a tax borne by capital owners, it will result in reduction of the supply of heavily taxed housing.

8. *State and Local Finances* (Washington: Advisory Commission on Intergovernmental Relations, 1969), p. 68.

9. *State-Local Taxation and Industrial Location* (Washington: Advisory Commission on Intergovernmental Relations, 1967).

10. Netzer, pp. 72–73.

11. Ibid., pp. 173–83.

12. *Federal-State-Local Finances*, p. 321.

13. *Financing Schools and Property Tax Relief* (Washington: Advisory Commission on Intergovernmental Relations, 1973), chap. 5.

14. The figures for the various states are adjusted to exclude from the published data the revenue from levies not of a retail sales tax nature (e.g., business taxes on gross receipts, taxes on mineral production) and to add revenue from levies on sale of automobiles and hotel and motel accommodations, which in most states are subject to the sales tax per se.

15. These rate figures, used in preparing Table 3, are those of July 1, 1973. As of July 1, 1974, the Connecticut 7 per cent rate had been cut to 6 per cent, the Indiana rate raised from 2 per cent to 4 per cent, the Arizona rate to 4 per cent. The California state rate was cut to 3.75 per cent while the local rate was raised from 1 to 1.25 per cent and the state raised again, to 4.75 per cent, April 1, 1974.

16. Most recently by J. M. Schaefer, "Sales Tax Regressivity under Alternative Tax Bases and Income Concepts," *National Tax Journal* 22 (December 1969):516–27.

17. Ibid.

18. "The Border Tax Problem in Washington," *National Tax Journal* 14 (December 1961):361–75.

19. "Sales Taxation: An Analysis of the Effects of Rate Increases in Two Contrasting Cases," *National Tax Journal* 19 (December 1966):411–20.

20. "An Analysis of Municipal Sales Taxation" (Ph.D. diss., University of Illinois, 1969); "Central Cities and Sales Tax Differentials," *National Tax Journal* 23 (June 1970):206–13.

21. *Federal-State-Local Finances*, p. 320.

22. This figure is based on the results of the study "Estimating Sales Tax Revenue Changes in Response to Changes in Personal Income and Sales Tax Rates," by A. F. Friedlaender, G. J. Swanson, and J. F. Due, *National Tax Journal* 26 (March 1973):103–10.

23. California, Connecticut, Florida, Indiana (as of May 1, 1973), Kentucky (as of October 1, 1972), Louisiana (as of January 1, 1974), Maine, Maryland, Massachusetts, Minnesota, New Jersey, New York, North Dakota (July 1, 1973), Ohio, Pennsylvania, Rhode Island, Texas, Vermont, and Wisconsin.

24. Schaefer, pp. 516–27.

25. The taxes in Hawaii and New Mexico apply to these services.

26. R. C. Brown, "Observations on the Distribution of Local Sales Taxes in California," *Proceedings of the National Tax Association for 1968*, pp. 27–39.

27. *Federal-State-Local Finances*, p. 64.

28. R. Barlow, H. E. Brazer, and J. N. Morgan, *Economic Behavior of the Affluent* (Washington: Brookings Institution, 1969).

29. *Federal-State-Local Finances*, p. 320.

30. Ibid., p. 260.

31. Connecticut, Florida, New Hampshire, and Tennessee.

32. *Federal-State-Local Finances*, p. 320.

33. A detailed discussion is found in *State-Local Taxation and Industrial Location* (Washington: Advisory Commission of Intergovernmental Relations, 1967).

Tax Effort for Education

The basic goal of any state school finance program is twofold: it should provide equality of educational opportunity for the students of the public schools and it should spread the tax burden for education equitably among residents of the state. Johns and Morphet have written that "any defensible plan for financing the schools of a state . . . should enable the people of the state . . . to provide essential and appropriate educational opportunity at a reasonable and equitable cost to the taxpayers."[1] Although other characteristics of a defensible state finance program have been suggested,[2] this twofold goal has received the most recent attention and has probably been the most difficult to attain. Most Americans have generally subscribed, in principle, to both aspects of this goal, but have seldom agreed as to how they can be achieved. What has been meant by equal educational opportunity or tax equity has been largely a matter of personal philosophy. Definitional problems have often obscured the issue.

For many people, equal educational opportunity has meant that a state or a local school system should spend the same amount of money for each child's education. Others have taken it to mean that the same facilities or the same program for each child would constitute equal educational opportunity. Johns and Morphet have helped to clarify this issue: "Equality of educational opportunity for all does not mean that every student should have the same program of education. Instead, it means that every person should have the opportunity for the kind and quality of education that will best meet his needs as an individual and as a member of the society in which he lives" (p. 164).

Two principles of taxation emerge in discussions of tax equity: the benefit principle and the ability-to-pay principle.[3] According to the benefit principle, taxes should be paid by those who benefit from the expenditure of tax revenue. This principle can be applied only where the beneficiaries can clearly be identified. This is not true of most public services, including public education. Therefore, the benefit principle may not be the most appropriate method to evaluate tax equity. The ability-to-pay principle has certain implications for the financing of public education: not only do the rich pay more but those who are similarly situated (e.g., have the same income) should pay the same taxes. This idea has come to be known as the "equal treatment of equals." It appears that this logic could be applied to financing of education.

Numerous studies in the past fifty years have demonstrated the existence of wide variations in the fiscal capacity and tax effort among and within the various states. Such variations have been an impediment to the achievement of the goals of equal educational opportunity and tax equity. Rossmiller, Hale, and Frohreich have described the essence of this problem: "A vision of equality of educational opportunity guided the leaders who worked to develop public school systems which exist today in the various states. Equally clear is the fact that the quality of educational opportunity a school district can provide is conditioned, at least in part, by the fiscal resources to which that school district has access. At the same time, the principle of equity requires that the burden of taxes in support of education be shared equitably by all the state's taxpayers."[4]

The concept of tax equity can be broadened to include a requirement of tax equity among the various states in the support of public education. The evidence submitted in recent court cases dealing with several state school finance programs and in various studies have shown that tax burdens for education are not being shared equitably; i.e., those states and local school districts with greater fiscal capacity often tend to exert a lesser tax effort to support their schools.

The Supreme Court of California recognized this problem as it relates to intrastate variations in fiscal capacity and tax effort for education. In its decision in the Serrano case, the court said, "Obviously the richer district is favored when it can provide the same educational quality for its children with less tax effort. Furthermore, as a statistical matter, the poor districts are financially unable to raise their taxes high enough to match the educational offerings of wealthier districts. Thus, affluent districts can have their cake and eat it too; they can provide a high quality education for their children while paying lower taxes. Poor districts, by contrast, have no cake at all."[5]

This same problem was recognized by Ashby in 1936 as it applied to interstate variations in capacity and effort: "It is unjust for the poor states to be overburdened in their attempts to support schools whereas the more able states are only lightly burdened. It is unfair that the children of the rich states should have adequate educational opportunities as a result of the little effort their states exert, whereas the children of the poor states have inadequate educational opportunities despite the fact that their states exert great effort to support schools. The fact that there are exceptions to this statement does not undermine its general truth."[6]

Although Ashby was writing in the midst of the Great Depression, his concerns are recognized by many today. Johns and Morphet reiterated this concern in 1969: "Insofar as financial support relates to educational opportunity, the most able states have a decided advantage over the least able. The most able states can finance a reasonably adequate quality of education with much lower tax effort than can the least able. This seems to mean that if schools are to be financed entirely from state and local funds, either the people in the least able states will have to make much greater effort to support their schools than the people in the most able, or the children in the states with the lowest ability inevitably will have to attend schools that are poorly financed" (p. 180).

In a study made for the National Educational Finance Project (NEFP), Rossmiller concluded that "the obvious consequences of permitting continued existence of marked disparities in fiscal capacity and effort among the school districts of a state is the continued existence of disparities in educational opportunities among districts."[7] One could conclude that such variations in fiscal capacity and effort at the state level would also result in marked disparities in educational opportunity and tax equity among the states.

In a report of the National Legislative Conference Special Committee on School Finance in 1972, the limitations of the states in providing for the demands for quality public education were recognized: "In practically every state in the nation, wide variations exist in the amount of taxable wealth available to local school districts. Because their taxing efforts have been limited to the availability of local revenues, the public school systems have been unable to provide equal educational opportunities to their children. Efforts by the states to eliminate, or at least reduce, these disparities in the delivery of educational resources have simply not been able to keep pace with the demands."[8]

The central policy issue that emerges from the problem of variations in fiscal capacity and tax effort is the extent to which these variations and resulting disparities should be allowed to influence the provision of a major government activity, public education.[9] If the American public is to be committed to the realization of the goals of equal educational opportunity and tax equity, the barriers created by such variations must be overcome. The question remains as to the appropriate level of government that should have the ultimate responsibility in providing proximate solutions to these problems.

The problem of unequal distribution of financial resources has two dimensions—fiscal capacity and tax effort. Fiscal capacity represents the resources of a government or taxing jurisdiction that are available for taxation. Tax effort indicates the extent to which a government is actually using the resources available to it for tax purposes.

This chapter will be concerned with the dimension of tax effort as it relates to the support of public education. Although there have been many studies of ability and effort, none has conclusively identified the nature of tax effort. Most studies have concentrated on the relative positions of states or local jurisdictions in regard to their tax efforts for education or other public purposes. Such studies have dealt with the various measurements of effort or the various factors that may be associated with relative degrees of effort. This chapter will provide an extensive review of the literature and related research in an attempt to clarify the nature of tax effort.

CONCEPTS OF TAX EFFORT

Tax effort is generally defined as the extent to which a taxing jurisdiction is using its fiscal capacity to raise revenues for public purposes. Measures of tax effort involve a ratio of tax revenues or expenditures to some measure of fiscal capacity. Specific measures of tax effort will be investigated.

Although fiscal capacity and tax effort are important aspects of the broader area of public finance, the emphasis here will be on tax effort for public education. It should be noted, however, that any measures or studies of tax effort for public education must be considered within the broader framework of the total economy.

Prior to a discussion of the various measures of tax effort, it would be helpful to establish a conceptual framework in order to better understand the purpose for which such effort measurements are used. In a study for the Social Security Board in 1944, Saundelson and Mushkin described three general concepts of tax effort—tax performance, tax severity, and the relative use of tax capacity.[10] These are important in that each describes a different aspect of tax effort and should help clarify the differences that result from the use of various measures. Their concepts are summarized.

Tax performance provides a comparison of tax yields for all levies or from specific types of taxes, thus showing comparative trends in tax collections and a state-by-state distribution of total tax yields. The yields of state and / or local taxes on a per capita basis are often used as indicators of tax performance. This tax index indicates the tax yields in absolute amounts or on a relative basis, with no specific relation to the fiscal capacity of the state or local jurisdiction or the tax burdens that fall on the citizens.

Tax severity attempts to compare the relative loads or burdens assumed by or falling upon the taxpayers within various jurisdictions by relating taxes paid to selected measures of taxable capacity or ability. Measurements of tax effort based upon this concept provide insight into the effect of a tax program upon individuals or families, industrial or business groups, or various income groups.

Relative use of tax capacity: The differences in the economic structures of state and local governments and in their tax resources calls for a tax effort series that relates tax yields to their capacity to pay taxes. This measures the relative degree to which taxing authorities exploit or utilize their tax capacity. This index does not indicate how the tax burdens are distributed or the differences in tax loads carried by individuals or by business groups. Measurements of capacity use may also attempt to recognize individual differences in the tax bases available to various jurisdictions and the degree of their exploitation. Effort studies based on this concept describe the extent to which different jurisdictions utilize their political and legal opportunities for taxation.

Each of these concepts of tax effort will be investigated, but the major emphasis will be on the concept of the relative use of tax capacity. Most of the studies and research used focused on this particular concept. Before the results of these studies and research are presented, it would be useful to review the relation of tax effort and fiscal capacity.

TAX EFFORT IN RELATION TO FISCAL CAPACITY

In order to understand the various measures of tax effort it is necessary to determine the fiscal capacity of the jurisdiction in question. Tax effort must always be considered in relationship to fiscal capacity, since, by definition, tax effort is a ratio of tax revenues to some measure of capacity. The terms fiscal capacity and tax ability will be used interchangeably throughout this chapter. However, it should be noted that the Advisory Commission on Intergovernmental Relations (ACIR) has distinguished between the terms.[11]

Fiscal capacity is generally thought of as being the total economic resources available to a government for tax purposes. Tax effort measures indicate how much of this capacity the government is actually using in the support of public functions. There are two general approaches which have been used in measuring fiscal capacity. One approach uses economic indicators, primarily measures of income or wealth, and compares the various states on the basis of such indicators. The other approach measures the tax bases available within a state and provides comparisons based on the revenues that could be raised against given rates of taxation or the revenues derived from the application of the actual rates to the various bases.

Examples of both approaches to measuring fiscal capacity can be found in the literature on school finance. As early as 1926, Norton defined effort as the percentage of the state's economic power annually devoted to education. The economic power of a state for a given year was defined as the income of the state plus one-tenth of its wealth.[12] The two classic examples of the second approach have been from the work of Chism and Newcomer. Chism's method of measuring the relative tax resources of the states involved the application of the "Model Tax Plan" of the National Tax Association to each state in order to estimate the tax resources available if the model tax plan had been in operation. Newcomer used the computed yield of a "model tax system" to develop an index of relative taxpaying ability of the states. She used a tax structure similar to that used by Chism, but the rates applied were different. According to Ashby, Newcomer's study also took account of certain tax resources specially benefiting some of the states; tax resources depending to a large extent on wealth or economic activities outside of these states. Ashby concluded that Newcomer's measures of tax resources more closely approximated the actual tax resources of the states under the actual tax conditions than did Chism's.[13]

Probably the index most widely used to measure relative fiscal capacity of the states is per capita personal income. Personal income figures are generally more readily available from governmental sources than are figures for specific state and local taxes. Holshouser has concluded that "although other measures of tax capacity have theoretical advantages, probably the best practical measure is personal income."[14]

Some writers have used more refined measures of personal income. The Commission on Intergovernmental Relations in 1955 used disposable income per child as a measure of tax capacity.[15] Disposable income is the income remaining after the payment of all personal taxes. The Educational Policy Commission of the National Education Association (NEA) recommended in 1959 that state fiscal capacity be measured by the income left people after payments for personal taxes and for the basic necessities of food, clothing, and shelter.[16] The amount suggested to be deducted for subsistence was $800. Johns and Morphet have used net personal income as a measure of capacity. This figure was obtained by deducting from the total personal income the federal personal income taxes paid and an amount of $600 per person for the basic necessities for subsistence.[17] The National Educational Finance Project (NEFP) used the net personal income concept of Johns and Morphet but increased the subsistence allowance to $750 per person.[18] It could be expected that as the cost of living continues to increase, those who use the net personal income concept will continue to increase the subsistence allowance to obtain comparable results.

The use of these income indicators (personal income and its derivatives) is based on the economic premise that all taxes are paid from current income or accumulated wealth. According to the ACIR, this reasoning fails to consider the fact that a substantial part of a state's tax revenue is derived from tapping the income stream at other stages in its flow from production to profit-taking.[19] To account for this situation, the ACIR has developed a composite income index. This method groups various state and local taxes into three categories—personal direct taxes, business taxes, and corporation income taxes. Each of these categories is then assigned to its appropriate income flow index—personal direct levies to personal income, business levies to income produced, and corporation net income taxes to corporation income in each state. The final step involves the determination of a weighted average for a combination of the three measures of income for each state. The weights assigned were determined by the proportion of state and local taxes paid out of each source of income. This composite index takes account of the different stages of the income flow at which taxes are imposed.[20] Such an index may yield a more valid measure than personal income but a difficulty occurs in securing current and adequate data about state and local tax collections.

The ACIR has also used a "representative tax system" approach in measuring fiscal capacity (see appendices). This approach requires the evaluation of the bases available for taxation in each state and the estimation of the amount of revenue that each state could raise if all applied a uniform tax system. The representative tax system that the ACIR constructed represented the then current state and local tax practice.[21]

The ACIR in 1971 measured fiscal capacity of the states as determined by an "average financing system." This approach estimates the revenue capacity of a state by the total amount of both tax and nontax revenues that would result by applying, within the state, the national average rate of each of the various kinds of state-local revenue sources. This method broadens the "representative tax system" used in the ACIR's 1962 study by including consideration of nontax revenues of the area under study.[22]

For tax capacity of local school districts, the convention has been to measure the full value of property per pupil in average daily attendance

(ADA) or average daily membership (ADM). This method is logical due to the large proportion of local school district revenues that come from the property tax. Most studies of the relative local taxpaying ability of school districts have utilized the full value of property per pupil. The problems encountered with this measure of tax ability are those associated with the shortcomings of the property tax. Due has indicated that property tax is not closely correlated with either income or net worth.[23] Another major problem with the property tax is the uneven assessment practices. Johns and Morphet have suggested two approaches to measuring local ability—the assessment ratio plan and an index of taxpaying ability. The purpose of these approaches is to minimize some of the problems associated with uneven assessment practices of local property. They conclude that the index of taxpaying ability is a more defensible measure of local capacity than the use of unadjusted assessed valuation, but it is not a perfect measure. According to them, "the sales-ratio method, supplemented by appraisals, is the best plan yet developed for measuring local taxpaying ability.[24]

The application of "economic indicators," such as income, wealth, consumption, and productivity, to measures of local taxpaying ability has had its proponents. Johns summarized several studies done in the 1930s and 1940s which attempted to measure the theoretical taxpaying ability of local school districts utilizing the various economic indicators.[25] Rossmiller and his associates used economic as well as tax base indicators in comparing the relative fiscal capacities of seven classes of school districts. Their measures of local capacity used the following variables: property value per pupil in ADM, retail sales per capita, retail sales per household, effective buying income per capita, and effective buying income per household.[26]

Although different measures of fiscal capacity have been developed and are currently being used to measure state and local taxpaying ability, a definite pattern has emerged. Since local school taxes consist primarily of property taxes, Johns concluded that "the relative value of property is about the only practical measure of local taxpaying ability for schools."[27] For measuring state fiscal capacity the most common approach has been the use of various income measures.

MEASUREMENTS OF TAX EFFORT

The various measures of tax effort that have been developed and used are based on one of the three concepts discussed earlier: tax performance, tax severity, and the relative use of tax capacity. I will in this section discuss the various measures of tax effort, how they were developed, and how they have been used. Some comparative charts will be used to contrast various measures. The primary emphasis will be on the concept of the relative use of tax capacity, although the concepts of tax performance and tax severity will be discussed briefly. The former concept of tax effort predominates in the literature and research of the subject.

Tax Performance

Probably the simplest method of comparing relative tax efforts among the various states is to compare per capita tax collections.[28] Comparisons can be made of either per capita state tax collections or per capita local collections, or the total of both state and local tax collections. A high per capita tax collection would indicate a corresponding high effort and a low per capita tax collection would be indicative of a low effort. As indicated earlier, the basic weakness of tax performance as a measure of effort is that it has no specific relation to the fiscal capacity of the jurisdiction or to the tax burdens that fall on the taxpayers. Table 1 was developed using 1969–70 per capita tax collection data. Per capita state tax collections in 1970 for all fifty states ranged from a high of $442.19 in Hawaii to a low of $128.46 in New Hampshire. The national average was $236.93. Per capita local taxes ranged from a high of $317.00 in New York to a low of $64.00 in South Carolina. The national average for local per capita tax collections was $191.00. When per capita total tax collections of both state and local governments were ranked, the range was from a high of $652.32 in New York to a low of $251.66 in Arkansas. The national average was $427.14.

Tax Severity

Frank has suggested an index of tax sacrifice as a useful device in comparing interstate tax burdens.[29] He indicated that the index of tax sacrifice is a synthesis of two tax effort measures, per capita taxes and taxes as a per cent of income. He criticized the use of per capita tax figures on the grounds that such figures indicated the amount of contribution assessed to the average resident of the jurisdiction without consideration of his ability to pay. He also criticized the use of taxes as a per cent of income as failing to indicate the efforts of the society in producing a given amount of income.

The index of tax sacrifice measures "the degree of sacrifice involved in each state, on the average, for the payment of state and local taxes."[30] The index was developed by taking the per capita state and local tax collections as a percentage of personal income and dividing by the per capita personal income. The result was multiplied by 1,000. Frank's index of tax sacrifice gives greater weight to income than to taxes as a result of the index equation which has the effect of squaring the income figure. In Table 2 1970

TABLE 1
TAX PERFORMANCE AS A MEASURE OF TAX EFFORT

State	Per Capita Local Tax Collections, 1969–70		Per Capita State Tax Revenue, Fiscal 1970		Per Capita Total Tax Collections of State and Local Governments, 1969–70	
	Amount	Ranking	Amount	Ranking	Amount	Ranking
Alabama	$ 68	49	$ 190.86	40	$ 258.73	49
Alaska	133	35	284.27	8	417.01	20
Arizona	162	29	267.57	13	425.33	18
Arkansas	69	48	182.73	43	251.66	50
California	284	2	275.52	10	249.33	3
Colorado	206	13	212.96	29	418.68	19
Connecticut	240	5	244.64	18	484.78	8
Delaware	93	42	356.95	2	449.87	12
Florida	138	32	209.31	31	346.97	34
Georgia	107	39	205.10	35	311.80	41
Hawaii	130	36	442.19	1	572.30	2
Idaho	129	37	218.62	27	347.28	33
Illinois	229	6	258.12	15	486.78	7
Indiana	164	28	193.01	38	357.09	32
Iowa	214	9	222.41	24	436.34	16
Kansas	203	16	191.62	39	394.60	27
Kentucky	81	44	218.38	28	299.05	45
Louisiana	101	41	230.24	23	331.01	39
Maine	171	23	208.94	32	380.13	28
Maryland	206	13	275.87	9	482.00	9
Massachusetts	252	4	244.97	17	497.14	6
Michigan	191	18	264.23	14	455.54	11
Minnesota	174	22	268.31	12	441.96	15
Mississippi	77	46	219.11	26	295.75	46
Missouri	167	24	175.49	46	342.77	36
Montana	212	10	185.51	42	397.92	25
Nebraska	220	8	176.11	45	396.50	26
Nevada	211	11	305.13	4	516.54	4
New Hampshire	204	15	128.46	50	332.95	38
New Jersey	261	3	185.86	41	447.25	13
New Mexico	90	43	269.16	11	359.30	31
New York	317	1	336.24	3	652.32	1
North Carolina	77	46	234.20	22	310.92	42
North Dakota	179	21	196.91	36	375.74	29
Ohio	183	19	159.84	49	343.24	35
Oklahoma	110	38	196.20	37	305.84	44
Oregon	196	17	205.93	33	399.80	23
Pennsylvania	166	27	235.51	21	401.40	22
Rhode Island	167	24	240.78	19	408.08	21
South Carolina	64	50	209.87	30	274.24	48
South Dakota	229	6	169.16	48	398.12	24
Tennessee	104	40	175.05	47	279.35	47
Texas	140	31	176.40	44	316.22	40
Utah	137	33	237.52	20	374.75	30
Vermont	167	24	303.95	5	470.62	10
Virginia	135	34	205.60	34	340.23	37
Washington	141	30	301.55	7	442.94	14

Continued

TABLE 1—*Continued*

State	Per Capita Local Tax Collections, 1969–70		Per Capita State Tax Revenue, Fiscal 1970		Per Capita Total Tax Collections of State and Local Governments, 1969–70	
	Amount	Ranking	Amount	Ranking	Amount	Ranking
West Virginia	$ 80	45	$ 220.72	25	$ 301.10	43
Wisconsin	207	12	301.55	7	508.51	5
Wyoming	180	20	254.12	16	433.63	17
United States	$ 191		$ 236.93		$ 427.14	

SOURCE: *Rankings of the States, 1972*, Research Division, National Education Association (1972).

data are applied to Frank's equation for his index of tax sacrifice. The five highest ranking states in tax sacrifice were Mississippi, North Dakota, South Dakota, Vermont, and Wisconsin. It is interesting that the five leading states in per capita personal income ranked near the bottom in tax sacrifice.

Relative Use of Tax Capacity

Given the definition of tax effort as a ratio of tax revenues to some measure of fiscal capacity, measurements of tax effort can be derived from the general formula tax effort = tax revenues / fiscal capacity. Many measures of tax effort have been developed, but they all rely on this general formula. Any measure of tax effort for education shows the extent to which a state or local school district is actually utilizing its fiscal capacity for that particular purpose. A more general effort measure can be derived by relating tax revenues from own sources to the measure of fiscal ability. Differences in tax effort indices result from the various values that can be used in the numerator and denominator of the general equation.

In one of the first major studies of tax effort as it related to the adequacy and ability of the states to support education, Ashby in 1936 described the general measure of state tax effort as a ratio of the amount spent for education to the financial resources of the state. For the amount-spent portion of his effort index, he used the total expenditures of the state and local school districts exclusive of interest charges, plus the cost of the state department of education less the federal funds and subsidies. In the denominator of the index he used the measures of tax resources as calculated by both Chism and Newcomer.

Ashby considered several possible alternatives for the numerator portion of the index but rejected them as an insufficient measure of the amount

TABLE 2
TAX SEVERITY

State	State / Local Tax Collections in 1969–70 as a Percentage of Personal Income 1970		Per Capita Personal Income 1970		Frank's Index of Tax Sacrifice A / B × 1,000	
	Per Cent	Ranking	Amount	Ranking	Index	Ranking
Alabama	9.1	45	$ 2,853	48	3.1896	17
Alaska	9.0	46	*4,592	4	1.9599	50
Arizona	11.7	11	3,591	28	3.2581	14
Arkansas	9.0	46	2,791	49	3.2246	15
California	12.6	5	4,426	8	2.8468	26
Colorado	10.9	22	3,816	19	2.8563	25
Connecticut	9.9	33	4,856	1	2.0378	49
Delaware	10.3	29	4,324	10	2.3820	46
Florida	9.4	37	3,642	26	2.5809	39
Georgia	9.3	40	3,332	34	2.7911	29
Hawaii	12.8	4	4,527	6	2.8274	27
Idaho	10.7	26	3,240	37	3.3024	13
Illinois	10.8	23	4,502	7	2.3989	45
Indiana	9.4	37	3,781	20	2.4861	42
Iowa	11.8	9	3,688	25	3.1995	16
Kansas	10.3	29	3,823	18	2.6942	33
Kentucky	9.7	34	3,073	43	3.1565	19
Louisiana	10.8	23	3,049	44	3.5421	9
Maine	11.7	11	3,257	36	3.5922	8
Maryland	11.3	18	4,255	11	2.6556	35
Massachusetts	11.4	17	4,360	9	2.6146	36
Michigan	11.2	19	4,059	12	2.7593	31
Minnesota	11.5	14	3,824	17	3.0073	21
Mississippi	11.5	14	2,575	50	4.4660	1
Missouri	9.2	42	3,704	23	2.4838	43
Montana	11.8	9	3,379	33	3.4921	10
Nebraska	10.6	27	3,751	21	2.8259	28
Nevada	11.1	20	4,562	5	2.4331	44
New Hampshire	9.2	42	3,590	29	2.5626	40
New Jersey	9.7	34	4,598	3	2.1096	48
New Mexico	11.5	14	3,131	41	3.6729	6
New York	13.7	1	4,769	2	2.8727	24
North Carolina	9.7	34	3,207	39	3.0246	20
North Dakota	12.6	5	2,995	46	4.2070	2
Ohio	8.6	50	3,972	14	2.1651	47
Oklahoma	9.2	42	$ 3,312	35	2.7777	30
Oregon	10.8	23	3,705	22	2.9149	23
Pennsylvania	10.2	31	3,927	15	2.5974	38
Rhode Island	10.4	28	3,902	16	2.6652	34
South Carolina	9.3	40	2,936	47	3.1675	18
South Dakota	12.6	5	3,165	40	3.9810	3
Tennessee	9.0	46	3,085	42	2.9173	22
Texas	8.9	49	3,531	31	2.5205	41
Utah	11.6	13	3,213	38	3.6103	7
Vermont	13.5	3	3,465	32	3.8961	4
Virginia	9.4	37	3,607	27	2.6060	37

Continued

TABLE 2—*Continued*

State	State / Local Tax Collections in 1969–70 as a Percentage of Personal Income 1970		Per Capita Personal Income 1970		Frank's Index of Tax Sacrifice A / B × 1,000	
	Per Cent	Ranking	Amount	Ranking	Index	Ranking
Washington	11.0	21	3,993	13	2.7548	32
West Virginia	10.0	32	3,021	45	3.3101	12
Wisconsin	13.7	1	3,693	24	3.7097	5
Wyoming	12.2	8	3,556	30	3.4308	11

SOURCE: *Ranking of the States, 1972*, Research Division, National Education Association.

*Reduce 30 per cent to make the purchasing power comparable to figures for other areas of the United States.

spent for education. Receipts from taxation and appropriation were rejected since part of these funds were used either as direct capital outlay or for the payment of debts and interest. According to Ashby, this did not indicate accurately the amount of money that actually went to provide educational opportunities in a given year. He also rejected total expenditures since they included expenditures for capital outlay and debt service and federal monies. Total expenditures for current expenses were rejected because of the inclusion of federal funds.

The amount-spent portion of his index reflected the exclusion of interest charges for debt service and federal funds and subsidies that were objectionable in the alternative figures. The cost of the state department of education was included, according to Ashby, because the money a state department spent for the supervision and improvement of education represented effort just as did money spent directly for schools.[31]

Ashby did cite four limitations to the effort formula that he proposed: it failed to allow for variations in the ratio of total government needs to tax resources; it failed to allow for variations in the ratio of needed educational services to other government needs; it failed to account for differences in standards of living in the various states; it failed to account for the varying costs of a given standard of living due to differences in the price range.[32]

In their 1944 study, Saundelson and Mushkin made a comprehensive analysis of the concepts and measurements of state and local tax effort. They used as a measure of tax effort a ratio of current yields of various tax bases to the actual values of that tax base. Although the fiscal capacity portion of their index was similar to the model tax program suggested by both Chism and Newcomer in that it relied on multiple tax bases, Saundelson and Mushkin used the value of the actual tax bases available. To improve on the model tax program, they made two variations: they used existing tax programs as the standard of comparison rather than a model or theoretically desirable tax (this was done to remove the subjectivity of the model tax plan), and they provided a comparison of the relative tax exploitation by each state with that of the states with comparable economic resources and backgrounds.[33]

In a paper for the National Conference on School Finance in 1965, Alkin proposed a modification of the traditional effort formula. This modification consisted of an allocation factor in the denominator of the effort ratio along with the measure of fiscal capacity. He developed three different indices utilizing different allocation factors as a means of recognizing various impediments in the traditional effort index.[34] His modified effort formula was tax effort = expenditure / allocation factor × fiscal ability. The expenditure portion of the formula represented current expenditures for general control, instructional services, operations, maintenance, and fixed charges at state, intermediate, and local levels of administration. In each of his indices, fiscal ability was defined as personal income of the state as measured by the Department of Commerce. A separate allocation factor was used in each index.

Index 1: The allocation factor was a constant equal to the national average per cent of income devoted to education. This assumed that all states should be expected to spend the same proportion of this income on education.

$$\text{Ind}_1 = \frac{E}{Q_1 \times I}$$

where: $Q_1 = \frac{\Sigma E}{\Sigma I}$

E, I = corresponding national totals
Ind_1 = the effort index
E = expenditure
Q = allocation factor
I = fiscal ability.

Index 2: The allocation factor was assumed to be proportional to the ratio of public school children to the total population in a state. This assumed that the per cent of the state's fiscal ability which was "expected" to be devoted to public education should be proportional to the per cent of public school children in the total population of the state.

$$\text{Ind}_2 = \frac{E}{Q_2 \times I}$$

where: $Q_2 = \dfrac{\Sigma E}{\Sigma I} \cdot \dfrac{A}{N} \cdot \dfrac{\Sigma N}{\Sigma A}$

N   = total population of a state

A   = total public elementary and secondary school enrollment of a state

$\Sigma N, \Sigma A$= corresponding national totals.

Index 3: The allocation factor was based upon the theoretical division of a state's total fiscal ability between schools and all other purposes (including feeding, clothing, and housing the total population of the state) in proportion respectively to public school attendance and total population.

$$\text{Ind}_3 = \frac{E}{Q_3 \times I}$$

where: $Q_3 = \dfrac{C \cdot A}{CA + N}$

$$C = \frac{\Sigma E}{\Sigma I - \Sigma E} \cdot \frac{\Sigma N}{\Sigma A}$$

In order to obtain comparability among the various effort indices, each index was adjusted mathematically with appropriate constants representing national data so that the national average index was 1 for each index. If an index is larger than 1, a state is considered to be exerting greater than national average effort. An index smaller than 1 would reflect an effort below the national average.

Alkin described (see appendices) the results obtained from using the three effort indices as:

Index 1, because of the way it was derived, is unaffected by the ratio of population to public school attendance. Indices 2 and 3 are related functions of N / A, the higher the ratio of N / A, the higher their measured effort. This bears a relationship to how states fare on the various indices. Consider Mississippi (N / A:3.84) and Rhode Island (N / A:6.41). The three indices rank Mississippi 8th, 28th, and 25th with scores of 1.236, .956, and .956, respectively. Rhode Island has ranks of 48, 15, and 15 with scores of .823, 1.062, and 1.056 respectively. On the other hand, Maine, which comes closest to the national average of N / A, obtains the same scores and ranks from all three indices.

As a basis for comparing the indices an analysis has been prepared which shows the relationship between index results and four situational factors. (1) per capita income; (2) percent enrollment increase

1950–60; (3) percent enrollment in private schools; and (4) percent urban population. . . . In the case of the first factor, per capita income, it appears that Index 1 strongly "favors" those states whose per capita income is low. Also, factors 2, 3, and 4 are favored by Indices 2 and 3. That is, each of these two indices has a greater positive relationship to percent enrollment increase, percent enrollment in private schools, and percent urban population.

Factor 2, percent increase in enrollment, shows consistent results among the three indices. In all three cases states with a high percent of increase received smaller effort measures. The differences are less with Indices 2 and 3, however. . . . Relative to the third factor, Index 1 shows opposite results from Indices 2 and 3, the former giving highest effort to the states with the highest relative public school enrollment. . . . Although the results of the relationship from Factor 4 is perhaps incidental, it should be noted that indices 2 and 3 favor urban states to a slight degree.

In a study of the relationships among centralization, ability, and effort in school finance among the continental states, Ratliff used as his measure of tax effort public school expenditures as a per cent of personal income.[35] Centralization was defined as the per cent of total state and local revenues from the state. Ability was determined by the personal income per pupil enrolled in the public schools. He concluded that among the continental states, those that were exerting the greatest effort to support public education had the least ability and that states with the least ability tended to have the greatest degree of centralization.

In Ratliff's rankings of the states, the five leading states in tax effort (New Mexico, South Dakota, North Dakota, Wyoming, and Louisiana) ranked low in ability with ranks of 40, 38, 33, 26, and 34, respectively. When ranked according to his definition of centralization, the five leading effort states ranked 5, 46, 38, 26, and 7, respectively. The five lowest ranking states in tax effort were Illinois, Missouri, Connecticut, Rhode Island, and Delaware. When these states were ranked according to ability, their respective ranks were 5, 16, 3, 6, and 1. Their centralization ranks were 37, 20, 32, 43, and 1. It is interesting to note that Delaware ranked first in centralization and ability, but last in tax effort.

Ratliff hypothesized that in those states where ability was lowest, or where the educational task was most burdensome, the people were most willing to shift the duty of financing the schools to the state government. He also hypothesized that the state governments in these low ability or heavy educational task states may have felt the necessity of participating in school finance to a greater degree to assure a certain minimum of educational services. The results of this analysis are shown in Table 3.

State	Centralization Total State and Local Revenue from State Per Cent	Ranking	Ability Personal Income Per Pupil Enrolled Amount	Ranking	Effort School Expenditure as Per Cent of Personal Income Per Cent	Ranking
Alabama	79.8	2	$ 5,056	45	3.28	15
Alaska	—	—	—	—	—	—
Arizona	33.8	29	7,320	32	3.65	6
Arkansas	47.7	17	4,617	47	2.99	22
California	43.6	18	12,290	8	2.68	30
Colorado	16.2	44	8,506	23	3.02	21
Connecticut	28.0	32	14,296	3	2.15	46
Delaware	85.9	1	16,071	1	2.00	48
Florida	57.8	11	8,294	24	2.68	29
Georgia	71.3	6	5,694	42	2.94	26
Hawaii	—	—	—	—	—	—
Idaho	25.2	35	6,320	37	3.51	7
Illinois	24.9	37	14,103	5	2.21	44
Indiana	34.7	28	9,392	17	2.62	32
Iowa	14.0	45	7,734	30	3.46	11
Kansas	20.3	40	7,956	29	3.25	17
Kentucky	39.4	24	6,321	36	2.38	40
Louisiana	71.2	7	6,652	34	3.76	5
Maine	27.9	33	8,217	25	2.50	36
Maryland	35.6	27	11,006	14	2.39	39
Massachusetts	23.4	39	13,130	7	2.25	42
Michigan	50.9	14	11,523	10	2.65	31
Minnesota	40.0	23	9,179	20	3.26	16
Mississippi	57.4	12	3,886	48	3.38	13
Missouri	40.9	20	10,208	16	2.20	45
Montana	19.0	42	9,022	21	3.50	9
Nebraska	2.2	48	8,536	22	2.99	23
Nevada	49.2	15	11,104	12	2.61	33
New Hampshire	5.8	47	10,538	15	2.41	38
New Jersey	25.2	36	14,285	4	2.37	41
New Mexico	74.3	5	6,236	40	4.40	1
New York	37.9	25	14,793	2	2.47	37
North Carolina	75.7	4	5,407	44	3.16	19
North Dakota	23.9	38	6,874	33	3.86	3
Ohio	31.6	31	11,490	11	2.23	43
Oklahoma	40.2	22	6,651	35	3.38	14
Oregon	32.8	30	9,269	19	3.39	12
Pennsylvania	48.4	16	11,672	9	2.59	34
Rhode Island	17.7	43	13,784	6	2.07	47
South Carolina	78.7	3	4,623	46	3.48	10
South Dakota	7.1	46	6,282	38	4.30	2
Tennessee	64.0	9	5,758	41	2.95	25
Texas	56.0	13	8,128	27	2.84	27
Utah	40.3	21	6,253	39	3.51	8
Vermont	27.8	34	7,966	28	2.99	24
Virginia	41.5	19	7,470	31	2.54	35

Continued

TABLE 3—*Continued*

State	Centralization Total State and Local Revenue from State Per Cent	Ranking	Ability Personal Income Per Pupil Enrolled Amount	Ranking	Effort School Expenditure as Per Cent of Personal Income Per Cent	Ranking
Washington	65.7	8	9,285	18	3.03	20
West Virginia	62.7	10	5,647	43	3.17	18
Wisconsin	20.0	41	11,096	13	2.77	28
Wyoming	37.0	26	8,142	26	3.85	4

Johns and Morphet, in a discussion of variations in tax effort for education, have analyzed several possible measures of state effort.[36] They are critical of using school expenditures, alone, as a measure of effort: "The expenditures may constitute a very rough indication of effort, but do not actually measure it, because a state or district with high ability may be able, with little effort, to expend a large amount of funds that a less wealthy state or district could expend with much higher effort. Expenditures therefore give some indication of the investment in education, but not necessarily of the effort being made to support the schools."

They suggested two other more feasible measures of tax effort: the percentage of personal income devoted to expenditures for schools, and the percentage of personal income per school-age child utilized to provide revenue from state and local sources for public schools. In the first method they recommended the use of current expenditures rather than total expenditures. They indicated that current expenditures are less likely to fluctuate from year to year since that figure does not include money from the sale of bonds to be retired over a period of years.[37]

The NEFP has suggested two indices of state effort to support education: the percentage of net personal income devoted to elementary and secondary schools, and the percentage of the tax revenue of the state and local governments that goes to education.[38] Both are based on the assumption that state revenue is largely based on net personal income. The derivation of the net personal income figure was explained in the earlier section on fiscal capacity. A ranking of the states based on these indices shows wide variations in state effort. Table 4 gives some examples.

The Advisory Commission on Intergovernmental Relations (ACIR) in 1962 measured the tax effort of the states according to the income and representative tax system approach.[39] The income approach measured tax effort as a ratio of tax revenues to various income indicators—personal income, income produced, corporate income, and a composite income index. The representative tax system approached measured effort as a ratio of tax revenues to the results of a uniform or representative tax system. These results are shown in Appendices A and B.

In 1971 the ACIR measured effort as the ratio of revenue amounts actually received by state and local governments to the revenue capacity of the state as determined by an "average financing system." This system broadened the "representative tax system" used in the ACIR's 1962 study of capacity and effort by including a consideration of nontax revenues of the area under study.[40]

The ACIR figures from the 1971 study showed wide variations in the states' functional efforts for education and other public services. Functional effort was defined as the expenditures from state-local sources as a per cent of overall fiscal capacity. Table 5 shows this variation.[41]

TABLE 4
VARIATIONS IN STATE EFFORT

Rank	State	Elementary-Secondary Education as a Per Cent of Net Personal Income, 1969
1	New Mexico	8.90
5	Mississippi	7.84
10	Minnesota	7.36
15	New York	6.99
20	Colorado	6.61
	Wisconsin	6.61
25	Michigan	6.44
30	Alaska	6.21
35	North Carolina	5.89
40	Oklahoma	5.66
45	Illinois	5.39
50	Nebraska	5.00

Rank	State	Per Cent of State and Local Tax Revenue Allocated to Elementary-Secondary Education, 1969
1	Utah	39.73
5	Pennsylvania	38.87
10	Illinois	37.38
15	Virginia	36.30
20	Maine	35.65
25	North Carolina	33.99
30	Texas	32.57
35	Idaho	32.11
	Georgia	32.11
40	California	30.43
45	Hawaii	29.18
50	Wyoming	25.51

In determining Alabama's relative tax effort among nine southeastern states, Leathers used four different measurements of state tax effort.[42] These effort measures were per capita state and local tax collections, state and local taxes as a percentage of personal income, Frank's index of tax sacrifice, and a composite index of tax effort.

The first three measurements have been discussed elsewhere in this chapter. The composite index of tax effort was explained by Leathers:

> The composite index of tax effort involves the computation of three different indexes: an economic ability index, a tax index, and the effort index. Each index is calculated by dividing the state per capita figure by the average per capita figure for the nation, and then multiplying by 100.
>
> The economic ability index is in itself a composite index, consisting of three equally weighted component indexes: a per capita personal income index, a per capita value of the output of basic industries index, and a per capita retail sales index. The per capita output index, in turn, has three equally weighted components: per capita value added by manufactures, per capita value of 78 basic farm crops, and the per capita value of mineral production, all of which must be calculated from aggregate data. Both the economic ability index and its component per capita output index are found by taking the simple arithmetic mean of the three component indexes.
>
> The tax index is simply obtained by dividing the state-local per capita figures for each state by the average per capita state-local figure for the nation, multiplied by 100. The tax effort index, finally is calculated by dividing the tax index by the economic ability index, multiplied by 100. An index number of 100.00 on any of the indexes indicates the national average, while a rating above 100.00 or below 100.00 indicates an index exceeding or falling below the national average.

Leathers indicated that an advantage of the composite index approach was that it enabled the observer to compare tax abilities as well as tax efforts. The primary disadvantage occurred as the result of the normal time lag in the availability of data needed for the calculations.

According to Leathers, the four methods used to measure Alabama's relative state-local tax effort gave somewhat conflicting results in both national and regional rankings. These results are shown in Table 6. When the various states' relative tax effort was measured by per capita state-local taxes, Alabama ranked forty-seventh among all states and seventh among the nine southeastern states. According to the second effort index, state-local taxes as a percentage of personal income, Alabama tied for fifth place in the southeast. The best overall tax effort rating was achieved using Frank's index of tax sacrifice. Using this index, Alabama was tied for eighth highest in the nation, but ranked only fifth out of nine in the region. According to the composite index approach, Leathers indicated that Alabama's tax effort index ranked the eighth lowest in the nation and seventh among the nine southeastern states.

In a study of state and local tax effort in Georgia, Holshouser briefly reviewed the tax effort studies of Leathers, Frank, and Quindry.[43] He concluded that the most commonly used and the most adequate measure of tax effort was state and local taxes as a percentage of total personal income. He was critical of Frank's index of tax sacrifice as possibly giving too much

TABLE 5
MEASURES OF FUNCTIONAL EFFORT
(expenditure from state-local sources as a per cent of overall fiscal capacity)

Function(s)	United States Average	Median State	Highest State	Lowest State	High-Low Range
Education	39	39	Utah, 62	Nevada, 26	2.5–1.0
Highways	11	13	Vermont, 27	Nevada, 7	4.1–1.0
Public welfare (health and hospitals)	12	10	New York, 20	N. Dakota, 6	3.5–1.0
Police and fire protection	5	4	New York, 8	N. Dakota, 2	3.8–1.0

weight to income, especially when the equation had the effect of squaring the personal income figure. He was also critical of Leathers' composite tax index as not yielding current enough data. Quindry's measure of tax effort used personal income supplemented with the estimated annual yield of property (12.5 per cent of the full assessed value) as a measure of tax capacity. Holshouser indicated that supplementing personal income with the estimated annual yield of property tax is theoretically superior to using only personal income. He suggests that the difficulty with Quindry's measure is the problem encountered in estimating accurately the full assessed value of property.

Holshouser applied his effort measure to Georgia and compared the results with the average effort of the United States and the southeastern states. He found that the estimated tax effort in Georgia for 1969–70 was slightly above the effort of the average southeastern state, below the effort

TABLE 6
LEATHERS' RELATIVE TAX EFFORTS OF NINE SOUTHEASTERN STATES BY FOUR METHODS OF MEASURE

| State | Per Capita State and Local Taxes, 1965 | | Indices | |
	Amount (dollars) and Ranking	Per cent of Per Capita Personal Income and Ranking	Frank's 1965 Index and Ranking	Tax Effort 1963 Index and Ranking
Alabama	167.55 7	8.8 5	4.6 5	84.7 7
Arkansas	159.47 9	8.6 6	4.7 3	88.3 5
Florida	233.01 1	9.6 3	4.0 9	103.7 1
Georgia	190.74 3	8.8 5	4.1 8	89.1 4
Louisiana	222.04 2	10.7 1	5.2 2	95.2 3
Mississippi	169.89 6	10.6 2	6.6 1	100.0 2
North Carolina	188.30 4	9.2 4	4.5 6	85.1 6
South Carolina	160.82 8	8.6 6	4.7 3	83.4 8
Tennessee	178.24 5	8.8 5	4.4 7	80.7 9

of the average of the four leading southeastern states (other than Georgia), and considerably below the effort of the average state in the nation.

The National Education Association (NEA), through its research division, produces regular reports of the tax ability and tax effort of the various states in the support of public education. The NEA utilized two measures of tax effort, both of which are related to personal income: the ratio of total current expenditures to personal income, and a ratio of state and local revenues for schools to personal income (see appendix).

The conventional method of measuring local tax effort has been the ratio of local school tax revenues of the school district to the equalized assessed valuation of property. This method has been suggested or used by Johns and Morphet, Johns and Kimbrough, Kay, and others in studies of local tax effort.[44]

As indicated in the section on local tax ability, a number of writers have suggested using economic indicators, primarily income, as a standard of local ability. Local effort measures could then be developed. *School Management* has used, as one of its measures of local effort, a ratio of current expenditures per pupil to the per capita personal income of the school district.[45] Johns and Kimbrough, in a study of fiscal relationships among selected school districts in four states, used both the equalized assessed valuation of property standard and a ratio of local revenue receipts of the local school district to the net effective buying income of that district as reported by *Sales Management*.[46] Net effective income is comparable to the economic definition of disposable income, that is, the income remaining after the payment of all personal taxes.

Rossmiller utilized various economic indicators and property values per pupil in ADM in comparing the relative fiscal capacities and efforts of several classes of school districts.[47]

Patton, in a study of fiscal relationships in South Dakota, used as a measure of local effort, a ratio of annual current operating expenses to the assessed valuation of property.[48]

INDICATORS OF TAX EFFORT

The purpose of this section is to review the relevant literature and to identify the indicators of tax effort. Many of the studies referred to have already been mentioned in the various sections of this paper.

Johns and Morphet have observed that there are many factors that influence the effort made by the people to support public education: "[the people's] interest in and attitude toward public education, their 'feelings' about government and taxes, the tax structure in the state in which they live, the amounts of taxes they pay for purposes other than public schools, whether they have children or grandchildren in schools, their reaction to the program provided by the schools in the communities in which they live, probably their reaction to the party in power and to the kind of leadership provided by prominent legislators and the governor, and so on.'' They also cited inadequate district structure as one of the important reasons for differences in effort, but they concluded that "even if all districts would be properly organized and a sound state plan of financial support developed there would still be variations in effort due to differences in the peoples' interest in their schools, in their attitudes towards taxes, and in their willingness to provide the financial support needed for a satisfactory program of education."[49]

In a study of socioeconomic variables affecting local tax effort in Kentucky, Kay identified twenty-four variables to study in relation to local effort. His research suggested that the degree of urbanization was the most important single factor in explaining the variance in local school tax effort. The second most important factor was the amount of wealth and income in the district. Other factors associated with local districts characterized by high tax effort were districts drawing much of their local taxes from residences, high levels of income, high levels of education, large number of people in white-collar occupations, substantial number of renters (mobile population), many Negro students, high average daily attendance (ADA), increasing enrollments, good school retention, and substantial number of students in nonpublic schools. Factors associated with low effort districts were those deriving a substantial portion of their local tax revenue from farms, low incomes and high unemployment, districts receiving substantial amounts of aid from the state and federal governments, and a stable population.

Kay concluded that in wealthy districts the socioeconomic variables and factors explained a substantial portion of the variance in tax effort. For all districts and for low-wealth districts, idiosyncratic variables, e.g., the attitudes of local opinion leaders regarding education, not identified in his study, were generally as important or more important than the socioeconomic factors and variables used.[50]

In a comprehensive study done for the Office of Education in 1968, Johns and Kimbrough investigated the interrelationships of socioeconomic factors, educational leadership, and the community power structure, and the relationships of these factors to local financial effort. The factors they found associated with high effort districts were high per capita wealth; competitive power structures; superintendents more politically active in resolving both educational and general community issues; community influentials, teachers, and registered voters all held more liberal civic beliefs but there were no significant differences in educational or economic beliefs; a larger percentage of the leaders were from the political category; leaders tended to produce open social systems; and the community influentials participated more in the resolution of civic and educational issues.

Low effort districts were characterized by noncompetitive power structure; superintendents less politically active in resolving both educational and general community issues; the power structure was dominated by leaders from the economic system; the community influentials tended to produce closed social systems; the higher percentage of leaders were native-born; and more leaders tended to be locals.

Johns and Kimbrough concluded that the evidence in their study indicated that "the level of local effort was determined largely by political decisions resulting from the interactions of power systems with each other, conditioned by the beliefs and value systems of the components of their environment and affected only occasionally at the present time by the activities of the superintendent of schools.[51]

An important aspect of their study was the fact that 88 of the 122 school districts studied followed relatively consistent effort patterns during the 18-year time span of the study. They found that the high effort districts continued as such throughout the time period, the median districts, in general, continued to make median effort, and the low effort districts consistently made low effort. They observed that "conceivably most districts select for themselves a high, low, or median financial effort norm which represents their educational aspiration level. Once a district has established its effort norm, it seems difficult to change it."[52]

In a study of informal county leadership structure and controls affecting educational policy decision-making, Kimbrough identified factors of community power structure associated with fiscal effort.[53] These power characteristics were associated with the low fiscal effort district: there was a monopolistic power structure; the educational policies were sanctioned by a small group of power wielders, none of whom held official position in the school system; public school officials held relatively low power status compared to those in the economic sphere of influence; the government structure was under the control of a small group of economic dominants in the power structure; the superintendent was not recognized as influential; citizen participation was low; there was only one active political party; there were few civic issues; and the political climate was very conservative.

The high effort county was characterized: there was a competitive power structure (multistructured); the power structure was influenced by professionals, retirees, and businessmen; local public officials held higher power status; the superintendent of schools was one of the nine most powerful officials; there was less differentiation in power roles; the political system was more open; there was greater citizen participation; there was a strong two-party political system; there was a high rate of population increase; there were more civic issues; and the political climate was moderately conservative.

Kimbrough concluded that the extreme conservatism of the low effort county leaders contributed to the county's lower financial effort. This conclusion was supported by the study of actions taken by the leaders of both counties on proposals which would have meant increased expenditure for education.

Johns wrote in 1952 that variations in local effort could be explained by differences in per capita wealth of local school districts or differences in the cultural level of the people or in the quality of educational leadership.[54]

In 1962 the ACIR suggested that possible differences in tax effort could result from differences in population density and urbanization. Differences could result from the higher cost of essential government services in the urban areas or the differences in the proportion of the population consisting of the dependent age groups: the unemployed, the aged, and those with needs for publicly assisted housing. The ACIR also observed that states at varying stages of economic development, experiencing different growth rates, may elect to allocate their resources differently between public and private uses. Methods of financing government functions employed by states or local jurisdictions could affect tax effort ranks over short periods of time.[55]

Saundelson and Mushkin identified a number of factors affecting relative tax effort. They indicated that variations in economic and political policies, in standards and costs of government services, and in methods of financing government functions are all reflected in tax effort. They concluded that the causes of tax effort variations must be explored more extensively to assess fully the significance of these variations. State differences in population density and urbanization, racial composition, needs for particular government programs, debt position, industrialization, and political and economic factors must be considered in turn in evaluating tax effort findings.[56]

In a study of suburban power structure and the relationship of values, influence, and tax effort, Bloomberg and Sunshine have developed a model of the determinants of local tax effort.[57] They identified three variables associated with strategic alternatives available to the supporters of the

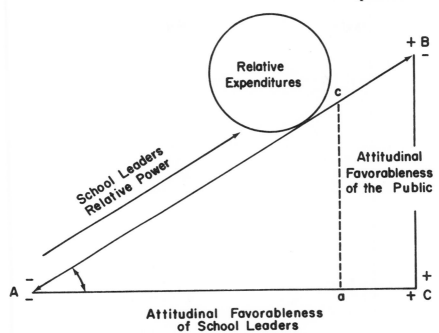

Fig. 1. Bloomberg-Sunshine model of the determinants of local tax effort

public schools: the power resources of school leaders relative to others involved, and how efficiently this potential is employed; the values and goals of school leaders—how favorable their attitudes are with respect to seeking greater local tax effort; and the attitudinal favorableness of citizens at large. Figure 1 is the model Bloomberg and Sunshine developed to demonstrate the interrelationships of the three identified variables. They describe how the model is used to explain tax effort:

The figure shows relationships among these three variables and the relative expenditure of a district, which locates it somewhere between the top and bottom alternative levels of relative expenditure for districts of that resource potential and thereby establishes its status for tax effort. The ends of the lines making up the figure are tagged with a plus and a minus to signify favorable and unfavorable directions. The ball on the incline represents current tax assessments on full property value relative to the size of the school enrollments. The higher the ball on the incline, of course, the closer this utilization of local resources is to the pragmatic maximum tax effort for districts of that level of property wealth.

The line AC indicates that the attitudes of the school leaders, to be located for favorableness on line AC, serve to set a limit on how far along the tax effort continuum the district could be pushed if there were no resistance whatever the power of the school leaders. It also shows the "distance" between their aspirations, as indexed by attitudinal favorableness, and the actual level of relative expenditure. The length of the line AB represents the total distance between top and bottom alternative levels of relative expenditures, indexed as described above. The slope of the line portrays the resistance faced by school leaders, which is determined essentially by the attitudes of the public, represented by the length of the line BC. This mechanical analogy makes it clear that the amount of power required to move the tax ball is a function of the angle BAC, or, more simply, the length of the line BC. If the citizens of the district have very unfavorable attitudes, line BC is lengthened, thereby increasing the slope and increasing the amount of power which school leaders would have to be able to apply to boost school taxes.

Bloomberg and Sunshine indicate that other strategic alternatives are available to school supporters to increase the support level, tax effort, besides those strategies aimed at influencing public attitudes. Nevertheless, the importance of public attitudes as shown in Bloomberg and Sunshine's model is consistent with Kay's conclusion in his study of tax effort in Kentucky. Kay found that the attitudes of local opinion leaders regarding education were generally as important or more important than the socioeconomic factors and variables used in his study.[58]

CONCLUSIONS

Although per capita personal income is probably the most widely used measure of tax capacity in tax effort indices, there are several limitations that must be recognized when personal income figures are used. The primary problem is that personal income tends to understate the actual tax capacity of certain areas. An understatement of tax capacity has the effect of inflating the tax effort index. This is especially true in those states that are able to shift the incidence of various taxes to nonresident consumers. An example of this occurs in tourist states, such as Florida, that rely heavily on sales taxes: "in an area with a large volume of tourist trade, heavy reliance on sales taxes may load onto nonresident visitors a considerable fraction of the financing of public requirements. For such an area one might find a comparatively high measure of relative revenue effort, even though locally borne tax burdens are only average or even low."[59]

According to the ACIR study of state revenue potential, personal income also understated the true taxable base of oil- and mineral-rich states like Louisiana, Texas, and Wyoming because of their ability to tax certain captive industries heavily.[60] Tax capacity measures based on personal income also understated those jurisdictions with a heavy concentration of large industries that pay corporate income taxes or local property taxes. Because these taxes can be shifted forward through higher prices to the wider buying public, the local residents enjoy the benefits of the tax contributions without the consequent tax burdens.

In these various situations per capita personal income is not a valid indicator of tax capacity. In an effort to avoid the problems associated with personal income, a tax effort index has been developed using the tax data provided by John Due in his chapter in this volume. Rather than devising a model tax system based on the many available state taxes, Due concentrated on the four major sources of state tax: sales, cigarettes and liquor, personal income, and corporate income. He estimated that a potential additional tax revenue of $37.7 billion could be realized if these four taxes were increased to a given rate, the tax structures broadened, and the tax administration made more effective.

This is a more realistic approach to tax capacity since it provides a method to compare states on the basis of their estimated tax revenue potential. This approach shows the tax revenues that states are capable of generating rather than what they actually raise. Table 7 shows the tax effort rankings using tax capacity based on Due's total tax revenue potential from the four major state taxes.

It is not surprising to note that tourist states such as Florida and Nevada rank 47 and 45, respectively, in tax effort when using this capacity measure. Both states rely heavily on the general sales tax as a major source of state revenues. The incidence of these taxes can readily be shifted forward to the nonresident tourist consumer. Neither state uses a personal income tax as a revenue source. States relying on their mineral production as a source of tax revenue also show a low tax effort for education. Louisiana, Wyoming, and Texas rank 30, 34, and 35 respectively. The incidence of these taxes can also be shifted forward through higher consumer prices.

According to the ACIR, fiscal effort measures are concerned with relationships in two ways: to measure for any particular area the actual fiscal performance of governments against their estimated financial reach, and to examine differences from area to area in this measure of relative government effort.[61] A variety of measures have been developed and used to determine state and local tax effort for education. The relative position that an area has in regard to its tax effort rank will depend, to a large extent, on the particular measure used. The comparative charts have demonstrated

TABLE 7
TAX EFFORT INDEX USING DUE'S POTENTIAL STATE TAX REVENUES AS THE TAX CAPACITY MEASURE

State	State and Local Revenue for Elementary and Secondary Education Per ADM (1972–73)[1] (A)	Due's Tax Capacity Per Capita (1972–73)[2] (B)	Tax Effort A / B (C)	Rank Order (D)
Alabama	$ 534.49	$296.82	1.8007	44
Alaska	1,575.54	370.46	4.2529	1
Arizona	906.65	429.95	2.1087	33
Arkansas	602.31	377.54	1.5953	48
California	1,230.74	439.65	2.7993	10
Colorado	1,093.52	339.17	3.2241	5
Connecticut	1,299.92	488.38	2.6616	14
Delaware	1,307.80	498.07	2.6257	19
Florida	885.74	517.59	1.7112	47
Georgia	637.01	424.89	1.4992	50
Hawaii	1,227.38	627.21	1.9568	40
Idaho	736.13	371.79	1.9799	39
Illinois	1,309.57	405.18	3.2320	3
Indiana	1,011.55	371.74	2.7211	13
Iowa	1,064.37	378.02	2.8156	9
Kansas	1,006.30	414.95	2.4251	24
Kentucky	691.55	394.59	1.7525	46
Louisiana	817.17	382.61	2.1357	30
Maine	804.32	388.21	2.0718	36
Maryland	1,369.29	441.67	3.1002	6
Massachusetts	1,123.93	427.50	2.6290	18
Michigan	1,085.11	446.10	2.4324	23
Minnesota	1,307.00	458.58	2.8501	8
Mississippi	562.49	356.87	1.5761	49
Missouri	978.74	355.76	2.7511	11
Montana	884.73	384.36	2.3018	26
Nebraska	840.39	386.19	2.1761	29
Nevada	958.12	542.21	1.7670	45
New Hampshire	905.62	440.18	2.0573	37
New Jersey	1,392.87	431.91	3.2249	4
New Mexico	779.17	410.41	1.8985	43
New York	1,644.53	404.99	4.0606	2
North Carolina	796.46	351.73	2.2644	28
North Dakota	863.66	407.57	2.1190	32
Ohio	930.87	379.08	2.4556	22
Oklahoma	778.08	364.41	2.1351	31
Oregon	1,128.67	441.05	2.5590	21
Pennsylvania	1,195.04	387.74	3.0820	7
Rhode Island	1,048.09	407.22	2.5737	20
South Carolina	717.98	373.81	1.9207	41
South Dakota	803.84	342.65	2.3459	25
Tennessee	695.36	349.48	1.9896	38
Texas	814.06	392.02	2.0765	35
Utah	794.89	418.01	1.9016	42
Vermont	1,241.61	540.43	2.2974	27

Continued

TABLE 7—*Continued*

State	State and Local Revenue for Elementary and Secondary Education Per ADM (1972–73)[1] (A)	Due's Tax Capacity Per Capita (1972–73)[2] (B)	Tax Effort A / B (C)	Rank Order (D)
Virginia	925.56	347.85	2.6608	15
Washington	1,120.58	422.18	2.6544	16
West Virginia	715.14	260.56	2.7446	12
Wisconsin	1,187.20	448.21	2.6487	17
Wyoming	1,034.48	494.22	2.0931	34

1. Revenue and enrollment data from the National Education Association, Research Division.
2. Tax capacity data from John Due, "Alternative State and Local Tax Sources for Education," in this volume.

the variations in the tax effort rankings of states as the result of given measures. In some cases, a given formula may tend to give greater weight to a particular factor in the effort measure. This was the case in the modifications in the traditional effort formula proposed by Alkin which was discussed earlier.

Questions remain as to the wider meaning of effort measures and the validity of the resulting indices. In order to evaluate measures of tax effort one must consider the related activities of the total economy. The collection and allocation of tax revenues for education do not occur in fiscal isolation. They occur within the wider parameters of the general economy. Saundelson and Mushkin have identified several aspects of the economy that should be considered when evaluating tax effort measures. These include a consideration of the relation of tax effort measures to governmental activities such as the total scope of the public economy, the costs of other government functions, and other methods of government financing available.[62] Each of these activities has a potential impact on measures of tax effort. Saundelson and Mushkin wrote, "In a sense, a composite measure of tax effort reflects the state of economic development in a particular jurisdiction and its decision on the desired allocation of its resources for the satisfaction of wants. Tax effort generally indicates not merely the extent to which taxes are imposed but also differences among jurisdictions in their emphasis on government activity and in the allocation of functions between the public and private economies. . . . Current differences among states in tax effort reflect in part variations in their industrialization and economic development and the different types of government activities considered essential. . . . Tax effort is a basic expression of social and economic policy and denotes more than the government's willingness to tax or the people's willingness to be taxed'' (p. 4). Tax effort measures should be carefully evaluated to determine what is actually being measured: the fiscal performance of particular governmental units as related to their revenue capacity or the resulting tax burdens that fall on the people. Tax effort measures have been used to show both situations.

The problem of securing current and adequate data should also be taken into consideration when evaluating tax effort measures. Data used in such measures are generally one to several years old. In most cases, these are probably the best data available for tax effort studies. There is generally a time lag between the collection, processing, and availability of government fiscal data. The tax effort rankings that are based on such data are therefore limited by such time constraints. This is not to imply, however, that such tax effort measures are invalid. Such measures provide a comparative ranking of the areas under consideration for a given point in time. Major changes in the fiscal relationship among the various levels of government or political and fiscal changes within a state or local government could have an important effect on the comparative tax effort rankings. Any such changes should be taken into consideration when evaluating tax effort measures.

Great variations exist among states and local areas in their tax effort for education. In some cases, those states making the greatest tax effort have the least fiscal ability. The converse is also true: some states making a low effort for education have the greatest fiscal ability. Although some writers have argued for "reward for effort," this method could potentially benefit more those states or districts who are already in a favorable position because of greater fiscal capacity. Those states or districts with greater fiscal capacity may be in a position to exert greater tax effort simply because they are more able to afford the additional effort which may not represent a burden for the people. In those states with high effort and low ability, any additional effort may be impossible because of other governmental needs or the tax burden placed upon the people. Low effort and low ability states or districts may be in a position in which even a modest effort has such meager returns that a pattern of low effort is perpetuated.

Several studies have indicated that idiosyncratic and power structure variables have an impact on tax effort. These considerations should also be made when evaluating tax effort measures. The degree to which these power structure variables act as a restraint of tax effort for education is not known at present. Additional study of the degree of impact of such variables is recommended.

State	Johns and Hamilton, 1969 State / Local Revenue for Elementary Per Cent Secondary Education as Per Cent of General Revenue of State / Local Government from Own Sources and Ranking		NEA, 1969–70 State and Local Revenues as a Per Cent of Total Personal Income and Ranking		NEA, 1969–70 Total Current Expenditures as a Per Cent of Personal Income and Ranking		ACIR, 1968–69 Tax Revenue As a Per Cent of Tax Capacity (average financing system) and Ranking		Johns and Lindman State / Local Revenue as a Per Cent of Net Personal Income ÷ 6.24 (United States Average Effort) 1969 and Ranking	
Alabama	27.81	47	4.0	48	3.9	46	84	38	.88	42
Alaska	32.24	32	5.0	23	6.6	3	99	20	1.00	29
Arizona	36.20	16	5.8	6	5.3	8	103	12	1.24	6
Arkansas	33.22	27	4.1	45	4.6	25	74	47	.99	31
California	30.42	40	4.3	36	4.1	39	116	5	1.04	23
Colorado	32.89	28	5.3	15	4.8	21	98	22	1.06	19
Connecticut	38.95	4	5.3	15	4.3	31	88	32	.90	41
Delaware	38.43	7	5.7	8	4.9	19	81	42	1.15	11
Florida	34.34	24	4.6	34	4.3	31	81	42	1.01	27
Georgia	32.11	34	4.1	45	4.1	39	87	33	.92	37
Hawaii	29.18	45	5.6	10	4.9	19	129	2	1.02	26
Idaho	32.11	34	4.7	29	4.6	25	100	18	1.14	12
Illinois	37.38	10	4.7	29	3.7	48	87	33	.86	45
Indiana	39.65	2	4.3	36	4.2	35	90	29	1.05	21
Iowa	35.80	17	5.4	12	5.5	7	103	12	1.13	14
Kansas	37.33	12	5.3	15	4.2	35	87	33	1.07	17
Kentucky	29.63	42	4.3	36	4.3	31	89	30	.92	37
Louisiana	32.19	33	5.0	23	5.1	12	83	40	1.19	9
Maine	35.65	20	5.4	12	5.1	12	102	14	1.03	24
Maryland	38.80	6	5.2	20	4.7	24	105	10	1.08	16
Massachusetts	29.57	43	4.1	45	3.4	50	119	4	.84	48
Michigan	33.30	26	4.7	29	4.8	21	109	8	1.03	24
Minnesota	35.36	21	5.8	6	5.2	11	112	7	1.18	10
Mississippi	31.32	37	4.7	29	5.0	15	98	22	1.26	5
Missouri	34.64	22	4.3	36	4.0	45	81	42	.88	42

Continued

APPENDIX A—*Continued*

State	Johns and Hamilton, 1969 State / Local Revenue for Elementary Per Cent Secondary Education as Per Cent of General Revenue of State / Local Government from Own Sources and Ranking		NEA, 1969–70 State and Local Revenues as a Per Cent of Total Personal Income and Ranking		NEA, 1969–70 Total Current Expenditures as a Per Cent of Personal Income and Ranking		ACIR, 1968–69 Tax Revenue As a Per Cent of Tax Capacity (average financing system) and Ranking		Johns and Lindman State / Local Revenue as a Per Cent of Net Personal Income ÷ 6.24 (United States Average Effort) 1969 and Ranking	
Montana	38.14	8	6.0	3	6.0	5	91	27	1.29	3
Nebraska	26.98	49	4.2	42	4.1	39	87	33	.80	50
Nevada	29.82	41	4.7	29	4.2	35	71	50	.95	33
New Hampshire	34.60	23	4.3	36	3.9	46	77	46	.86	45
New Jersey	36.64	14	4.9	25	4.4	29	100	18	.92	37
New Mexico	35.73	18	5.9	4	6.1	4	91	27	1.43	1
New York	32.53	31	5.3	15	4.8	21	139	1	1.12	15
North Carolina	33.99	25	4.4	35	4.3	31	87	33	.94	35
North Dakota	27.95	46	5.4	12	5.0	15	95	25	1.14	12
Ohio	35.72	19	4.3	36	4.1	39	82	41	.85	47
Oklahoma	29.26	44	3.8	50	4.1	39	74	47	.91	40
Oregon	39.32	3	5.9	4	5.3	8	101	16	1.29	3
Pennsylvania	38.87	5	4.9	25	4.4	29	99	20	.99	31
Rhode Island	30.77	39	4.0	48	4.1	39	107	9	.83	49
South Carolina	37.02	13	5.1	22	5.1	12	89	30	1.07	17
South Dakota	27.15	48	4.9	25	5.3	8	101	16	.95	33
Tennessee	32.87	29	4.2	42	4.2	35	84	38	.94	35
Texas	32.57	30	4.2	42	3.6	49	72	49	.87	44
Utah	38.73	1	6.3	2	5.6	6	104	11	1.35	2
Vermont	37.37	11	6.5	1	6.7	1	116	5	1.21	8
Virginia	36.30	15	4.8	28	4.5	27	96	24	1.01	27
Washington	30.95	38	5.3	15	4.5	27	102	14	1.00	29
West Virginia	37.54	9	5.2	20	5.0	15	95	25	1.22	7
Wisconsin	31.52	36	5.7	8	5.0	15	123	3	1.06	19
Wyoming	25.51	50	5.6	10	6.7	1	78	45	1.05	21

APPENDIX B
COMPARATIVE MEASURES OF TAX EFFORT BY STATE

State	Alkin, Index 1 1960 and Ranking		Alkin, Index 2 1960 and Ranking		Alkin, Index 3 1960 and Ranking		ACIR 1962: Actual Tax Collections in 1960 as a Per Cent of Selected Income Series in 1959 and of Yield under Representative Tax System: Per Cent Related to U.S. Average and Ranking								
Alabama	1.121	15	.936	32	.942	29	8.6	91	40	6.9	92	38	7.9	92	36
Alaska	.794	50	.803	48	.803	48	6.7	71	50	5.3	71	50	6.0	70	50
Arizona	1.180	9	1.021	19	1.027	19	11.5	121	6	8.4	112	16	9.8	114	14
Arkansas	1.082	22	.918	35	.923	36	9.5	100	30	8.4	112	17	9.2	107	24
California	1.120	16	1.108	10	1.108	10	10.8	114	15	8.7	116	9	9.9	115	11
Colorado	1.074	24	.963	26	.966	24	10.8	114	16	8.6	115	13	9.8	114	15
Connecticut	.839	43	.898	39	.880	42	7.8	82	46	7.0	93	36	7.7	90	40
Delaware	.825	45	.915	36	.913	37	6.9	73	49	7.7	103	30	8.0	93	35
Florida	.904	37	.908	37	.908	38	9.8	103	26	8.5	113	15	9.4	109	20
Georgia	1.026	27	.858	46	.864	46	9.2	97	32	7.1	95	35	8.2	95	33
Hawaii	.852	41	.781	50	.784	50	11.8	124	5	9.4	125	4	10.6	123	6
Idaho	1.120	17	.929	33	.935	32	11.0	116	12	8.6	115	14	9.9	115	12
Illinois	.825	46	.936	31	.933	33	8.1	85	42	6.1	81	46	7.1	83	46
Indiana	1.026	28	.974	23	.976	23	8.7	92	37	6.6	88	42	7.6	88	41
Iowa	1.153	13	1.070	13	1.074	13	10.7	113	17	8.1	108	25	9.3	108	21
Kansas	1.098	19	1.006	20	1.009	20	11.0	116	13	9.3	124	5	10.4	121	7
Kentucky	.892	39	.865	45	.866	45	7.9	83	45	6.0	80	48	6.9	80	47
Louisiana	1.428	1	1.352	1	1.355	1	12.0	126	4	8.7	116	10	10.1	117	9
Maine	.904	38	.905	38	.904	39	11.3	119	9	10.4	139	2	11.3	131	2
Maryland	.887	40	.929	33	.928	34	8.7	92	38	7.9	105	28	8.8	102	29
Massachusetts	.804	49	.968	24	.964	26	9.8	103	27	8.3	111	22	9.3	108	22
Michigan	1.098	20	1.065	14	1.065	4	9.9	104	24	8.1	108	26	9.2	107	25
Minnesota	1.240	6	1.265	2	1.247	2	11.3	119	10	8.4	112	14	9.8	114	16
Mississippi	1.236	8	.956	28	.965	25	11.4	120	8	10.4	133	3	10.9	127	3
Missouri	.825	47	.874	43	.873	44	7.1	75	48	5.5	73	49	6.3	73	49

Continued

APPENDIX B—*Continued*

ACIR 1962: Actual Tax Collections in 1960 as a Per Cent of Selected Income Series in 1959 and of Yield under Representative Tax System:

State	Alkin, Index 1 1960	Rank	Alkin, Index 2 1960	Rank	Alkin, Index 3 1960	Rank	Per Cent Related to U.S. Average	Related	Rank	Per Cent Related to U.S. Average	Related	Rank	Per Cent Related to U.S. Average	Related	Rank
Montana	1.239	7	1.162	6	1.164	5	11.5	121	7	8.7	116	11	10.0	116	10
Nebraska	.938	33	.942	29	.942	30	8.9	94	36	6.5	87	44	7.3	85	44
Nevada	.907	36	.789	49	.793	49	10.4	109	21	7.3	97	32	8.7	101	30
New Hampshire	.836	44	.964	25	.960	28	9.6	101	29	8.4	112	19	9.3	108	23
New Jersey	.938	34	1.091	12	1.086	12	8.1	85	45	7.0	93	37	7.9	92	37
New Mexico	1.249	5	1.036	18	1.042	18	9.9	104	25	7.2	96	33	8.4	98	32
New York	.983	30	1.174	3	1.169	3	10.7	113	18	8.4	112	20	9.7	113	17
North Carolina	1.063	25	.883	42	.888	41	9.4	99	31	6.8	91	39	7.9	92	38
North Dakota	1.161	12	1.048	16	1.052	16	12.9	136	2	9.3	124	6	10.8	126	4
Ohio	.916	35	.940	30	.939	31	8.4	88	41	6.6	88	43	7.6	88	42
Oklahoma	1.090	21	.957	27	.961	27	10.0	105	23	7.4	99	31	8.6	100	31
Oregon	1.270	4	1.163	4	1.167	4	10.7	113	19	9.2	123	7	10.3	120	8
Pennsylvania	.943	32	1.116	8	1.110	8	8.1	85	44	6.7	89	41	7.6	88	43
Rhode Island	.823	48	1.062	15	1.056	15	9.1	96	34	8.2	109	24	9.0	105	27
South Carolina	1.109	18	.873	44	.880	43	9.8	103	28	8.0	107	27	9.0	105	28
South Dakota	1.168	11	1.047	17	1.051	17	13.3	140	1	9.1	121	8	10.8	126	5
Tennessee	1.007	29	.892	41	.895	40	9.0	95	35	7.2	96	34	8.2	95	34
Texas	1.051	26	.980	22	.982	22	8.7	92	39	6.3	84	45	7.3	85	45
Utah	1.300	3	.988	21	.998	21	11.1	117	11	7.8	104	29	9.2	107	26
Vermont	1.081	23	1.163	5	1.161	6	12.5	132	3	10.6	141	1	11.8	137	1
Virginia	.848	42	.806	47	.807	47	7.8	82	47	6.1	81	47	6.9	80	48
Washington	1.169	10	1.103	11	1.105	11	10.7	113	20	8.7	116	12	9.9	115	13
West Virginia	1.132	14	.920	34	.926	35	9.2	97	33	6.8	91	40	7.9	92	39
Wisconsin	.978	31	1.114	9	1.110	9	10.3	108	22	8.4	112	21	9.5	110	19
Wyoming	1.361	2	1.117	7	1.124	7	10.9	115	14	8.3	111	23	9.6	112	18

REFERENCES

1. Roe L. Johns and Edgar L. Morphet, *The Economics and Financing of Education: A Systems Approach* (Englewood Cliffs, N.J.: Prentice-Hall, Inc., 1969), p. 283.

2. Ibid., pp. 283–86.

3. Otto Eckstein, *Public Finance*, 2d ed., Foundations of Modern Economic Series (Englewood Cliffs, N.J.: Prentice-Hall, Inc., 1967), pp. 59–60.

4. Richard A. Rossmiller, James A. Hale, and Lloyd E. Frohreich, *Fiscal Capacity and Educational Finance: Variations among States, School Districts, and Municipalities*, Special Study no. 10 (Gainesville, Fla.: National Educational Finance Project, 1970), p. 2.

5. Serrano v. Priest, 96 Cal. Rptr. 601, 487 P. 2d 1241 (1971).

6. Lyle W. Ashby, "The Effects of the States to Support Education as Related to Adequacy and Ability," *Research Bulletin*, National Education Association (Washington, May 1936), p. 155.

7. Richard Rossmiller, "Variations in Ability and Effort to Support Education," in *Financing Education: Fiscal and Legal Alternatives*, ed. R. L. Johns, K. Alexander, and K. F. Jordan (Columbus, Ohio: Charles E. Merrill Publishing Co., 1972), p. 124.

8. *A Legislator's Guide to School Finance*, Education Commission of the States (Denver, Col., February 1973), p. vii.

9. *State-Local Revenue Systems and Educational Finance* (Washington: Advisory Commission on Intergovernmental Relations, 1971), pp. 1–7; *Report of the President's Commission on School Finance* (Washington, 1971), pp. 1–8.

10. Wilner Saundelson and S. J. Mushkin, *The Measurement of State and Local Tax Effort*, Bureau Memorandum no. 58., Federal Security Agency, Social Security Board, Bureau of Research and Statistics (Washington, June 1944), pp. 3, 5.

11. To the ACIR, "fiscal capacity" includes revenue from both tax and nontax sources, while "tax capacity" refers only to revenue derived from tax sources. See Allen D. Manual, "Tax Capacity Versus Tax Performance: A Comment," *National Tax Journal* (June 1973), pp. 293–94.

12. Ashby, p. 108.

13. Ibid., p. 114.

14. Eugene C. Holshouser, "State-Local Tax Effort in Georgia," *Atlanta Economic Review* (June 1970), p. 40.

15. Advisory Commission on Intergovernmental Relations, *Federal Responsibility in the Field of Education* (Washington, June 1955), pp. 66–67.

16. Cited in Marvin D. Alkin, *Measurement of State Effort to Support Education*, Institute of Government and Public Affairs (Los Angeles: University of California, April 1965), p. 11.

17. Johns and Morphet, p. 185.

18. *Future Directions for School Financing* (Gainesville, Fla.: National Educational Finance Project, 1971), p. 15.

19. *Measures of State and Local Fiscal Capacity and Tax Effort* (Washington: Advisory Commission on Intergovernmental Relations, 1962), p. 13.

20. Ibid., p. 29.

21. Ibid., pp. 88–89.

22. *Measuring the Fiscal Capacity and Efforts of States and Local Areas* (Washington: Advisory Commission on Intergovernmental Relations, 1971), p. 7.

23. John Due, "Alternative Tax Sources for Education," in *Financing Education: Legal and Fiscal Alternatives*, p. 132.

24. Johns and Morphet, pp. 181–83.

25. R. L. Johns, "Local Ability and Effort to Support Schools," in *Problems and Issues in School Finance*, ed. R. L. Johns and E. L. Morphet (New York: National Conference of Professors of Educational Administration, 1952), p. 221.

26. Rossmiller, Hale, and Frohreich, p. 79.

27. Johns, "Local Ability and Effort to Support Schools," p. 222.

28. Charles Leathers, "Some Comments on Alabama's Relative Tax Effort," *Alabama Business*, October 15, 1968, p. 3.

29. Henry J. Frank, "Measuring State Tax Burdens," *National Tax Journal* (June 1959), p. 179.

30. Ibid., p. 182.

31. Ashby, pp. 111–13.

32. Ibid., pp. 157–59.

33. Saundelson and Mushkin, pp. 82–83.

34. Alkin, *Measurement of State Effort to Support Education*, pp. 12–15.

35. Charles E. Ratliff, Jr., "Centralization, Ability and Effort in School Finance," *National Tax Journal* (March 1960), pp. 41, 43–44.

36. Johns and Morphet, pp. 184–85.

37. Ibid., p. 84.

38. *Future Directions for School Financing*, p. 16.

39. *Measures of State and Local Fiscal Capacity and Tax Effort*, pp. 75–76.

40. *Measuring the Fiscal Capacity and Efforts of State and Local Areas*, p. 7.

41. Ibid., p. 114.

42. Leathers, pp. 4–5.

43. Holshouser, pp. 39–40.

44. Johns and Morphet, p. 185; Roe L. Johns and Ralph B. Kimbrough, *The Relationships of Socioeconomic Factors, Educational Leadership Patterns and Elements of Community Power Structure to Local School Fiscal Policy*, USOE Project no. 2842 (May 1968), p. 27; Harold B. Kay, *A Study of the Relationship between Selected Socioeconomic Variables and Local Tax Effort to Support Education in Kentucky* (Ed.D. diss., University of Florida, 1973).

45. "How to Evaluate Your District's Financial Effort," *School Management* (January 1965), p. 112.

46. Johns and Kimbrough, pp. 25–26.

47. Rossmiller, Hale, and Frohreich, p. 79.

48. Don C. Patton, "Fiscal Ability and Fiscal Effort in Financing the Public Schools of South Dakota," in *Financing the Public Schools of South Dakota*, Special Study (Gainesville, Fla.: National Educational Finance Project, 1973), p. 44.

49. Johns and Morphet, pp. 176, 185.

50. Kay, p. 94.

51. Johns and Kimbrough, p. 193.

52. Ibid., pp. 187–88.

53. Ralph B. Kimbrough, *Informal County Leadership Structure and Controls Affecting Educational Policy Decision Making* (University of Florida, Cooperative Research Project No. 1324, September 1961–October 1964).

54. Johns, "Local Ability and Effort to Support Schools," pp. 236–37.

55. *Measures of State and Local Fiscal Capacity and Tax Effort*, pp. 88–89.

56. Saundelson and Mushkin, pp. 96, 101.

57. Warner Bloomberg, Jr., and Morris Sunshine, "Suburban Power Structure and Public Education: A Study of Values, Influence, and Tax Effort," vol. 10, *The Economics and Politics of Public Education* (Syracuse, N.Y.: Syracuse University Press, 1963), pp. 159–63.

58. Page 94.

59. *Measuring the Fiscal Capacity and Efforts of State and Local Areas*, p. 4.

60. Will S. Myers, "The ACIR Study of State Revenue Potential" (paper presented to the National School Finance Conference, Orlando, Fla., March 18, 1974), p. 5.

61. *Measuring the Fiscal Capacity and Efforts of State and Local Areas*, p. 4.

62. Saundelson and Mushkin, pp. 4–11.

Equitable State School Financing

Kern Alexander

K. Forbis Jordan

A comprehensive and equitable state school financing system must have four essential elements. First, it should contain an adequate determination of the *fiscal ability* of the local school district and should adjust each district's allocation in terms of its relationship to the state established standard. No child should suffer educational disadvantage due to the fiscal incapacity of the local school district. Variations in wealth of school districts should be properly measured and fully equalized. Second, the adequacy of funds for a child's educational opportunity should not be compromised by the local citizenry's lack of educational aspirations as reflected in the local tax rate or *effort,* nor should education be predicated on the exigencies of political restraints. Third, a finance formula should recognize as nearly as possible the individual *educational needs* of all children throughout the state. While it is, of course, impractical or impossible to finance each child's education individually, it is nevertheless fully within the realm of feasibility for the state to finance many different types of educational programs with widely varying costs by simply recognizing the programmatic costs in the state formula. The development of a reasonable finance program requires that the local school district identify children with various needs and provide an appropriate education program. The state must then respond to the need by making formula adjustments where high cost programs demand greater funding. The fourth element necessary to provide maximum equity in treatment is for the state to provide greater funding to those school districts which, because of the high *cost of delivering education,* cannot provide equal services. In districts which must spend more to provide equal services, the state should fully supplement the differences. Care should be taken not to provide additional funding to local school districts simply because they choose to spend more for education. Under no circumstances should a differential be allowed for the cost of delivering education until proper research provides adequate assurance that such high expenditures have not been created by greater district wealth rather than conditions requiring high costs.

In this chapter we will discuss briefly each of these elements and conclude by examining a state school finance plan that includes the elements discussed below.

MEASURES OF FISCAL CAPACITY

One of the most elusive problems in designing state school support programs has been the determination of an equitable measure of local fiscal capacity. The term fiscal capacity refers to a quantitative measure intended to reflect the resources which a taxpaying jurisdiction can tax to raise revenue for public purposes.[1] Principal sources of public wealth subject to taxation have been property, income, and sales.[2] If a level of government has the power to tax all of these sources, writers have been in general agreement that these sources can then be used in developing the indicator of wealth, or measure of fiscal capacity, for that level of government. Since real property has been the primary tax base available to local school districts, most state support programs have used equalized property value per pupil in average daily attendance (ADA) or average daily membership (ADM) as the common measure of wealth among local school districts.[3]

No single measure of wealth is wholly adequate for describing the ability of a community to support education.[4] Even though the district may only be permitted to tax property, it is generally agreed that actual tax payments must be made from income. As greater attention has been devoted to municipal overburden and other financing problems of urban school districts, some consideration also has been given to utilizing the total municipal tax rate as an adjustment in a measure of local fiscal capacity. The net effect of including this factor has been that the relative wealth position of urban school districts when compared to all districts in a state has been reduced. Cities usually have had higher total tax rates for all governmental services than rural and suburban districts throughout a state.[5]

Attributes of a Measure

One of the attributes of a measure of fiscal capacity for a local school district is that the measure should be predictive of the district's ability to support education; the measure should reflect the degree to which the community can supply the funds which are required to support public services.[6] A high incidence of property wealth in a taxing jurisdiction should not be interpreted to indicate that the locality also has available resources from which to pay the levy.

An additional consideration is that the capacity measure reflect the relationships between revenue sources and characteristics of the population. The common pattern has been to determine the local district's relative position by dividing its wealth by the ADA, ADM, or a similar measure. Some support has been expressed for using per capita or school age population as the divisor; however, each choice has certain public policy implications. Careful consideration should be given to the impact of various choices on individual districts and the resultant equity implications. Any capacity measure should be based on some index of population so that a unit of measure may be comparable among local districts within a state.

Common Measures of Capacity

Measures of local district fiscal capacity to support schools normally have been grouped into four categories: property wealth, sales tax receipts, personal income, and indices of fiscal capacity. The established measure for fiscal capacity has been the value of real property. This choice may have been more the result of a lack of fiscal information needed for more sophisticated analyses than an indication that property was an adequate and desirable indicator of fiscal capacity.

Of the three measures—real property, personal income, and retail sales—property yields the least amount of revenue with the greatest amount of fiscal inequity, economic inefficiency, and administrative difficulty.[7] The property tax itself has unpopular features which generally produce a drag on the school revenues. No other major tax places such a burden on the low income families or, as Shannon has observed, is so capriciously "related to the flow of cash into the household." The tax is probably in effect an anti-home ownership tax discouraging low income families from owning their homes. Taxpayer shocks are more common with the property tax in that reappraisals coupled with lump sum yearly payments produce a painful effect on the taxpayer. Other major taxes such as income and sales do not possess either of these irritating features. In spite of these and other defects the property tax has certain saving graces; the most obvious advantage is that the tax constitutes a large and available revenue source to local government and schools. The tax also allows citizens in the local community to retain the revenues gained from bearing the incidence of the tax. Additionally, with proper reassessment, the tax provides additional school revenues by imposing a levy on unrealized capital gains. Most economists classify this latter attribute as important and necessary for wealth redistribution purposes.

Regardless of the pros and cons education is generally attached to the local property tax, both legally and in the public eye. Realism mandates that it be used and that its faults be corrected as efficaciously as possible.

The quest for property tax equity to the taxpayer as well as to the student in the public school may be at least partially achieved by better tax administration and by equalized allocation procedures combining property and nonproperty revenues. Here, the measurement of fiscal capacity becomes vital. Since the property tax is the major local revenue source for schools, it must be a primary determinant of fiscal wealth for equalization purposes.

Retail sales receipts provide another measure of fiscal capacity which can serve as an indicator of the economic activity in a community. The principal problem with using retail sales as an indicator of local district fiscal capacity is that economic activity is not uniformly distributed among the school districts. Various studies have reported wide variations in the sales tax yield among school districts with the difference between rich and poor being at least as great as variations in property wealth.[8]

As a measure of fiscal capacity, income provides an accurate measure not only of capacity but also of the ability to pay the taxes which have been levied. Rhode Island, Kansas, and Virginia have included income in combination with property valuations as a measure of fiscal capacity. Income as a measure of fiscal capacity tends to shift rather substantially the wealth positions of school districts in most states. Farner and Edmundson reported this conclusion in their study of eleven western states in which income and sales were used to predict the taxpaying ability of local school districts.[9] Whether income is predictive of property values should not be the sine qua non of its use; the mere fact that a wide divergence exists between property value and income tends to reinforce the necessity of combining the two to assure more adequate identification of the true taxpaying capacity of the school district. A principal problem in utilizing income is the difficulty of obtaining reliable data on a school district basis since income-reporting systems do not provide information on a local school district basis. As more sophisticated reporting systems are developed, the possibility of using income as an indicator of local district fiscal capacity will be considerably enhanced. The technical feasibility of securing the needed data for local school districts was demonstrated in earlier NEFP research activities which revealed that a common reporting system could be developed for all states.[10]

The authors of a University of Wisconsin study observed that no single measure of wealth adequately or fully describes the ability of a community to support public services.[11] They did conclude, however, that of the alternative variables analyzed, personal income tax paid was the most adequate measure available. Since the true capacity of a governmental unit is determined by economic activity or flow of resources as well as the taxable resources available, the use of a broadly based measure of fiscal ability rather than a narrow one is probably more desirable.

The impact of introducing income into the determination of school district wealth holds important implications for equalization. The relative wealth position of cities, suburbs, and rural districts may be shifted substantially depending on the type of wealth measure used in a formula. In equalizing fiscal ability, a school district may be above the state average in either property or income wealth, but its position relative to the state average may be greatly altered to either its benefit or detriment.[12]

Fisher has made a comprehensive study of 28 standard metropolitan statistical areas (SMSA), and found that the cities typically had higher personal income than the majority of the school districts in the SMSA.[13] For example, of 327 suburban school districts in the Chicago SMSA, only 98 had higher adjusted gross personal income than Chicago. Of 97 suburban districts in the Detroit SMSA, the central city was exceeded by only 24. Only 40 of New York City's suburbs exceeded the city proper. Similar results were found in other major SMSAs except for Newark; in this instance 80 per cent of the suburbs were wealthier than the city.

The assessed valuation of property per pupil presented somewhat the same picture; the wealth per pupil in the cities was generally higher than in the suburbs. Of 57 school districts in the Cleveland SMSA, Cleveland ranked seventh from the top in assessed valuation of property per pupil. Cities tended to rank relatively higher on assessed valuation of property than on adjusted gross personal income when compared to their suburbs. On the basis of these data, the use of a personal income factor as a measure of wealth would appear to make the cities poorer and would therefore increase their state allotments if an equalization formula were to be utilized by the state. However, this generalization can only be tested when all school districts in a state are analyzed together. Callahan and Goettel found that a composite index of full value of taxable property and personal income tended to reduce equalization support to New York City when calculations were based on allocations to regions within the state.[14]

The impact of a composite index of personal income and property values would undoubtedly fluctuate greatly depending on the distribution of wealth related to the location of industry, residential areas, and agriculture. In certain midwestern states, farm areas have high assessed value, but farmers have very low adjusted gross income. Under these circumstances the inclusion of personal income *as a measure of wealth* would result in more state aid for rural areas.

Property valuation may be a suitable measure of wealth, but it is much less satisfactory as a measure of potential revenue to support local governmental services.[15] An issue which bears on this discussion is the majority opinion in Rodriguez, in which the justices of the U.S. Supreme Court expressed doubts that average property values of districts alone were predictive of the income level of persons residing there.[16] Justice Powell noted, "Yet recent studies have indicated that the poorest families are not invariably clustered in the most impecunious school districts. Nor does it now appear that there is any more than a random chance that racial minorities are concentrated in property-poor districts."

The number or per cent of low-income families in a school district is an important variable in measuring capacity. Measuring capacity by mean incomes is probably feasible at this point in time; however, the possibilities are very remote that a more sophisticated method can be presently developed which takes into account the median income of individuals or families. An alternative would be to adjust indices of mean property values and mean incomes by using income level and educational deficiencies to weight the numbers of children by which the measures are determined.

Measurement Units Affecting Fiscal Capacity

Once the basis for local school district wealth is determined, whether it be property values, income, both, or some other quantification, a further decision must be made regarding the units by which the wealth will be interpreted. Should the measure of wealth for each district be the district's total wealth compared to the state's total wealth or should wealth be interpreted reflecting some measure of need? A different result is achieved depending on whether total wealth is compared to wealth per ADM, wealth per ADA, or wealth per capita. A school district may appear to be affluent if no wealth divisor is employed or if relative wealth is determined by dividing by ADA; however, the same school district may become, in relation to other school districts, much poorer if ADM, total population, or some weighted pupil standard is used as a divisor.

Among the alternative units of measure which might be used to assess the educational needs of the school district are ADA, ADM, population, proportion of total wealth, school-age child, school-attending child, weighted average daily attendance (WADA), and weighted full-time equivalent (WFTE).

Average daily attendance.—Average daily attendance has been the typical measure used as the divisor in many state support programs to calculate a district's relative wealth. The aggregate number of days in attendance for a given period of time is divided by the number of days in the period, and the result is the ADA for the school district. The method rewards the district which has the highest percentage of attendance and encourages the district to take positive action to assure that absenteeism is kept to a minimum. As an end result, the state school support program is used to enforce compulsory attendance laws.

Even though this measure may appear to have some merits in that the district is rewarded for having pupils in attendance, the measure may actually have little relationship to the ability of the district to support education. If significant portions of the district's school-age population are attending nonpublic schools, the measure may not reflect the district's fiscal capacity. If large numbers of the students are culturally deprived and their parents do not encourage them to attend schools, the measure may not be indicative of the district's population to be served. Also, if the age distribution of total population departs from the norm for the state, the measure may be deficient.

Average daily membership.—This measure is very similar to ADA except that the aggregate days' membership is used as the divisor rather than the aggregate days of attendance. The problems of using the measure as a vehicle to enforce compulsory school attendance and to cope with the low attendance of culturally deprived pupils have been removed. However, relief is not provided for districts with a higher than state average percentage of population in nonschool-attending age categories.

Population.—A third alternative is to use the total population as the divisor. This option provides for recognition of demand for all governmental services in the calculation of a local district's fiscal capacity. The incidence of pupils of school age or attending school is not recognized. Support for this alternative may be found among those who contend that the funding of school support programs should not be considered independent of the total demands for governmental services. Others might contend that the purpose of the school support program is to provide funds for education; therefore, the measure should be oriented toward a unit of need which is related to the program's purpose. This approach has some rather profound effects, depending upon the differing relationships between the number of students and the total population among school districts.

An additional problem with this measure is that the only source of reliable data will be the decennial census, and even that information often is not reported in a pattern which conforms to local school district boundaries. Steps are being taken to resolve the latter, but the data are not presently available on an annual basis.

Proportion of total wealth.—A limited number of states compute a local district's fiscal capacity on the basis of the district's proportional share of the total wealth of the state. A total local share is determined for the entire state and each local district's share of the total is that district's percentage of the total wealth of the state. In contrast to the previous alternatives, this measure does not recognize either the pupils to be educated or the total population requiring governmental services. The measure's merits are in its simplicity; it is not dependent upon local district reports or on census information which may be outdated.

School-age child.—A technique for compensating those districts with higher than state average percentages of nonpublic school attendance is to use the number of school-age children in the district as the divisor in calculating each local district's wealth. The most obvious problems with this measure are that it fails to provide any incentive to encourage the district to serve its school-age population, that it does not recognize the total population requiring governmental services, and that the data must be obtained from either the decennial census or a locally conducted school census. For these reasons, little support can be found for this alternative.

School-attending child.—If the public policy is to recognize both public and nonpublic school-attending pupils in calculating a local district's relative wealth, the total number of school-attending children may be used as the divisor. Most of the negative factors associated with the school-age-child method are alleviated through this alternative. Its chief handicaps are that reports must be secured from nonpublic schools and that the state often does not have the manpower to assure that the reports are accurate. Nonpublic school officials may not be supportive, for they do not receive any direct reward for filing and certifying the information.

Weighted average daily attendance.—The only difference between using WADA and ADA as the divisor is that the incidence of pupils requiring high-cost programs is recognized in the calculation. Under this alternative, educational needs of students become a factor in the calculation of a district's fiscal capacity. Funding weights for programs are multiplied by the ADA of the pupils in the program to obtain the WADA for each local school district. The demand for other governmental services is not recognized, nor is the number of pupils attending nonpublic schools. All of the criticisms associated with ADA also apply to this alternative.

Weighted full-time equivalent pupils.—The use of WFTE as the divisor permits the recognition of the educational need factor and the number of pupils in average daily membership. The calculation process is similar to WADA except that the number of full-time equivalent pupils is used as a multiplier. WFTE is subject to the criticisms and the merits of ADM, but does represent an additional refinement. Funding weights for programs are multiplied by the ADM of full-time equivalent pupils in the program. The number of units is an indicator of the number of pupils served by the program. The addition of the weights provides for recognition of the variations in costs associated with each program. If the state seeks to secure maximum recognition of the factors associated with educational programs in the public schools, this alternative has considerable merit over several of the other options.

The preceding discussion illustrates that no single unit of measure is obviously preferable to others. Rather than being objective decisions, choices must be made in terms of the public policy position prevalent in the state. If the unit measure of fiscal capacity is to be neutral of educational need, or if simplicity is the desired goal, the best measure will be proportion of total wealth. If maximum recognition is to be given to the incidence of educational need, WFTE will be preferred. If maximum recognition is to be given to the number of pupils attending nonpublic schools, the choice will be school-attending child. If the desire is to recognize the demand for all governmental services, population may well be the best unit of measure. If the intent is to use the unit measure of fiscal capacity to encourage compulsory school attendance, ADA or WADA will be selected.

Irrespective of the option which may be selected, consideration should be given to the simplicity of procedures required to gather the data and the predicted accuracy of the information. If multiple uses cannot be made of the data or if they are not easily available, an overly cumbersome system may require excessive paperwork in local school districts and extensive checking from the state education agency. Often, both agencies will have limited resources and could profit more by devoting their efforts to other endeavors.

In determining an appropriate unit measure of local district fiscal capacity, attention must be given to the necessity for the measure to serve as a technique for recognizing differences in educational need among school districts. For this reason, WFTE has distinct advantages. Further, the use of this measure in determining local fiscal capacity and the level of educational need reduces the possibility of inequities in the calculation process.

MEASURES OF EDUCATIONAL NEED

As discussed in great detail in another chapter of this book, varying education needs of children place diverse educational cost burdens on local school districts. States have commonly allocated funds through weighted or unweighted classroom units and / or pupil counts. Of course, classroom units are basically derived from pupil counts and generally have approximately the same funding effect.

Much of the work of the NEFP has been devoted to the analysis of incidence rates of types of educational need and the corresponding cost differentials for funding vital services. As indicated by Stultz and Jordan, the cost differentials evolving from cost accounting of ongoing programs present a rather reliable picture of the relative educational financial burden accompanying the implementation of high cost educational programs. Cost analyses such as this and other similar efforts have diminished the uncertainty which existed a few years ago when the federal courts in McInnis[17] and Burruss[18] held that the lack of "manageable standards" prevented a definitive judgment on whether certain educational needs were being adequately recognized by the state school finance formulas. States are in a much better position today to quantify accurate objective measures of educational need than ever before; several states have moved in this direction.[19] In these instances the educational needs of children have been assessed, programs have been identified, and cost differentials or weightings have been applied. This procedure has resulted in the establishment of minimum program cost standards for a state upon which all such programs statewide may be based. To assure adequate data, the state should assume an active role in assessing educational needs and program costs. In these programs expenditures for instructional salaries and other current operations have been identified and included in the composite cost of the educational program.

Under this system pupils are counted only once, e.g., if a child attends a regular class for three hours a day and a vocational class for the remainder of the day, his time is allocated between the two programs and the appropriate cost is determined without double counting. The calculation of full-time equivalent pupils for each program eliminates the possibility of duplicate pupil counts which have produced allocation inefficiencies between categorical and basic general aid formulas. The benefits of the cost differential or pupil-cost-unit approach have been variously described, but can be summarized in five points.

Local school districts are encouraged to explore alternative instructional methods based on educational needs because greater flexibility is provided in program operation when funding is based on the pupil to be educated rather than on numbers of teachers, numbers of supervisors, or a standardized self-contained classroom unit.

A uniform and comprehensive system of funding is established for all local school districts within a given state. Variations in allocations are dependent only on the differences in educational need among children, rather than on administrative or organizational arrangements.

The cost differential method of weighting pupils increases the rationality and objectivity of the distribution system because allocation is based on actual cost analysis of educational programs rather than on politics, geography, or other extraneous considerations.

A balanced program is created whereby the entire program is interactive with each component of the unit cost of the basic program; therefore, a definitive relationship exists among all elements of the educational finance program.

Adoption of this system facilitates evaluation by establishing the basic framework through which programmatic budgeting can transpire. Costs of programs are easily determined when the allocation procedure creates a full cycle of programmatic funding.

SCHOOL DISTRICT FISCAL EFFORT

When states provide local school districts with the discretion to increase or reduce tax rates, an implicit assumption is that local decisions will be on the whole reasonable and rational. To maintain, however, that local exercise of discretion is prima facie rationale is a mistake which many states have made in designing school finance systems. The result has been that the vagaries of the local social, economic, or political conditions have sometimes worked to retard worthwhile education, and the citizens of the community have, without due consideration to the consequences, deprived their own children of equal educational opportunity.

No good pattern exists whereby one can pinpoint the reasons for low local fiscal effort for education. Some have maintained that a certain political power structure will produce low effort and bad schools; some have maintained that the nature of the populace, e.g., education, race, or nationality, will determine the level of the fiscal effort; others have suggested that effort is associated with the tax structure or the economic condition of the people. Research to date is inconclusive as to the nature of the school district fiscal effort. A state school system which is dependent on local funds for general support must address the problems created by variations in fiscal effort. A child's education may be seriously impaired if local aspiration levels prevent local school authorities from utilizing resources which are present in the tax base of the community. Only in a system of full state funding is the issue of effort diminished; however, typical state school finance programs historically have been calculated by foundation program or percentage equalizing formulas. In either of these, if local option is allowed to establish the funding floors and ceilings, the dilemma of effort presents itself regardless of the level of fiscal equalization. The state can only diminish the impact of disequalization through variations in local effort by mandating uniform taxation requirements throughout the state. Such uniformity has been rejected in many instances, but the question of state-enforced uniformity continues to be a major source of controversy. At what level should equalization be established, and at what point should local discretion take precedence over state uniformity?

With the foundation program supplemented by equalized grants based on each district's levied tax rate, the local district retains taxing power to exceed the state-mandated minimum. Even though additional local tax leeway is fully equalized, wide variations in effort may be expected beyond the minimum, resulting in substantial differences in expenditures per pupil among the school districts. The dilemma is to determine a reasonable level of allowable local tax leeway. Should it be set high above the floor established by the foundation program, or should it be limited?

The importance of knowing the nature and impact of effort is even more acute if the state chooses not to establish a minimum required local effort or a maximum level of tax effort. This open-endedness may provide full equalization of all funds raised, but it does not require that the local districts put forth any effort at all, nor does it limit those districts that want to exercise unrestricted high effort. Under such a system the level of funding for the child's education would be a function of effort.[20]

In attempting to explore the essence of effort, several studies have discovered an interesting relationship between wealth and effort.[21] Hopper, in a Florida study in 1950, found that significantly high correlations existed between net effective buying income per capita and effort. Quick found significant relationships between net effective buying income per capita and effort in Illinois. Ranney's research supports the conclusions that income level of the community is a major determinant of local school fiscal effort. Hatley observed that high income groups tended to support all school funding proposals, but low income groups tended to support only tax measures promising direct, job-related benefits.

Variables other than income which have been found to have important relationships with effort are numerous and sometimes confusing, but an NEFP study of Kentucky provides a profile of the nature of effort which may be of assistance.[22]

The low effort school district will typically have a high per cent of its income derived from farm property, a high per cent of low income families with deprived children, including Negro children, a high per cent unemployed, and a high per cent of persons 65 years or older. On the other hand, the high effort district will typically have high adjusted gross income, high median years of educational attainment among its citizenry, high per cent of tax paid by commercial and industrial property, high per cent of white collar workers, and a high incidence of renter-occupied housing, along with relatively high population mobility.

Local tax effort for schools is largely a function of wealth, good jobs, education, youth, and mobility. Children who happen to attend schools in districts not having these attributes are probably destined to receive a lower level of education. Education, income and effort are inextricably intertwined, producing a cycle of education which is a function of community affluence and knowledge.

While this profile provides insight into the nature of effort and probably identifies some of the determinants of high and low effort, it would be foolhardy to assume that this is descriptive of all or even most circumstances. As Johns and Kimbrough have observed from exhaustive research, the more nebulous but nevertheless important factors of community power structure, characteristics of community influentials, community beliefs, and the interaction of all these factors are the real determinants of fiscal effort. They found, for example, that districts with noncompetitive power structures tended to make less tax effort, while those with competitive power structures tended to have high effort. Community influentials were more likely to be involved in educational issues in high effort districts. The power structures of low effort school districts tended to be dominated by leaders of the economic community.

Little evidence exists that school tax effort is responsive to the educational needs of the community. It tends to be more closely associated with extra-educational considerations such as political beliefs of the community influentials or the make-up of the community power structure.[23] Other noncontrollable and constitutionally questionable determinants may also be identified, e.g., income level, racial make-up of community, age of voters, or even percentage of population which is of a certain religion. If local discretion hinges on these questionable determinants, there would appear to be a certain legitimacy in limiting or controlling tax effort variations from the state level and certainly a legitimate state interest in seeking funding alternatives which would limit the impact of irrational local educational taxing judgments.

COST OF DELIVERING EDUCATION

In the past, little discussion has focused on the importance of cost variations among school districts for the same educational services. The variation in expenditures per pupil between rich and poor school districts has usually been of such magnitude as to mask the smaller differences which exist due to educational cost differences. It is not unusual even today for fiscal inequality to create such wide disparity in expenditures that the first and foremost consideration must be devoted to equalizing access to resources. In terms of equalization priorities, fiscal equalization should be realized, educational needs should be met through uniform programs and services, and effort variations should be diminished; then, costs of delivering educational services should be used as a correction factor to assure more fully equalized educational opportunity. The National Urban Coalition has observed that "Wealth, need, and effort being equal, high cost districts should receive more aid than low cost districts."[24] The need for indices of educational costs in state-aid formulas was recognized by the President's Commission on School Finance: "Distribution of educational resources equally requires that the value of the resources at the receiving end be equal."[25]

Recently the State of Florida, in reforming its state school finance program, incorporated a cost-of-living factor providing for a cost index ranging from 0.90 for low cost districts to 1.10 for high cost districts.[26] This index was developed from a price survey of consumer goods and services for twelve selected Florida counties. Weightings for the price list were established from data routinely utilized by the Bureau of Labor Statistics (BLS). Data from the sampled counties were used to establish a regression plane estimating the price level of the remaining fifty-five counties in Florida.[27] The resulting price level estimates for each county were then used as a multiplier in the Florida Act to determine the school district's final allocation. This study technique was replicated in 1973 with the sample expanded to thirty-one counties.

The Florida study was certainly a significant step forward in establishing reliable cost data; nevertheless, the study has some serious shortcomings. Johns observed that the price level index established by the two studies had a Pearson coefficient of correlation of 0.86 with average family income; he further concluded that "The Florida Price Level Index now incorporated in the Florida School Finance Act of 1973 measures differences in consumption which are a function of differences in average family income rather than differences in the cost of living for the same standard of living." The result of the act was to allocate more funds to counties with high family income than to counties with low family income. To this extent the index was disequalizing and made it more difficult for low income counties to compete on an equal basis for instructional personnel. Further, the Florida studies on which the act was based made no attempt to establish the actual differences among school districts in the cost of living for school personnel for the same standard of living. Johns admonished against utilizing price indices until more definitive research reveals the portion of the teacher's salary, the major portion of the school budget, affected by cost of living differentials. Major questions are: how much does the teacher spend on items affected by cost of living; how much is invested, saved, or paid on debts; and is the same standard of living available to the teachers regardless of location?[28]

After the passage of the Florida Act, Wood of the University of Georgia surveyed 12,257 teachers in forty-two Florida counties and found that the Florida index discriminated most heavily against smaller counties because their teachers spend the largest per cent of their income in counties with higher cost of living factors.[29] He found that over 26 per cent of total personal expenditures were made outside the county of employment. Further, Wood found that 1,634 of the teachers responding to the survey lived outside of their county of employment. Population mobility serves to magnify the problems of determining a valid cost of education index. Cost adjustments for automobile gas, oil, and maintenance become increasingly important with teacher mobility; the accuracy of costs is further diminished by teachers shopping in adjacent school districts. Since Florida has only sixty-seven county unit school districts, the complexity of the mobility issue is not as great as in states which have a large number of school districts. In these, the reliability of market basket cost projections is substantially reduced. These observations are supported by research performed by McDonald in Connecticut where he found that in small communities teachers purchased 44 per cent of their food and 91 per cent of their clothing and personal services in communities other than the ones in which they taught.[30] He concluded that "Since teachers do purchase goods and services in communities other than the one in which they teach, the variations in the cost of living between communities are not important factors on which to base the adjustments in teachers' salaries."

A major unresolved element of the cost of living market basket approach is the difficulty in identifying identical purchases. Housing quality from place to place is generally not comparable. Structurally similar houses found in different school districts may, in fact, have much different location conditions. A person purchasing or renting a dwelling pays not only for structure but also for location. Fox, in reacting to the Florida studies, has observed that, with two similar structures in two districts, one may be surrounded by tenements in a high crime area overlooking a brick wall and the other may be located in a high income area nestled among palm trees overlooking the Atlantic ocean.[31] Since about one-third of a consumer's expenditures are devoted to shelter, the overall standard of living is greatly affected by this one factor. Comparability must therefore be established if an accurate estimate of cost of living is to be made.

All of the studies testify to the difficulty of identifying a reliable measure for the cost of delivering education. While equal educational opportunity cannot be fully achieved until the cost dilemma is resolved, it nevertheless would do further damage to an already inequitable system to establish cost indices which tend to reward wealthy school districts because they already have more. Careful attention must be given to identifying costs for the *same standard of living*. Moreover, the same standard of educational opportunity is governed to a great extent by teacher supply and demand. A teacher's selection of a certain school district may be related to a number of variables, each of which represents a cost function. For example, Fox has observed that the cost of living alone is surely inadequate as a measure of cost of delivering education when a combination of such factors as difficulty of assignment (combat or battle pay), district location (boredom pay), and price differentials (cost of living) are all significant contributors.[32]

The National Educational Finance Project recommends that provisions be made in the state school finance plan for variations among districts in the cost of living for the *same standard of living*. In the educational sense, this means that cost variations should only reflect true and valid differentials and be unrelated to wealth of school district. The state formula should recognize only those factors which create inequality of educational services because of variations in the cost of delivering education.

EDUCATIONAL PROGRAM AND TAX RESOURCE EQUALIZATION

Equal treatment of equals, a concept engendered by the American heritage and promoted by constitutional precepts, establishes a goal toward which state educational programs are slowly but surely moving. Equalization of educational opportunity is more advanced today than ever before. Much of the increase in fiscal equality may be attributable to school district reorganization and to special curricular offerings and innovations, but to a large degree the new equity has been enhanced by improvements in state school fund distribution formulas. In very recent years new recognition of the necessity for equalization has been brought to the forefront of political thought by numerous court actions dealing with almost every aspect of school finance. Resulting inquiries into inequality within and among states have laid the groundwork for modernization of distribution processes.

The purpose of this section is to illustrate some of these advancements by constructing an equalization aid plan which, with certain modifications, is adaptable to conditions in most states. Many diverse elements of education, economics, and politics must be considered in any major legislation, and, while the plan below attempts to resolve only a small number of these problems, this approach is educationally, economically, and politically plausible. In any equalization plan it is always necessary to have in play affirmative political forces which are seeking to resolve problems of inequity.

As observed previously, the essential elements of a desirable school finance system require the equalization of *fiscal ability,* uniformity of *effort,* recognition of the differences in *educational need* of children, and compensation for the differences among districts in the *cost of delivering* education. Each of these, with the probable exception of the cost of delivering education, is presently measurable, and techniques for application are available. The various elements are in use in several states, although no state fully equalizes under all of the elements.

The following formula may be viewed basically as percentage-equalizing with effort limitations and educational needs and cost adjustments. The calculation utilizes personal income as well as equalized property valuations as the measure of tax resource equalization. Further, it includes weighted full-time equivalents as the measure of educational need and adjusts both the program cost and the local school district wealth by this standard.

Basic State Allocation

$$1 - 0.5 \left(\frac{\dfrac{I_d + V_d}{W_d}}{\dfrac{I_s + V_s}{W_s}} \right) \times D_s \times W_d \times C_d = \text{Basic State Allocation}$$

where:
- 0.5 = predetermined constant representing approximate local share in district of average wealth
- s = state
- d = local school district
- I = total personal income
- V = total equalized valuation of property
- D = dollars per full-time equivalent student as determined by previous year's average state and local expenditure per FTE
- W = weighted full-time equivalent students
- C = cost of delivering education factor.

Should the state be able to justify, through valid research, the use of a cost-of-delivering-education index, then the index should be included as a multiplier in calculating the Basic State Allocation.

The Basic State Allocation should then be supplemented by a Leeway Equalizing provision which equalizes the dollars earned from a district's effort above the Basic State Allocation requirement. This formula is precisely the same as the Basic State Allocation formula except that there is no state-established minimum. The state equalizes each dollar raised by local effort beyond the dollar amount required for the Basic State Allocation up to a maximum millage limit which should be imposed by the state.

Leeway Equalization Allocation

$$1 - 0.5 \left(\frac{\dfrac{I_d + V_d}{W_d}}{\dfrac{I_s + V_s}{W_s}} \right) \times L \times W_d = \text{Leeway Equalization Allocation}$$

where:

L = leeway tax rate in local school district multiplied by the yield per FTE from that tax rate in district of average wealth in the state.

What are some of the assumptions on which this illustration is based and how does it compare with other recommended formulas? It is assumed in this formula that the present most frequently used measure of wealth property valuations is generally inadequate for equalization purposes. The lack of uniformity in property tax administration procedures is well documented throughout the country, and assessment practices may generally be classified as very poor. Even in states such as Kentucky and Florida, where courts have repeatedly required assessment at 100 per cent of fair cash value, many discrepancies exist. The use of income in the formula may interject a more accurate measure of ability of taxpayers of the district as a whole to support schools. If no local nonproperty taxes are in use in a state, the value of using income as an ability measure is diminished and it then becomes necessary for policy makers to decide if the use of income is justified if it serves only as a proxy for ability in the absence of accurate property valuations.[33]

The goal of equality of educational opportunity is recognized in the formula through the incorporation of the weights as derived from the identification of educational needs and program costs. In the example, the level of state aid in the district of average wealth has been fixed at 50 per cent. If the policy decision is to raise the level of state share, the constant should be reduced so that the sum of the expected state and local shares equals 1.0.

COMPARISON WITH OTHER PLANS

Unique characteristics of every state require tailoring financial plans to meet the special historical, economic, political, organizational, and informational conditions. Each finance formula will have a different effect on each state. Generally, however, there are some commonalities regarding the basic types of state finance programs which may be observed.

Of the finance programs presently in use, most can be classified into three basic types: flat grant formulas, Strayer-Haig-Mort foundation programs, and percentage-equalizing formulas. Each of these may have one or more elements in common with the proposed plan, but none of them possesses all of the variables necessary to assure full equalization. First, the flat grant type formula can be dismissed because of its lack of fiscal equalization. While the flat grant could be a viable alternative if all school districts had equal or near equal fiscal capacity, no state, with the possible exception of Hawaii, presents this fortuitous circumstance. The flat grant could be considered as a reasonable alternative if it were large enough to approach full state funding. This would provide a solution to inequalities created by fiscal incapacity and low effort, but it would not necessarily address itself to the problem of high incidence of educational need and program costs. While a full state funding flat grant based on weighted pupils and costs would answer most of the questions surrounding fiscal and educational need capacity, it nevertheless is not as politically feasible as the illustrated formula.

The traditional Strayer-Haig-Mort foundation program approach has definite advantages over the flat grant, but its major shortcoming is that it does not provide for fiscal equalization of local leeway beyond the required local effort. It does not provide full fiscal equalization nor does it limit or encourage local effort beyond a minimal level. It has the advantage, when used with the Morphet-Johns adaptations, of addressing the issue of educational need through the use of weighted pupil or weighted classroom units. The extent of equalization afforded by the foundation program rests on the establishment of the working minimum. Typically, the minimum level of funding has been inadequate in terms of providing for substantial fiscal inequity or sufficient funds to support an adequate educational program.

Another feature of the foundation program found objectional in many states has been the necessity, in order to participate, of requiring a local millage levy. The psychology of the state mandating a local effort expressed in terms of a definite tax rate many times has needlessly induced a controversy over local control. The above plan, even though it does not have a local effort provision, does not express local participation in terms of a *required* local tax rate, but instead simply prescribes a residual amount of dollars which must come from the local level. This is not unique and is the nature of the percentage-equalizing formula which has been used in several states for many years. The local dollar requirement and the required local tax rate as expressions of local effort have the same fiscal impact, but they have a different psychological effect on the taxpayer.

Substantial improvements have been made over the years in the foundation program approach primarily emanating from the Morphet-Johns inclusion of educational needs and programs in the determination of the allocation amount. In addition, Morphet and Johns have included a type of budgetary model foundation program which includes instruction, transportation, other current expenses, and capital outlay under one umbrella formula. This system typically provides for a more rational allocation of the various budgetary components and for fiscal equalization of each according to the property wealth of the local school district. This feature, which one may term as program-budget oriented, is certainly the strongest feature of the foundation program approach to the extent that it determines program costs based on educational need for all school costs relating to administration, instruction, and other current operation, except for pupil transportation. The methods of allocation for transportation, debt service, and capital outlay are discussed in another chapter of this book.

The percentage-equalizing concept has some distinct advantages and disadvantages, none of which are by nature significant. As Johns has observed, when certain conditions are constant, "the percentage grant or state aid ratio formula is only a mathematical manipulation of the Strayer-Haig-Mort formula."[34] The foundation program approach, though, is a "fixed level" program, while the percentage-equalizing formula may or may not be fixed. The percentage-equalizing formula, therefore, is more easily applied to "varying levels" of local dollars raised allowing full fiscal equalization with local effort being the determinant of the state allocation.[35] Whether one believes that a child's education should be determined by local fiscal effort may serve to determine his preference for the minimum foundation program or percentage-equalizing formula. To allow for full equalization under the fixed level foundation program, it is necessary to establish a maximum millage cap and raise the required local effort to that level. In other words, full fiscal equalization under the foundation program provides for no variance between total tax rate and the required local effort; "the maximum is the minimum." With percentage-equalizing the effort may vary, and equalization occurs as a function of local effort. It should be pointed out that the percentage-equalizing formula has in actual use always had a minimum or a fixed dollar amount, or percentage, to which it has been applied. No state has permitted percentage-equalizing to be applied entirely at the whim of the local taxpayer. States, generally, have not been willing to allow unrestrained local determination of fiscal effort with no regulation or minimum at all. For the state to establish no local fiscal standard at all would be for the state to abdicate its responsibility to provide for a rationally equal or uniform system of public education. This is the distinguishing point between the proposed percentage-equalizing formula and the district power-equalizing formula as proposed by Coons and others.[36] As Coons stated, the district power-equalizing formula "operates by making dollars per pupil a function of effort alone." Presumably under district power equalization, a district could opt for no educational program and put forth no local effort; then, the state would equalize nothing. This is the questionable characteristic which is unique to district power equalization; the child's education may be totally a function of local effort.[37]

Historically, percentage-equalizing formulas have not accommodated educational needs and program costs as well as the foundation program concept. A review of the history of state finance plans does not reveal, except for minor weighting adjustments between elementary school and high school, such need and cost accommodations. This severe limitation has been detrimental to school districts having high incidence of educational need, such as core cities and some rural areas.

Any proposed formula, in summary, should combine the best features of each of the various methods of allocation. Fiscal ability should be based on an accurate and realistic measurement, whether it is property valuation alone, property and income, some combination thereof, or some other reasonable proxy. A good formula allows for local initiative to expand tax effort but does not condemn the child because of inadequate exercise of local aspiration. The formula should include a quantification of educational needs and interpret them into program costs, and, in addition, it should be dynamic and responsive to inflation in that the amount for the basic program floats with the estimated financial needs beyond the previous year's expenditures. Finally, the formula accommodates those legitimate costs associated with delivering educational services.

REFERENCES

1. R. L. Johns, S. K. Alexander, and D. H. Stollar, *Status and Impact of Educational Finance Programs*, vol. 4 (Gainesville, Fla.: National Educational Finance Project, 1971), p. 122.

2. Richard A. Rossmiller, James A. Hale, and Lloyd E. Frohreich, *Fiscal Capacity and Educational Finance*, Special Study no. 10 (Gainesville, Fla.: National Educational Finance Project, 1970).

3. Clyde H. Reeves, *1968 School Finance Law Handbook* (Evanston, Ill.: National School Board Association, 1968).

4. R. L. Johns, S. K. Alexander, and K. F. Jordan, eds., *Financing Education: Fiscal and Legal Alternatives* (Columbus, Ohio: Charles E. Merrill Publishing Company, 1972).

358/Equitable State School Financing

5. Leroy J. Peterson et al., *Economic Impact of State Support Models on Education* (Madison: University of Wisconsin, School of Finance, 1963).

6. Paul R. Mort and Walter C. Reusser, *Public School Finance: Its Background, Structure and Operation* (New York: McGraw Hill, 1951).

7. John Shannon, "The Property Tax: Reform or Relief," in *Property Tax Reform*, ed. George E. Peterson (Washington: The Urban Institute, 1973), pp. 26–27.

8. See William R. Wilkerson, "Potential Impact of County Sales and Income Taxes on Public School Finance," unpublished paper, Indiana University, 1970, pp. 3–5; Kern Alexander and Charles Whaley, *Beyond the Minimum* (Kentucky Education Association, 1967), pp. 126–31; Duane O. Moore, "Local Nonproperty Taxes for Schools," in *Status and Impact of Educational Finance Programs*, ed. Johns, Alexander, and Stollar, pp. 209–21.

9. Frank Farner and John Edmundson, *Relationships of Principal Tax Bases for Public School Support in the Counties of the Eleven Western States* (Eugene: University of Oregon, 1969), p. 12.

10. Dewey Stollar and Gerald Boardman, *Personal Income by School Districts in the United States* (Gainesville, Fla.: National Educational Finance Project, 1971).

11. Peterson et al., pp. 41–42.

12. John J. Callahan and Robert J. Goettel, "Regionalism in School Finance Concept, Practice, and Analysis," in *Financing Equal Educational Opportunity Alternatives for State Finance* (Berkeley, Calif.: McCutchan, 1972), p. 94.

13. Jack E. Fisher, "A Comparison between Central Cities Suburbs on Local Ability to Support Education" (Ed.D. diss., University of Florida, 1972).

14. Callahan and Goettel, p. 110.

15. Ibid., p. 111.

16. San Antonio Independent School District v. Rodriguez, 93 S.Ct. 1278 (1973).

17. McInnis v. Shapiro, 293 F. Supp. 327, affd. mem. 394 U.S. 322, 89 S. Ct. 1197 (1969).

18. Burruss v. Wilkerson, 310 F. Supp. 572, affd. mem. 397 U.S. 44, 90 S. Ct. 812 (1970).

19. Kentucky, Florida, New Mexico, Rhode Island, and Utah.

20. The operation of the new Kansas school finance formula has revealed that, although much greater equalization has transpired, the expenditure range is still excessive because of local determination of the level of tax effort.

21. Harold H. Hopper, "Socio-Economic Factors Associated with Pattern of School Fiscal Policy in Florida" (Ed.D. diss., University of Florida, 1965); Walter J. Quick, "Socio-Economic Factors Associated with Pattern of School Fiscal Policy in Illinois" (Ed.D. diss., University of Florida, 1965); David C. Ranney, *School Government and the Determinants of the Fiscal Support for Large City Education Systems* (Edwardsville: Southern Illinois University, 1967); Richard Von Hatley, Dissertation Abstracts International 31 (1970): 5703–A.

22. Kern Alexander and Harold Kay, "The Nature of School District Fiscal Effort in Kentucky," in *Financing the Public Schools of Kentucky*, vol. 1 (Gainesville, Fla.: National Educational Finance Project, 1973), pp. 40–75.

23. Roe L. Johns and Ralph B. Kimbrough, "The Relationships of Socio-Economic Factors, Educational Leadership Patterns and Elements of Community Power Structure to Local Fiscal Policy," U.S. Office of Education Project No. 2842 (May 1968).

24. John J. Callahan, William K. Wilken, and M. Tracy Sillerman, *Urban Schools and School Finance Reform: Promise and Reality* (Washington: National Urban Coalition, 1973), p. 18.

25. *Schools, People, and Money, The Need for Educational Reform*, Final Report (1972), p. 35.

26. Florida Statutes, 236.081(4).

27. James C. Simmons, *Florida Cost of Living Research Study: Florida Counties Price Level Index* (State of Florida, June 1973), p. 33.

28. R. L. Johns, "The Cost of Delivering Equivalent Educational Services" (Paper prepared for the National Educational Finance Project, Gainesville, Fla., 1973), p. 3.

29. Norman J. Wood, "Survey of Florida Teacher Purchases, 42 Counties, Results and Analysis" (unpublished paper, University of Georgia).

30. Everett A. McDonald, *Salaries and Living Costs of Teachers in Connecticut* (New Haven: Yale University).

31. James N. Fox, "Cost of Living Adjustments in School Finance: Righteous Intent Wrong Technique" (unpublished paper, 1974), pp. 3–4.

32. Ibid., p. 14. See also Harvey E. Brazer, *Adjusting for Differences among School Districts in Costs of Educational Inputs, A Feasibility Study* (Washington: U.S. Office of Education, 1974).

33. R. L. Johns and William McLure argue convincingly that no measure of fiscal capacity should be utilized if no tax exists to tap the resource directly. This is the prevailing view in most states.

34. R. L. Johns, "The Economics and Financing of Education," in *Designing Education for the Future No. 5*, ed. Edgar L. Morphet and David L. Jessen (New York: Citation Press, 1968), p. 227.

35. See Florida Statutes, 1973.

36. John E. Coons, William H. Clune III, and Stephen D. Sugarman, *Private and Public Education* (Cambridge: Harvard University Press, 1970), p. 202.

37. The recapture provision in the district power-equalizing proposal is not unique, having been in use in Utah for many years.